THE SOCIAL PSYCHOLOGY OF EVERYDAY POLITICS

The Social Psychology of Everyday Politics examines the ways in which politics permeates everyday life, from the ordinary interactions we have with others to the sense of belonging and identity developed within social groups and communities. From discrimination and prejudice to inclusion and social change, politics is an ongoing process that is not solely the domain of the elected and the powerful.

Using a social and political psychological lens to examine how politics is enacted in contemporary societies, the book takes an explicitly critical approach that places political activity within collective processes rather than individual behaviours. While the studies covered in the book do not ignore the importance of the individual, they underscore the need to examine the roles of culture, history, ideology and social context as integral to psychological processes. Individuals act, but they do not act in isolation from the groups and societies to which they belong.

Drawing on extensive international research, with contributions from leaders in the field as well as emerging scholars, the book is divided into three interrelated parts which cover:

- The politics of intercultural relations
- Political agency and social change
- Political discourse and practice

Offering insights into how psychology can be applied to some of the most pressing social issues we face, this will be fascinating reading for students of psychology, political science, sociology and cultural studies, as well as anyone working in the area of public policy.

Caroline Howarth is Associate Professor in Social Psychology at the London School of Economics and Political Science, University of London, UK.

Eleni Andreouli is Lecturer in the School of Psychology at the Open University, UK.

THE SOCIAL PSYCHOLOGY OF EVERYDAY POLITICS

Edited by Caroline Howarth and Eleni Andreouli

LONDON AND NEW YORK

First published 2017
by Routledge
2 Park Square, Milton Park, Abingdon, Oxon OX14 4RN

and by Routledge
711 Third Avenue, New York, NY 10017

Routledge is an imprint of the Taylor & Francis Group, an informa business

© 2017 selection and editorial matter, Caroline Howarth and Eleni Andreouli; individual chapters, the contributors

The right of the editors to be identified as the authors of the editorial material, and of the authors for their individual chapters, has been asserted in accordance with sections 77 and 78 of the Copyright, Designs and Patents Act 1988.

All rights reserved. No part of this book may be reprinted or reproduced or utilised in any form or by any electronic, mechanical, or other means, now known or hereafter invented, including photocopying and recording, or in any information storage or retrieval system, without permission in writing from the publishers.

Trademark notice: Product or corporate names may be trademarks or registered trademarks, and are used only for identification and explanation without intent to infringe.

British Library Cataloguing in Publication Data
A catalogue record for this book is available from the British Library

Library of Congress Cataloging-in-Publication Data
Names: Howarth, Caroline (Caroline Susannah), editor. | Andreouli, Eleni, editor.
Title: The social psychology of everyday politics / edited by Caroline Howarth and Eleni Andreouli.
Description: Abingdon, Oxon ; New York, NY : Routledge, 2016. | Includes bibliographical references and index.
Identifiers: LCCN 2016007718 (print) | LCCN 2016016882 (ebook) | ISBN 9781138814448 (hardback) | ISBN 9781138814455 (pbk.) | ISBN 9781315747460 (ebk.) | ISBN 9781315747460 (ebook)
Subjects: LCSH: Political sociology—Case studies. | Social psychology—Case studies.
Classification: LCC JA76 .S6224 2016 (print) | LCC JA76 (ebook) | DDC 306.2—dc23
LC record available at https://lccn.loc.gov/2016007718

ISBN: 978-1-138-81444-8 (hbk)
ISBN: 978-1-138-81445-5 (pbk)
ISBN: 978-1-315-74746-0 (ebk)

Typeset in Bembo
by Apex CoVantage, LLC

CONTENTS

Preface: Everyday politics   viii

PART I
The politics of intercultural relations   1

1 Everyday multiculturalism as critical nationalism   3
    Caroline Howarth

2 Political leadership and social diversity: The everyday
    politics of race and gender   18
    *Martha Augoustinos, Peta Callaghan, Jasmin Sorrentino
      and Anna Worth*

3 Everyday politics, everyday racism: Censure and
    management of racist talk   34
    Stephen Gibson

4 Essence politics: Identity work and stereotyping
    in intergroup relations   49
    *Wolfgang Wagner, Maaris Raudsepp, Peter Holtz
      and Ragini Sen*

5 The social and political psychology of globalisation
   and global identities   65
   Ilka H. Gleibs and Geetha Reddy

   Commentary on Part I: Politics, identities and social
   representations in multicultural societies   79
   Xenia Chryssochoou

PART II
Political agency and social change   85

6 Citizenship and social psychology: An analysis of
   constructions of Greek citizenship   87
   Eleni Andreouli, Irini Kadianaki and Maria Xenitidou

7 Identity, emotion and mobilisation   102
   Stephen Reicher and Yashpal Jogdand

8 Resistance and transformation in postcolonial contexts   116
   Shose Kessi and Floretta Boonzaier

9 Everyday reconciliation   131
   Sandra Obradović and Caroline Howarth

10 Climate change activism between weak and strong
   environmentalism: Advocating social change with moderate
   argumentation strategies   146
   Paula Castro, Mehmet ali Uzelgun and Raquel Bertoldo

   Commentary on Part II: Culture, narrative and the
   everyday dynamics of identity   163
   Helen Haste

PART III
Political discourse and practice   171

11 The precariat, everyday life and objects of despair   173
   *Darrin Hodgetts, Shiloh Groot, Emily Garden and Kerry
   Chamberlain*

12 Public opinion and the problem of information 189
    Susan Condor

13 Everyday politics and the extreme right: Lay explanations
    of the electoral performance of the neo-Nazi political
    party Golden Dawn in Greece 206
    Lia Figgou

14 Political beliefs and political behaviour 222
    Isabelle Goncalves-Portelinha, Christian Staerklé,
        and Guy Elcheroth

15 Social policy in everyday contexts 237
    Jenevieve Mannell

    Commentary on Part III: Political discourse and practice 253
    Michelle Fine

    Conclusion: The social psychology of everyday politics:
    Beyond binaries and banality 261
    Paul Nesbitt-Larking

Index 275

PREFACE

Everyday politics

We often think about politics as the world of politicians, those in government who influence government policy. However there is a politics evident in everyday life: the ways in which we deal with others in everyday interactions; form communities and social movements; and find a sense of belonging, national identity and difference to others – these are all political processes. They are bound up with processes of inclusion and exclusion, the defence of certain perspectives over others, discrimination and prejudice, as well as possibilities for social and political change.

This focus on sociopolitical phenomena from the perspective of the everyday is gaining ground in the social sciences. Increasingly, there are calls for the study of key social scientific concepts, such as citizenship, multiculturalism and cosmopolitanism, in terms of everyday practices in order to complement the more traditional top-down approaches that social scientists routinely employ. Inevitably, this trend brings about a new conception of politics – one that not only focuses on states and governments but also takes under consideration the perspectives of other political actors, such as those of citizens themselves.

This book makes a case for the relevance and value of the discipline of psychology in this broader field. Psychology, particularly social and political psychology, is uniquely positioned to study the intricacies and complexities of the everyday in its sociopolitical context, and it therefore has much to offer to these recent developments. The aim of this book is to use psychology to extend our understanding of politics as processes of power struggle and claims-making which take place not just in the sphere of official politics but also in the domain of everyday social interactions. The chapters in this volume shed light on the mundane and ordinary ways in which politics is enacted in contemporary societies.

The book also aims to offer a more explicitly social and critical approach to the study of politics in psychology, which has been dominated by individual-level approaches. Many would see political psychology as the use of psychology to study political behaviours. For the most part, research and teaching in this field construct political behaviours as *individual* behaviours, for example, by examining the psychological profiles of different leaders or differences in cognitive styles or individual differences in voting, prejudice attitudes and social protest more generally. Clearly, political psychology needs to incorporate this focus on the individual and on cognitive processes. However, what we also need to examine are the roles of culture, history, ideology and social context, more broadly, as integral to psychological processes, even at the level of the individual. Hence, political behaviours also need to be understood as social or collective behaviours and the products of particular contexts, histories and ideologies. This is what is distinctive about many of the chapters in this collection: a fundamentally societal form of psychology to examine everyday politics.

The chapters of this volume combine theoretical development of the everyday as a conceptual tool in social and political psychology with empirical work from a range of fields. As a whole, the book draws on extensive research on the politics of the everyday, from voting behaviours in Europe to the politics of resistance in postcolonial settings; from different strategies for dealing with diversity in political leadership in Australia to lay explanations of electoral patterns in Greece; from the gendered inequalities of South Africa to racist discourse and the symbolic exclusion of 'cultural others' in the UK; from social movements and protest across the globe to the ways in which public policy filters into everyday social relations.

The book is divided in three parts, each with five chapters: The Politics of Intercultural Relations (Part 1); Political Agency and Social Change (Part 2); and Political Discourse and Practice (Part 3). Together, these highlight the significance of politics for everyday social relations, social identities, knowledge systems and possibilities for social and political transformation. Each part of the book concludes with commentary from a leading scholar in the field (Xenia Chryssochoou, Helen Haste and Michelle Fine). Alongside an overall conclusion by Paul Nesbitt-Larking, these complementary chapters provide a critical overview of the chapters in relation to the broader field of social and political psychology and discuss avenues for the future study of everyday politics.

We hope that this volume will be a valuable tool for students and scholars interested in exploring traditional psychological topics, such as prejudice, identity and intergroup relations, from the perspective of everyday political life. Furthermore, the chapters of this volume should appeal to a wider range of social science scholars and students with an interest in the micropolitics of everyday life, such as colleagues working in political science, sociology and geography. We hope that this volume will inspire work in previously unexplored facets of political life that transcend the psychology of traditional political behaviours. Given the increasing complexity and scope of contemporary politics, the variety of political actors and the multiplicity of ways of doing politics, this is a fertile way forward for the study of politics. In doing so, such ventures should produce a psychology that has real social and political significance in today's complex world.

PART I
The politics of intercultural relations

Part I

The politics of intercultural relations

1
EVERYDAY MULTICULTURALISM AS CRITICAL NATIONALISM

Caroline Howarth

While many politicians assert the importance of national identities and affiliation to the nation, most politicians around the globe from across the political spectrum agree that multiculturalism has failed. And yet despite this political rejection of multiculturalism, for certain scholars multiculturalism is alive and well (Harris, 2013). They cite evidence including examination results in highly diverse schools and measures of citizenship and creativity. While the horrific attacks on *Charlie Hebdo* in Paris in 2015 are regarded by extreme right parties as proof that multiculturalism has failed, there is evidence of broad multicultural support in the marches of sympathy and protest across Europe. While some minoritised groups no doubt feel under pressure to 'display' their patriotism and loyalty, in such events others are there with the same set of political attitudes as peers from majority groups.

So has multiculturalism failed, or is it part of our national cultures to uphold and cherish it? Part of the problem is that we use different definitions of both nationalism and multiculturalism; sometimes these collide, sometimes these concur. For some, multiculturalism is a description of a demographic fact and "an inescapable reality" (Green & Staerkle, 2013), particularly when we recognise the 'super-diversity' of many contemporary cities (Vertovec, 2010). This 'de facto multiculturalism' (Nesbitt-Larking, 2014) or 'everyday multiculturalism' examines mundane intercultural encounters and practices, showing the very real, practical and embodied ways in which identities and cultures are negotiated in everyday micro-interactions in markets, through the media, commercial exchanges and social relationships (Harris, 2013; Wise & Velayutham, 2009). This resonates with Gilroy's work on the conviviality of contemporary intercultural exchanges – those "ordinary experiences of contact, cooperation and conflict across the supposedly impermeable boundaries of race, culture, identity and ethnicity" (Gilroy, 2004). Such mundane, pragmatic experiences of cultural diversity are often far removed from top-down understandings of 'panicked multiculturalism' (Noble, 2009).

While recognising the 'apparentness' of multiculturalism in the everyday, it is important to recognise the different forms of multiculturalism as public policy and governance strategy that generally are "designed to cope with already divided communities in order to sustain peace and promote equality" (Nesbitt-Larking, 2014, p. 281). An array of texts (e.g., Kinnvall & Nesbitt-Larking, 2011) outline the different policies related to multiculturalism in different countries on a continuum from accommodationist to integrationist. What these works demonstrate are the ways in which different policies in different nations connect to everyday practices of multiculturalism in the everyday, as a form of 'emotional governance'. Richards (2007) developed this concept in examining political leadership as emotional management, particularly in connection to political discourse on terrorism and nationalism in the media and how this relates to public emotions. Kinnvall (2014) uses this in a broader Foucauldian sense to include the surveillance and manipulation of emotions, particularly around otherness and cultural diversity. Here we can see that multiculturalism can be understood as political discourse or as public sentiment in relation to cultural diversity, and we need to examine the connections between the two.

The same is true for nationalism: we can take a top-down approach that examines nationalism as a political principle (Gellner, 1983) and we can take a more bottom-up everyday approach that examines the ways in which explicit and often implicit symbols of the nation shape everyday interactions and relationships (Billig, 1995; Howarth, Andreouli & Kessi, 2014). Furthermore, in addition to a bottom-up, everyday level and a top-down, policy level of both multiculturalism and nationalism, some psychological works on both multiculturalism and nationalism examine these as *individual* psychological traits and develop scales of support for multiculturalism and/or nationalism (e.g. Berry & Kalin, 1995; Verkuyten, 2014). For example, Dekker, Malová and Hoogendoorn (2003) define nationalism as an individual's attitude consisting of national liking, national pride, national preference and national superiority, and they depict multicultural attitudes and nationalistic attitudes as oppositional. We return to this point later.

Clearly, these three levels of analysis (top-down, everyday and psychological) need to be integrated. Politicians claim that multiculturalism has failed, the media often amplify this and people often assert this in the context of their everyday lives (Verkuyten, 2014). Yet there is also some evidence for the opposite. The UK legislature is becoming increasingly diverse, there is increased cultural diversity in the media (Al Jazeera English, for example, is followed by 220 million people in over 100 different countries and is by no means limited to Muslim or Arabic audiences), and there is increased diversity in what we eat, what music we listen to and our social networks and friendships. Our children even are evidence of the success of multicultural relationships and communities. More than this, some are mobilised into displaying a sense of connection and allegiance across assumed (or constructed) divisions of difference (Gilroy, 2004), such as the 2014 "I'll ride with you" Twitter campaign from Australia that went viral within hours and which demonstrated support for Muslims and a stand against Islamophobia. Given these examples that suggest that our world is simply multicultural, why do many insist that multiculturalism has failed?

The answer is surprisingly simple. Multiculturalism has succeeded. Multiculturalism is changing aspects of citizenship, participation and governance. Indeed multiculturalism, for some, is *too* successful. Its success now means that those 'othered' in previously marginalised communities are now part of all systems of decision making and governance, from school governors, to university councils, to police associations, to local government and national politicians, even if they still experience prejudice in these contexts. No longer is multiculturalism imagined as angry black men rampaging on the streets (who can be contained or imprisoned) or submissive Asian women who can't speak English properly (who can be ignored); now 'the problem' is that it is clear these people are just like 'us' – they care about their children's education, they care about doing well in life, they vote, they produce comedy, they make us reflect on 'our' own cultural values and points of hypocrisy. Furthermore, they teach our children, they treat us in hospitals, they police our streets, they inform us about political decisions. More than this, not only do they participate in all forms of civic society, but they want to participate in the fullest sense of the term, that is, they want their representations to have consequence (Howarth, Andreouli & Kessi, 2014). And finally we begin to see that this distinction between 'us' and 'them' is ideologically constructed, politically motivated and sometimes reinforced in academic studies of cultural differences (Gunaratnam, 2003; Howarth, 2009).

Take, for example, the so-called Trojan Horse Affair which was a major issue of national debate in the UK. An investigation was launched into local schools after an anonymous (probably hoax) letter was received in 2014 that outlined a Muslim 'Trojan Horse' plan to take over school governance. In response, the government, official educational bodies and the media maintained that this was about reducing the threat of extremism, safeguarding our children and promoting British values. Yet if we look carefully at the evidence produced, we see something quite different. Far from being construed as a Muslim plot, the affair can be regarded as an attack on Muslim communities. For many, the assumed privileges of whiteness of all political institutions and systems of governance are under threat (see also Van Oudenhoven & Ward, 2013). Hence debates about multiculturalism have become debates about nationalism or at least threats to the nation, and they currently produce a problematic form of nationalism as we see later in the chapter. What is needed is a clear examination of the points of tension and connection between these concepts in order to see whether there is a more constructive way to address the inherent diversity of all nations that involves both majority and minoritised groups.

In order to achieve this, the next section of the chapter provides a detailed examination of the conceptual tensions between multiculturalism and nationalism and includes a discussion on postnationalism, banal nationalism and cultural essentialism. The following section explores the ways in which we can connect multiculturalism and nationalism through critical identities, counternarratives and critical nationalism. Throughout the chapter I draw on a range of studies from social and political psychology and related disciplines to illustrate the points of connection and tension. Many of these studies concern ways in which young people are positioned in discussions about the nation and multiculturalism. This is partly because this is my own focus in research, but also because many studies with young people examine what we can call the 'political imaginary' – how we not only make but also imagine future worlds (Moscovici, 1988), imagine our own place within these and therefore contribute to the mobilisation of different possibilities (Sirin & Fine, 2007) and different politics (Phoenix, Howarth & Philogene, forthcoming).

Connecting multiculturalism and nationalism: An ideological dilemma

In drawing nationalism and multiculturalism together, there are at least three conceptual and practical challenges to address that are evident in social science as well as everyday debates:

1 The idea that global, multicultural, cosmopolitan or even postnational identities may be more significant today than national identities
2 The assumption that nationalism is a feature of violent conflicts and prejudices between different cultural groups
3 The claim that multiculturalism 'ignores' majority national groups as well as sustains a problematic form of cultural essentialism.

Are contemporary identities multicultural and thereby postnational?

When thinking about the everyday level of intergroup relations, some argue that nationalism (as discourses of proud affiliation to the nation) and national identities (as overtly identifying in national terms) are of diminishing significance in today's world. This is a global world where "individuals, through diverse neighbourhoods, foreign travel, work abroad, global media and online social networks, will be in constant interaction across cultural and national boundaries" (Modood, 2014, p. 2), although this may be more true for middle-class migrants than others. As Gleibs and Reddy discuss in Chapter 5, globalisation has fundamentally changed daily life – what we eat, what we listen to, what we believe in (Vertovec, 2010). As we increasingly live in a world of everyday multiculturalism (Harris, 2013), have national identities become less significant? Some theorists argue that actual and symbolic (through consumption and intercultural exchange) movements across borders and the development of more globalised connections mean that collective identities and loyalties will become more salient at human and global levels, where cosmopolitanism replaces the nation state and we enter an age of postnationalism (Nesbitt-Larking, 2014) with commitments to a single human community and a shared morality (Appiah, 1997). Hence, community and national bonds may weaken as more cosmopolitan, multicultural or intercultural identities emerge (Barrett, 2013; Moghaddam, 2008).

However, when national identities are threatened by transnational and global encounters and identities, they may be fiercely (re)asserted, defended and fought over (Wagner, et al., 2012). Thus, as Calhoun has argued, "globalization has not put an end to nationalism. . . . Indeed, globalization fuels resurgence in nationalism among people who feel threatened or anxious as much as it drives efforts to transcend nationalism in new structures of political-legal organisations or thinking about transnational connections" (Calhoun, 2007, p. 171). Hence, just as nationalism can be seen (and experienced) as a dialectic of difference and commonality, so too is globalisation – it is a broader, more expansive and more complex form of the dialectic of categorisation and particularisation (Billig, 1985), and so too is an ideological dilemma (Billig, 1988) for both global citizens and nation states. As Billig outlines in his work on ideological dilemmas, which abound in everyday and political discourse, these are productive and invite people to consider the contradictory tensions in sense-making and social debate. It is not then that multiculturalism has eroded nationalism, but that it can make nationalism more assertive and more complex as different groups with different claims to the nation assert and defend different versions of the nation.

Is nationalism more evident in violent claims to the nation and less evident in everyday life?

The second challenge to address is the fact that some would argue that nationalism is not experienced as a salient issue in everyday politics, particularly in intensely multicultural or cosmopolitan contexts. In the course of our everyday lives, nationalism is irrelevant, unseen and unheard. We see it, feel, it and care about it in violent confrontations with others – on football pitches, in terrorist attacks, in extreme political movements and in contexts of war. Nationalism appears violent and hostile and is 'othered out' to white working-class communities, football hooligans, extremists and right-wing politicians. Hence 'they' are nationalistic (as bad nationalism) when we are patriotic (as good nationalism). In this way, nationalism is often seen as "extraordinary, politically charged and emotionally driven" (Billig, 1995, p. 44). But as Billig explains, we can compare (and connect) this 'hot' nationalistic passion to a 'cold' or 'banal' nationalism that is a form of life so entrenched and taken-for-granted that it is rarely seen or commented upon.

Hence we often "fail to see the everyday nationalism that organises people's sense of belonging in the world and to particular states" (Calhoun, 2007, p. 27). We also may fail to see how this everyday nationalism is also a politics of cultural privilege, exclusion and denigration of particular cultural 'others'. In the subtle politics of constructing national identities in schools, for instance, it is possible to find a more symbolic form of cultural exclusion – where certain cultural groups are equated to the nation and other groups are tolerated at best, generally marginalised and sometimes forcibly excluded (Howarth, 2004). Banal nationalism therefore is no more inclusive or progressive than hot nationalism, and its banality is in fact part of its power and privilege in much the same way as whiteness is often unseen and unnamed (Garner, 2007), at least to 'white' bodies and institutions (Ahmed, 2004). Hence the privileges of both hot and banal forms of nationalism are wrapped up in a politics of who is seen to belong and rightfully govern, and so privilege is implicated in claims to and rejections of multiculturalism as policy.

What is increasingly evident in contemporary national and international politics, as documented in a range of studies inspired by Billig's banal nationalism approach (e.g., Condor, 2000; Gibson, this volume), is that rather than displays of nationalism being either hot or banal nationalism, there is a connection between the two, and one fuels the other. Increasingly, we see how hostile claims to nationalism are made in cold or banal actions and everyday encounters (as Billig himself recognised). As the extreme right moves towards the centre of mainstream politics across Europe, hot forms of nationalism becomes less extraordinary, more everyday, more mainstream and therefore more banal (Kinnvall, 2004, 2014). Hence, in contemporary politics, the distinction between hot and banal nationalism is diminishing. Furthermore, nationalism, even in its banal forms, appears more acceptably exclusive, racialised and increasingly Islamophobic. We could say that there is a racialisation of nationalism, and that this racialisation includes Muslim communities as targets of exclusion and the denial of national recognition (Hopkins & Kahani-Hopkins, 2009; Modood, 2014). Hence, nationalism both as a political principle and within everyday practice sometimes appears as a simple rejection of multiculturalism.

Can multiculturalism really include majority groups?

Open, inclusive and more multicultural versions of nationalism that include 'othered' cultural groups such as black Britons, British Muslims, Scottish Asians and so forth, have provoked a sense of loss, insecurity and uncertainty for majority groups (Calhoun, 2007; Gilroy, 2004), as they "may feel anxious about a sense of cultural loss, of losing control of the pace of identity change" (Modood, 2014, p. 8) as well as losing power and status (Verkuyten, 2014). This is the third challenge in connecting nationalism and multiculturalism – the idea that majority cultures are fading (Van Oudenhoven & Ward, 2013) and that multiculturalism 'ignores' majority groups and is a political ideology for 'minoritised' groups.

This creates a vacuum around nationalism, a space, as we have seen, for the far right to emerge as the voice of the nation. Here multiculturalism and nationalism are seen in opposition; one can be pronationalism or promulticulturalism, but not both. Hence, again as evident in Europe's move to the far right, nationalism becomes essentially anti-immigration. In fact, all major parties move to endorse tighter controls on migrants as political support increasingly becomes a battle for representing the nation and loyalty to 'the people'. Here immigration and so multiculturalism become increasingly more threatening for many.

Identities become defined by insecurity (Kinnvall, 2004) and a sense of nostalgia for a past (Gilroy, 2004; Hage, 2003) where communities were seen to be more homogeneous (Howarth, 2001) and more 'pure' (Dekker et al., 2003), and asserting in-group loyalty and pride was not deemed problematic (Condor, 2000).

Multiculturalism in this context is seen as responsible for diminishing national identities, national cohesion and national pride. This rests on an ideology of 'us' and 'them' (Bouchard, 2011) with binary notions of majority and minority, 'who belongs' and who has citizenship rights ('us') and duties ('them' – and this in the main is to prove allegiance) as well as racialised binaries of white and black, and increasingly Muslim and non-Muslim. Furthermore, we can see how the reification of difference is produced in political and social institutions. If we examine practices and discourses about multiculturalism in very different schools across Britain, for instance, we see that there is a tendency to reify cultural difference in displays of celebrating, tolerating and including 'others' in ways that mark them as essentially and forever 'other' to national identities (Howarth & Andreouli, 2016; Howarth, Wagner, Magnusson & Sammut, 2014; see also Philips, 2007). In such studies we see that there are often two contradictory positions to multiculturalism that support either:

1   A version of multiculturalism as threatening to the nation and to national identities that is problematic in the production of social cohesion, *or*
2   A version of multiculturalism that produces the nation and national identities that ensures social cohesion and invites national belonging, inclusion and productive forms of citizenship.

Thus far we have examined the former: how multiculturalism is constructed in ways that are seen as problematic for nationalism. Let us now turn to the latter: multiculturalism as constructive for the production of national identities and essential for inclusive and democratic forms of nationalism. We need also to examine the ways in which this version of multiculturalism addresses the challenges raised earlier in the chapter and incorporate majority identities, challenge cultural essentialism and exclusion and provoke a more inclusive or critical form of nationalism.

Towards a political psychology of multiculturalism as critical nationalism

To do this, we need an integrated political psychology of the connections between nationalism and multiculturalism. This needs to examine (a) the production of critical forms of national identity and political subjectivity, (b) the production of both narratives and counternarratives of the nation, as well as (c) the role of governance structures in supporting a more inclusive form of both nationalism and multiculturalism. We shall take each in turn.

The role of critical identities in debates that connect nationalism and multiculturalism

In connecting nationalism and multiculturalism, we need to recognise the diversity of communities and nations as well as the hybridisation of identity as distinctive features of contemporary society. The negotiation of identity is not a simple matter of rejecting old identities and adopting new ones (Hall, 1988), so we cannot simply develop an additive model of national identities where we 'add on' or 'switch on' (Tajfel, 1978) different layers of identity, such as black British, black Muslim British, black Muslim British mother living in Scotland and so on. Furthermore, for most of us, even those generally seen as from majority groups, it is not a matter of 'choosing' between different identities or different types of identities as racialised, classed, connected to parenting, occupations and so on – all identities are intercultural and intersectional (Brah & Phoenix, 2004).

From research into identities in multicultural settings (Back, 1996; Brah, 1996; Phoenix & Tizard, 2001) as well as national identities (Condor, 2000) we know that identities are co-constructed through and against the representations that others have of us (Howarth, 2004). Most centrally, we employ social representations *of* the groups we are associated with, elaborating, challenging or rejecting these ways of being seen and constructed. Re-presentations of socially significant categories such as nation, gender, ethnicity and religion play a crucial role in the co-construction of identity and in this process of re-presentation of these identities and the categories on which they are based, questioned, elaborated and sometimes transformed. Hence there is a political psychology of the production of identities, particularly critical identities and how young people today experience belonging, contest particular versions of nationalism and assert a claim on nationalism.

Parents of children on the 'borders' of national identities – positioned by race or religion as 'others' – sometimes assert that their children have a weak sense of identity because they are excluded from the national culture and also because they are not taught about their 'home' cultures at school. As a response to this, community activities, alternative education centres, language courses and religious events become significant ways parents endeavour to share their cultural associations with their children (Howarth, 2004). Such studies highlight the creative ways young people living in some multicultural communities develop assertive and dynamic forms of identity that both integrate and reject aspects of their parents' cultures and 'majority' cultures, and so cultivate their own versions of national identity (e.g. Howarth, Wagner, Magnusson & Sammut, 2014). This highlights the possibilities for 'multiculturalism without culture' (Philips, 2007), or at least multiculturalism without imposed, reified versions of what particular cultures should be.

Clearly we need to see the ongoing production of national culture and national identities as a collective and contested enterprise, not only a process of contestation by the minoritised and not only a process of defence by those seen as 'the majority'. It is a process in which we all are invested, and we have contradictory claims and ambitions. Sometimes we fear others who seem to threaten the stability and security of the categories we orientate ourselves around (Kinnvall, 2004); sometimes we are drawn into the allure of difference; sometimes any such (constructed) differences melt away in the conviviality of lived social relationships. Sometimes we imagine and assert new forms of attachment, belonging and national inclusion. These are fluid, contested and creative processes that draw in and draw on the histories and politics of both nationalism and multiculturalism. As Modood emphasises: "... each new generation does not simply add a new chapter to an ever-expanding book, but it re-thinks the whole story" (Modood, 2014, pp. 10–11).

Social subjectivity (Calhoun, 2004) is part of this, and it enables us to examine the agency of individuals and communities in positioning themselves in discourses that connect (and sometimes disconnect) nationalism and multiculturalism. More than a social imaginary, however, there is also then a *political imaginary* or *political subjectivity* to the tensions between multiculturalism and nationalism (Kinnvall, 2014). People debate these tensions, position themselves in relation to policy debates on nationalism, patriotism and multiculturalism, and develop their own subjective and agentic sense of belonging, commonalities and difference. They may be aware of the ways in which they are excluded; they may be aware of threats to the social categories they hold dear; they may find ways to assert belonging and a national identity even in the face of narrow and prejudiced representations of the nation. But political subjectivity is also framed by the dominant representations in society (see Kessi and Boonziar, this volume). The question is, how are counternarratives of nationalism and multiculturalism developed and asserted?

Developing counternarratives that connect multiculturalism and nationalism

As "identity can only be constructed from those narratives which are available" (Wetherell and Potter, 1992, p. 79), what narratives *are* available in any context? Particularly, what narratives of the nation are available? Are these narratives of inclusion or exclusion? Much work on nationalism, and indeed some chapters in this volume, demonstrates the ways in which nationalism converges with racism and other forms of exclusion.

Hence, national identities depend on the claims which people themselves make in different contexts and at different times. These claims are limited by the dominant narratives of the nation. However, while many may simply take their identities and these narratives for granted, as banal nationalists (Billig, 1995), others are passionate and mobilised by a sense of national identification in producing counternarratives of nationalism. Indeed, as Andreouli argues (2015), nationalism is not equally banal for everyone. For some, national borders and boundaries cannot be taken for granted: crossing boundaries can be a very conscious process particularly for those who have trouble crossing them. While Anderson (1983) powerfully argued that a nation "is an imagined political community" (p. 138) and is imagined as a community with "deep, horizontal comradeship" (ibid), nations are also reimagined as sites of struggle over meanings, ideologies and identity positions (Howarth & Andreouli, 2016).

This needs careful and critical examination. How, for example, is 'Britishness' collectively imagined at school in Anderson's (1983) sense of imagined communities? Does it enable young people to challenge exclusive or racialising versions of the nation? Does it encourage them to develop assertive ways of claiming a British identity even in the face of otherising representations? At a time when the British government is calling for affirmations of Britishness from communities often constructed as 'other' and is establishing educational policies to apparently foster a sense of citizenship, cultural understanding and belonging, these are pressing concerns. Take this press release on citizenship education from the Home Office, September 2002:

> David Blunkett: We want British citizenship to embrace positively the diversity of background, culture and faiths that living in modern Britain involves. . . . British citizens should have a sense of belonging to a wider community.

Over a decade later, this inclusive form of nationalism is far less common in political discourse. We have seen a move to a top-down form of nationalism: nationalism or Britishness as defined by policymakers and their advisors and taught through monitored school curricula. What this can do, however, is provoke resistance and contestation, as "different factions, whether classes, religions, regions, genders or ethnicities, always struggle for the power to speak for the nation, and to present their particular voice as the voice of the national whole" (Billig, 1995, p. 71). This more bottom-up nationalism relates to the diverse ways in which nationalism is experienced, rejected and claimed by different groups and individuals in diverse societies. Such counternarratives evident in 'everyday' nationalism go hand-in-hand with narratives about multiculturalism.

Connecting critical nationalism, governance and care

In developing an everyday politics of nationalism, "we need to consider the changing meanings of nationalism" (Calhoun, 2007, p. 9) and also consider how *should* it change? As Calhoun (ibid) continues: "It matters whether nationalist appeals mobilise citizens for ethnic cleansing, external war, or internal loyalty to regrettable regimes. It matters whether nationalist appeals mobilise citizens for democratic projects, mutual care, or redistribution of wealth".

At the heart of Kymlicka's (2010, p. 103) vision of multiculturalism is a political subjectivity that is reflective, agentic, transformative and critical. Multicultural citizens from minority and majority groups are engaged in a dialogue that transforms the relationship and encounters between them. They are attached to the nation, focused on new forms of belonging and inclusion but open to discussions on inequalities and prejudices. This connects multiculturalism to a politics of engagement (Nesbitt-Larking, 2014) and a progressive or critical nationalism, which Johanson and Glow (2009) define as both a critique and a caring for the nation. They stress the ways in which such critical nationalists may love the nation, but also how they "recognise and attempt to improve on the shortcomings of the nation" (p. 387) and hence "not to eschew the possibility of national values, but to reflect on the process necessary to achieve them" (ibid). This can be seen as a constructive patriotism or the ability to question and criticise national norms and practices (Schatz, Staub &

Lavine, 1999) as a form of 'everyday reconciliation' (Obradović and Howarth, this volume).

For Johanson and Glow (2009), this is a caring nationalism that cares for the nation through a critical lens or critical attachment (Penic, Elcheroth & Reicher, 2015). What Penic et al. (2015) show is that critically attached minority voices are dependent on the larger societal context, in that different sociopolitical contexts enable or delegitimise critique of the nation. This also connects to Scuzzarello's (2015) concept of caring multiculturalism, where governance structures are attentive to immigrant minorities, responsive to others and aware of the consequences of their policies. It is more open, gives legitimacy to critique (Penic et al., 2015) and promotes deliberative democracy. There is a danger that concepts of 'caring nationalism' and 'caring multiculturalism' may fall into binary and unhelpful distinctions between 'good' and 'bad' nationalism (as discussed previously and critiqued by Billig, 1995). Clearly, critical nationalism is an evaluative and ideological position, as is critical multiculturalism. However, while this may seem problematic and naively hopeful, Hage (2003) argues that we need to develop a 'good' form of nationalism as an inclusive social force that is in fact grounded in hope. The alternative is a melancholic, paranoid nationalism (Gilroy, 2004) or blind patriotism (Schatz et al., 1999) built on insecurity, an ongoing sense of threat and an inability to accept critique (Kinnvall, 2014). Such blind nationalists assert that if you criticise a past or present associated with the nation, you are also criticising the values or essence of society (Hage, 2003). The need to value the nation so highly and reject all critique means also that valuing other nations or cultures becomes impossible. As we have known for some time, ethnocentrism and patriotism often go together (Andreouli, 2015; Pratto, Sidianus & Levin, 2006), as both require an uncritical conformity to prevailing societal norms and rejection of other nations or outgroups.

While there are significant examples of governments and political leaders asserting forms of critical nationalism, such as from Bulgaria (Reicher, Cassidy, Wolpert, Hopkins & Levine, 2006) and reparation movements in Australia (Hastie & Augoustinos, 2012), in the current turn against multiculturalism and proimmigration politics, governments generally fail to produce critical nationalism and this may lead to the internalisation of noncritical attitudes (Penic et al., 2015). Yet even in these spaces where critical nationalism and promulticultural discourses are discouraged, we see examples of individuals, families, communities and even social institutions taking a stand and finding ways of encouraging a more critical approach to constructing the nation that is de-essentialising, inclusive and fundamentally more democratic. For instance, some schools find ways to examine, critique and transform top-down, governmental definitions of nationalism and national loyalty (Andreouli et al., 2014; Howarth & Andreouli, 2016).

There is evidence of a bottom-up form of engagement, identification with national culture and even governance that shows the ways in which claims to multiculturalism are often claims to nationalism. And this is precisely what is so successful about multiculturalism; it is so successful that it becomes a threat. It is not that 'they' want to be 'us' or that 'we' are becoming more like 'them', as political rhetoric from the far right about the so-called Islamification of society would suggest (Kinnvall, 2014); they are already us. They always have been a part of us, as diverse societies are as old as humanity (Kymlicka, 2010). Cultural or national essentialism is a political construction, and it is one that ill serves a constructive and democratic form of nationalism. Combining multiculturalism and nationalism limits the extent to which nationalism can flourish as an exclusive and hierarchical form of governance and ideology.

Conclusion: Critical nationalism as a world-making possibility

Certain forms of nationalism and multiculturalism may incorporate ideologies of difference, exclusion and prejudice. However, as Calhoun (2007) asserts, we still need to recognise the possibilities for national solidarities. I have argued that in combination with a critical and everyday form of multiculturalism, nationalism can offer protection from racism and Islamophobia, reject assimilationist politics and assert the recognition of diverse identities within claims to the nation. Modood has argued that multiculturalism is about "replacing national identity if closed, and for embracing if plural" (2014, p. 13). Somewhat unconventionally, let me end this chapter on a personal note. Politics is always personal, and to address this can help open up discussions on the kinds of worlds we not only think are possible, but that we strive for as we collectively (re)imagine futures for our children. This also demonstrates the ways in which claims to the nation are future oriented and about what worlds we construct for future generations.

When my four-year-old came home from nursery with a Union Jack painted on his face, I had a profound sense that my representations of the British flag as a symbol of colonialism (from my childhood in Fiji and Papua New Guinea), of overt racism (from experiences on the football terraces of Burnley in the north of England) or of a more banal sense of national superiority (from experiences at institutions of privilege in Cambridge and London) were not and really *should not* be relevant. The dilemmas of nationalism in parenting, in promoting a confident sense of national identity that is not blind to its past, came back to me in 2014 when Emily Thornberry was forced to resign from the British shadow cabinet after posting a photo of a house draped in the English St George's flag in what appeared to be a condescending comment on working-class expressions of nationalism. I wondered how the parents in the community explained to their children the media storm that developed about the intersections of class, whiteness and belonging in representations of who has the 'right' to display nationalism in particular ways. Certain expressions of nationalism are not really accepted in middle-class and political circles, where there are preferences for the more banal or understated forms of nationalism or as commodified statements of fashion and style. We are encouraged to be quite careful about how we do claim national attachment – not to be too patriotic, too superior. What does this mean for our children and future generations? Do we simply accept that nationalism is always problematic or always about prejudice? Do we sit back and let others define how Britishness or any form of nationalism is to be celebrated and nurtured? This is a dangerous situation, and in this chapter I have suggested that it is one we need to address. We need to reclaim nationalism and reclaim the right to collectively define what our nation is (or should be), not in a way to reject the politics of difference and multiculturalism, but in a way that makes explicit the productive connections *between* nationalism and multiculturalism. This has been the main aim of this chapter.

Let me emphasise: nationalism, as Calhoun has asserted, "is not moral mistake" (2007, p. 1). We need to find ways for young children to grow up proud of their national identities, curious about the wealth of cultures that make up nations and aware of the ways nationalism can tip over into discriminatory attitudes and behaviours. And as Verkuyten (2014, p. 169) argues, "a well-functioning society needs a sense of commitment and common belonging, making it important to foster a spirit of shared national identity." To avoid nationalism, it seems to me, is to create this political vacuum which is then filled by extremist political discourses that defend a morally problematic nationalism. Hence, we need to give public legitimacy to more inclusive nationalism that takes in all groups in society including majorities (Modood, 2014) in an ethnic of care and so claim everyday multiculturalism as a productive form of critical nationalism.

References

Ahmed, S. (2004). Declarations of whiteness: The non-performativity of anti-racism. *Borderlands ejournal, 3*(2), 1–59.
Anderson, B. (1983). *Imagined communities*. London: Verso.
Andreouli, E. (2015). Nations and immigration. In J. Turner, C. Hewson, K. Mahendran, & P. Stevens (Eds.), *Living psychology: From the everyday to the extraordinary* (pp. 237–279). Milton Keynes, UK: The Open University.
Andreouli, E., Howarth, C., & Sonn, C. (2014). Promoting inclusive communities in contexts of diversity. *Journal of Health Psychology, 19*(1), 16–21.
Appiah, A. K. (1997). Cosmopolitan patriots. *Critical Inquiry, 23*(3), 617–639.
Back, L. (1996). *New ethnicities and urban culture: Racisms and multiculture in young lives*. (Vol. 2). London: UCL Press Limited.
Barrett, M. (2013). *Interculturalism and multiculturalism: Similarities and differences*. Strasbourg: Council of Europe Publishing.
Berry, J. W., & Kalin, R. (1995). Multicultural and ethnic attitudes in Canada: An overview of the 1991 National survey. *Canadian Journal of Behavioural Science/Revue canadienne des sciences du comportement, 27*(3), 301–320.
Billig, M. (1985). Prejudice, categorisation and particularisation: From a perceptual to a rhetorical approach. *European Journal of Social Psychology, 15*, 79–103.
Billig, M. (1988). *Ideological dilemmas: A social psychology of everyday thinking*. London: Sage.
Billig, M. (1995). *Banal nationalism*. London: Sage.
Bouchard, G. (2011). What is interculturalism? *McGill Law Journal, 56*, 2.
Brah, A. (1996). *Cartographies of diaspora: contesting identities*. London: Routledge.
Brah, A., & Phoenix, A. (2004). Ain't I a woman? Revisiting intersectionality. *Journal of International Women Studies, 5*(3), 75–86.

Calhoun, C. (2004). Is it time to be postnational? In S. May, T. Modood, & J. Squires (Eds.), *Ethnicity, nationalism and minority rights* (pp. 231–256). Cambridge, UK: Cambridge University Press.

Calhoun, C. (2007). *Nations matter: Citizenship, solidarity, and the cosmopolitan dream.* Oxford, UK: Routledge.

Condor, S. (2000). Pride and prejudice: Identity management in English people's talk about this country. *Discourse & Society, 11*(2), 175–205.

Dekker, H., Malová, D., & Hoogendoorn, S. (2003). *Political Psychology, 24*(2), 345–376.

Garner, S. (2007). *Whiteness: An introduction.* New York: Routledge.

Gellner, E. (1983). *Nations and nationalism.* Ithaca, NY: Cornell University Press.

Gilroy, P. (2004). *After empire: Melancholia or convicial culture.* London: Routledge.

Green, E., & Staerkle, C. (2013). Migration and multiculturalism. In L. Huddy, D. O. Sears & J. Levy (Eds.), *Oxford handbook of political psychology* (pp. 852–889). Oxford: Oxford University Press.

Gunaratnam, Y. (2003). *Researching 'race' and ethnicity: Methods, knowledge and power.* London: Sage.

Hage, G. (2003). *Against paranoid nationalism: Searching for hope in a shrinking society.* Annandale, Australia: Pluto Press.

Hall, S. (1988). New ethnicities. In K. Mercer (Ed.), *Black film, British cinema* (pp. 27–31). London: Institute for Contemporary Arts.

Harris, A. (2013). *Young people and everyday multiculturalism.* London: Routledge.

Hastie, B., & Augoustinos, M. (2012). Rudd's apology to the stolen generations: Challenging self-sufficient arguments in 'race' discourse. *Australian Psychologist, 47*, 118–126.

Hopkins, N., & Kahani-Hopkins, V. (2009) Reconceptualising 'extremism' and 'moderation': From categories of analysis to categories of practice in the construction of a collective identity. *British Journal of Social Psychology, 49*, 99–113.

Howarth, C. (2001). Towards a social psychology of community. *Journal for the Theory of Social Behaviour, 31*(2), 223–238.

Howarth, C. (2004). Re-presentation and resistance in the context of school exclusion: Reasons to be critical. *Journal of Community & Applied Social Psychology, 14*, 356–377.

Howarth, C. (2009). 'I hope we won't have to understand racism one day': Researching or reproducing 'race' in social psychological research? *British Journal of Social Psychology, 48*(3), 407–426.

Howarth, C., & Andreouli, C. (2016). 'Nobody wants to be an outsider': From diversity management to diversity engagement. *Political Psychology, 37*, 327–340.

Howarth, C., Andreouli, C., & Kessi, S. (2014). Social representations and the politics of participation. In T. Capelos, H. Dekker, C. Kinnvall & P. Nesbitt-Larking (Eds.), *Political psychology in Europe and the world* (pp. 21–42). London: Palgrave Macmillan.

Howarth, C., Wagner, W., Magnusson, N., & Sammut, G. (2014). 'It's only other people who make me feel black': Acculturation, identity and agency in a multicultural community. *Political Psychology, 35*, 81–95.

Johanson, K., & Glow, H. (2009). Honour bound in Australia: From defence nationalism to critical nationalism. *National Identities, 11*(4), 385–396.

Kinnvall, C. (2004). Globalisation and religious nationalism: Self, identity, and the search for ontological security. *Political Psychology, 25*(5), 741–767.

Kinnvall, C. (2014). Fear, insecurity and the (re)emergence of the far right in Europe. In P. Nesbitt-Larking, C. Kinnvall, T. Capelos & H. Dekker (Eds.), *The Palgrave handbook of global political psychology* (pp. 316–335). Basingstoke: Palgrave Macmillan.

Kinnvall, C., & Nesbitt-Larking, P. (2011). *The political psychology of globalization.* Oxford: Oxford University Press

Kymlicka, W. (2010). The rise and fall of multiculturalism? New debates on inclusion and accommodation in diverse societies. *International Social Science Journal, 61*(199), 97–112.

Modood, T. (2014). Multiculturalism, interculturalisms and the majority. *Journal of Moral Education*. Early view, 1–14.

Moghaddam, F. M. (2008). *Multiculturalism and intergroup relations: Psychological implications for democracy in a global context*. Washington, DC: APA.

Moscovici, S. (1988). Notes towards a description of social representations. *European Journal of Social Psychology, 18*, 211–250.

Nesbitt-Larking, P. (2014). Migration and multiculturalism. In P. Nesbitt-Larking, C. Kinnvall, T. Capelos & H. Dekker (Eds.), *The Palgrave handbook of global political psychology* (pp. 279–296). Basingstoke: Palgrave Macmillan.

Noble, G. (2009). Everyday cosmopolitanism and the labour of intercultural community. In A. Wise & S. Velayutham (Eds.), *Everyday multiculturalism* (pp. 47–67). Basingstoke: Palgrave Macmillan.

Penic, S., Elcheroth, G., & Reicher, S. (2015). Can patriots be critical after a nationalist war? The struggle between recognition and marginalisation of dissenting voices. *Political Psychology*. Early view.

Philips, A. (2007). *Multiculturalism without culture*. Oxford: Princeton University Press.

Phoenix, A., & Tizard, B. (2001). *Black, white or mixed race? Race and racism in the lives of young people of mixed parentage*. London: Routledge.

Phoenix, A., Howarth C., & Philogene, G. (forthcoming). The everyday politics of identities and social representations: A critical approach. *Papers on Social Representations*.

Pratto, F., Sidianus, J., & Levin, S. (2006). Social dominance theory and the dynamics of intergroup relations: Taking stock and looking forward. *European Review of Social Psychology, 17*, 51–68.

Reicher, S. Cassidy, S., Wolpert, I., Hopkins, N., & Levine, M. (2006). Saving Bulgaria's Jews: An analysis of social identity and the mobilisation of social solidarity. *European Journal of Social Psychology, 36*, 49–72.

Richards, B. (2007). *Emotional governance: Politics, media and terror*. Basingstoke: Palgrave.

Schatz, R., Staub, E., & Lavine, H. (1999). On the varieties of national attachment: Blind versus constructive patriotism. *Political Psychology, 20*, 151–174.

Scuzzarello, S. (2015). Caring multiculturalism: Power and transformation in diverse societies. *Feminist Theory, 16*(1), 67–86.

Sirin, S., & Fine, M. (2007). Hyphenated selves: Muslim American youth negotiating Identities on the fault lines of global conflict. *Applied Development Science, 11*(3), 151–163.

Tajfel, H. (1978). *Differentiation between social groups: Studies in the social psychology of intergroup relations*. London: Academic Press.

Van Oudenhoven, J., & Ward, C. (2013). Fading majority cultures: The implications of transnationalism and demographic changes for immigrant acculturation. *Journal of Community & Applied Social Psychology, 23*(2), 81–97.

Verkuyten, M. (2014). *Identity and cultural diversity*. London: Routledge.

Vertovec, S. (2010). Towards post-multiculturalism? Changing communities, conditions and contexts of diversity. *International Social Science Journal, 61*(199).

Wagner, W., Sen, R., Permanadeli, R., & Howarth, C. (2012). The veil and Muslim women's identity: Cultural pressures and resistance to stereotyping. *Culture & Psychology, 18*(4), 521–541.

Wetherell, M., & Potter, J. (1992). *Mapping the language of racism: Discourse and the legitimation of exploitation*. Hemel Hempstead: Harvester-Wheatsheaf.

Wise, A., & Velayutham, S. (2009). *Everyday multiculturalism*. New York: Palgrave MacMillan.

2
POLITICAL LEADERSHIP AND SOCIAL DIVERSITY

The everyday politics of race and gender

Martha Augoustinos, Peta Callaghan, Jasmin Sorrentino and Anna Worth

Increasing cultural diversity and norms of social equality in liberal democratic nations have made the emergence of national leaders from minority backgrounds, such as Barack Obama in the United States and Julia Gillard in Australia, more likely. Such leaders not only face special challenges in mobilising widespread social identification and political support from the wider polity, they also make salient how minorities must manage and negotiate their marginalised identities in everyday social life. Indeed the elevation of Obama and Gillard to positions of political leadership was associated with widespread debates in their respective nations about race and identity in America and gender and sexism in Australia. These public debates were not limited to formal institutional settings but also proliferated into everyday life where issues such as racial and gender inequality became salient concerns for ordinary people. Using a discursive psychological approach (Potter, 1996; Potter & Edwards, 2001), this chapter examines how the first African American president of the United States and the first female prime minister of Australia attended to their minority group memberships in their political discourse and discursively managed the categories of race and gender, respectively, when they emerged as contested topics in public debate. In conclusion, we discuss the potential such leaders with minority identities have in generating more complex and inclusive categories of national and civic identification in order to reflect the reality of increasing social diversity and for the purposes of social change.

Barack Obama and social identity

President Obama's mixed racial identity, while distinctive, is not uncommon in today's ethnically and racially diverse America. The increasing number of people who identify as multiracial was reflected in the US Census in 2013, where over 9 million people identified with two or more racial categories (US Census Bureau, 2013). This increasing diversity has led to new theoretical understandings about multiracial identity that have produced new perspectives with regard to race. According to Shih and Sanchez (2009), these new perspectives are "forcing scholars to generate new ideas about intergroup relations, racial stigmatization, social identity, social perception, discrimination, and the intersectionality of race with other social categories such as social class" (p. 1).

Despite the increasing number of Americans identifying with two or more racial categories, Obama's racial heritage is not typical of the significant African-American minority in the US. The son of a Kenyan father and a white American mother, several black critics have argued that Obama is not really an African American, as that category is commonly understood (see Walters, 2007), with one African-American columnist arguing that "other than colour, Obama did not – does not – share a heritage with the majority of black-Americans, who are descendants of plantation slaves" (Crouch, 2006). This cautious attitude toward Obama by sections of the African-American community who had questioned Obama's 'blackness' clearly demonstrates the dilemma Obama faced in gaining support from African-American voters, let alone white voters (Walters, 2007). Obama himself acknowledged this dilemma in his speech, "A More Perfect Union" (2008b), where he expressed that he had often been criticised for either being 'too black' or 'not black enough'.

Ironically, some authors have argued that Obama's atypical African-American heritage worked in his favour by allowing him to appeal to the dominant white majority. Scheiber (2004) suggests that Obama's background enabled him to neutralise the stereotypical African-American identity, thereby downplaying race as an issue. Moreover, it has been argued that Obama's cautious negotiation of his biracial heritage and his "perceived ability to transcend race: that is, not to be a Black candidate but simply an American one" (Mazama, 2007, p. 3) enabled him to run as a candidate "who represented all Americans" (Novkov, 2008, p. 649).

Obama's mixed racial heritage and unique background made it essential for him to strategically craft an identity that appealed not only to both white and black America, both of whom had expressed reservations about 'who he was', but also to an increasingly culturally diverse America – a diversity that he himself personified. A new model of leadership proposed by Haslam, Reicher and Platow (2011) premised on the tenets of social identity theory argues that in order to be perceived as best representing the group, leaders need to actively define themselves in group prototypical ways: to be effective, leaders must be 'entrepreneurs of identity' and proactively work towards constructing an identity that comes to represent the group as a whole (see also Van Knippenberg, 2011). Thus, Obama needed to forge a shared social identity with which the majority of Americans could identify and that he could embody as leader. Paradoxically, although Obama's multiracial identity presented him with various dilemmas about how to represent himself, the complexity of his social identity also provided him with the rhetorical resources to appeal to an increasingly socially and culturally diverse constituency in the US.

Next we analyse a sample of Obama's speeches during his first candidacy for President (February 10, 2007, to November 20, 2008), to demonstrate how he managed this dilemma around his identity. Having examined 58 potential speeches that were delivered during this period, 8 keynote speeches were selected for detailed discursive analysis specifically because Obama oriented to his personal and social identity in these speeches. The extracts are representative exemplars of how he managed his potentially problematic identity by shifting flexibly between representing himself as a prototypical in-group member – as part of the 'larger American story' – and representing social diversity as the very basis upon which to build a sense of commonality and identification with himself as the very exemplar of that category.

Obama's personal narrative

The following extract is taken from the beginning of Barack Obama's speech entitled "Reclaiming the American Dream" (January 29, 2008). Obama tells this personal story on a number of occasions, including in a speech of the same name delivered in November 2007. The narrative traces his family's history, simultaneously interweaving it with significant historical moments of the 20th century.

Extract 1

```
31
32   Obama(O):    now (.) it's a st↑ory that began HE↑re (1.1) in E:L DO:ra↓do (0.4)
33                when a young man (0.5) fell in love with a young woman (.) who grew u↑p
34                (0.3) down the road in Augusta
35   Audience (A):         [xx(1.8)xx]
36   O:           he::y (0.6) we got some August folks here (0.4) [there you
37                g↓o
38   A:                                                [xxXX(2.3)XXxx]
39   O:           so they came of age in the mi:dst (.) of the De↓pression
40                (1.5) a::nd this young man found odd jobs on small farms
41                and oil rigs (0.6) ah always dodging the bank failures and
42                foreclosures that were sweeping the nation at the time
43                (1.4) ah the young couple married just after wa:r broke (.)
44                out in Europe (0.8) he enlisted in Patton's army after the
45                bombing (0.5) of Pearl Har↓bor(1.1) she gave birth to their
46                daugh↑ter (0.7) on the base at (0.8) Fort Leavenworth a::nd
47                she worked o:n a bomber assembly line (0.6) when he le↑ft
48                (.) for wa↓r (1.5) in a ti::me of great uncertain↓ty (0.9)
49                and great anxie↓ty (1.1) my grandparents held on to a
50                simple dream (0.7) that they could rai↑se my mother in a
51                la:nd of bo↑undless opportunity (1.3) that their
52                generation's struggle (.) and sacrifice (.3) could give
53                he:r (0.3) the FR↑eedom (0.9) to be what she wanted to be
54                (0.8) to li::ve how she wanted to li↓ve (1.6) I am
55                sta:nding here today (.) because that dream (.) was
56                rea↓lized (1.0) [because
```

57	A:	[xxxXXX(8.9)XXXxx]
58	O:	because m↑y grandfather got the chance to go to scho:ol on
59		the GI Bill (1.0) buy a house (.) through the federal
60		housing authority (0.2) and move his family west (0.9) a:ll
61		the way to Hawaii
62	A:	[hhHH(4.4)HHhh]
63	O:	the weather is a little warm↑er in Hawaii
64	A:	[hh(2.0)hh]
65	O:	where my mother would go to college and one day fall in
66		love (.) with another (0.6) young man (0.8) ah from Kenya
67		(1.2) I am here because that dream (0.2) made my parents'
68		love possible even th↓en (0.8) because it meant that after
69		my father left (0.9) when my mother struggled as a single
70		parent (0.5) and even had to turn to fo↑od stamps (.) for a
71		time >while she was still going to school and working at
72		the same ti↓me< (.) she was still able to send m:y (.)
73		sister and me to the best scho:ols in the country [and I
74		am ...
75	A:	[xxxXXXXXXX(7.1)XXXXXXXxxx]

(Obama, 2008a)

Here Obama recounts a narrative that is shaped by culturally valued activities and endpoints (Gergen, 1988) that include significant moments in American history: the Depression, the Second World War, geographical and social mobility and of course, rising up over adversity. This narrative positions Obama's family as underdogs – strong, resilient and determined to succeed. Vandello, Goldschmied and Richards (2007) identify this 'underdog' narrative as a strategy that emphasises triumph over adversity, and it is grounded in the principles of justice, fairness and deservingness. It is a narrative that is frequently drawn upon by politicians as it has great audience appeal. Notably, it elicits applause from the audience on line 57.

The two points where extended applause is elicited also signify Obama's invocation of the well-known narrative of the American Dream. This narrative is defined by stories of aspiration and social mobility, and the United States is predominantly characterised as a 'land of boundless opportunities' (ll. 51–52). Obama cites the realisation of both his grandparents' and mother's aspirations for themselves and their children, thereby representing himself as the product of two generations who held onto this 'simple dream'. It was through hard work, struggle and sacrifice that his candidacy for president was made possible.

What is most significant about Extract 1 is the absence of any explicit reference to Obama's racial identity. Obama refers to race only implicitly when telling his family's story; for example, he describes his father as a "young man from Kenya" (ll. 66–67) thus, only alluding to race implicitly by the use of this ethnic category. Similarly, the categories he uses to describe his family include "young man" (ll. 32; 40; 66), "young woman" (l. 33), "the young couple" (l. 43), "my grandparents" (l. 50), "my grandfather" (l. 58), "my father" (l. 69), "my mother" (ll. 51; 65; 69) and "my sister" (l. 73). Thus, Obama avoids explicit references to racial categories by using membership categories that predominantly relate to age ('young') and family ('grandparents').

Another implicit reference to race can be seen when Obama describes the "dream that made my parents love possible even then" (ll. 67–68). Whilst there is no explicit reference to the fact that his parents were a mixed-race couple, he orients to the fact that his parents' love at that time (the 1960s) was unusual. In short, in the "Reclaiming the American Dream" speech, Obama avoids using racial categories when attending to his identity to instead emphasise a story that appeals to the category of the common people: an American story that draws on widely shared collective narratives of American history and American values – narratives that make salient his *American* ancestry and roots.

Indeed such indirect and implicit references to racial categories were typical in other speeches during Obama's presidential campaign. Thus, throughout Obama's political campaign he avoided and downplayed explicit reference to his racial identity. We are not claiming, however, that Obama did not mention or discuss issues of race (see, for example, Obama's speech "Changing the Odds for Urban America", July 18, 2007), but rather that when attending to his own identity (i.e. telling 'his story'), racial category memberships are primarily implicit rather than explicit – an avoidance which led to criticism from sections of the African-American community. However, in March 2008, it emerged that the Reverend Jeremiah White – Obama's minister – delivered sermons in which he vehemently criticised the entrenched nature of racism in America and appeared to be justifying the attacks of September 11, 2001, on the basis of US foreign policy. The ensuing public condemnation of Reverend Wright forced Barack Obama to attend to his racial identity.

Obama's speech "A More Perfect Union", which came to be known as the 'Race Speech', was the first time Obama explicitly attended to his racial identity during the presidential campaign. A content analysis of the 58 speeches in the data corpus we examined indicated that Obama rarely made explicit references to his racial identity during the campaign before the Race Speech, with only one other explicit reference to his racial identity (in a speech addressing racial inequality and civil rights injustices related to the Jena Six incident), compared to eight implicit references. After the Race Speech, two explicit and five implicit references were made to his racial identity.

Extract 2

```
59  O:   ...I am the so↓n of a black man (0.5) from Kenya and er
60        (0.4) a white wo↑man from Kansas (1.1) I was ra::ised
61        with the help of a white grandfather who survived a
62        Depress↓ion to serve in (0.5) Patton's Army during World
63        War Tw↑o (0.6) and a wh= =white grandmother who worked on
64        a bomber assembly li↓ne at (.) Fort Leavenworth (0.4)
65        while he was overseas (1.0) I've gone to some of the best
66        schools in Amer↑ica and lived in one of the world's
67        poorest nations (1.1) I am married to a black American
```

```
68      who carries within her the blood of sla::ves and
69      slave:own↓ers (0.7) an inher↑itanc::e we pass on to our
70      two precious daughters (1.1) I have brothers (.) sisters (.) nieces (.) nephews
71      uncles a↑nd cousins of every race
72      (.hhh) and every hu↓e (0.5) scattered across three
73      continents and for as LO:ng as I LI↑ve I will never
74      forget (0.5) that in no other country on ea::rth (0.8) is
75      my story even poss↓ible (1.8) it's a sto::ry (0.4) that
76      hasn't made me (.) the most COnvention↓al (0.4) of
77      candidates (1.2) But it is a sto::ry that has sea↑red
78      into my genetic makeup (0.4) the id↑ea that this nation
79      is mo::re than the sum of its parts (1.1) that out of
80      ma↑ny (0.4) we are tru::ly one
```
(Obama, 2008b)

In this extract Obama employs the familiar narrative evident in Extract 1. However, in this instance, Obama makes explicit reference to racial categories, adding the category 'black' or 'white' to reference his parents' racial identities; "a black man from Kenya and a white woman from Kansas" (ll. 59–60). The strategically placed pauses and emphasis make these colour categories more explicit. Following this, Obama also refers to his grandparents' racial identities; he was "raised with the help of a white grandfather" (ll. 60–61) and "a white grandmother" (l. 63). Again, Obama emphasises these colour categories to make his racial identity salient. In this way Obama is explicitly constructing a multiracial identity for himself.

Obama describes a number of varied and contrasting social locations to emphasise the *diversity* of his background and experience, such as the descriptions of his grandparents surviving the Depression and of life in America during World War II (ll. 62–63), which also appeared in Extract 1. Obama also makes reference to having attended some of the best schools in America while also having lived in one of the world's poorest nations (ll. 66–67). He also highlights that he has "brothers, sisters, nieces, nephews, uncles and cousins of every race and every hue scattered across three continents" (ll. 70–73). Thus Obama constructs a version of himself that draws on a repertoire of not only racial but also social diversity.

In Extract 2, we can also see Obama attend to the criticism that he is 'not black enough' because his African heritage was not borne out of slavery. He strategically positions himself in relation to this potentially problematic identity by highlighting his connection to slavery indirectly through his marriage (ll. 67–69). In this extract, Obama explicitly recognises that he is an unconventional candidate and also an unconventional American. However, rather than minimising or discounting his difference, Obama represents it here as an actual strength in current day America: "out of many we are truly one" (ll. 79–80). Thus Obama draws upon a nationalist discourse that we see recurrently throughout his speeches, where the American people are constituted as one people, despite the social and cultural differences within the nation's borders.

Representing social diversity

In this section we examine how Barack Obama was able to represent himself as a prototypical ingroup member despite his own admissions that he was not a 'conventional candidate'. We have already detailed some of the ways Obama accomplished this. For example, by threading and weaving his story with significant moments in American history, he fused his self-identity with that of the nation (Reicher & Hopkins, 2001). In addition, Obama worked proactively to position himself as embodying the American Dream by aligning his life and experiences with the central and core values of the nation.

Extract 3 comes from Obama's "American Promise" speech delivered in August 2008. Here we see Obama positioning himself as not only understanding the diverse interests of different social groups within American society, but also identifying with their aspirations. As we saw in Extract 1, Obama integrates and connects the aspirations of diverse social groups into his own family's story and lived experience. In so doing, Obama depicts himself as the embodiment of diversity. He is capable of listening and empathising with diverse interest groups *because* he is both a prototypical ingroup member and the very exemplar of social diversity.

Extract 3

```
153
154   O:   ... the fundamentals we use to measure economic strength (.)
155        are whether we are (0.6) living up to that fund↑amental
156        promis:e that has made this country gr↓eat (0.3) a
157        promis::e (0.3) that is the only reason I am standing (0.2)
158        he:re to↓night (1.2) because (.) in the FAces of those
159        young veterans who (0.2) come back from Iraq and
160        Afghani↑stan (0.9) I see my grand↓father (0.7) who signed
161        up after Pearl Har↓bor (0.7) marched in Patton's Army (0.4)
162        and was reward↑ed by a grateful nation (0.5) with the
163        chance to go to college on the GI Bill (1.3) in the fa:ce
164        of [that young stu↑dENT (0.9)
165   A:      [xxx(4.4)xxx]
166   O:   who SLEeps JUst THree hours beFORe working the night]
167        sh↓ift (0.6) I think about my mo↓m (0.4) who rai::sed (.)
168        my sister and me (0.3) on her own while she worked and
169        earned her deg↓ree (0.8)
170   A:   [right]
171   O:   who once tu::rned to food stamps but was still able to send
172        us to the best scho:ols in the country (0.6)
173   A:   [right]
174   O:   with the help of [student loans and scholarships (2.6) when
175        I (3.9)
176   A:      [xxxXXXXX(9.7)XXXXXxxx]
177   O:   when I lis↑ten] (0.3) to ano↓ther worker tell me that his
178        (.) factory has shut down (.) I remem↑ber all those men and
179        women on the south side of Chica↓go who (.hhh) I stood by
```

```
180      and fought for tw:o decades ago (0.3) after the local steel
181      plant clo↓sed (1.3) and wh↑en I he:ar a woman talk about
182      the difficulties of (0.3) starting her own business (.) or
183      making her way in the world I think about my grandmother
184      (0.8) who wo:rked her way u↑p from the secretarial po↓ol to
185      middle management (0.7) despite years of being passed over
186      for promotions because she was a wo↓man (1.2) SHe's the one
187      who taught me about ha:rd work (1.0) she's the one who put
188      o↑ff (.) bu:ying a new car (0.5) or a new dress (.) for
189      herself (0.7) so that I could ha:ve a better life (1.1) she
190      po::ured everything she had (.) into m↓e . . .
```
(Obama, 2008c)

In this extract, Obama once again integrates his personal story with the lives and experiences of everyday Americans. Obama represents himself as embodying and personifying typical American stories told to him by the American people by voicing these stories through his own lived experience. This allows him to depict himself as a prototypical ingroup member who has lived, experienced and embodied such hardships whilst simultaneously establishing collective and shared values with his audience. Whilst Obama arguably constructs his identity as an *exceptional* prototypical American, he simultaneously constructs himself as someone who is truly representative of the diverse and varied experiences within America.

As the first black president of the United States, Obama actively crafted an identity that appealed to a broad constituency, sections of which had problematised his identity as either 'too black' or 'not black enough'. We demonstrated earlier how Obama responded to the 'challenge of his blackness' (McIlwain, 2007) by proactively working towards constructing an identity for himself as the prototypical American who could represent America as a whole (Van Knippenberg, 2011). He achieved this by making only implicit references to his racial identity: significantly explicit references to his racial identity were rare during the presidential campaign, even after the Race Speech (Extract 2). More importantly, Obama strategically emphasised the diversity of his group memberships and allegiances, a diversity that he commonly referenced as constituting the very nature of contemporary American society. By doing so, Obama's identity discourse can be seen to be both oriented towards depicting himself as an exemplar of the increasing social diversity of American society and simultaneously constituting that diversity as an identity marker.

Prime Minister Julia Gillard and gender

It is unquestionable that political leadership has been predominantly a male prerogative. Although women's representation in senior leadership roles has increased since the 1970s, they remain significantly underrepresented in elite leadership positions (Eagly & Karau, 2002). Moreover, while the legitimisation of discrimination against women has decreased over time (Jetten, Branscombe, Iyer & Asai, 2013), women in leadership roles are judged by different standards, which makes it difficult for them to succeed in higher level leadership positions despite their individual abilities and achievements (Ryan & Haslam, 2005).

In 2010, Julia Gillard became Australia's first female prime minister. Despite this historical milestone and the wider symbolic significance for gender politics in Australia, Gillard's prime ministership was dogged by controversy from the outset: her elevation to the position was achieved by a leadership challenge to the incumbent prime minister, Kevin Rudd, an act that many in the media represented as treacherous and 'unbecoming' of a woman (Hall & Donaghue, 2012). Moreover, when she did lead the Labor Party to an election victory in August of the same year, it was only after negotiating a coalition with the Greens and with minor independents to form what many perceived as a precarious minority government. Perhaps what generated the most controversy and media coverage nationally and internationally, however, was a speech she made in the Australian parliament on October 9, 2012, where she accused the leader of the Opposition, Tony Abbot, of sexism and misogyny. This speech was made after a protracted period in which the prime minister was subjected to a daily barrage of offensive sexist abuse by her political opponents and through social media (for details see Summers, 2013). This speech generated polarised responses: the majority of the political commentariat in Australia condemned the speech, accusing Gillard of playing the 'gender card' for strategic political purposes and igniting what was referred to as the 'gender wars'. In contrast, women all over the world, primarily via social media, applauded Gillard's stand against sexism. These contradictory public responses demonstrated the highly contested meanings and significance attached to sexism and misogyny as social issues and how different social groups oriented to these concerns as either 'real' social problems that needed to be addressed or irrelevant distractions from the practical concerns of ordinary people (see Worth, Augoustinos & Hastie, in press).

More importantly for the purposes of the present analysis, Gillard's landmark speech on sexism and misogyny stands in stark contrast to the first 18 months of her incumbency during which she actively downplayed the relevance of gender to her role and status as prime minister. Specifically, in the following analysis we present naturalistic data during this time to demonstrate how Gillard oriented to, resisted and negotiated her identity as a woman when questions regarding her gender were put to her directly. A comprehensive search of the Internet for publicly available television, radio and web interviews during this period in which questions about gender were put directly to Gillard were selected for detailed analysis. The search produced a corpus of 10 such instances. The following extracts are representative exemplars of how Gillard managed and negotiated such questions.

Australia's first female prime minister: Downplaying gender

In Extract 4, Gillard is being interviewed by Liz Jackson from the ABC documentary program *Four Corners* (Jackson, 2011), seven months after becoming PM. In this extract Jackson asks Gillard whether she is proud to be "Australia's first female Prime Minister". Here, Jackson immediately orients to Gillard's gender, therefore making it discursively relevant.

Extract 4

```
37  LJ:  Are you proud to be Australia's first female Prime Minister?
38       (.6)
39  JG:  well I'm proud to be prime minister and I'm conscious((smiley
40       talk))ah that it's a:: a record being the first ah woman. hhh
41       ah to hold this job. hhh but I don't (.) really in my own
42       mind (.) put a big emphasis on that. hhh ah I've said it in
43       the past and I genuinely feel it I don't. hhh view myself as
44       a. hhh woman politician. hhh I view myself as a politician
45       (.) who's a woman. hhh I didn't (.) go into politics
46       predominantly. hhh to make a point about (.) women and
47       equality. hhh I went into politics to make a point about
48       opportunity and change
```

(Jackson, 2011)

Gillard's relatively long delay in responding to the question is followed by a well-prefaced short utterance and then an agreement token "I'm proud to be prime minister" (l. 39), which is then constituted by a qualification of the agreement: although recognising that it is a "record being the first woman to hold this job" (ll. 40–41) she does not "put a big emphasis on" it (l. 42). This particular construction functions to mitigate the role her gender plays in her own evaluation and is further supported at lines 42 and 43, where Gillard goes on to say that she has "said it in the past", implying that her position is recurrent rather than being spontaneously invoked by the current interaction. Gillard proceeds to further solidify her position by stating that she views herself, first and foremost, as a "politician who's a woman" (ll. 44–45) rather than a "woman politician" (l. 44). Here, Gillard privileges her role as a politician first and foremost and once again downplays her gender as merely inconsequential. Through this delicate management of the membership category 'woman', Gillard plays down her gender by separating it from her identity as PM. Moreover, she makes clear that what drives her politically is not to "make a point about women and equality" but about "opportunity and change" (ll. 45–48). Thus not only does Gillard play down her own identity as a woman, she also distances herself from what may be perceived as a potentially problematic *feminist* identity.

The next extract comes from an internationally live web broadcast (Interview with Julia Gillard, 2012) in which Gillard is taking questions from a wide audience. In this extract the speaker positions Gillard as a role model for "young women" and "little girls" around the world. As in the previous extract, Gillard again is explicitly asked to attend to her status as Australia's first female PM.

Extract 5

```
 7  OP:  hi (.3) I'm Orsi Parkanyi founder and director of women as
 8         entrepreneurs. hhh and my question to the Prime Minister
 9         today (.4) is how does it feel to be the first female Prime
10         Minster (.) in Australi::a. hhh and what message would you
11         send (.) to little girl::s (.) and young women (.) around
12         Australia and all around the world (.4) who are dreaming of
13         becoming leaders (.3) or perhaps (.) even Prime Ministers
14         (.3) thank you
15         (1.8)
16  JG:  oh-I hope there are a lot of a::h girls and women around
17         the world and in Australia dreaming of becoming Prime
18         Minister. hhh I think that would be a fantastic thing
19         if they're doing that in very very large numbers. hhh ah
20         I don't (.) real::ly ah (.) wake up in the morning and think to
21         myself "gee (.3) y'know I'm the first woman to do this job"
22         (.) ah I get out there and I do the job ah guided by (.)
23         y'know my values my labour values by the things that
24         brought me to join the labour party a long long time ago
25         when I was a. hhh much younger woman. hhh um (.) so(.)
26         y'know I'm not (.4) sort of out there (.) thinking day
27         after day (.) first woman to do the job. hhh
```
(Interview with Julia Gillard, 2012)

Gillard's response again occurs following a very long delay at lines 14–15. Gillard begins by constructing an account that demonstrates her support for women's self-determination and describes the idea of women pursing positions of leadership as "a fantastic thing" (l. 17). This is made more robust through the deployment of the extreme case formulation (Pomerantz, 1986) "very large numbers" at line 18. However, rather than follow on with a discussion about what it's like to be the first female PM, Gillard claims that being "the first woman to do the job" (l. 20) does not privilege her thinking. This works to present herself as someone who supports women's opportunities and success, however mitigates her own success and accomplishments as the first woman to do the job. Furthermore, Gillard's "I get out there and I do the job guided by y'know my values my labour values" at lines 20 to 22 again emphasises how her motivation to get into politics was based on her egalitarian ideals, values that motivated her to join the Labor Party.

Once again Gillard mitigates the relevance and significance of her identity as a woman to her role as PM, but at the same time encourages and supports women who may choose to pursue positions of leadership. The structure of her turn is interesting as it involves complex paradoxes between supporting the empowerment of women, on the one hand, whilst simultaneously downplaying the symbolic significance others may attach to her being the first female PM, on the other. Although this could be seen as a form of modesty on Gillard's part to downplay her own achievements, it can also be seen as a delicate management of her image as leader – as someone who represents everyone's interests and not women's interests alone.

'You have no family': Emphasising social diversity

Extract 6 is an interaction between Gillard and an audience member on ABC's Q&A (Jones, 2010) program in August 2010. In the following example, Gillard's purported lack of a family is positioned by the audience member as the chief reason for Gillard's perceived inability to relate to Australian families. Such an account highlights Gillard's deviation from what is understood to be normative gendered behaviour.

Extract 6

```
218   MH:   Prime Minister u::h some of the Australians think (.) you
219         have no family (.5) so you will not really (.) understand
220         their concerns (.5) ah my question is (.) how will you
221         persuade these people (.5) to believe that (.) their
222         worries (.) their worries are not necessary (.8) thank you
223         (.4)
224   JG:   .hhh oka::y um (.)thank you and thank you for asking the
225         question because I think it's a question on a lot of
226         people's. hhh minds but sometimes people think they
227         shouldn't .hhh ask questions about (.) y'know personal
228         circumstances but I think it's good to talk about it .hhh
229         and I suppose what I would sa:y first and foremost is .hhh
230         is there's never going to b:e ah one Australian who can
231         encapsulate in their own life experience. hhh the story of
232         every other Australian .hhh ah you've always got to be
233         prepared to listen and learn from other people's
234         experiences .hhh I'm never gonna to know what it's like to
235         be an Indigenous Australian I'm never go (.) going to know
236         what it's like to be someone who has .hhh a disabil::ity
237         and has had to negotiate the world with that disability
238         .hhh ah John Howard didn't know what it was like to be a
239         mother. hhh and so the list goe:s on
```

(Jones, 2010)

Gillard's response to Han's question is prefaced by considerable delay (l. 223) and a hedged "okay" (l. 224), suggesting that a delicate issue has been broached. In what might be seen as an attempt to normalise the interactional trouble Han's question introduces, Gillard thanks Han "for asking the question" (ll. 224–225). Gillard's account is interesting in two ways. First, Gillard's "there's never going to be one Australian who can encapsulate in their own life experience the story of every other Australian" (ll. 229–231) is a rhetorically robust one which is difficult to undermine. It also simultaneously defends Gillard's identity, which has been tainted by the stigma associated with being childless. Gillard's argument is further strengthened by the use of extreme case formulations (Pomerantz, 1986) such as "never" (ll. 229; 233; 234), "every" (l. 231) and "always" (l. 232). Second, it is noteworthy that, unlike Obama, Gillard does not attempt to construct an identity for herself as having lived and embraced a diverse range of experiences, but rather accentuates and embraces the fact that people have varied and unique experiences.

What is interesting to note about this exchange is how Gillard has turned a gendered account into a predominantly gender neutral one by emphasising social and cultural diversity ("Indigenous Australian", ll. 233–234; "someone who has a disability", l. 235). Therefore, by redirecting the interaction towards the importance of diversity, Gillard is able to avoid further discussion about her perceived transgression of conventional norms (marriage and children). Unlike Obama though, who was able to transcend his non-normative identity by emphasising his embodiment and personification of America's increasing social diversity, Gillard invokes diversity as a rhetorically robust bottom-line argument to neutralise her childless and unmarried status.

Minority leadership and social change

Like Obama's Race Speech, Gillard's misogyny speech was made after increasing public pressure to defend herself from relentless criticism she faced on a daily basis and to address sexism and misogyny as a significant social issue not just for herself but for all women. As we have demonstrated, up to that point in time, like Obama, Gillard actively downplayed the significance of her gender as prime minister and avoided gender politics even when speaking to feminist audiences (Summers, 2013). Clearly then, leaders from minority category memberships face special challenges in managing their identities that leaders from dominant groups do not need to manage.

Notwithstanding these challenges, minority leaders like Obama and Gillard have the potential to generate more complex and inclusive categories of national and civic identification in order to reflect the reality of increasing social diversity and for the purposes of social change. For example, Obama's entrepreneurial identity work has been to craft and project an identity that has the potential to radically transform what it means to be a prototypical American; Obama's own embodiment of racial and social diversity could become the basis upon which to build an alternative national identity that the dominant majority may come to value over time. Obama's presidency has provided the necessary political conditions to facilitate more complex constructions of social identity (Brewer, 2010) so that projections of the national self-image become more inclusive of the increasing diversity of American society. As Brewer (2010) argues, the increasing reality of socially diverse societies does not guarantee this, and prevailing norms must be consistent with this diversity: it is here where political leadership can be instrumental in providing a political climate that values social diversity and inclusiveness.

Despite Obama's reluctance to explicitly address racial issues during his first term as president, his second term has enabled him to discuss racial issues more openly (Shapiro, 2013). As several black scholars have cogently argued, however, the fact that race remains a socially divisive issue in the US exposes the myth of post-racism in America (Greene, 2010; Reed, 2010; Teasley & Ikard, 2010). It will take much more than one black president to transform the entrenched racial fabric of American society.

Female national leaders also have the same potential to challenge normative understandings of everyday politics and identities. It is clear, however, that female national leaders face unique challenges that male leaders, regardless of race, class or ethnicity, do not. Female leaders face a 'double bind' which requires them to display high levels of traditional masculine qualities whilst maintaining sufficient femininity so as not to be disliked (Hall & Donaghue, 2012). Characteristics that are traditionally understood as vital to successful leadership (such as assertiveness, confidence and ambition) tend to be associated with coldness and unfemininity, and therefore come at a substantial cost to the popularity and electoral success of female politicians (Jamieson, 1995). Much has been written and speculated as to the role that gender played in Gillard's political demise, but what is clear is that unlike her male counterparts, Gillard was constantly required to attend to and strategically manage gender as a significant identity marker. Like Obama, who lamented that he was either 'too black' or 'not black enough', Gillard too had to tread a fine line between affirming her identity as a woman and rendering it irrelevant to her position as national leader. Despite the criticisms that Gillard's sexism and misogyny speech received by the mainstream press, many ordinary men and women perceived it as a "landmark speech for the nation", and one that would "define her prime ministership" (Summers, 2013, p. 98).

As we write this chapter, Hilary Clinton just became the Democratic nominee for the US presidency. Gender has already featured as a salient concern during her campaign, most notably by attacks made against her by her Republican rival, Donald Trump. As social and political psychologists, we have a tremendous opportunity to examine and analyse how and when gender will feature during the campaign as a salient social issue and how Clinton manages her identity as a woman when it becomes relevant in social interaction and public discourse. An important goal for future research is to determine how leaders from minority backgrounds negotiate this tricky terrain of garnering widespread public support without compromising their valued minority identities.

References

Brewer, M. B. (2010). Social identity complexity and acceptance of diversity. In R. J. Crisp (Ed.), *The psychology of social and cultural diversity* (pp. 11–33). Oxford: Wiley-Blackwell.

Crouch, S. (2006, November 2nd). What Obama isn't: Black like me on race. *New York Daily News*. Retrieved March 16, 2009, from www.nydailynews.com/opinions/2006/11/02/2006-11-02what_obama_isnt_black_like_me_on_race.html

Eagly, A. H., & Karau, S. J. (2002). Role congruity theory of prejudice toward female leaders. *Psychological Review, 109*, 573–598.

Gergen, M. (1988). Narrative structures in social explanation. In C. Antaki (Ed.), *Analysing everyday explanations* (pp. 94–112). London: Sage.

Gillard, J. (2012, October 10). Transcript of Julia Gillard's speech. *Sydney Morning Herald*. Retrieved May 27, 2016, from www.smh.com.au/federal-politics/political-news/transcript-of-julia-gillards-speech-20121009-27c36.html#ixzz49omif66B

Greene, B. (2010). 2009 Carolyn Wood Sherif award address: Riding Trojan horses from symbolism to structural change: In feminist psychology context matters. *Psychology of Women Quarterly, 34*, 443–457.

Hall, L.J., & Donaghue, N. (2012). 'Nice girls don't carry knives': Constructions of ambition in media coverage of Australia's first female Prime Minister. *British Journal of Social Psychology, 52*, 631–647.

Haslam, A., Reicher, S., & Platow, M. (2011). *A new psychology of leadership*. East Sussex: Psychology Press.

Interview with Julia Gillard. (2012, July 20). Prime Minister Julia Gillard answers Google+ Hangout with OurSay, Desakin University and Fairfax Media. Retrieved from www.youtube.com/watch?v=NhUOmfVT0SU

Jackson, L. (Presenter). (2011). The real Julia Gillard [Television series episode]. Four Corners, Australia Broadcasting Corporation.

Jamieson, K. H. (1995). *Beyond the double bind: Women and leadership*. New York: Oxford University Press.

Jetten, J., Branscombe, N. R., Iyer, A., & Asai, N. (2013). Appraising gender discrimination as legitimate or illegitimate: Antecedents and consequences. In M. K. Ryan & N. R. Branscombe (Eds.), *Handbook of gender and psychology* (pp. 306–322). London: Sage.

Jones, T. (Presenter). (2010). Julia Gillard special [Television series episode]. Q&A, Australian Broadcasting Corporation.

Mazama, A. (2007). The Barack Obama phenomenon. *Journal of Black Studies, 38*, 3–6.

McIlwain, C. D. (2007). Perceptions of leadership and the challenge of Obama's blackness. *Journal of Black Studies, 38*, 64–74.

Novkov, J. (2008). Rethinking race in American politics. *Political Research Quarterly, 61*, 648–659.

Obama, B. (2007, November 7). *Reclaiming the American dream*. Retrieved April 8, 2009, from www.barackobama.com/2007/11/07/remarks of senator barack obam 31.php

Obama, B. (2008a, January 29). *Reclaiming the American dream*. Retrieved July 10, 2009, from www.youtube.com/watch?v=t1lt_xABGcM&NR=l

Obama, B. (2008b, March 18). *A more perfect union*. Retrieved July 10, 2009, from www.youtube.com/watch?v=pWe7wTVbLUU

Obama, B. (2008c, August, 28). *The American promise*. Retrieved July 10, 2009, from www.youtube.com/watch?v=ato7BtisXzE

Pomerantz, A. M. (1986). Extreme case formulations: A way of legitimizing claims. *Human Studies, 9*, 219–230.

Potter, J. (1996). *Representing reality: Discourse, rhetoric and social construction*. London: Sage.

Potter, J., & Edwards, D. (2001). Discursive social psychology. In W. P. Robinson & H. Giles (Eds.), *The new handbook of language and social psychology* (pp. 103–118). Chichester: John Wiley & Sons.

Reed, P. D. (2010). Barack Obama's improbable election and the question of race and racism in contemporary America. *Journal of Black Studies, 40*, 373–379.

Reicher, S., & Hopkins, N. (2001). *Self and nation*. London: Sage.

Ryan, M. K., & Haslam, S. A. (2005). The glass cliff: Evidence that women are over-represented in precarious leadership positions. *British Journal of Management, 16*, 81–90.

Scheiber, N. (2004). Race against history. *The New Republic, 230*(20), 21–26.

Shapiro, A. (2013). Obama warms to speaking openly about race. *Code switch: Frontiers of race, culture and ethnicity*. Retrieved July 16, 2014, from www.npr.org/blogs/codeswitch/2013/08/03/208358153/has-obama-changed-his-stance-on-speaking-about-race

Shih, M., & Sanchez, D. (2009). When race becomes even more complex: Toward understanding the landscape of multiracial identity and experience. *Journal of Social Issues, 65*(1), 1–11.
Summers, A. (2013). *The misogyny factor*. Sydney: New South.
Teasley, M., & Ikard, D. (2010). Barack Obama and the politics of race: The myth of postracism in America. *Journal of Black Studies, 40,* 411–425.
United States Census Bureau. (2013). ACS demographic and housing estimates. Retrieved from http://factfinder.census.gov/faces/tableservices/jsf/pages/productview.xhtml?pid=ACS_13_3YR_DP05&prodType=table
Vandello, J., Goldschmied, N., & Richards, D. (2007). The appeal of the underdog. *Personality and Social Psychology Bulletin, 33,* 1603–1616.
Van Knippenberg, D. (2011). Embodying who we are: Leader group prototypicality and leadership effectiveness. *Leadership Quarterly, 22,* 1078–1091.
Walters, R. (2007). Barack Obama and the politics of blackness. *Journal of Black Studies, 38*(1), 7–29.
Worth, A., Augoustinos, M., & Hastie, B. (in press). Playing the gender card: Media representations of Julia Gillard's sexism and misogyny speech. *Feminism and Psychology.*

Transcription Notation

Symbol	Function
1	Line number.
[text]	Indicates the start and end point of overlapping speech.
(# of seconds)	A number in parentheses indicates the length, in seconds, of a pause in speech.
(.)	A micro pause of less than 0.2 seconds.
↓	Indicates falling pitch or intonation.
↑	Indicates rising pitch or intonation.
>text<	Indicates that the enclosed speech was delivered more rapidly than usual for the speaker.
<text>	Indicates that the enclosed speech was delivered more slowly than usual for the speaker.
ALL CAPS	Indicates shouted or increased volume in speech.
Underlined	Indicates that the speaker is emphasising or stressing the speech.
:	Indicates prolongation of sound.
(.hhh)	Audible inhalation.
...	Indicates that the speech continues.
=	Indicates the break and subsequent continuation of a single utterance.
[xxx(length in sec)xxx]	Applause
[hh(length in sec)hh]	Laughter

3

EVERYDAY POLITICS, EVERYDAY RACISM

Censure and management of racist talk

Stephen Gibson

Since the so-called discursive turn of the 1980s, a great deal of social psychological work has been directed at trying to deconstruct contemporary talk and text around 'race'. Classic early work – notably that of Potter and Wetherell (1987) and Wetherell and Potter (1992) – used the topic of racism to outline many of the central methods and concepts of the discursive approach. At the same time, other scholars were drawing on work in classical rhetorical scholarship, sociology and political science to challenge some long-held theoretical and methodological assumptions concerning racism and prejudice in social psychology (e.g. Billig, 1988; Billig et al., 1988; Condor, 1988). These developments led to a rich tradition of work exploring race talk, which has sought to understand the ways in which exclusion continued to be legitimated in western liberal democracies characterised by an apparent norm against prejudice, and in particular against racism (see Augoustinos & Every, 2007; Goodman, 2014 for reviews).

This tradition of work can be understood as an exemplar *par excellence* of the study of everyday political reasoning. However, despite this extensive literature, it has been suggested that discursive work has yet to engage fully with the dialogical production of racism (Condor, 2006; Condor et al., 2006; Condor & Figgou, 2012). Similarly, it is only recently that the well-established finding that there is a taboo against racism (i.e. 'I'm not racist but. . . .'; van Dijk, 1992) has been matched by serious analytic attention to an apparent taboo against *accusations* of racism.

In arguing that much discursive work fails to take seriously the dialogical nature of prejudice, Condor (2006) and Condor et al. (2006) have noted that many analyses assume an individual actor engaged in acts of self-presentation on their own behalf. In contrast, Condor argues that racist discourse should be theorised as being produced in social contexts characterised by complex networks of social relationships and interactions between individuals. Because of this, not only does appearing to be racist pose problems, but challenging racism is extremely problematic as well.

> For ordinary social actors to openly challenge prejudiced talk as it arises incidentally in the flow of mundane conversation might seriously jeopardize their relationships with others, which might in turn have ramifications well beyond the particular local context in which the 'scene' takes place.
> *(Condor, 2006, p. 16)*

This suggests a need to further explore how, in practice, accusations of racism might actually be accomplished.

> A consideration of the process by which charges of racism are made, accepted, challenged, denied or ignored in the course of social interaction might afford a perspective in which the status of any particular utterance, action or event as 'racist' or 'prejudiced' may itself be treated as a social accomplishment.
> *(Condor et al., 2006, p. 445)*

This injunction to attend to what counts as 'racist' or 'prejudiced' is related to a similar concern to avoid reifying race categories in research and instead to explore how these are constructed (Condor, 1988; Howarth, 2009). Work on the ways in which accusations of racism are made and responded to is still at a relatively early stage, although there is preliminary evidence that in the UK context at least there has been a striking inversion of the norm against racism whereby speakers can position themselves as speaking uncomfortable truths by highlighting and challenging the norm (e.g. Capdevila & Callaghan, 2008; Goodman, 2010).

In what follows, I want to illustrate how an approach which takes seriously the dialogical management of racist talk can be used to explore an extended case example in which a speaker is explicitly censured for racism. The aim is to show how this particular censure is occasioned, how it is enacted and how it is responded to. My aim is not to offer this as a typical or general case of censure for racism, but in drawing attention to this I want to highlight (a) the possibilities of such an approach to extend individual-level analyses of racism, and (b) the value of paying close attention to the unfolding of discursive events over an extended sequence of interaction. In doing this, the focus of the present analysis will be on the dialogical dynamics of the interview interaction. Space constraints preclude a fuller analysis of the extent to which the interview talk draws on historically embedded interpretative repertoires, but following Wetherell (2003, p. 13), it is important to note that although '[t]he interview is a highly specific social production, . . . it also draws on routine and highly consensual (cultural/normative) resources that carry beyond the immediate local context, connecting local talk with discursive history' (see Gibson, in press; Gibson & Hamilton, 2011 for analyses of race talk based on the wider dataset which engage more fully with the implications of this line of argument).

It should be noted that the data to be presented in the following sections include some extremely offensive ethnophaulisms (disparaging terms for ethnic or national groups), including what Billig (2001, p. 272) describes as 'the ultimate hate word'. It is arguable that the presentation of such terms in academic analyses should be edited – through the use of asterisks, for example – but doing so risks creating the impression that the language was somehow less offensive than it actually was. There is no straightforward resolution to this matter, but following Billig I have decided here to present these terms in full to preserve the original character of the interaction.

Empirical example

The discussion which follows is taken from a group interview conducted as part of a project which explored young people's conceptions of citizenship and related concepts (for other analyses based on the wider dataset, see Gibson, 2011, in press; Gibson & Hamilton, 2011, 2013). The interview was conducted by the author with four young people, all of whom were fifteen years of age at the time of the interview, and who are here referred to by the pseudonyms Amy, Craig, Claire and Sharon. The interview took place at their school, a state comprehensive school in North Yorkshire. The interview covered a range of topics broadly related to the concept of citizenship, and discussion was prompted with the use of question cards which the participants were encouraged to read out and discuss.

In the extract to be considered here, the discussion was prompted by the question, 'Is social inequality a problem today?' The extract begins after the participants have discussed poverty, social housing and other issues related to economic inequalities. There has also been a discussion of Polish migrants, with some rather crude physical stereotyping from one participant in particular (Amy) who characterises Polish people as 'sweaty', with 'big noses' and as having 'ten hundred diseases'. Tellingly, this resulted in an accusation of racism from Craig, which was swiftly softened: 'You can't say that – that's like racist – not racist but like disrespectful or something'. This self-correction points to the difficulty in making accusations of racism and would be worthy of detailed analysis in itself, but for present purposes I want to focus on a subsequent section of the interview in which racism again becomes a live issue. As we join the interview, the participants have been considering the issue of gender inequality, which has led into a discussion of linguistic hygiene (see the end of the chapter for transcription notations):

```
1   AM    you can't say policeman now it's police person cos (.)
2         you- [((inaudible))]
3   ?          [yeah ((inaudible))]
4   ?                                    [but I don't think I
5         don't think [people treat policewomen]
6   AM                [it's like it's not fireman it's fire person (.h)
7         you can't say to someone [((inaudible))]
8   SH                             [policewomen] don't get the same
9         respect though [(0.2)] if you think about it=
```

```
10   CL                      [°no°]
11   AM   =you know when you have a coffee you can- in a café 'n that
12        you can't say black or white either it's racist now
13   ?    °°yeah°°
14   AM   you just say
15   CL   this is about inequality not racism
16   AM   yeah I know but I'm just telling you you can't say d'you
17        want black or white [cos its- it's racist]
18   CR                       [°racism can be involved in soci-°]
19        °°social inequality°°
20   AM   ye[ah:]
21   ?      [°it] can°
22   ?    °°mm°°
23              (0.5)
24   CR   °like (0.5) people are extremely racist I think
25        [          (0.5)      ] today°
26   AM   [it's like white or black]
27   I    yeah?
28              (0.4)
29   SH   they ↑a:re↑=
30   CR   =cos [if you walk round this school it's disgusting]=
31   CL        [<the world revolves around racism>]
32   CR   =[°the amount of people that are racist°]
```

There is much that might be said about this stretch of talk, but for present purposes I simply want to note that we see here the participants spontaneously making matters of racism relevant to the discussion of linguistic hygiene, with Amy constructing a rule against saying 'black coffee' on the grounds that it is racist (ll. 11–12). This is significant insofar as the specific term 'black' becomes a matter of contention later on in the discussion.

The participants subsequently enter into a discussion of whether racism is relevant to matters of social inequality, prompted by Claire's distinction between racism and inequality on line 15. Following Craig's response that 'racism can be involved in . . . social inequality', Amy agrees, before the participants move on to consider matters of race and racism more directly, with Craig adopting an explicitly antiracist stance and suggesting that racism is indeed widespread and problematic (ll. 24 and 30). Claire responds not by explicitly aligning or challenging Craig's view, but with the somewhat ambiguous statement 'the world revolves around racism' (l. 31). In context, this appears to function as a way of suggesting that racism is inevitable, natural even. Such assumed naturalness is a hallmark of what has been termed 'new racism' (e.g. Hopkins, Reicher & Levine, 1997), and yet here it appears alongside the assumption that what counts as racism has actually changed and is therefore historically specific. Amy's complaint about the strictures against ordering 'black or white' coffee includes a clear temporal dimension (l. 12: 'it's racist *now*'), and thus her argument concerns something that was not treated as racism in the past but is now treated as racism.

So, here we have the outcome of a negotiation between the participants concerning whether racism is relevant to the topic that they have been asked to discuss ('social inequality') and an initial contrast between a strident condemnation of racism (Craig) and an apparent acceptance that racism is inevitable (Claire). This sets the scene for what comes next, which will be analysed in greater detail.

```
33    SH        [but (.) when you think about it] black people- I °mean°
34              (0.1) Benjamin he's got (0.4) black family. (0.4) but
35              ↑they↑ all call each other black people all call each other
36              ↑ni↓ggers (0.2) but if a white person called them
37              [((inaudible))]
38    CL        [we'd get arrest[ed 'n'] shot
39    SH                        [↑yeah↑]
40    SH        [but black people are allowed to call themselves niggers]
41    AM        [but we- pe- some people say right] cos we call them pakis
42              an' niggers right=
43    SH/CL    =[            ((laughter))                                ]
44    AM         [((inaudible)) no:! I'm sorry right but they don't-] they
45              don't think owt of it (0.2) but they call us ((laughing))
46              milky bar people ((laughs))
47    I         do you think that [er]
48    SH                          ((laughing))[[↑mi↑]lky ba:r!
49    AM        th- they call us milky bar so why not us call
50              them [     (0.7)     ] black!
51    I              [d- do you think]
```

Here we see the beginnings of an escalation in the use of ethnophaulisms. Sharon begins by developing the previous discussion of linguistic hygiene to focus on something that she constructs as a disparity between black and white people. There are a couple of interesting self-corrections in Sharon's turn which point to the delicacy of the talk. First, on lines 33–34, she corrects the general category 'black people' to provide a specific example of Benjamin – someone about whom common knowledge is assumed on the part of her fellow interviewees. The correction is marked by an abrupt halt after 'black people', a meta-discursive comment ('I mean'), and a short pause prior to the invocation of Benjamin. This concrete example functions as a way of legitimising the observation by grounding it in a specific instance about which privileged insider knowledge can be claimed. It also allows Sharon to avoid the impression that she is generalising to *all* black people. However, the problem is then glossed in terms which reintroduce this generalisation by virtue of a further correction. Immediately after introducing Benjamin and his 'black family', Sharon begins to say that 'they all call each other' something, but this is not completed. At this stage 'they' refers to Benjamin and his 'black family'. This is subsequently corrected to ensure that the remark that is about to follow is heard specifically as referring to 'black people' as a category, rather than one particular 'black family'.

Having initially worked so hard to move away from explicit generalisation, why might Sharon be seeking to reinstantiate the general category so soon afterwards? I would suggest that there are two likely explanations which are not mutually exclusive: first, while it is useful to claim firsthand experience of a 'black family' who do what she is about to describe, the point Sharon is about to make requires it to be generalised to the racial category 'black people' to legitimate her complaint. Whilst the particularisation involved in citing a specific example may be useful, it also carries the risk that the practice she describes will be seen as being confined to only one family. In fact, multiple corrections and backtracking arguably perform important rhetorical buttressing here insofar as they allow Sharon to have the best of both worlds – she can ensure that her point is seen as applying to 'black people' as a group, whilst also having indicated that she has firsthand knowledge of actual occurrences to back this claim up. Second, the way in which Benjamin and his 'black family' are introduced suggests that they may not fit the prototypical image of members of the category 'black people' or 'black family'. Note that whereas Benjamin is introduced without explanation, his family – and only his family – are glossed explicitly as 'black'. Thus the other participants do not need a reminder of who Benjamin is, but they do need to be informed that his family is 'black'. Moreover, the 'black family' is something that Benjamin has, not something of which he is a *member*. There is thus a contrast here between Benjamin and his family – Benjamin is not readily categorised as 'black', whereas his family is. Thus, if Benjamin has 'got black family', then the contrast implies that he also has family who are not black – his family may thus not be particularly good exemplars of Sharon's general point here. To strengthen her position, a return to the categorical serves the function of ensuring that the practices she goes on to describe are clearly offered as applying unambiguously to 'black people'. Furthermore, the use of extreme case formulation (l. 35: '*all* call each other') emphasises that this applies to the entire category.

Sharon then draws a contrast between the acceptability of 'black people' calling each other 'nigger', and 'a white person' using this term (l. 36). Her gloss on the consequences is inaudible as Claire interjects to assert that 'we'd get arrested 'n' shot' (l. 38). Note here that whereas Sharon initially invoked the contrast between 'black people' and 'a white person' without positioning herself and others present in one or other group, in Claire's formulation it is not 'a white person' who would suffer the severe consequences she suggests, but 'we' who would 'get arrested 'n' shot'. This deixical referent places Claire – and by extension, the others present – firmly in a white ingroup. Claire has thus shifted the footing (Goffman, 1979) of the discussion onto a firmly intergroup level with the speakers as members of one of the groups.

Amy's first contribution on this issue, on lines 41–42, features a series of false starts – marking this as a delicate matter (van Dijk, 1984) – before she uses a combination of strategic vagueness, reported speech and the construction of consensus: 'some people say' (see Potter, 1996, for a detailed discussion of how these discursive devices are used in buttressing claims). Invoking others enables her to externalise what she is about to say, so that it is not seen as purely and solely her personal view (and thus potentially more easily dismissible), nor is it something for which she is herself accountable – it is what 'some [other] people say'. The vagueness of this formulation (Which other people? How many? In what context?) also ensures that what she is about to claim is more difficult to refute – the details of a claim cannot be challenged quite so readily if those details are not presented. Amy goes on to begin to articulate her claim, but this is never completed. This is because of the reaction that the initial part of her claim elicits from (at least one of) her peers.

Amy states that 'cos we call them pakis an' niggers'. She is clearly about to outline a consequence of this statement – indicated both by its formulation as the first part of a causal statement (*because of X, Y follows*) and by the way in which she is cut off by the immediate laughter which follows from either (or possibly both – the recording is ambiguous) Sharon and Claire. The laughter is instructive here – there was none following Sharon's initial use of the word 'niggers' on line 36, so why now? I would argue that there are two relevant features of Amy's talk here that mark this as an exercise in explicit boundary-pushing. First, and perhaps most obviously, Amy adds a second ethnophaulism. If the shock value of uttering the n-word would thus be negated given that Sharon has already used it, the p-word constitutes a taboo still to be broken in the context of the present conversation. Second, the shift in footing enacted by Amy is crucial here. Whereas Sharon referred to 'a white person' – a hypothetical individual – Amy says that '*we* call them pakis and niggers'. The strategic vagueness of the deixical referent *we* here is important. There is no clear criteria for who is included – the bridging assumption is that *we* are white, but this could also be a much more localised *we* – it could be *we* (white) people at this school or here in this room. The frisson of taboo-breaking excitement is thus raised insofar as the impression is made available to the interviewer that *this group* of young (white) people use these offensive racist terms.

On line 44, Amy responds to the laughter with an emphatic 'no!' followed by 'I'm sorry right but', which serves not so much to apologise for the disclosure that 'we' use these terms, but to complain that 'they [black people] don't think owt [a colloquialism meaning 'anything'] of it' when 'they call us milky bar people'. This latter phrase is a reference to a popular white chocolate bar (Milky Bar). At this point, the interviewer attempts to interject (l. 47), only to be cut off by Sharon laughing and repeating the phrase 'milky bar' (l. 48). Again, the frisson of taboo-breaking elicits laughter before Amy completes her point that a certain level of symmetry is called for: if 'they call us milky bar … why not us call them … black!' (ll. 49–50). The argument flattens power relations between 'us' and 'them', treating the use of racial terms as a straightforward matter of fairness. Furthermore, the implication here is that 'we' are the ones who are treated unfairly by virtue of not being accorded the same linguistic freedom as 'them'. Notably, Amy is claiming that 'we' should be able to call 'them' black at this point, something which follows from her earlier suggestion (ll. 11–12) that the term 'black' has become taboo even in contexts which are ostensibly far removed from matters of race. There is thus no attempt at this stage to claim rights to the use of any other – potentially more offensive – terms.

Subsequently, however, Amy uses a further ethnophaulism which leads to her explicit censure by her fellow interviewees:

```
52  I    do you think maybe because they've had (0.1) a lot of
53       [     (0.5)        ][racism n stuff against them]=
54  CR   [they've had [a lot of]
55  SH               [ yeah ] [they're fighting back at us]
56  I    = they're sort of (.) reclaiming that °maybe they're°=
57  SH   =yeah they're just get- clai[ming what]
58  CL                               [((inaudible))]
59  AM                       [I don't ((inaudible))]right I
60       just call them minstre:ls,
61            (0.1)
62  ?    shsh[shsh!]
63  AM       [↑it's better than using that [horrible↑]word though
64  CL                                     [shush!]
65  AM   innit=
66  CL   °↑shut [up↑°]
67  SH          [((inaudible))!]
68  CL   °↑shut up↑°!
69  AM   [I know but it's better than saying] (.) a black person
70  CR   [°(no) I am- I am not°]
71  AM   [I'd rather say:: (.) li:ke,]
72  CR   [°°you don't think you're racist at ↑all↑] do you?°°
73  AM   ah! you know what I mean
74  SH   it's just like the >inequality< of pol↑ice↑women (0.3) if
75       a=
76  CL   =you don't [get treated the same as a man]
77  SH              [if you got- if you got like a] ↑thug↑ (0.6) an'
78       a policewoman comes to arr↑est↑ 'em (0.2) (.hh) they'll
79       laugh at [you]
80  SH            [look at-] yeah they'd (..) like spit at 'em and
81       think you can't arrest me you're a ↑wo↑man
82           (0.4)
83  CR   'n they'll get their trun[cheon out] [and beat (°°em up°°)]
84  ?                             [well yeah-]
85  CL                                        [then a big [butch]]
86  ?                                                    [yeah!]
87  CL   lesbian comes along (.h) proves 'em ↑wrong↑=
88  AM   = a big butch lesbian! ((laughs))
89  ??   ((laughter))
90  I    so what what do you ↑think↑ (.) cos we've (.) sort of
91       established there are various different. (0.3) forms
92       [of inequality (that) are a problem] (0.1) think there's
93  AM   [     ((laughs))                   ]
94  I    owt that can be done about [it? like you]
95  AM                              [((laughing in-breath))]
```

```
96   I    were saying? of you kn- you know (0.1) changing [people's]
97   ?                                                    [((laugh))]
98   I    [attitudes is it?]
99   ?    [((increased laughter))]
100               (0.8)
101  SH   is [there any ↑way↑ you can]
102  AM   [I don't think there's owt]I don't think there's owt
103       wrong with black people.=
104  SH   =can you change people's attitu:des (.) I mean there's so
105       many black people that've got bad ↑na:mes↑=
106  AM   =they're just the same as us but a different colour
107  SH   ex↑act↑ly:
```

Again, there is much to comment on here, but for present purposes I want to draw attention to two key features of this stretch of talk and its relationship with the talk in lines 33–51. First is Amy's shift in footing and the way in which she *uses* an ethnophaulism whereas these have previously been *mentioned*. Second is the central role of the interviewer in occasioning both the ethnophaulism that leads to censure, and the censure itself.

Footing and the use-mention distinction

On lines 33–50, it is notable that the participants (specifically Sharon, and subsequently Amy) mention a range of ethnophaulisms ('niggers', 'pakis', 'milky bar people', 'minstrels'). However, the only occasion on which the articulation of such a term leads to censure from the other group members comes subsequently, on lines 59–60, where – crucially – Amy speaks from a personal footing (Goffman, 1979). Whereas previous utterances have dealt with the linguistic terms used by the racialised outgroup (e.g. ll. 33 and 40: 'black people'), the usage of such terms by a hypothetical 'white person' (l. 36) and a non-specific ingroup (ll. 41–42: 'we call them pakis and niggers'), Amy now declares her own naming practices: 'I just call them minstrels' (ll. 59–60).[1] The censure from her peers is immediate and extensive, with Claire in particular telling Amy repeatedly to 'shush' and 'shut up', and Craig challenging her remark as indicative of a racism of which she is herself not cognizant (l. 72: 'you don't think you're racist at all do you?'). At this point it is worth recalling that earlier in the interview (as summarised above), Craig had made a previous accusation of racism against Amy, but then swiftly softened it. The rhetorical question can thus be read as referring back to this previous occasion when Amy's status as potentially racist became a live issue.

It therefore appears that at least part of the reason for the censure visited upon Amy arises as a result of her articulating the ethnophaulism from a personal footing, reporting that she herself uses this term to refer to black people. This draws attention to the significance of the distinction between use and mention (see Garver, 1965, on the origins of this distinction, and see Potter & Litton, 1985, for its relevance to discourse analysis in psychology). Whereas some articulations of a term may simply be *mentioned* – as in the case of talking about somebody else having talked about something – on other occasions those terms may be *used* – invoked by a speaker as indicating something about their own beliefs, practices, feelings and so on.

The previous invocations of ethnophaulisms are marked by an avoidance of personal footing – they are thus mentioned rather than used. In this respect, we might say that until Amy's remark for which she is censured, the interviewees are displaying recognition of a social rule and are complaining about that rule, without actually breaking it explicitly. So even though Sharon and Claire both complain about linguistic hygiene, they nevertheless stick to its proscriptions. Amy's mistake is to actually transgress this rule, and for this she is censured. Despite complaining about the rule, Claire and Sharon nevertheless enforce it.

The role of the interviewer

However, this may not be the whole story. It is notable that it is the interviewer's attempt at offering a counterargument between lines 52–56 which occasions Amy's shift in footing. In offering the counterargument, the interviewer enacts a subtle shift from elicitor of views ('Why?'; 'What do you think?') to participant in debate (and note the various ways in which this is constructed in order to attend to the possibility that it may be received as an accusation of racism [Condor, 2006] – e.g. the tagged softener 'racism and stuff'; the repeated use of 'maybe'; the use of 'sort of'). This subtle shift in the interviewer's footing does not, however, close down the debate. Instead, it can be seen as effectively challenging Amy's 'face' (Goffman, 1955). Amy's response to this challenge is to push the boundaries further. However, on this occasion her remarks are not met with a subtle challenge from the interviewer, but with explicit censure from her peers. This does not produce further envelope-pushing from Amy, but produces a range of identity management strategies:

- Framing her claimed usage of the term 'minstrels' as a preferable alternative to 'black' (the term that she focussed on in her original complaint about linguistic hygiene on ll. 11–12, but which is now offered as *more offensive* than 'minstrels')
- Claiming that her aberration is a matter of semantics, of 'meaning' (l. 73: 'ah! you know what I mean').
- Several lines later, after the interviewer's subsequent question, she makes a series of explicit claims to nonprejudiced character (ll. 102–103; l. 106).

It is thus the opprobrium attracted from her peers, rather than the interviewer's attempt to critique her position, which elicits Amy's backtracking. Interestingly, though, the interviewer's challenge occasions the utterance which occasions the peer group censure and displays to the other speakers what lines of argument the interviewer may be likely to challenge and support.

We might argue, then, that this opens up a discursive space in which to challenge racist talk. The interviewer displays a willingness to formulate and consider this alternative account of the processes described by the interviewees, and in doing so actually invites the interviewees to agree with him. Indeed, both Craig and Sharon can be heard aligning themselves with the interviewer here. First, Craig (on line 54) interrupts the interviewer to facilitate the completion of his utterance. Sharon comes in on line 55 with an agreement followed by 'they're fighting back at us'. This utterance, with its reference to 'fighting back', is not necessarily one which is designed to display sympathy with 'them'. However, at this point the interviewer continues with 'they're sort of (.) reclaiming that °maybe they're°' (l. 56). This, in common with the first part of this turn at talk on lines 52–53, features several hedges, softeners and pauses (e.g. l. 52: 'maybe'; l. 53 'racism n stuff'; l. 56: 'sort of'; 'maybe'; and pauses on ll. 52, 53 and 56). These features mark this stretch of talk out as delicate, something which is perhaps to be expected when an interviewer is engaging in talk which may be heard as displaying disapproval of participants' responses. Furthermore, the continuation of these hedges after both Craig and Sharon have displayed at least partial alignment with the interviewer is received by Sharon as requiring a modification of her 'fighting back' utterance on line 55. Subsequently, therefore, on line 57, she latches her agreement onto the interviewer's 'reclaiming' utterance and suggests 'they're just get-claiming what' before being interrupted and tailing off. We might suggest therefore that Sharon orients to the interviewer as challenging her gloss on the situation as one which involves 'fighting back'. Whereas 'fighting back' may be construed as legitimate, but nevertheless as antagonistic, 'reclaiming' is a more unproblematically favourable gloss on 'their' actions – the act of reclaiming implies that that which is to be reclaimed was rightfully 'theirs' all along. Sharon's use of 'just' here also marks her utterance as a downgrading of her previous formulation – 'they' are not 'fighting back', they are 'just claiming' (see Lee, 1987, on uses of *just*).

However, in drawing attention to what is subject to peer group censure, our attention should equally be drawn to that which is allowed to pass without censure. I have already analysed in detail the stretch of talk in which the participants are complaining about linguistic hygiene and shown that the careful management of this talk allows them to jointly produce a complaint whilst 'dodging the identity of prejudice' (Wetherell & Potter, 1992, p. 211). However, two other points are worth noting here. First, Amy's attempts at claiming a nonprejudiced character on lines 102–103 and 106 actually garner support from Sharon, who begins to formulate racism as the fault of the outgroup (ll. 104–105: 'I mean there's so many black people that've got bad names'). The utterance which occasioned censure might therefore be a momentary aberration, made and then censured, with the participants free to continue the more delicate task of rationalising exclusions whilst avoiding anything that might appear to their peers as obviously racist. Second, the censure elicited by the use of 'minstrels' is not matched by a similar censure when Claire uses the term 'big butch lesbian' to refer to female police officers (ll. 84–87). Instead, we are back to the laughter which was elicited by the initial escalation in the use of ethnophaulisms. It is beyond the scope of the present chapter to compare race talk and sexuality talk, but it is notable that this highlights the extent to which normal service has been resumed. The moment of accusation and censure has passed, Amy has done her little bit of backtracking and identity management work, and she is now back in the fold, laughing along with stereotypical constructions of lesbian women. If justice was almost instantly administered for Amy's transgression, her conversational rehabilitation is similarly swift.

Concluding remarks

By way of conclusion, I want to make three broader points about the implications of the analysis presented here. The first concerns the role of laughter in much of the talk preceding the censure and its absence at the point of censure. It is notable that Amy's peers react to her escalation in the use of ethnophaulisms with laughter. Taken at face value, it may seem rather odd that in a matter of seconds, Amy's peers go from laughing at her use of the terms 'pakis', 'niggers' and 'milky bar people' to censuring her for the use of 'minstrels'. However, the laughter occasioned by Amy's remarks can be understood in terms of Billig's (2002, 2005) observations on laughter, humour and bigotry. Building on his rhetorical respecification of the Freudian concept of repression (Billig, 1999), Billig (2002, 2005) argues that laughter can be understood as a display of recognition – and indeed enjoyment – of the pushing of boundaries, the saying of the unsayable (see also Condor, 2006, extract 2). In everyday parlance, the participants are *egging each other on*, pushing the boundaries further and further, with Amy as boundary-pusher-in-chief. But we should be cautious about the idea that the boundaries are in any way fixed. Where the boundaries lie in any given interaction is therefore a matter for joint production by the participants in the interaction.

Second, recent attempts to respecify the distinction between old and new racism (Leach, 2005; Pehrson & Leach, 2012) have suggested that 'old' racism may not be quite so old as is often assumed, with old-fashioned racist bigotry still very much in evidence. Similarly, new racism may not be particularly new. If 'old' and 'new' racisms coexist, then from a discursive or dialogical perspective, the concern becomes one of how such distinctions are managed by participants in interactions. We may not find too many people using these terms explicitly – the participants here certainly don't – but we nevertheless see the policing of debate such that certain terms or practices are ruled out and treated as racist, whereas others – still with exclusionary upshots – are a matter of more or less consensual agreement. In glossing racism as understandable (if regrettable), as Sharon does, but then also censuring Amy for her confession that 'I just call them minstrels', we are therefore seeing a *participants'* distinction being made between a racism which is caused by 'black people' themselves and a racism which is to be censured. We may not want to use the terms 'old' and 'new', but we see a distinction between the acceptable and unacceptable (see also Goodman & Rowe, 2014, for examples of people distinguishing between acceptable prejudice and unacceptable racism).

Finally, it is worth returning to the implications of this style of analysis for social psychological approaches to the 'everyday'. Much psychological work on racism in social and political psychology relies on one or another form of an attitudes paradigm, in which an individual speaker's utterances are conceptualised as reflections of internal psychological entities. The contrast with the approach presented here is striking. Can we treat what Amy says as reflective of her 'attitudes'? Or are her utterances so inextricably bound up with the context that it is difficult to attribute any single utterance to her and her alone? Isn't her moment of censure just as much a product of her fellow interviewees' laughing and egging her on? Isn't it similarly a function of the interviewer's ham-fisted attempts to shoehorn in a gentle challenge to the complaints concerning linguistic hygiene? These possibilities have important conceptual and methodological implications for how we study everyday politics. Danziger (1992) made the point some time ago that, when faced with the complexities of the world, the developing field of social psychology simply remade the world in the image of the laboratory. As we attempt to study the everyday, we may be faced with a similar dilemma. We can embrace the everyday in all its complexity, but to do so means radically rethinking the nature of our subject matter such that phenomena cease to be primarily located at the level of the individual. This must surely be preferable to the alternative, which is to continue to neglect the everyday because it doesn't fit in with our ideas of the primacy of the individual.

Note

1 The term 'minstrels' again has connotations with a popular item of chocolate confectionary, but it can also be heard as a reference to the tradition of 'blackface' minstrelsy, exemplified in the UK by the now infamous *Black & White Minstrel Show*, a staple of the television schedules from the late 1950s until the late 1970s, and which attracted huge audiences in its heyday.

References

Augoustinos, M., & Every, D. (2007). The language of 'race' and prejudice: A discourse of denial, reason, and liberal-practical politics. *Journal of Language & Social Psychology, 26*, 123–141.
Billig, M. (1988). The notion of 'prejudice': Some rhetorical and ideological aspects. *Text, 8*, 91–110.
Billig, M. (1999). *Freudian repression: Conversation creating the unconscious*. Cambridge: Cambridge University Press.
Billig, M. (2001). Humour and hatred: The racist jokes of the Ku Klux Klan. *Discourse and Society, 12*, 267–289.
Billig, M. (2002). Henri Tajfel's 'cognitive aspects of prejudice' and the psychology of bigotry. *British Journal of Social Psychology, 41*, 171–188.
Billig, M. (2005). *Laughter and ridicule: Towards a social critique of humour*. London: Sage.
Billig, M., Condor, S., Edwards, D., Gane, M., Middleton, D., & Radley, A. (1988). *Ideological dilemmas: A social psychology of everyday thinking*. London: Sage.
Capdevila, R., & Callaghan, J. M. (2008). 'It's not racist. It's common sense': A critical discourse analysis of political discourse around asylum and immigration in the UK. *Journal of Community and Applied Social Psychology, 18*, 1–16.
Condor, S. (1988). 'Race stereotypes' and racist discourse. *Text, 8*, 69–89.

Condor, S. (2006). Public prejudice as collaborative accomplishment: Towards a dialogic social psychology of racism. *Journal of Community & Applied Social Psychology, 16,* 1–18.
Condor, S., & Figgou, L. (2012). Rethinking the prejudice problematic: A collaborative cognition approach. In J. Dixon & M. Levine (Eds.), *Beyond prejudice: Extending the social psychology of conflict, inequality and social change* (pp. 200–221). Cambridge: Cambridge University Press.
Condor, S., Figgou, L., Abell, J., Gibson, S., & Stevenson, C. (2006). 'They're not racist': Prejudice denial, mitigation and suppression in dialogue. *British Journal of Social Psychology, 45,* 441–462.
Danziger, K. (1992). The project of an experimental social psychology: Historical perspectives. *Science in Context, 5,* 309–328.
Garver, N. (1965). Varieties of use and mention. *Philosophy and Phenomenological Research, 26,* 230–238.
Gibson, S. (2011). Dilemmas of citizenship: Young people's conceptions of un/employment rights and responsibilities. *British Journal of Social Psychology, 50,* 450–468.
Gibson, S. (in press). Constructions of 'the Polish' in northern England: Findings from a qualitative interview study. *Journal of Social and Political Psychology.*
Gibson, S., & Hamilton, L. (2011). The rhetorical construction of polity membership: Identity, culture and citizenship in young people's discussions of immigration in northern England. *Journal of Community and Applied Social Psychology, 21,* 228–242.
Gibson, S., & Hamilton, L. (2013). Knowledge, autonomy and maturity: Developmental and educational concerns as rhetorical resources in adolescents' discussions regarding the age of electoral majority in England. *Journal of Youth Studies, 16,* 34–53.
Goffman, E. (1955). On face-work. *Psychiatry, 18,* 213–231.
Goffman, E. (1979). Footing. *Semiotica, 25,* 1–30.
Goodman, S. (2010). 'It's not racist to impose limits on immigration': Constructing the boundaries of racism in the asylum and immigration debate. *Critical Approaches to Discourse Analysis Across Disciplines, 4,* 1–17.
Goodman, S. (2014). Developing an understanding of race talk. *Social & Personality Psychology Compass, 8,* 147–155.
Goodman, S., & Rowe, L. (2014). 'Maybe it is prejudice ... But it is NOT racism': Negotiating racism in discussion forums about gypsies. *Discourse & Society, 25,* 32–46.
Hopkins, N., Reicher, S., & Levine, M. (1997). On the parallels between social cognition and the 'new racism'. *British Journal of Social Psychology, 36,* 305–329.
Howarth, C. (2009). 'I hope we won't have to understand racism one day': Researching or reproducing 'race' in social psychological research? *British Journal of Social Psychology, 48,* 207–426.
Hutchby, I., & Wooffitt, R. (1998). *Conversation analysis: Principles, practices and applications.* Cambridge: Polity.
Leach, C. W. (2005). Against the notion of a 'new racism'. *Journal of Community and Applied Social Psychology, 15,* 432–445.
Lee, D. (1987). The semantics of just. *Journal of Pragmatics, 11,* 377–398.
Pehrson, S., & Leach, C. W. (2012). Beyond 'old' and 'new': For a social psychology of racism. In J. Dixon & M. Levine (Eds.), *Beyond prejudice: Extending the social psychology of conflict, inequality and social change* (pp. 120–138). Cambridge: Cambridge University Press.
Potter, J. (1996). *Representing reality: Discourse, rhetoric and social construction.* London: Sage.
Potter, J., & Litton, I. (1985). Some problems underlying the theory of social representations. *British Journal of Social Psychology, 24,* 81–90.
Potter, J., & Wetherell, M. (1987). *Discourse and social psychology: Beyond attitudes and behaviour.* London: Sage.

van Dijk, T. A. (1984). *Prejudice in discourse*. Amsterdam: John Benjamins.
van Dijk, T. A. (1992). Discourse and the denial of racism. *Discourse & Society*, *3*, 87–118.
Wetherell, M. (2003). Racism and the analysis of cultural resources in interviews. In H. van den Berg, M. Wetherell & H. Houtkoop-Steenstra (Eds.), *Analyzing race talk: Multidisciplinary approaches to the interview* (pp. 11–30). Cambridge: Cambridge University Press.
Wetherell, M., & Potter, J. (1992). *Mapping the language of racism*. Brighton: Harvester Wheatsheaf.

Transcription Notations (adapted from Hutchby & Wooffitt, 1998, pp. vi–vii)

(1.0)	The number in parentheses indicates a time gap to the nearest tenth of a second.
(.)	A dot enclosed in parentheses indicates a pause in the talk of less than two-tenths of a second.
[]	Square brackets between adjacent lines of concurrent speech indicate the onset and end of a spate of overlapping talk.
.hh	A dot before an *h* indicates speaker in-breath. The more *h*s, the longer the in-breath.
hh	An *h* indicates an out-breath. The more *h*s, the longer the breath.
(())	A description enclosed in double parentheses indicates a nonverbal activity, such as ((pointing)). Alternatively, double parentheses may enclose the transcriber's comments on contextual or other features.
-	A hyphen indicates the sharp cut-off of the prior word or sound.
:	Colons indicate that the speaker has stretched the preceding sound. The more colons, the greater the extent of stretching.
!	Exclamation points are used to indicate an animated or emphatic tone.
that	Underlined fragments indicate speaker emphasis.
° °	Degree signs are used to indicate that the talk they encompass is spoken noticeably quieter than the surrounding talk.
> <	Greater than and less than signs indicate that the talk they encompass was produced noticeably quicker than the surrounding talk.

4
ESSENCE POLITICS

Identity work and stereotyping in intergroup relations

*Wolfgang Wagner, Maaris Raudsepp,
Peter Holtz and Ragini Sen*

Setting identity straight

A young Muslim woman living in Hindu, India, when asked what reason she had for wearing a *hijab*, gave an elaborate explanation. She answered that her Hindu friends "always considered her to be one of *them* (non-Muslim)", while she felt that she "belonged to *them* (Muslims)". In contrast to what could be expected of a positive embrace, she "started feeling bit of a cheat". She was faced with an existential dilemma: "Why was I lying to them about my identity?" So she started contemplating the idea of wearing a scarf, "My way of asserting an identity of being the person I was.... [and that's what] I wanted to tell them." This woman made a bold statement about what it felt like when one was attributed a wrong ethnic identity. She felt the need to be and make visible her Muslim identity in a context where members of the majority embraced her in an amicable but also paternalistic way by valuing her as "being one of them", that is a Hindu. She did not want to be a clone of majoritarinism for being accepted. She had her own Muslim identity, was proud of it and wanted to assert it (Wagner et al., 2012).

This interview highlights the interdependence between social and ethnic identities and how they are enacted and stereotyped by the outgroup. In fact, the friends of this woman embraced her as one of them as a means to protect her from the negative stereotyping that Hindu Indians by and large maintain against Muslims, and she knew that "even if my friends knew that I was a Muslim, they would say, but *you* are *not* one of *them*." But the vexed situation for her was that she was one of them, and she did not want to distance herself from that identity. For her, this acceptance was not an upwardly mobile route as the much-discussed westernisation and Sanskritisation; it negated a core element of her identity. At the end, she responded by changing her attire to make a visible statement of her identity and to carve out her own unique niche within the local majority culture. She did not wish to be assimilated.

The example demonstrates the dynamic processes through which an identity-conscious person may deal with blatant or implicit stereotyping: being embraced and unjustly assimilated into another group in the present case. The young woman perceives this embrace as negating her real identity that obviously was not deemed as appropriate by her ethnically outgroup friends. Her reaction is a political statement and response to resist discrimination – a reaction that is intended to reestablish her self-worth and ethnic standing as a Muslim woman with all her culture's signifiers. She made a political statement of identity, belonging and difference.

We observe a confluence of feelings of identity, stereotyping and discriminatory behaviours and how they depend on each other as shown in people's coping responses. Because this process of coping potentially changes the wider social environment, it will be called 'politics' in our chapter. It describes means and measures groups and individuals use in their struggle for acknowledgement, social worthiness and social standing. Our understanding of interpersonal and intergroup politics may not resonate with popular parlance, where the term *politics* denotes the activities associated with intrastate governance and international relationships. Similar to what governance is for the large sphere of a state, in the present use, everyday-folk politics is the governance of the relationship between individuals in everyday life as well as the relationship between groups in a society.

Identity and stereotyping in intergroup relationships are highly related to perceiving group-related essences; that is, struggling for recognition and identity and countering stereotypes necessarily involves managing perceived essence that objectifies these precepts. In the following we will discuss the everyday political aspects of these issues in ethnic, religious, gender and sexual interest contexts.

Psychological essentialism and social processes

The idea of an essence

We think that a large part of intergroup behaviour and perception is governed by the implicit use of an idea that is called 'psychological essentialism'. When children state that a cat cannot be transformed into a dog even with chemical and surgical methods (Keil, 1992), they implicitly entertain the idea of a deep-seated substance in living beings that determines its category membership, be it a cat, a human or a dog. This substance or 'essence', in other words, resists external intervention and once and for all defines the living being's category identity. Translated into social life, the idea of essence lends itself also for thinking about social groups, ethnic categories and races.

Psychological essentialism (Medin & Ortony, 1989) is defined as the belief in something hidden and invisible which is inherent to its carriers and causes them (at least in important regards) to be as they are. Basically, an imagined essence cannot (or can hardly) be acquired or dispensed with. Its causal implications are important for the identity of the essence's carrier insofar as by carrying the essence he or she either belongs to a certain natural or does not. Furthermore, attributing an essence is coextensive with being natural. The perceived meaning of 'natural' in this case is close to a 'biologically given', that is a state that resists change of the deep-seated characteristics; attributing essence is equivalent to naturalising the social entity (e.g. Ahn et al., 2001).

The vernacular idea of essence consists of two components: essentialised categories can be characterised as being natural, on one hand, and entitative, on the other. These two components are complementary in the sense of a category being perceived as either natural (i.e. distinct, unalterable) or entitative (i.e. homogeneous, sharing a common goal). Differences between ethnic groups and racial categories are perceived as being natural; differences between religious groups, among others, are perceived as being due to their identity and common goal, that is, their apparent entitativity (Haslam et al., 2000).

Three predictions result from these ideas for everyday thinking. First, stereotypes based on physical, language and other conspicuous differences are perceived as being supported by difference in essence. Second, ascribing essence naturalises social groups, which leads to the impression of ethnic categories being mutually exclusive. Third, by virtue of the naturalising consequence of an essence, significant attributes that a group ascribes to themselves or to outsiders, be they 'positive' or 'negative' attributes, become inalterable markers. These can be intended for one's own group's positive characteristics or for an outgroup's negative characteristics in the case of conflict.

In the following we will analyse political uses of the everyday idea of essence in group life. The role and importance of essentialist attributions for group identities and the creation of stereotypes has been extensively documented. There has been less attention devoted to the interdependence between self-attributed and other-attributed essentialist notions in identity and stereotype construction and the dynamics that originate therefrom. Our basic assumption is that social groups in contact develop a sense for other groups' self-definition in the form of an identity, which in turn informs the stereotypical representation of that group. This implies that the outgroup's stereotypes can be changed when active group members first change their own group's self-image and then project this image as a changed or newly acquired identity to the outside world. Whether identity politics can achieve the desired goal by de-essentializing one's image or by re-essentializing depends on the group's particular situation. This is an important means of changing power relationships within societies and between minorities and majorities.

Essentialism in stereotyping and prejudice

Social entities or groups can be divided into those whose membership can be more or less freely chosen and those where membership is forced by birth. Most cases of forced categories comprise races, ethnic and religious belonging, and language units. It is these latter groups that interest us here because they best reflect stereotyping and prejudice in its most conspicuous form.

In 2007, when the Estonian government relocated a formerly Soviet Bronze Soldier monument that commemorates the liberation of Estonia from German Nazi rule by Soviet troops, an emotional storm thundered amidst a section of the large Russian population. Many of them had been living in Estonia for decades, and they vehemently protested against the desecration of 'their' monument. Some of the indigenous Estonians responded vehemently in the media. For one night, violence between Russians and the police loomed.

On the Internet, a fierce debate between the Estonian and the Russian factions of the population accompanied these events. In this debate one topic popped up over and over again: what constitutes a real Estonian and what is a real Russian? Group members defined each other using terms such as our versus their 'blood', language and nationality; in other words, what constitutes each group's essence and what can be inferred from that (Raudsepp & Wagner, 2012).

The example of the Estonians and Russians living in Estonia shows an intricate relationship between mutual ascriptions of essence and self-definition based on language and citizenship. Language and ethnic belonging are easily detectable attributes of forced social categories. As a rule, ethnic descent and maternal language use endow individuals with strong feelings of belonging, a long-term tradition, a shared habitus and sometimes even shared biological features.

Consequently, in the aforementioned Estonian case, the right-wing factions of the two groups attributed to each other characteristics that were deemed pivotal for understanding their mutual behaviour. In doing so, both groups drew upon old stereotypes of each other: ethnic Estonians called Russians uncivilised, emotional and easily swayed by ideologies. Conversely, Russians called Estonians peasant barbarians and fascists. These characteristics, together with a few others, were considered stable and determined by the respective shared group essences (Raudsepp & Wagner, 2012).

In another instance, a study of extreme right-wing Internet postings showcases a particularly strong example of biologically based essentialism (Holtz & Wagner, 2009). The discourse developing in the threads demonstrates a strong tendency to essentialize the categories of Jews and Africans/Blacks and to ascribe them immutable attributes caused by an essence that effectively makes them 'natural kinds'. The group of Jews appeared as a kind of their own with superhuman powers and influence that are outcomes of their group's essence. Africans and Blacks are despised and discriminated against on two levels: first, when they are seen as unfit to being awarded German citizenship due to their incompatible African essence and, second, when they are deemed unsuitable to procreate with Whites. It is believed that such procreation produces 'bastards' – or 'monsters' – and the posters reflect this as disgust. Procreation between different 'natural kinds' appears impossible due to their incompatible essences that make the offspring a hybrid without 'natural' identity. Similar results were also found in an experiment with Austrian participants. Politically right-leaning respondents tended to judge the children of 'mixed' Austrian-African or Austrian-Turkish couples living in Austria significantly more negatively than the offspring of 'pure' Austrian, Turkish or African couples living in Austria. This effect did not hold for left-leaning respondents (Wagner et al., 2010).

Objectifying social identities

Social groups in societies rarely partake in an equal status of power. More often than not, there is a dominant majority and one or more ethnic minority groups that are either suffering discrimination or pressure towards integration or even assimilation. In many societies, minorities that are conspicuously different from the majority are not welcome and have to face prejudice. In fact, some sectors of the majority public reject assimilation of minority members. But minorities also often have an interest in maintaining their distinct identities and ethnic habits and therefore resist assimilation to the majority's lifestyle.

From the position of minority interests, essentialist self-ascriptions have been shown to differ depending on the minority's feeling of group denial and discrimination by the majority. Homosexuals, for example, tend to self-essentialize more when they deem their group status to be at stake than when they feel that they are being individually devalued (Morton et al., 2009). In a similar way, ethnic minority members endorse self-essentialization when they emphasise their ethnic identity in the context of multiculturalism and de-essentialize themselves when they feel threatened (Verkuyten, 2003). Likewise, American Jews recently put a high value on their identification as a group and emphasised their essentialist uniqueness (Tenenbaum & Davidman, 2007). By emphasising an ingroup essence in their discourse, the group members effectively objectify their group identity, entitativity and bounds. Apparently, psychological essentialism can and is being put to variable use in political discourses about identity conservation and societal status (Hopkins & Greenwood, 2013).

Mutual awareness of group images

Perceiving other groups' self-essentialization

Ethnic groups composing a society relate to each other usually as a majority comprising one or more minorities when accosted by a majority that dominates and the ethnic minority meets prejudice and suffers discrimination. This asymmetric relationship kindles specific identity interests in the minority. Consequently, a minority's self-essentialization has been shown to differ depending on its feeling of group denial and discrimination by the majority (Verkuyten, 2003).

Minorities' strategic construction of their images can take two forms: they think that either emphasising their essence or de-essentializing will make a positive difference in their social standing and for their relationship with the majority. This presupposes that an outgroup is aware of a minority's degree of self-essentialization.

If the majority were blind to the minority's projected identity and the dominant stereotype about the minority was completely arbitrary, no identity work on the part of the minority could possibly ameliorate their social standing.

Knowledge of another group's self-image and self-essentialization and the resulting hetero-essentialization can be expected when groups live in daily contact that also allows for conflict to arise. Such proximal groups are likely to attain a feeling of the outgroup's identity construction and group cohesion. Hence, we posit that attributing group essence onto others in many cases will not be arbitrary but will match the target group's self-ascribed essence to a certain degree. In other words, we expect groups to mutually acknowledge their proximal partner group's level of self-essentialization. This can be assessed by simultaneously investigating a majority and a proximal minority in the real-life context.

We ran two such studies to show that groups' mutual hetero-essentialization matches the target's self-essentialization; one was on majority-minority relationships in Estonia and the other one was in Austria. In Estonia, native Estonian majority members face a minority of Estonian Russophones, while in Austria we considered the relationship between members of the Austrian mainstream majority and members of the Turkish immigrant community. The studies are presented in the following sections.

For both studies we expected members of the majority to judge their own group as less essentialized than members of the minority judge their group's level of essence. More importantly, we expected a mirror effect such that the minority's and the majority's essentialization of the other will, more or less, reflect the level of the other group's self-essentialization. If minority members show a high and majority members show a low self-ascribed group essence, minority members – Russians in Estonia, Turks in Austria – will perceive the majority group as less essentialized than their own group, and the majority will essentialize the minority group more than themselves.

Estonian majority and Russian minority

Participants were ethnic Estonians and members of the Russophone section of the Estonian population. Potential participants were identified by their names being either Estonian or Russophone. We collected data from 122 Estonians and 81 Russophones.

The experiment was presented online. Among others, the respondents were presented an item on essentialization to be answered on a 5-point scale ranging from 'not at all' to 'absolutely'. The item was presented twice, first referring to the ingroup and then to the outgroup. The item read "Some people think that the members of ethnic groups share an underlying characteristic that is invisible and that cannot be shed even when living away from home for a long time. How much, do you think, do people from [ingroup/outgroup] possess such an underlying essence of [ingroupness/outgroupness]?"

At the end respondents were asked sociostatistical questions. All items were presented in the respective ethnic group's language and writing, that is, Estonian Latin

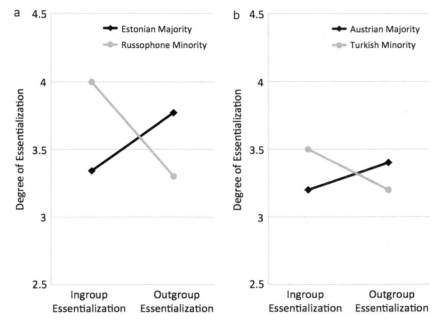

FIGURE 4.1 Degree of attributed group essence by majority vs. minority members and by ingroup vs. outgroup target: (1a) Estonians and Russophone minority, (1b) Austrians and Turkish minority.

and Russian Cyrillic. Participants were approached personally or by e-mail and given a URL pointing to the website that was in the appropriate language, Estonian or Russian.

According to our hypothesis, we calculated a 2 × 2 mixed MANOVA with the dependent essence attribution item and respondents' ethnic group (Estonians vs. Russophones) and ingroup versus outgroup attribution of essence (repeated measure) as factors. As hypothesised, the interaction 'respondents' ethnicity' by 'attribution target' was significant [$F(1, 201) = 51.20, p \leq 0.001$, eta^2 = 0.20]: the essence Estonians attribute onto the Russian minority mirrors the Russians' self-ascribed essence, and Russians attribute to the Estonian majority approximately the same degree of essentialization as the Estonians do to themselves. We consider this a strong finding as the interaction explains 20% of variance (Figure 4.1a).

Austrian majority and Turkish minority

For this we approached 154 Austrians and 122 Turkish migrants living in Austria and had them answer a questionnaire. The respondents were presented the same essence-related questionnaire items as mentioned in the foregoing section. However, instead of being presented online, an interviewer approached the respondents personally. All items were presented in the respective ethnic group's language and writing, that is, German and Turkish, where Turks had the choice between the Turkish and the German version.

We tested the same hypothesis as in study 1 and calculated a 2 × 2 mixed MANOVA with the dependent essence attribution item and respondents' ethnic group (Austrians vs. Turks) and ingroup versus outgroup attribution of essence (repeated measure) as factors. According to the hypothesis, the interaction 'respondents' ethnicity' by 'attribution target' was significant [$F(1, 274) = 4.92$, $p \leq 0.05$, $eta^2 = 0.02$]: the essence that Austrians attribute to the Turkish minority mirrors approximately the Turkish self-ascribed essence, and Turks attribute to the Austrian majority approximately the same degree of essentialization as the Austrians do to themselves (Figure 4.1b).

Mutual recognition of ingroup essentialization

Study 1 shows the Estonians' stereotype of Russophones to reflect the Russophone minority's self-attributed essence, and the Russians' stereotype of Estonians reflects the majority's self-attributed essence relatively accurately. The same is true for the Austrians' stereotype of Turkish self-essentialization and the Turks' perception of Austrians' self-essentialization in study. Taken together, the findings indicate that proximal majority and minority groups do perceive or judge their 'fellow' groups' self-essentialization relatively accurately.

Estonia is a good case for studying mutual essentialization as it can be characterised as an 'ethnic democracy' and there is a lively minority that feels threatened and a majority whose ethnic groupness is officially propagated. The fact that the mutual outgroups' stereotype of self-essentialization matches this self-essentialization was shown for both countries and contexts. Every group maintains a self-image of which self-essentialization is a central part. An essentialized groupness is a means to negotiate the group's standing in society as well as signalling unity, worth and the group's perpetuity, notwithstanding the flexible use of group essence under pressure or threat.

We consider stereotyping of and identity formation in proximal ethnic groups to be interrelated processes that cannot be separated in real-life settings. As members of groups interact in their daily errands, they wittingly or unwittingly enact their habitus and identity characteristics, which in turn are easily discerned by members of proximal other groups. These, in turn, partake in shaping the stereotypes about themselves. Self-essentialization and groupness, being part of the self-image, hence enter in the process of stereotyping and form the mutual understanding – and at times, misunderstanding – of groups. If this were not so, attempts by groups and their members to manage and change apparent group homogeneity in situations of inclusion or exclusion would not make sense. 'Essence politics' presupposes a feedback loop of perception between groups as well as meta-knowledge about what others know about the group.

Our present studies do not show that stereotyped attributes in general – that is, projecting positive or negative characteristics onto outgroups – has an analogy in self-attributed identity attributes of the respective groups in the majority of cases. Neither do we imply that essentialization by the outgroup is driven by the target's identity alone or that self-essentialization is primarily driven by outgroup stereotypes. There are examples of both. As groups are dynamic and adaptive structures in interaction with others, any causal direction is conceivable and may temporarily drive identity reconstruction and stereotyping in one or the other direction. Certainly, mutual representations of groups in many instances and during historical times can be unchanging, but that does not mean that they will always remain immune to change. In any case, however, the degree of attributed essence – read: naturalisation – will determine how easily or not a minority will be able to manage stereotyped characteristics and change their identity in the eyes of the majority.

Political shades of essence ascriptions

In our view, groupness and identity construction, as well as essentializing and stereotyping processes, are two sides of the same coin. Their dynamics and interrelationship are part of society's ongoing discourse where groups position themselves according to political needs and pressures. In the course of societal changes, each side of the coin may change, but probably more often than not it will match the other side to a certain degree. Without such mutual reference (Sen, 2012) and related dynamics, groups could barely adapt their identities and positioning to changing social conditions and political developments (Stoler, 1997).

The findings of the previously reported studies are prerequisites for discussing the dynamics of essence politics, but how, in fact, does 'politics' enter the picture in the present context? Let's look at some examples that show different political entailments of psychological essentialism.

Many people consider racism to be a set of negative attitudes toward members of a certain race or ethnic group. This set of attitudes goes hand in hand with a tendency to essentialize the other. By doing so, people make the target's attributes appear as natural and immutable. The aforementioned study of neo-Nazi websites, for example, shows the discriminatory aspects of racist essentialism in discourse (Holtz & Wagner, 2009). This 'oppressive' aspect of stereotyping clearly is essentialism in political action.

Quite an opposite political aspect of essentialization is when a group of politically minded people attributed a strong indigenous cultural essence onto one of the last Indian tribes in the Amazon territory. Indeed, every culture harbours a large corpus of knowledge about the outside world that enables their survival for centuries and often millennia. Even if it were just for the indigenous knowledge about pharmaceutical effects of plants and other things, this knowledge could significantly enrich the modern world's armamentarium to fight diseases. This corpus would be in danger of being lost if tribes with distinct cultures were being 'modernised' more or less forcefully and their cultural knowledge was not protected and preserved. In this case, any political activist destined to protect the tribe is well advised to point to its uniqueness and, indeed, cultural essence in their discourse, making them distinct but of great value to modern society. This could be called the 'progressive' or 'emancipatory' aspect of psychological essentialism (Verkuyten, 2003).

Now let's consider the case of an ethnic group that maintains a distinct self-identity that is used to elevate their own worth compared to outsiders. In a certain sense, identity work is almost always meant to positively distinguish one's own group from others. By itself, an essentialist distinction from others must not necessarily result in an aggressive devaluation of outsiders. Emphasising one's own ethnic superiority and maintaining deprecating attitudes towards others, however, illustrates another 'oppressive' or 'self-aggrandising' aspect of employing essentialization and naturalisation in identity work. This would be sourced by an inflated positive self-essentialization and entail a complementary negative prejudice against others. Quite often, such self-aggrandising identities are justified by religious arguments or by mythical descent. Expressions like 'God's own country', frequently applied to the USA; the orthodox Jewish folklore of being the 'chosen people'; and the extremist Islamists' claim of a religious superiority and the consequent physical elimination of nonbelievers in jihad terrorism, among many others, spring to mind.

As long as the members and opinion leaders of a group are content with their self-definition and the corresponding outside stereotypes, there is no need to act. The situation changes, however, if due to societal developments group members perceive a discrepancy between their own claim of identity and the view maintained by others.

Making politics by managing essence perception

Deconstructing an essentialized outgroup representation

Motivated by societal developments, there have always been groups engaged in discourses that attempt to change cultural patterns of perception. As shown before, essentialized identities can be considered positive or negative depending on the situation and the interests of the groups in positioning themselves in society.

Of course, societies are subject to change and so are mentalities, ideologies and representational systems, which are often driven by interest-guided politics. Some groups may perceive it as advantageous to denaturalise an identity that was seemingly forced upon individuals at birth. Others may struggle to consolidate their group in the eyes of outsiders by inventing and emphasising an essentialized or 'natural' identity. Hence, the relative stability of natural categories does not preclude that they are the result of discursive construction in the long run and that they might undergo change in the course of history.

One important contemporary political movement is feminism. This movement aims to achieve formal equality between men and women in all relevant realms of life. It faces a traditional commonsense representation where men and women are perceived as different not only biologically but also in mentality, tastes and behaviour, constituting a natural kind of man and a natural kind of woman. As this representation refers to a natural basis of sexual differences, it engages the strongest version of essence, that is, of an immutable natural endowment of men and a different one of women. This representation is often perceived as standing in gross opposition to granting both sexes equal spaces and chances.

As a consequence, large parts of the feminist movement are engaged in replacing this representation with an explanation of gender differences that allows women and men to occupy all social roles and professions in society on equal terms. In this case, societal progress is seen in de-essentializing and de-naturalising a social category. In discourse, this is accompanied by switching terminology from 'sex' to 'gender'.

In their struggle, feminists engage in heated debates about the roles of essence versus constructionism in their theorising that perfectly highlights the political consequences of essentializing or de-essentializing the social category of women (Fuss, 1989; Mahalingam, 2007). In these discourses, it becomes clear that projecting or self-attributing essence to a category or social group has significant political consequences. On one hand, it impedes social change, particularly in favour of groups whose members want to shed perceived discrimination; on the other hand, it is pivotal if one wants to create groups, in order to give them identity and visibility in political struggles. This tension between perceived essence as an impediment and essence as a political tool underlines the centrality that this notion seems to be deeply ingrained in humankind's intuitive cognitive functioning; it can hardly be overcome, as Fuss (1989, p. 2) states: "Essentialism emerges perhaps most strongly within the very discourse of feminism, a discourse which presumes upon the unity of its object of inquiry (women) *even* when it is at pains to demonstrate the differences within this admittedly generalising and imprecise category." Fuss, hence, expresses doubts regarding the success of feminist political essence discourse.

Denaturalisation, that is fighting against a stereotypical representation in the public, is indeed a discursive instrument for many social movements. The emancipatory impetus of discursively constructing a less essentialist social identity, for example, can also be observed with immigrants. A study in the wake of the 2009 ban on building minarets in Switzerland (Holtz et al., in press) describes a process where perceived discrimination by an outgroup lead to a discourse about de-essentializing one's self-identity. At that moment, European Muslims were strongly divided on how to properly respond to this event, which was felt to be clear prejudice and discrimination. Many German-Turks or Turkish-Germans felt their so-called 'hyphen identity' under threat by the discrimination, and they tended towards a de-essentializing strategy.

Bracing one's political positioning by naturalisation

As elaborated earlier, minorities not only struggle for recognition but need to resist pressure towards assimilation. Recall our initial example of the Muslim woman in the first paragraph of this chapter. Her response to being protected by her Hindu friends was setting her identity straight: she started to follow traditional Muslim rules of attire. She clearly marked the difference by drawing on the inference potential of a symbolically laden and essentialist identity as a Muslim.

From the position of minority interests, essentialist self-ascriptions have been shown to depend on how a group feels when they are either denied a standing and discriminated against by the majority or embraced as part of the society. In the former case, ethnic minority members endorse self-essentialization if they emphasise their ethnic identity in the context of multiculturalism and de-essentialize themselves when they feel threatened. Equally, when the majority embraces the minority, essentialization is a strategy to maintain uniqueness and rescue the minority's culture. Likewise, in the aforementioned study on Muslim responses to the Swiss minaret ban (Holtz et al., in press), more radical factions of German Muslims were shown to respond to discrimination by feeling that this event confirmed their radical thinking and exclusiveness. They constructed their identity as purely Muslim to the core and not as hyphenated Turkish-German or Arab-German or Muslim-German. They were neither attached to the culture or nationality of their country of origin nor to their host country. In the face of outgroup discrimination, they re-confirmed their identity as immutable and immune to cultural hybridisation.

We mentioned that besides ethnic and religious minorities struggling to find a fine line between resisting essentializing tendencies by others and finding comfort in self-essentialization, sexual minorities face similar challenges. Many cultures uphold that a homosexual relationship results from a conscious sexual preference by same-sex partners. Due to real or assumed sexual practices, homosexuality is frequently viewed as repugnant (Norton & Herek, 2013; West & Hewstone, 2012). Homosexuality is prosecuted in many countries, but England and Wales lifted their legal ban on male homosexuality in 1967, Ireland lifted theirs in 1993, and Cyprus lifted theirs in 1998 (Itaborahy & Zhu, 2013).

In an attempt to counteract this widespread representation of homosexuality as a chosen sexual practice that stands in the way of achieving full equality before the law in terms of marriage and child adoption, some activist groups have taken up an essentializing strategy. They have been eager to pick findings of genetic, physiological and neurological correlates of homosexuality with the aim of representing gay people's sexual behaviour as natural instead of as an arbitrary personal preference (Bailey et al., 1999; Conrad & Markens, 2001; Epstein, 1987; Servick, 2014). This group's interest to naturalise itself is particularly strong when facing marginalisation, that is, when the majority denies attributing them a status as a group. Indeed it has been shown that essentialist beliefs reduce the heterosexual majority's negative attitudes. Specifically, a belief in the inalterability and biological basis of homosexuality is associated with lower levels of antigay attitudes (Haslam et al., 2002).

Another case in point is aristocracy and its abolishment or decline in various parts of Europe. Traditionally, the self-representation of nobility and its outgroup representation converge in attributing this category of people an exceptional position in society. It encompasses political dominance, wealth, elitism, distinguished manners and separation from the general population. The core of this representation is the belief in 'blue blood' being shared among such dynasties, where blue blood is just another term for essence and relationship by common descent, the consequences of which attracted some scientific interest at the beginning of the 20th century. It was only a matter of time until aristocracy and its blood-related and feudal self-definitions collided with the development of democratic rule and human equality.

The 19th century republican politics attempted to de-essentialize this category of people, and the aristocracy's representatives tried to maintain their traditional image as being *essentially* different from the common man; they had some success, as testified by the unending reporting in the yellow press. The ways of achieving this were different in various parts of Europe, but the goal was the same: for example, by replacing nobility by blood through so-called state elites in France (Doyle, 2007). In Germany, aristocracy maintained a remarkable degree of homogamy, but in the Netherlands the postfeudal nobility attempted to absorb some 'blue blood' by marrying into the 'traditional elites' (Dronkers, 2008). Most of these attempts were successful, if not in maintaining the spirit of blue-bloodedness, then in replacing the essence of biological descent by the essence of money and wealth (Dronkers, 2008).

Conclusion: The interplay between identity, stereotyping and social positioning

All too often it is forgotten that groups exist in relation to outgroups (Tajfel, 1978). They relate to each other by renegotiating their identities to change their positions in society like feminists attempting to de-essentialize the category of women and aristocracy in renaturalising their group. They relate because groups have an image of themselves but also have a feeling of how they are stereotyped by others. They also relate because a stereotype maintained by an outgroup is not completely arbitrary but is co-determined by the characteristics that the target group projects to the outside. The stereotype will be biased to a certain degree, but more often than not it reflects how the ingroup enacts its identity.

In other words, a group stereotype can be understood as a social representation that unites relevant characteristics of the stereotyping actors as well as of the target in a circular fashion. These representations are a social fact in the sense that they are the result of a 'concert of interaction' where their mutual identity work and stereotype construction endow the representations in interaction with evidence.

A study about ethnic relationships in Brixton with a mixed African and Caribbean population – which outsiders know as a notorious place of racial turmoil – shows how judgmental stereotypes impact the transformation of identities. The study shows how young inhabitants of Brixton attempt to convert their negative image in the British majority into an identity that makes their belonging to a geographic and racial category a group that allows them to collectively resist the essentializing stigma of otherness (Howarth et al., 2014). It illustrates the close rapport between outgroup and ingroup representations as well as the role of social meta-knowledge, where a group's identity work is triggered and informed by a stereotype.

The aforementioned study on the Swiss minaret ban describes a process where discrimination by the outgroup makes fundamentalist Muslims reconfirm their identities. They tended towards affirming their religious essence by emphasising dress codes, beards and public prayer. More secular Muslims show variance in how they respond to this discrimination and vacillate between suggesting re-essentializing and de-essentializing strategies (Holtz et al., in press). The discourse of all factions, however, was a marked illustration of how outside stereotyping and prejudice are interdependent with political identity construction.

The interdependence and inclusiveness of identity- and stereotype-related representations has been called 'holomorphism' (Wagner, 2012). This is the simultaneous and mutual knowledge and meta-knowledge of the group's and others' identities and stereotypes, which are pivotal for essence politics. Renegotiating identities would be incomprehensible if it was not used as a response to outside stereotypes and the intended change of a group's societal standing for the better.

Wrapping up we may ask: where and for what purpose do people essentialize? As an instrument to naturalise attributes of groups and social categories and thereby to homogenise the individual variability of their members implies stability and status quo. There is little that may appear more stable and immutable to the occasional observer than nature. Hence, representing a social group as natural and endowed with an unalienable essence gives its members a unique identity. Neither the term 'natural', with its 'physiomorphic' allusion, nor the term 'essence' can be thought of as independent of the other; being natural implies having an essence by necessity in the eyes of the perceiver.

Essentializing strategies applied to a group's identity project are meant to enhance the standing, power and social value of the group and to counteract discrimination. Homogeneous groups are the intended construction of social actors where members as much as outsiders participate in a process of confirming the group's representation irrespective of whether the outsiders confront the group positively or negatively. Social groups are not contingent but necessary given their respective status in a social system. This co-construction of social categories does indeed signal that the group is an entity – a unit that sets itself apart from others and that exhibits uniformity, informativeness, inherence and exclusivity. It is exactly those attributes that define entitative groups; this entitativity is not a passive perceptual feature, as insinuated in experimental studies, but is first and foremost intended and signalled as such to the outside.

On the one hand, naturalisation legitimises a group's position in society, as we know from the example of aristocracy. On the other hand, naturalising a social category in terms of stigma and devalued status legitimises exclusion, discrimination and inequality; it embodies the difference and fosters stigmatisation. Assigning the members of a social category a 'natural' status comes with a host of symbolic and behavioural consequences: nature, as opposed to culture, is truculent and barely controllable. These consequences can be negative for the essentialized outgroup, as in the case of ethnic or racial minorities, or positive for the ingroup, as in the case of aristocracy, as long as its members constitute a dominant minority. In any case, essence politics illustrates the volatile and discursive character of psychological essentialism in the discourse of societies where the idea of essence is employed or contested as a representational tool in the social groups' unceasing interactions and mutual relating.

References

Ahn, W.-K., Kalish, C., Gelman, S. A., Medin, D. L., Luhmann, C., Atran, S., . . . Shafto, P. (2001). Why essences are essential in the psychology of concepts. *Cognition*, *82*, 59–69.

Bailey, J. M., Pillard, R. C., Dawood, K., Miller, M. B., Farrer, L. A., Trivedi, S., & Murphy, R. L. (1999). A family history study of male sexual orientation using three independent samples. *Behavior Genetics*, *29*(2), 79–86.

Conrad, P., & Markens, S. (2001). Constructing the 'gay gene' in the news: optimism and skepticism in the US and British press. *Health*, *5*(3), 373–400.

Doyle, W. (2007). French and Polish nobility: Memory, identity, culture, XVI–XX century. *English Historical Review*, *122*(498), 1046–1048.

Dronkers, J. (2008). Declining homogamy of Austrian-German nobility in the 20th century? A comparison with the Dutch nobility. *Historical Social Research-Historische Sozialforschung*, *33*(2), 262–284.

Epstein, S. (1987). Gay politics, ethnic-identity – the limits of social constructionism. *Socialist Review*, *93–94*, 9–54.

Fuss, D. (1989). *Essentially speaking: Feminism, nature and difference*. New York, NY: Routledge.

Haslam, N., Rothschild, L., & Ernst, D. (2000). Essentialist beliefs about social categories. *British Journal of Social Psychology*, *39*(1), 113–127.

Haslam, N., Rothschild, L., & Ernst, D. (2002). Are essentialist beliefs associated with prejudice? *British Journal of Social Psychology*, *41*, 87–100.

Holtz, P., & Wagner, W. (2009). Essentialism and attribution of monstrosity in racist discourse: Right-wing internet postings about Africans and Jews. *Journal of Community & Applied Social Psychology*, *19*(6), 411–425.

Holtz, P., Wagner, W., & Sartawi, M. (in press). Discrimination and immigrant identity work: Fundamentalist and secular Muslims facing the Swiss minaret ban. *Journal of the Social Sciences*.

Hopkins, N., & Greenwood, R. M. (2013). Hijab, visibility and the performance of identity. *European Journal of Social Psychology*, *43*(5), 438–447.

Howarth, C., Wagner, W., Magnusson, N., & Sammut, G. (2014). 'It's only other people who make me feel black': Acculturation, identity and agency in a multicultural community. *Political Psychology*, *35*(1), 81–95.

Itaborahy, L. P., & Zhu, J. (2013). *State-sponsored homophobia*. Brussels: International Lesbian Gay Bisexual Trans and Intersex Association.

Keil, F. C. (1992). *Concepts, kinds, and cognitive development*. Cambridge, MA: MIT Press.

Mahalingam, R. (2007). Essentialism, power, and the representation of social categories: A folk sociology perspective. *Human Development*, *50*(6), 300–319.

Medin, D. L., & Ortony, A. (1989). Psychological essentialism. In S. Vosniadou & A. Ortony (Eds.), *Similarity and analogical reasoning* (pp. 179–195). Cambridge: Cambridge University Press.

Morton, T. A., Hornsey, M. J., & Postmes, T. (2009). Shifting ground: The variable use of essentialism in contexts of inclusion and exclusion. *British Journal of Social Psychology*, *48*(1), 35–59.

Norton, A. T., & Herek, G. M. (2013). Heterosexuals' attitudes toward transgender people: Findings from a national probability sample of US adults. *Sex Roles*, *68*(11–12), 738–753.

Raudsepp, M., & Wagner, W. (2012). The essentially other – representational processes that divide groups. In I. Marková & A. Gillespie (Eds.), *Trust and conflict: Representation, culture and dialogue* (pp. 105–122). London: Routledge.

Sen, R. (2012). Hetero-referentiality and divided societies. In D. J. Christie (Ed.), *The encyclopedia of peace psychology, Volume II* (pp. 506–510). Malden, MA: Wiley-Blackwell.

Servick, K. (2014). New support for 'gay gene'. *Science, 346*(6212), 902.

Stoler, A. L. (1997). On political and psychological essentialisms. *Ethos, 25*(1), 101–106.

Tajfel, H. (1978). *Differentiation between social groups.* London: Academic Press.

Tenenbaum, S., & Davidman, L. (2007). It's in my genes: Biological discourse and essentialist views of identity among contemporary American Jews. *The Sociological Quarterly, 48*(3), 435–450.

Verkuyten, M. (2003). Discourses about ethnic group (de-)essentialism: Oppressive and progressive aspects. *British Journal of Social Psychology, 42*, 371–391.

Wagner, W. (2012). Social representation theory. In D. J. Christie (Ed.), *The encyclopedia of peace psychology, Volume III* (pp. 1041–1046). Malden, MA: Wiley-Blackwell.

Wagner, W., Kronberger, N., Nagata, M., Sen, R., Holtz, P., & Flores Palacios, F. (2010). Essentialist theory of 'hybrids': From animal kinds to ethnic categories and race. *Asian Journal of Social Psychology, 13*(4), 232–246.

Wagner, W., Sen, R., Permanadeli, R., & Howarth, C. S. (2012). The veil and Muslim women's identity: Cultural pressures and resistance to stereotyping. *Culture & Psychology, 18*(4), 521–541.

West, K., & Hewstone, M. (2012). Culture and contact in the promotion and reduction of anti-gay prejudice: Evidence from Jamaica and Britain. *Journal of Homosexuality, 59*(1), 44–66.

5

THE SOCIAL AND POLITICAL PSYCHOLOGY OF GLOBALISATION AND GLOBAL IDENTITIES

Ilka H. Gleibs and Geetha Reddy

Introduction

Globalisation is a process by which cultures influence and change one another through trade, mobility and migration, and communication – both in terms of material goods and the exchange of people, information, worldviews and ideas. The speed and breadth of these processes have accelerated over the last decades, resulting in profound social, technological and informational change that is transforming the nature, reach, speed and loci of human influence. Hence, as globalisation seemingly intensifies, societies as we know them change constantly and there are mixed reactions to this. For some, globalisation is often perceived as a potential threat to the viability of local cultures, cultural identities and social cohesion. However, it can also be seen as a process that opens minds to new experiences, removes cultural barriers and accelerates cultural innovations. This tension between resisting and embracing globalisation will be focus of this chapter, and we argue that regardless of whether globalisation relates to desirable or undesirable consequences, it has a profound impact on everyday experiences influencing how people perceive themselves and others; thus it has profound effects on our collective identities.

Globalisation has undoubtedly transformed the cultures and life practices of many societies, but the flow of resources, wealth and sociocultural practices has been asymmetrical. For example, the United States has had major cultural influence, whereas China is one important beneficiary of global trade. Social science scholars have studied the processes of globalisation and its relationship to global inequalities, citizenship, migration, resistance and so forth (e.g., Guillen, 2001; Lechner, 2009; Martell, 2010). These analyses are primarily based on sociological theories and economical approaches that focus on mechanisms on a macro level, such as institutions, states or trade unions. However, studies of social groups or individual agents (i.e., citizens of developed versus developing countries) are still scarce. A psychological analysis of globalisation that provides a theoretically and empirically based understanding of human behaviour on the level of individuals and social groups is relatively new, and these new developments will be our starting point (e.g., Chiu, Gries, Torelli & Cheng, 2011).

More specifically, the focus of this chapter is on the social and political psychology of globalisation, which examines the psychological impact of globalisation on individuals situated in a sociopolitical context. With this, we aim to bridge the gap between the macro level (e.g., systems) and the micro level (e.g., individuals) and examine the interaction between the changing system on macro level – for example through global business, international regulations, global mobility – and the individual on the micro level. We will first define what we mean by a social and political psychology of globalisation. We will then focus on the tension between assimilation and fragmentation that is often associated with globalisation processes and focus on its psychological consequences especially with regard to identities. Moreover, we will concentrate on the question whether and how we can meaningfully conceptualise a 'global identity'. Thus, we will focus on how people undergo a change through globalisation and how they position themselves and others within a globalised world. Our main argument is that a social and political psychology of globalisation benefits from a multidimensional definition of global identities that moves away from a definition of identity around specific, fixed categories (e.g., ethnicity, nationality).

A social and political psychology of globalisation

There is no single accepted definition of the term globalisation despite its widespread use. Thus, for this chapter we take point of departure from an early (but very useful) definition:

> Globalisation refers to the multiplicity of linkages and interconnections that transcend the nation-states (and by implication the societies) which make up the modern world system. It defines a *process* [emphasis added] through which events, decisions, and activities in one part of the world can come to have significant consequences for individuals and communities in quite distant parts of the globe. Nowadays, goods, capital, people, knowledge, images, communications, crime, culture, pollutants, drugs, fashions, and beliefs all readily flow across territorial boundaries. Transnational networks, social movements and relationships are extensive in virtually all areas of human activity from the academic to the sexual.
> *(McGrew, 1992, pp. 65–66; see also Berry, 2008)*

This is a complex definition which focuses on cultural globalisation and points to important concepts that are defining for globalisation, such as multiplicity, interconnectedness and, significantly, the emphasis of globalisation being a process rather than an outcome.

Arnett (2002) further defined globalisation from a psychological perspective as an *exchange process* that has its primary influence on issues of identity and how we perceive others and ourselves. This includes how we are (politically, economically and also culturally) influencing and being influenced by the increased connectivity with those distant people and places around the world. Taking a cue from these two perspectives, we conceptualise globalisation as a process that involves a flow of cultural elements and the maintenance, establishing of, and change in social relationships and our connections with those (see also Berry, 2008).

Bringing this outlook together with a simple definition of social psychology (see, for example, Allport, 1954), we can establish a working definition for the social psychology of globalisation as:

> A social psychology of globalisation examines how we negotiate our understanding of how we think about, feel about and relate to others and ourselves vis-à-vis a more globalised world.

With this definition in mind, we will argue that a social psychological analysis of globalisation is important for understanding how individuals deal with the social change perpetuated through globalisation. The social psychological analysis of globalisation aims at examining the perspective of the individuals within the system and how the globalisation process influences the psychological understanding of self, identity, intergroup behaviours and so on. Therefore, creating a link between behaviour on an individual or group level and examining the problem on a systemic level is necessary for understanding efforts for structural change. This 'globalised' thinking of the social being should apply to how individuals are interconnected in social, political and economic contexts. From this standpoint, we might want to broaden the analysis of a social psychology of globalisation to a political psychological one that also takes into account "psychological understanding that involves a political dimension in the sense being embedded in a wider understanding of how social relations are organised in a world" (Elcheroth, Doise & Reicher, 2011, p. 730). Thus, we seek to include social and political lenses in examining globalisation processes and their influence on us that take into account multiple perspectives and levels of analysis. This broadens our definition to:

> A social and political psychological of globalisation examines how we negotiate our understanding of how we think about, feel about and relate to others and ourselves vis-à-vis a more globalised world by taking into account how individuals are interconnected in a social, political and economic contexts.

From this initial perspective we will further elaborate on the social processes of globalisation and their influence on identities.

Between assimilation and fragmentation: People in a globalised world

Globalisation is, on the one hand, characterised by unification and assimilation, thus the creation of one global world (O'Byrne & Hensby, 2011). For example, on a political level we observe that the importance and influence of global/transnational institutions such as EU, NATO, UNO, the IWF or the World Bank are increasing, leading to a debate in social science as to whether these global governance structures are undermining or transforming the authority of the nation-state (see Guillen, 2001, for a review). We witness a similar trend of increased assimilation on a cultural level. People all over the world are watching the same TV programs, listening to the same music and consuming similar goods, often made by US companies. One could argue that humans today are culturally and linguistically more homogeneous and group-based differences are decreasing (Moghaddam, 2009; Ritzer, 2007). From this perspective, the world is becoming a 'global village' (McLuhan, 1964) in which lifestyles become more unified and cultural experiences become similar whether they take place in Dhaka, London or Beijing. This trend is often perceived as diminishing local products, diversity and alternative views (Martell, 2010). On the other hand – and some would argue this is not independent from the assimilation processes through global institutions (Conversi, 2013) – we see an emerging trend of fragmentation or increased localism exemplified by the recent discussion about Scottish, Catalan or Basque independence.

Similar to the fragmentation processes on the political level, we observe a trend of 'ethnical revival' that highlights cultural differences and group differentiation on a cultural level (Moghaddam, 2012). For example, in April 2014 it was announced that Cornish people in the UK would be granted minority status under European rules for the protection of national minorities with the aim to strengthen their distinct Cornish identity. Moghaddam (2008, p. 4) argued, "just as globalization speeds ahead and group-based differences seem to be disappearing, there is also an ethnic revival and the re-emergence of ethnic pride and 'being different'". Taken together, it seems that the processes of globalisation on the cultural (macro) level enhance assimilation and inclusiveness, which as a consequence activates the need for differentiation, fragmentation and emphasis of localism (see also Geertz, 1998; Guillen, 2001).

This tension between assimilation and fragmentation is similar to what Brewer defined as an intrapersonal process in the *optimal distinctiveness theory* (Brewer, 1991), which argues that people (on an individual or micro level) search for optimal distinctiveness of being unique but also share a collective identity. Notably, individuals will attempt to restore the balance of these two identity motives (Vignoles, Regalia, Manzi, Golledge & Scabini, 2006) once it is disturbed. Bringing this together with changes on the cultural level, we argue that globalisation might disturb the balance between being unique and being similar at the same time, resulting in attempts to restore *optimal distinctiveness*. One strategy that people use to do so could be an increased differentiation between whom we define as 'us' and 'them' (van Stekelenburg & Klandermans, 2010). Importantly, the accentuation of different cultural/ethical identities might increase through the perception that specific collective identities (i.e., religious, political, ethical, cultural) are threatened by clashing ideologies or because they are marginalised in an economically and politically homogenised world (Moghaddam, 2008, 2012; van Stekelenburg & Klandermans, 2010). This is what Moghaddam (2008) defined as a process of "fractured globalisation" that accordingly describes "the tendency for sociocultural disintegration to pull in a local direction at the same time that macroeconomic and political systems are set up to accelerate globalization" (p. 13).

Hence, across these different levels of analysis, we observe a tension between assimilation (becoming one and creating a 'global' culture or democracy) and fragmentation and localisation (the focus on small units/communities with a distinct 'identity') that has an influence on how individuals negotiate their own identities and how they relate to others. Both processes put different emphases on transforming relationships between places that we inhibit and our identities within this social context. The key question for a social psychological analysis of globalisation and identity is then to ask what happens to our identity development when we are presented with these multiple, and sometimes contradicting, cultural contexts that, on the one hand, stress unification/humanity and, on the other hand, stress fragmentation/conflict (Jensen, Arnett & McKenzie, 2011)? Hence, how can people make sense of these 'global' changes and how can they incorporate these changes into a sense of who they are?

Between a 'local' and a 'global' identity

Adaptation to 'global changes' is often discussed in terms of negotiating our local (e.g., national, ethnic, or cultural identities) with a 'global' (superordinate, all humanity) identity. One question that researchers focus on is whether a global identity enhances or is in conflict with a local identity/identities. For example, Sharma and Sharma (2010) argued that globalisation as a process has positive consequences for the development of a bicultural identity (global *and* local) when a global identity confirms and reinforces other social identities and therefore provides individuals with stability, self-esteem and empowerment and may give rise to internal harmony and acceptance of oneself, enabling one to be accepting of others as well. Thus, if global and local identities are to a certain degree complementary and there is synergy among the person's multiple identities, it might increase openness to others and enhance complex decision making and navigation in a 'global' world (Ramarajan, 2014). This can be exemplified in the context of multicultural Singapore. In Singapore, English is the official language and might represent a 'global' identity. Moreover, one also develops the local ethnic identity of Chinese, Indian or Malay. The global 'English speaking' identity allows the Singaporeans to participate in a much larger worldwide community, while maintaining competency in their own ethnocultural language allows them to remain grounded in their local identity (Clammer, 1998).

However, it is argued that globalisation and the associated global identity 'threatens' and devalues other social identities and it has detrimental effects on well-being and adaptation. For example, it is argued that if global and local identities are experienced as being in tension and opposition with one another, it creates intrapersonal tension (Benet-Martinez & Haritatos, 2005; Benet-Martinez, Leu, Lee & Morris, 2002) and this conflict then influences how the person resolves conflict within themselves and with others (Ramarajan, 2014). Thus, when experienced as conflict, the processes of identity integration associated with globalisation disrupts principles of continuity, distinctiveness and self-esteem (Vignoles et al., 2006) of (local) identities, which in its consequence leads to what Sharma and Sharma (2010) call *identity dislocation*, which decreases psychological well-being. In addition, it might be related to perceptions of discrimination and the loss of traditional individual and kinship identities that clash with the global identity. This is exemplified in the loss of first language proficiency of Turkish migrants in Australia, who with the loss of their language also lose part of their ethnic identity (Yagmur, de Bot & Korzilius, 1999). This tension between local and global identity mirrors the tension of the assimilation-fragmentation process that we described earlier.

Defining a 'global identity'

What exactly is a 'global' identity, however, remains fuzzy, and not many attempts have been made to psychologically conceptualise or measure a global identity. Among the few, Sam McFarland argued that a global identity could be conceptualised as *identification with all humanity* (IWAH), which reflects viewing all humanity as 'family' or one (McFarland, Webb & Brown, 2012; McFarland, Brown & Webb, 2013; for similar concepts, see Buchan et al., 2011). Theoretically, the authors think about this concept as an individual difference measure that is related to a proactive care and concern for others. Moreover, it is theoretically also anchored in the self-categorisation literature (Turner et al., 1987), which states that the cognitive structure of the self is defined by multiple (social) categories (a woman, an academic, a daughter, fun-loving, German, Singaporean, Chindian etc.); these categories are hierarchically structured and their salience is context dependent. For example, when the category *academic* is activated, I might differentiate between psychologists and sociologists on a basic level, two categories that are nested in the superordinate category of social scientists. These activated categories and different levels of abstraction help me determine whom I perceive as ingroup or outgroup members at a given point in time (Turner et al., 1987). From this it follows that identification with all humanity is based on the categorisation of individuals on a highest and most abstract level of abstraction (namely humanity) and that, if constructed as an individual difference, some individuals are more prone to use this level of abstraction than others.

Thus, this concept of a global identity focuses on unification and an innate similarity between all humans stressing a common identity as 'we are all one'. In addition, McFarland and colleagues argue that this form of identification with all humanity portrays a 'moral ideal' that we all should strive for, as it might enhance global harmony and decrease intergroup tensions (McFarland et al., 2013). With this, IWAH is in line with the universalist beliefs about progress and common humanity and with this, the concept of identification with all humanity belongs to a larger tradition of social psychological research that stresses the importance and benefits of highly inclusive social categories for intergroup relations (Gaertner et al., 2000; Maslow, 1954; Turner et al., 1987; see also the concept of *omniculturalism*, Moghaddam, 2012).

The research on identification with all humanity is still in its infancy. However, McFarland et al. (2012) found that it is negatively related to right-wing authoritarianism, social dominance orientation, ethnocentrism and general prejudice; furthermore, IWAH is a distinct and positive predictor for human right commitments. Reese, Proch and Cohrs (2014) also showed that IWAH is significantly related to behavioural intentions to reduce global inequality (see also Buchan et al., 2011).

Yet, there are several shortcomings with this concept. The main problem with it is how we define 'all humanity'. One could reasonably ask: who is entitled to define the content of humanity? What will make such a definition universal, legitimate and supported by all groups? Previous empirical work and the theoretical concept of ingroup projection makes it is likely that we construct 'humans everywhere' to be either similar to us or we regard the ingroup as being prototypical for the superordinate category (Cheryan & Monin, 2005; Devos & Banaji, 2005; Wenzel, Mummendey, Weber & Waldzus, 2003). For example, whenever group members (e.g., Cornish) focus on superordinate categories (e.g., British, European human), their source of knowledge about the superordinate category is their knowledge about their own subgroup (in this case, Cornish). Such *pars pro toto* reasoning about superordinate social categories is known in social psychology as *ingroup projection* – a widely observed cognitive bias in processing information about higher level social categories (Kessler et al., 2010; Wenzel, Mummendey & Waldzus, 2008; see also Bilewicz & Bilewicz, 2012).

Second, one might argue that identifying with all humanity might be favoured by and favourable for members of advantaged or dominant groups but less so for members of disadvantaged groups. Recent research has shown that positive intergroup contact and the perception of one identity is beneficial and desirable to members of the high-status or dominant group, but it may lead the low-status or disadvantaged group to underestimate social inequalities, injustice and discrimination (e.g., Saguy & Chernyak-Hai, 2012; Saguy, Dovidio & Pratto, 2008). Intergroup harmony that is caused by commonality-focused encounters can blur impressions about discriminatory intergroup relations and, as such, harmony, a concept that focuses on the benefits of a commonality, hinders resolving social inequality (Bilewicz & Bilewicz, 2012; Dixon, Levine, Reicher & Durrheim, 2012; Dixon, Tropp, Durrheim & Tredoux, 2010; Wright & Lubensky, 2009). So far, research on IWAH has looked at its consequences on prejudice and behavioural intentions for members of relatively privileged societies such as the US or Germany. In light of the criticism we just highlighted, more research would be needed to see how the concept is understood and reflected in less advantageous societies and in different cultures.

Third, IWAH treats human commonality as a dispositional variable of an individual (micro level) rather than as a contextual and situational framing of an intercultural encounter. As such, it neglects the sociopolitical context from which identification emerges.

To summarise, we started from the notion that globalisation entails both integration and fragmentation, and we further outlined how globalisation can be construed as enriching and as an 'identity threat' at the same time. Thus, participating in a global society could be associated with ideas of integration, acceptance, tolerance and safety. Likewise (and sometimes simultaneously), it accelerates complexity and diversity of cultural identity development and, under certain circumstances, it leads to fragmentations and it threatens people's distinct 'ethnic/cultural' identities and what we connect with those (see also Jensen, Arnett & McKenzie, 2011). While acknowledging this tension, previously reviewed concepts of local versus global identities and of IWAH oscillate between interpersonal (within a shared social identity) and intrapersonal (an individual understanding of an identity) and therefore mostly allocate the challenge of dealing with a globalised world within the individual. Thus, from this perspective, global identities are mainly defined as a complex mixture of cultural identities, and it appears that any tension arising from identity negotiation needs to be solved within the individual.

However, this view on global identities neglects the focus on the social and political context in which identities (such as a 'global and local' one) help or hinder people navigating who they are. Moreover, it often defines these identities as being opposing ends of a continuum without focusing on how different identities are intertwined and define each other (see Howarth, 2002). In addition, identity in a globalised world is not only a 'problem' of identity integration or negotiation experienced by specific individuals, such as migrants or minority members, but it becomes increasingly important for everyone who experiences more diverse societies. In essence, identity in a globalised world should be studied in its social and political complexity, and understanding the multiplicity of identities and their consequences for individuals and social relations is important. With that, we propose that to understand identity in a global world, it might be fruitful to focus not only on identities that are based around specific social categories (such as ethnicity and culture) and complex mixtures of those, but also on those that take into account collective struggles or political projects.

Reconceptualising global identities

Thus, we argue that speaking of one global identity in the singular or the idea of one global culture and identity is a practical impossibility.

Instead of thinking of a global identity as a one-dimensional concept that entails, for example, a specific shared identity around a global culture and/or is conceptualised as an individual difference (thus, individuals being high or low 'global identifiers'), it might be more fruitful to think of it as a multidimensional concept that takes into account the fluidity and dynamics of global *identities* that recognise the process of 'hybridisation' (Croucher, 2009), intersectionality (Gillespie, Howarth & Cornish, 2012) and a more differentiated perception of political context and culture (Bilewicz & Bilewicz, 2012; Tripathi & Mishra, 2012). As such, it is important to stress that commonalities (or what our representation of a global identity entails) is differently understood in diverse cultures. Put differently, for studying global identities, it is important to examine that these are socially represented in different settings (e.g., Kashima et al., 2011). Second, it becomes important to understand global identities beyond fixed geographical space and national boundaries and to take into account the multiple identities that we inhabit (occupation, political attitudes etc.) and that are intertwined with our cultural identities (e.g., Jaspal & Cinnirella, 2010; see also McGarty, Thomas, Lala, Smith & Bliuc, 2013).

Hence, we propose that if we want to examine the formation of global identities and how globalisation impacts identity processes, our understanding of a global space should be built around the fact that we can expect disagreement and tensions but also acknowledge the inherent connectivity and interdependence. A social and political psychology of globalisation and global identities might be most useful when it recognises that social categories are human constructs and that they change and evolve and people are moving between them. Instead of a concept of identity constructed on a global/all human level, it might be more fruitful to focus on the dialectic nature of different identities (e.g., Cornish, British, gay, academic) and the differential representations that stem from the social world and the individual within the context (Howarth, 2002). The focus of understanding global identities is then not simply on how individuals negotiate their local and global cultures or on individual differences in identification, but on integrating the social aspects of the different contents and sociopolitical realities of what global identities mean in Kiev, Damascus or Berlin.

Moreover, to further develop another perspective of global identities that takes into account the politics of globalisation, it might be useful to focus on a conceptualisation of identity, which includes shared political attitudes that emerge in a globalised world (e.g., increasing inequality, climate change, poverty, discrimination), and not necessarily focus on differences or communalities around relatively fixed social categories (such as ethnicity, gender, race), as we discussed previously. This difference is nicely demonstrated in a quote by Harpies and Quines (quoted in Hopkins, Kahani-Hopkins & Reicher, 2006): "I am a feminist, not a woman, and a socialist first, not a Scot . . . unite with people who share your ideas not your accents [or] your genitals."

To this end, it might be useful to look at *politicised collective identities*, which in their conceptualisation explicitly include power struggles in society (Simon & Klandermans, 2001). When people have a politicised collective identity, we expect them to have a political understanding of a particular movement, and they negotiate this identity and its content in a tripolar setting that often includes the activists group (i.e., anti-globalisation movement), the authorities, government or other 'opponents' and the general public. When group members' politicised collective identities are salient, they intentionally engage in a power struggle that is embedded in a more inclusive societal context in which this struggle takes place (Simon & Grabow, 2010). Necessary for such activation are an awareness of shared grievance, adversarial attribution to blame opponents and the involvement of society. How these three factors work together could be illustrated in the example of the Occupy movement, which created a global identity for those who are questioning current power distribution. A group of activists (first in New York, but then also in Berlin, London, Tel Aviv and so forth) realises that for many people it is increasingly difficult to find a job, have a job that pays a living wage, or have a job that helps pay off their student loans and so forth, whereas 'the upper 1%' get increasingly richer and were hardly affected by the economic recession of the last years (see, for example, Leonhardt & Quealy, 2014). The activists then make adversarial attributions by blaming 'the bankers', and they make them responsible for the difficulties and demand a change in the system. Finally, for the triangulation of the power struggle, they occupy a public space and involve the wider society as a third party that is encouraged to take sides.

The important aspect of this concept is that politicised collective identities explicitly focus on actions aimed at a third party and changes in wider society and not exclusively on a bipolar ingroup/outgroup perspective. Moreover, a politicised identity is by definition an inclusive and nested identity (Simon & Grabow, 2010) that does not necessarily rest on specific ethnic or cultural affiliation. It entails both identification with the upset ingroup (i.e., the Occupy movement) and identification with the more inclusive entity (i.e., a global society) that provides the context for shared grievances, adversarial attributions and the ensuing power struggle for social change and takes into account the sociopolitical context in which globalised identities are constructed. In this sense, it is a useful concept to consider when examining global identities and how collective identities are used to make sense in a globalised world.

Thus, global identities, which are conceptualised around politicised collective identities and not only multiple cultural identities, explicitly acknowledge global (or local) inequalities and political contexts in which identities are embedded instead of masking group differences in an attempt to increase intergroup harmony. However, politicised, collective identities are not per se 'positive' and necessarily aimed at positive social change. One could argue, for example, that identification with the Islamic State is a politicised, global identity that people might adopt to make sense of a changing, global world (e.g., Becker, Tausch, Spears & Christ, 2011). Such a global and politicised identity is not aimed at increasing intergroup harmony or world peace, but is associated with terror and war and the extinction of 'nonbelievers'. Here, by constructing this specific global identity, misunderstanding and conflict between communities are maintained through segregation, which increases mutual ignorance and hate (Hewstone et al., 2005; Sharma & Sharma, 2010) and perpetuates intergroup conflict to extreme measures.

Conclusion

A social and political psychology of globalisation that focuses on the multiplicity of global identities explicitly needs a societal and political approach. Thus, studying social psychological processes of change and globalisation not only has to emphasise interindividual differences in adaptation and acculturation but also acknowledge the role of economics, politics and social contexts, as well as their constraints on identities, social relations and systems of inclusion and exclusion (Howarth et al., 2013). Thus, identities in a global world should be studied as a complex notion that takes into account the multiplicity of experiences that we have in a globalised world whereby one step among other concepts (see Ferguson, Tran, Mendez & van de Vijver, in press; Jensen, Arnett & McKenzie, 2011) might be studying how people make sense of their identities as politicised collective identities.

Importantly then, how we construct our identities in a globalised world impacts not only our self and other image and our own well-being (Chen et al., 2008), but it also has consequences for intergroup relations and political action. However, in the process of collapsing boundaries between different groups of people and countries and constructing an identity that takes into account diverse social context, individuals may find that their perspectives, which may have been construed to be normative to their own culture, could in fact be shared with other cultures around the world. Encountering different knowledge systems and ways of understanding the world can, under the right circumstances, lead to more positive intergroup contact that might help us to overcome the tensions and fragmentations that are created through globalisation.

Taken together, we can perceive our psychological reaction to globalisation as a complex negotiation between push-and-pull forces of maintaining and changing one's society and attached identities and a balance between assimilation and fragmentation. In this way, globalisation and attached identities are not 'given' or 'objective' but are socially constructed and socially embedded concepts that are constructed and co-constructed in our daily, global encounters.

References

Allport, G. W. (1954). *The nature of prejudice.* Reading, MA: Addison-Wesley.
Arnett, J. J. (2002). The psychology of globalization. *American Psychologist, 57*(10), 774–783.
Becker, J. C., Tausch, N., Spears, R., & Christ, O. (2011). Committed dis(s)idents: Participation in radical collective action fosters disidentification with the broader in-group but enhances political identification. *Personality and Social Psychology Bulletin, 37*(8), 1104–1116.
Benet-Martínez, V., & Haritatos, J. (2005). Bicultural identity integration (BII): Components and psychosocial antecedents. *Journal of Personality, 73*(4), 1015–1050.
Benet-Martínez, V., Leu, J., Lee, F., & Morris, M. W. (2002). Negotiating biculturalism cultural frame switching in biculturals with oppositional versus compatible cultural identities. *Journal of Cross-Cultural Psychology, 33*(5), 492–516.
Berry, J. W. (2008). Globalisation and acculturation. *International Journal of Intercultural Relations, 32*(4), 328–336.

Bilewicz, M., & Bilewicz, A. (2012). Who defines humanity? Psychological and cultural obstacles to omniculturalism. *Culture & Psychology, 18*(3), 1–14.

Brewer, M. B. (1991). The social self: On being the same and different at the same time. *Personality and Social Psychology Bulletin, 17*(5), 475–482.

Buchan, N. R., Brewer, M. B., Grimalda, G., Wilson, R. K., Fatas, E., & Foddy, M. (2011). Global social identity and global cooperation. *Psychological Science, 22*(6), 821–828.

Chen, S. X., Benet-Martínez, V., & Harris Bond, M. (2008). Bicultural identity, bilingualism, and psychological adjustment in multicultural societies: Immigration-based and globalization-based acculturation. *Journal of Personality, 76*(4), 803–838.

Cheryan, S., & Monin, B. (2005). 'Where are you really from?': Asian Americans and identity denial. *Journal of Personality and Social Psychology, 89*, 717–730.

Chiu, C., Gries, P., Torelli, C. J., & Cheng, S. Y. Y. (2011). Toward a social psychology of globalization. *Journal of Social Issues, 67*, 663–676.

Clammer, J. R. (1998). *Race and state in independent Singapore, 1965–1990: The cultural politics of pluralism in a multiethnic society.* Brookfield, VT: Ashgate.

Conversi, D. (2013). Between the hammer of globalization and the anvil of nationalism: Is Europe's complex diversity under threat? *Ethnicities, 14*(1), 25–49.

Croucher, S. (2009). Migrants of privilege: The political transnationalism of Americans in Mexico. *Identities, 16*(4), 463–491.

Devos, T., & Banaji, M. R. (2005). American = White? *Journal of Personality and Social Psychology, 88*(3), 447–466.

Dixon, J., Levine, M., Reicher, S., & Durrheim, K. (2012). Beyond prejudice: Are negative evaluations the problem and is getting us to like one another more the solution? *Behavioral Brain Sciences, 35*(6), 411–425.

Dixon, J., Tropp, L. R., Durrheim, K., & Tredoux, C. (2010). 'Let them eat harmony': Prejudice-reduction strategies and attitudes of historically disadvantaged groups. *Current Directions in Psychological Science, 19*(2), 76–80.

Elcheroth, G., Doise, W., & Reicher, S. (2011). On the knowledge of politics and the politics of knowledge: How a social representations approach helps us rethink the subject of political psychology. *Political Psychology, 32*, 729–758.

Ferguson, G. M., Tran, S. P., Mendez, S. N., & van de Vijver, F. J. R. (in press). Remote acculturation: Conceptualization, measurement, and implications for health outcomes. In S. J. Schwartz & J. B. Unger (Eds.), *Oxford Handbook of Acculturation and Health.*

Gaertner, S. L., Dovidio, J. F., Nier, J. A., Banker, B. S., Ward, C. M., Houlette, M., & Loux, S. (2000). *The common ingroup identity model for reducing intergroup bias: Progress and challenges* (pp. 133–148). Thousand Oaks, CA: Sage.

Geertz, C. (1998). The world in pieces: Culture and politics at the end of the century. *Focaal: Tijdschr. Antropology, 32*, 91–117.

Gillespie, A., Howarth, C., & Cornish, F. (2012). Four problems for researchers using social categories. *Culture and Psychology, 18*(3), 391–402.

Guillen, M. F. (2001). Is globalization civilizing, destructive or feeble? A critique of five key debates in the social science literature. *Annual Review of Sociology, 27*, 235–260.

Hewstone, M., Cairns, E., Voci, A., Paolini, S., McLernon, F., Crisp, R., . . . Craig, J. (2005). Intergroup contact in a divided society: Challenging segregation in Northern Ireland. In D. Abrams, J.M. Marques, & M.A. Hogg (Eds.), *The social psychology of inclusion and exclusion* (pp. 265–292). Philadelphia: Psychology Press.

Hopkins, N., Kahani-Hopkins, V., & Reicher, S. (2006). Identity and social change: Contextualizing agency. *Feminism & Psychology, 16*(1), 52–57.

Howarth, C. (2002). Identity in whose eyes? The role of representations in identity construction. *Journal for the Theory of Social Behaviour, 32*(2), 145–162.

Howarth, C., Campbell, C., Cornish, F., Franks, B., Garcia-Lorenzo, L., Gillespie, A., . . . Tennant, C. (2013). Insights from societal psychology: A contextual politics of societal change. *Journal of Social and Political Psychology, 1*(1), 364–384.

Jaspal, R., & Cinnirella, M. (2010). Coping with potentially incompatible identities: Accounts of religious, ethnic, and sexual identities from British Pakistani men who identify as Muslim and gay. *British Journal of Social Psychology, 49*, 849–870.

Jensen, L. A., Arnett, J. J., & McKenzie, J. (2011). Globalization and cultural identity. In S.J. Schwartz, K. Luyckx, & V.L. Vignoles (Eds.), *Handbook of identity theory and research* (pp. 285–301). New York: Springer.

Kashima, Y., Shi, J., Tsuchiya, K., Kashima, E. S., Cheng, S.Y., Chao, M. M., & Shin, S. H. (2011). Globalization and folk theory of social change: How globalization relates to societal perceptions about the past and future. *Journal of Social Issues, 67*(4), 696–715.

Kessler, R. C., McLaughlin, K. A., Green, J. G., Gruber, M. J., Sampson, N. A., Zaslavsky, A. M., . . . Williams, D. R. (2010). Childhood adversities and adult psychopathology in the WHO World Mental Health Surveys. *The British Journal of Psychiatry, 197*(5), 378–385.

Lechner, F. J. (2009). *Globalization: The making of world society.* London: John Wiley & Sons.

Leonhardt, D., & Quealy, K. (2014). The American middle class is no longer the world's richest. Retrieved April 22, 2014, from www.nytimes.com/2014/04/23/upshot/the-american-middle-class-is-no-longer-the-worlds-richest.html?_r=0

McFarland, S., Brown, D., & Webb, M. (2013). 'Identification with all humanity' as a moral concept and psychological construct. *Current Directions in Psychological Science, 22*, 192–196.

McFarland, S. G., Webb, M., & Brown, D. (2012). All humanity is my ingroup: A measure and studies of identification with all humanity. *Journal of Personality and Social Psychology, 103*, 830–853.

McGarty, C., Thomas, E. F., Lala, G., Smith, L. G. E., & Bliuc, A.-M. (2013). New technologies, new identities, and the growth of mass opposition in the Arab spring. *Political Psychology, 35*, 1–16.

McGrew, A. (1992). A global society? In S. Hall, D. Held, & T. McGrew (Eds.), *Modernity and its futures* (pp. 61–116). Cambridge: Polity Press.

McLuhan, M. (1964). *Understanding media.* New York: Mentor.

Martell, L. (2010). *The sociology of globalization.* Cambridge: Polity Press.

Maslow, A. H. (1954). *Motivation and personality.* New York: Harper and Row.

Moghaddam, F. M. (2008). *Multiculturalism, democracy, and intergroup relations: International and national contexts.* Washington: American Psychological Association.

Moghaddam, F. M. (2009). Commentary: Omniculturalism: Policy solutions to fundamentalism in the era of fractured globalization. *Culture & Psychology, 15*(3), 337–347.

Moghaddam, F. M. (2012). The omnicultural imperative. *Culture & Psychology, 18*(3), 304–330.

O'Byrne, D. J., & Hensby, A. (2011). *Theorizing global studies.* Basingstoke, England: Palgrave Macmillan.

Ramarajan, L. (2014). Past, present and future research on multiple identities: Toward an intrapersonal network approach. *The Academy of Management Annals, 8*, 589–659.

Reese, G., Proch, J., & Cohrs, J. C. (2014). Individual differences in responses to global inequality. *Analyses of Social Issues and Public Policy, 14*, 217–238.

Ritzer, G. (Ed.). (2007). *The Blackwell encyclopedia of sociology* (Vol. 1479). Malden, MA: Blackwell Publishing.

Saguy, T., & Chernyak-Hai, L. (2012). Intergroup contact can undermine disadvantaged group members' attributions to discrimination. *Journal of Experimental Social Psychology, 48*(3), 714–720.

Saguy, T., Dovidio, J. F., & Pratto, F. (2008). Beyond contact: Intergroup contact in the context of power relations. *Personality and Social Psychology Bulletin, 34*(3), 432–445.

Sharma, S., & Sharma, M. (2010). Globalization, threatened identities, coping and well-being. *Psychological Studies, 55*(4), 313–322.

Simon, B., & Grabow, O. (2010). The politicization of migrants: Further evidence that politicized collective identity is a dual identity. *Political Psychology, 31*(5), 717–738.

Simon, B., & Klandermans, B. (2001). Politicized collective identity. *American Psychologist, 56*(4), 319–331.

Tripathi, R. C., & Mishra, R. C. (2012). The 'other' truth of culture and omniculturalism. *Culture & Psychology, 18*(3), 359–374.

Turner, J. C, Hogg, M., Oakes, P., Reicher, S., & Wetherell, M. (1987). *Rediscovering the social group: A self-categorization theory*. Oxford, England: Basil Blackwell.

Van Stekelenburg, J., & Klandermans, B. (2010). Radicalization: Identity and participation in culturally diverse societies. In A. Azzi, X. Chryssochoou, B. Klandermans, & B. B. Simon (Eds.), *Identity and participation in culturally diverse societies: A multidisciplinary perspective* (pp. 181–194). Oxford: Blackwell Wiley.

Vignoles, V. L., Regalia, C., Manzi, C., Golledge, J., & Scabini, E. (2006). Beyond self-esteem: Influence of multiple motives on identity construction. *Journal of Personality and Social Psychology, 90*(2), 308.

Wenzel, M., Mummendey, A., & Waldzus, S. (2008). Superordinate identities and intergroup conflict: The ingroup projection model. *European Review of Social Psychology, 18*, 331–372.

Wenzel, M., Mummendey, A., Weber, U., & Waldzus, S. (2003). The ingroup as pars pro toto: Projection from the ingroup onto the inclusive category as a precursor to social discrimination. *Personality and Social Psychology Bulletin, 29*(4), 461–473.

Wright, S. C., & Lubensky, M. (2009). The struggle for social equality: Collective action versus prejudice reduction. In S. Demoulin, J. P. Leyens & J. F. Dovidio (Eds.), *Intergroup misunderstandings: Impact of divergent social realities* (pp. 291–310). New York: Psychology Press.

Yagmur, K., De Bot, K., & Korzilius, H. (1999). Language attrition, language shift and ethnolinguistic vitality of Turkish in Australia. *Journal of Multilingual and Multicultural Development, 20*, 51–69.

COMMENTARY ON PART I

Politics, identities and social representations in multicultural societies

Xenia Chryssochoou

Politics, according to Rancière (2005), are a permanent debate about reality. They involve a conflict that cannot be solved rationally – a conflict that opens a discussion about what is possible, who has the right to speak and who sets the agenda of the discussion. The chapters in this part aim to grasp aspects of this debate in relation to current societies that become increasingly multicultural. They discuss how different groups and individuals construct social reality and new "*we*"s, how leaders inscribe themselves into different groups in order to be able to lead, how intergroup relations are represented and how political action is expressed. Inevitably, even without making an explicit reference to it, they inscribe themselves within the theoretical framework of social representations.

In his attempt to describe the "phenomenon of social representations", Moscovici (1984) suggested that the distinction between sacred and profane sciences has been replaced in this era by another distinction: that between consensual and reified universes. In the consensual universe, society is a continuous creation permeated with meaning and purpose, a society of individuals of equal competence that can speak in the name of the group. In this universe, communication, conversation and exchange of views are necessary ingredients, and it is the functional value of the answers provided to the societal questions that is of interest. In the reified universe, on the contrary, society is characterized by invariant objects, by an environment that impacts human actions. It is a society where people have different statuses based on their competencies, and in particular on their competence to talk about the objects that form society and the world. In this universe, what is necessary is the correct information processing and the answers given are measured on a dimension that opposes "right" to "wrong". The two universes have different means for understanding the world: science for the reified universe and social representations for the consensual. Positioning oneself into one or the other universe has implications for how one sees thinking and knowledge production. For the consensual universe, thinking is a social process and not an information processing mechanism, as it is considered in the reified universe. In this universe, the interest is in how the social subject *acts* upon and not how it *reacts* to the social environment.

In which universe are politics? The chapters in this part take a clear stance and position politics in the consensual universe. In that sense, they are concerned with "everyday politics". I think it is important to emphasize this aspect, otherwise we run the risk of considering that there are politics that are not "everyday". The merit of this approach is to highlight that there are scientific endeavors that focus on how people construct and act upon social environments, and on how and, in particular, on why they inscribe themselves in them. These approaches that are socially embedded and do not reject the epistemology of common sense are necessary in order to understand the consequences of these actions and how societies remain stable or change.

Indeed, in the last years our societies have changed, and we can witness both trends of globalization and of particularization. One thing that is evident is that societies are not monocultural anymore. They were probably not in the past, either. However, what is felt as a change is that people with diverse cultural backgrounds claim participation to the national polity and thus claim rights and resources (Chryssochoou, 2000a). The old schemata about the nation are challenged both from global and particular perspectives (Chryssochoou, 2004). The multicultural nature of our societies is problematized. The chapters present different aspects of this reality and bring to the forefront questions raised by an "everyday" approach to politics. Not surprisingly, identity issues are present in all chapters as an important element of the changing social environment.

Identity is a concept much discussed in the social psychological literature, and it is beyond the scope of this brief commentary to present the multiple ways identities are involved in multicultural societies (Andreouli & Chryssochoou, 2015; Chryssochoou, 2009, 2011, 2014, 2015; Chryssochoou & Lyons, 2011). I would like though to highlight one aspect that is important and is implicit in the preceding chapters: the fact that identities are carriers of projects and, thus, they can be strategically mobilized (Reicher, 2004; Reicher & Hopkins, 2001). People construct superordinate identities that might become politicized (Gleibs and Reddy), leaders claim different identifications and mobilize different categories in order to lead (Augoustinos, Callaghan, Sorrentino and Worth), identity conflicts are negotiated in the public space (Gibson), new contents are constructed for nationhood in response to multiculturalism (Howarth) and the essence of categories attributed to self and others is strategically used (Wagner, Raudsepp, Holtz and Sen).

If one takes the perspective of a consensual universe, then it is evident that the way people speak and act within their social environment relates to the way they see themselves in it. Identity can be seen as the representation of the self that links individuals to their social world. It does that by mediating the relationship between individuals and the social world and it expresses the relationship between the "I" and the "we" and the relationship between the "I" and the "they". These relationships bind individuals with others and give meaning and purpose to their social environment. In other words, I would argue, because identity is socially constructed and represented, people are able to build shared realities and act upon the social world. These identities are not individual constructions but follow the mechanisms of social representations even in their phenomenology (Chryssochoou, 2003, 2014). Thus, in my view, there is no point arguing whether social representations precede identities or vice versa. We need to study the strategic aspects of identity construction in parallel with the construction of social representations of societies and societal orders.

One of the issues that the chapters raise, although in some it is implicit, is the new societal order implied by the presence of multicultural societies. Is this representation antagonistic to a monocultural nation? Do different global identities presume different representations of the social order? Have we moved from race to social diversity? In this new era, how can one avoid being considered nationalist or racist? What is the "allowed" content of the different categories one can affiliate with? Are minorities in power and, if so, how can they negotiate their positions? Has multiculturalism succeeded or failed? All these are questions asked in the chapters, and I am sure that the reader will find food for thought about the processes in action in current societies. These are questions of concern for every citizen, and in that respect, they constitute questions of everyday politics. It is not a matter of specialists like us, social psychologists and other social scientists, to say, for example, whether multiculturalism has failed or not. The answer to this question for politicians and citizens alike is strategic and ideological and thus political.

As Howarth rightly observes, multiculturalism enters the political arena because it challenges the hegemonic view that only monocultural societies are cohesive. Is this idea a social psychological fact? Inasmuch as it is the outcome of anchoring and objectification processes that translate social regulations into ways of thinking, I would say that we are in the presence of a social representational mechanism. Can we imagine that another social psychological outcome is possible? The answer is definitively positive, but this could happen in the presence of other social regulations.

It is important, in my view, to take into consideration that we are studying social psychological phenomena in a context where neoliberal capitalism prevails. In that respect, the social regulations that guide, at the level of the metasystem (Doise, 2012; Doise & Valentim, 2015; Moscovici, 1976), the way people give meaning to their identities and social environments are those of the capitalistic system. We therefore need to investigate the hegemonic and polemical representations (Moscovici, 1988) that fight each other today and understand who is producing them and for what purpose. The choice of the nation or of a global sphere as the arena of politics depends on the constraints that the system imposes and the interests of the different social agents.

Within the approach developed here, embracing a consensual universe, social categories cannot be treated in their cognitive aspect without embedding them into the social system and the ideologies that emerge. Thus, talking about less or more inclusive, superordinate categories corresponds to the projects that social agents have and the opportunities offered to pursue them. Different superordinate categories might refer to different representations of the social order and therefore might have different social psychological consequences and societal implications. As it is discussed in the chapter by Gleibs and Reddy, both anticapitalistic and Muslim identities make reference to supranational categories, but they have different societal implications. I would argue that this is because they refer to different representations of the social order.

Following Touraine (2005), I have argued elsewhere that two social representations of societal organization coexist with different implications for status, values and justice attribution. One representation organizes society and builds hierarchies in terms of merit. This representation emphasizes structural inequalities and constructs social categories such as social class. The other representation organizes society in terms of cultural differences and organizes hierarchies in terms of cultural group membership. It emphasizes cultural diversity and promotes cultural categories such as ethnicity. Part of my argument is that the adoption and use of each representation implies different criteria for distributive and procedural justice and emphasizes conflicts based on different memberships.

In that respect, we could argue that an emphasis from the dominant groups on cultural diversity could hide class membership and at the same time obstruct social mobility for people of different ethnicity than the ethnicity of the national majority (Chryssochoou, 2015). Unable to fight in terms of class in the national arena, people from cultural minorities therefore have as a sole opportunity, in order to seek justice and equal treatment, to fight adopting an ethno-cultural or religious identity. Seemingly, when people refer to national attachment and reject a more global European identity (Chryssochoou, 2000bc, 2013), it is probably because they cannot pursue claims of rights and prosperity within the European arena of unequal social relationships.

It is in this context that we observe representatives of the dominant groups saying that "multiculturalism has failed" and thus rejecting a more inclusive representation of the nation, and at the same time we hear them praising a more inclusive European identity that would subsume a national identity, apparently contradicting their first stance. In my view, in order to do everyday politics, we need to bring into the forefront not only the claims of the polemical representations but also the contradictions of the dominant and the hegemonic ones. The chapter by Augoustinos et al. shows, for example, how leaders who have a minoritized membership, in order to be able to stay in power, should "play" with their identity and embed it within dominant narratives which, thus, they consolidate and develop further.

Thus, I would argue that the representations and actions of those in power need our utmost attention. We need to investigate how power is exerted and how it sets the scene of the different intragroup and intergroup encounters. In micro encounters, such as in Gibson's chapter, we could see how the power of words, the power of the ingroup and the power of what is socially allowed shape the encounters and the claims for power of those who feel powerless, even if they seem to belong to the dominant group. In macro encounters (see the chapter by Wagner et al.), we could see how decisions from those in power to relocate symbols can impact the way memberships are sustained and essentialized and how conflicts are translated into intergroup perceptions.

To conclude, in this brief commentary I have tried to show that the chapters included in Part 1 "do everyday politics" because they started a debate on social reality and they discuss aspects of it that challenge or sustain the status quo. They inscribe themselves in a consensual universe where social knowledge is produced by thinking societies and where individuals and groups are considered agents of stability and of change. Since the social subject is heteroclite and heterogeneous, with different interests, everyday politics invite us to look at the politics of the dominant in combination with the politics of the dominated. We need to investigate the way different groups represent the social world, their antithesis and their contradictions, to look at the different identities and their interplay within the ideological context and the material conditions of the current system: neoliberal capitalism. The social implications of this system affect the everyday lives of people around the globe and call for everyday politics in action.

I had finished this commentary and was about to send it to the editors when the deadly attacks of November 13, 2015, happened in Paris. I looked at my text again, under the inevitable emotional shock because the city I lived in and loved was attacked. Social psychology cannot predict when and how these acts will happen. What it can certainly predict is that they *will* happen. Reading my text again, I stand by everything I said and I did not change a word. Maybe another version of multiculturalism has won: the one that wants people to identify with essentialized memberships that distinguish people between high and low cultural status. The "we" becomes global, a war of civilization starts and the arena of politics opens at a level beyond everyday claims where the system in power stays unharmed. By hiding the structural inequalities and transforming them into cultural differences, those in power opened the Pandora's box. Working in a consensual universe of knowledge production, let's hope that thinking societies will not fall into the trap and will be able to reverse what seems to be an inevitable route of barbarism.

References

Andreouli, E., & Chryssochoou, X. (2015). Social representations of national identity in culturally diverse societies. In G. Sammut, E. Andreouli, G. Gaskell & J. Valsiner (Eds.), *Handbook of social representations* (pp. 309–322). Cambridge: Cambridge University Press.

Chryssochoou, X. (2000a). Multicultural societies: Making sense of new environments and identities. *Journal of Community and Applied Social Psychology*, *10*(5), 343–354.

Chryssochoou, X. (2000b). Memberships in a super-ordinate level. Re-thinking European Union as a multi-national society. *Journal of Community and Applied Social Psychology*, *10*(5), 403–420.

Chryssochoou, X. (2003). Studying identity in social psychology. Some thoughts on the definition of identity and its relation to action. *Language and Politics*, *22*, 225–242.

Chryssochoou, X. (2004). *Cultural diversity. Its social psychology*. Oxford: Blackwell.

Chryssochoou, X. (2009). Identity projects in multicultural nation-states. In I. Jasinskaja-Lahti & T. A. Mahonen (Eds.), *Identities, intergroup relations and acculturation. The cornerstones of intercultural encounters* (pp. 81–93). Helsinki: Gaudeamus Helsinki University Press.

Chryssochoou, X. (2011). Development, (Re)construction and expression of collective identities. In A. Azzi, X. Chryssochoou, B. Klandermans & B. Simon (Eds.), *Identity and participation in culturally diverse societies: A multidisciplinary perspective* (pp. 5–8). Oxford: Wiley-Blackwell.

Chryssochoou, X. (2013). European identity: Lessons from 20 years of social psychological inquiry. In R. McMahon (Ed.), *Post identity? Culture and European integration* (pp. 122–140). Oxford: Routledge.

Chryssochoou, X. (2014). Identity processes in culturally diverse societies. How cultural diversity is reflected in the self? In R. Jaspal & G. M. Breakwell (Eds.), *Identity process theory: Identity, social action and social change* (pp. 135–154). Cambridge: Cambridge University Press.

Chryssochoou, X. (2015). Le paradoxe de la promotion des identités doubles à l'école. In M. Sanchez-Mazas, N. Changakoti & M. Broyon (Eds.), *Education à la diversité. Décalages, impensés, avancées.collection: Espaces Interculturels*. Paris: L'Harmattan.

Chryssochoou, X., & Lyons, E. (2011). Perceptions of (in)compatibility between identities and participation of ethnic minorities to the national polity. In A. Azzi, X. Chryssochoou, B. Klandermans & B. Simon (Eds.), *Identity and participation in culturally diverse societies: A multidisciplinary perspective* (pp. 69–88). Oxford: Wiley-Blackwell.

Doise, W. (2012). The homecoming of society in social psychology. In J. Pires Valentim (Ed.), *Societal approaches in social psychology* (pp. 9–34). Bern: Peter Lang.

Doise, W., & Valentim, J. P. (2015). Levels of analysis in social psychology. In J. D. Wright (Ed.), *International encyclopedia of the social & behavioral sciences* (2nd ed., Vol. 13, pp. 899–903). Oxford: Elsevier.

Moscovici, S. (1961/1976). *La psychanalyse, son image et son public*. Paris: PUF. English edition (2008) *Psychoanalysis: Its image and its public*. Cambridge: Polity.

Moscovici, S. (1984). The phenomenon of social representations. In R. Farr & S. Moscovici (Eds.), *Social representations* (pp. 3–69). Cambridge: Cambridge University Press.

Moscovici, S. (1988). Notes towards the description of social representations. *European Journal of Social Psychology, 18*(3), 211–250.

Rancière, J. (2005). *La Haine de la Démocratie*. Paris: Editions La Fabrique.

Reicher, S. (2004). The context of social identity: Domination, resistance, and change. *Political Psychology, 25*(6), 921–945.

Reicher, S., & Hopkins, N. (2001). *Self and nation*. London: Sage.

Touraine, A. (2005). *Un nouveau paradigme pour comprendre le monde d'aujourd'hui*. Paris: Fayard.

PART II
Political agency and social change

6
CITIZENSHIP AND SOCIAL PSYCHOLOGY
An analysis of constructions of Greek citizenship

Eleni Andreouli, Irini Kadianaki and Maria Xenitidou

In this chapter, we advance a social psychological approach to citizenship. We pay particular attention to the dynamics of constructing citizenship and to the relationship between state policies and lay practices of claims-making. The chapter is structured in four parts. In the first section, we outline a definition of citizenship that is in line with a dynamic social psychological framework. In the second section, we propose a social psychological framework of citizenship that acknowledges the interconnection between citizenship regimes and lay citizens' perspectives. To illustrate our approach, in the third section we discuss a study on Greek citizenship following new legislation that opened up citizenship to the children of migrants for the first time in Greek history. We conclude the chapter with a summary and some ideas about future avenues of research in the social psychology of citizenship.

What is citizenship?

The concept of citizenship has been the subject of study of many social science disciplines, such as political science, sociology and political theory, among others. Yet, citizenship resists a simple definition. Indeed, citizenship has been described as an 'essentially contested concept' (Condor, 2011). We propose here that it is precisely this contestability that should be the object of the study of citizenship. We also propose that social psychology offers suitable conceptual tools towards this aim.

Most commonly, citizenship has been studied as a state institution, that is, as a type of membership that is managed by the state. Joppke (2010), in a brief outline of key approaches to the study of citizenship in social and political theory, made a distinction between analyses of social, national, postnational and multicultural citizenship. Social citizenship is associated with the work of Marshall (1964) and focuses on the historical development of citizenship rights, from civil to political to social rights. Analyses of national citizenship (e.g. Brubaker's 1992 work) focus on the dynamics between inclusion and exclusion in different citizenship regimes, for instance, in states with ethnic or civic regimes of citizenship. Postnational citizenship, associated with the work of Soysal (1994), among others, refers to new articulations of rights that are unlinked from national citizenship, such as human rights. Finally, work on multicultural citizenship, associated most notably with the work of Kymlicka (1995), is concerned with the accommodation of minority rights within a national society. These analyses approach citizenship as an institution of the state, and it is state (or inter-state) policies, structures and practices that they seek to explain, analyse or challenge.

However illuminating, such state-centric approaches are not sufficient on their own for unpacking the complexity of citizenship, because they leave out of the analysis the perspectives of citizens themselves. While the state is a very powerful political actor, lay citizens are also key actors who need to be taken under consideration in analyses of citizenship. In this regard, we welcome Isin's (2009; Isin & Nielsen, 2008) work on how citizenship is enacted from the bottom up. Isin (2009) proposes a dynamic, actor-oriented approach to citizenship that focuses on 'acts' of citizenship. The starting point of this analysis is that we need a way of conceptualising citizenship that corresponds to contemporary forms of politics: a conceptualisation which is based on agents' efforts to advance political claims.

From the onset, this framework opens up the study of citizenship to a wide range of actors. Political actors are not just citizens in the formal sense of the term; these are anyone who engages in political action, irrespective of legal status. Political action and participation are understood here as acts of claims-making, not simply as a set of behaviours that have traditionally been seen as part of citizenship (e.g. voting). Isin (2009) uses the example of the '*sans-papiers*' movement in France. The movement, consisting of undocumented or irregular migrants, was mobilised on the basis of claiming the right to stay in France on a regularised status.

This emphasis on enacting citizenship through claims-making processes is aligned with a social and political psychological perspective. Indeed, some work from this field has focused on the ways in which group-level political claims and politicised group identities are key elements in processes of collective action. Notably, the social psychology of protest and collective mobilisation has recently focused on the ways that people, fuelled by a sense of common grievances, act as members of disadvantaged groups and engage in political action in order to challenge power asymmetries in existing intergroup relations (see Klandermans, 2014).

From our perspective, there are two main reasons why social psychology is suitable for the study of citizenship. First, social psychology is concerned with the politics of everyday knowledge. That is, social psychology is concerned with the processes through which systems of knowledge are constructed, negotiated and transformed in social encounters (Jovchelovitch, 2007). The politics of claims-making within specific political and intergroup contexts are thus central to the discipline. Second, social psychology has much to offer in connecting the level of everyday politics (as enacted by lay citizens and social groups) and official politics (as performed by official political structures). In fact, the tension between agency and structure is one of the most long-standing considerations in the discipline (Farr, 1996). These two points are interconnected. Systems of knowledge are institutionalised and prescriptive, but they can also be disrupted, resisted and changed. Indeed, we argue that it is in moments of social disruption that claims-making about citizenship becomes important. In what follows, we outline this social psychological perspective in more detail.

A social psychological approach to citizenship

In outlining a social psychological framework for the study of citizenship, we draw from two traditions of research that have been particularly concerned with the politics of knowledge construction: social representations and discourse analysis approaches. While there are recognised differences between the two approaches, they share much in common (Gibson, 2015; Voelklein & Howarth, 2005), notably a social constructionist and action-oriented approach towards social phenomena and a concern with the politics involved in processes of knowledge construction.

In the following three subsections, we first discuss social psychological work on how meanings of citizenship are negotiated by lay actors. We then move on to discuss the role of state citizenship regimes as nation-building projects. Finally, we explore the links between state and lay perspectives on citizenship.

The everyday level: Perspectives of lay citizens

One of the first social psychological explorations of citizenship was by Shotter (1993), who argued that citizenship is a 'living ideology'. Shotter (1993) drew attention to the dynamics of citizen identities in the politics of everyday life. He suggested that argumentation and debate over identity and belonging are central when studying citizenship in practice. Taking the lead from Shotter, several social-political psychologists analysed citizenship from a discursive psychology perspective (e.g. Barnes et al., 2004; Haste, 2004). Instead of taking a definition of citizenship as a given, the emphasis has been on how the category of citizenship is constructed and negotiated by social actors and what the ideological and rhetorical functions of these constructions in particular contexts are.

In line with Isin, who suggested that we shift "our attention from fixed categories by which we have come to understand or inherit citizenship to the struggles through which these categories themselves have become stakes" (2009, p. 383), claims-making has been central in these analyses. In one of the most commonly cited studies in this field, Barnes, Auburn and Lea (2004) studied how local residents mobilised citizen identities to claim entitlement over the management of the local area and to argue against the settling of travellers. Other authors have taken a more explicitly rhetorical approach, studying the ideological dilemmas (Billig et al., 1988) played out in constructions of citizenship (e.g. Andreouli & Dashtipour,

2014; Condor & Gibson, 2007; Gibson & Hamilton, 2011). For example, Gibson and Hamilton (2011), in their analysis of young people's talk about polity membership and immigration, found that participants managed the ideological dilemma of 'multiculturalism versus protecting the national culture' by advancing arguments for having a single, monocultural legal system, thus discursively marginalising minority cultures into the realm of private life.

In this body of research, it is evident that constructions of citizenship by lay actors depend on the positioning of these actors within a specific intergroup context. For example, in Greece, which is the empirical focus of this chapter, it has been found that representations of Greek citizenship in public debates vary, to a large extent, according to the ways that actors are positioned within a majority-minority intergroup structure. While native Greek citizens commonly essentialise citizenship as an ethnic category of membership seeking to maintain an established social order of 'insiders' (ethnic Greeks) and 'outsiders' (non-coethnic migrants), migrants challenge this social order by putting forward alternative conceptions of Greek citizenship based on criteria of cultural assimilation and civic participation (Kadianaki & Andreouli, 2015).

What this social psychological perspective highlights is that the 'ordinary', 'lay' or 'everyday' is political. Politics are not the preserve of official political structures. Rather, the politics of representation take place in everyday lives and interactions. Claims-making about citizenship and belonging is about claiming the power to construct and convey particular representations over others (Howarth, Andreouli & Kesi, 2014) in a way that allows social actors to participate in the public sphere on terms that are one's own (Hopkins & Blackwood, 2011).

The institutional level: The role of the state

Everyday citizenship, as outlined previously, is only part of the story. Citizenship is also institutionally demarcated through concrete policies. State practices and policies often echo historical constructions of nationhood in different societies. Favell (2001), for instance, traced Britain's 'multicultural' approach towards integration and citizenship to its tradition of paternalistic tolerance towards the colonised populations. The state can be seen as an 'entrepreneur of identity' (Reicher & Hopkins, 2001) that produces national and citizen identities through the policies it enforces. State citizenship regimes *can* therefore be understood as nation-building projects (Andreouli & Chryssochoou, 2015).

There is some social psychological research that analyses state constructions of citizenship. For example, Andreouli and Howarth (2013) analysed policy documents from Britain's 'earned citizenship' framework and found that they advance a fundamental distinction between 'worthy' and 'unworthy' migrants based on their ability to integrate and contribute to the economy, thus subtly rehearsing a 'good versus bad' immigrant dichotomy and an 'immigrants as a burden' narrative. Similarly, Gray and Griffin (2014) analysed how citizenship as an identity is discursively constructed in Britain's citizenship test. They showed, for instance, that the test constructs citizen identity as something that can be learnt and assessed. This transforms "citizenship from a set of universal rights to a matter of technical expertise", constituting "some citizens as more 'qualified' than others" (p. 311).

Hence, state discourses are equally discursively rich as everyday discourses about citizenship. What differentiates the two, however, is that state discourses enjoy a higher level of legitimation and can more easily acquire a hegemonic (c.f. Moscovici, 1998) status. Given that the state holds ultimate authority on how citizenship is to be understood and practiced, we conceptualise state discourses and practices as representations that are not easily challenged (Andreouli & Howarth, 2013). We do not suggest that the state necessarily operates as an oppressor, but that institutionalised discourses can convert from prescriptive to descriptive (Castro, 2012) and solidify into 'the way things are'.

Connecting the two levels

We suggest that a social psychological perspective takes into consideration both levels: (1) how state policies and practices construct citizenship and have an effect on lay citizens' understandings and enactments of citizenship; and (2) how citizens themselves negotiate the meanings of citizenship and may possibly influence state policies. Regarding the first level, we presented some research on state citizenship regimes that examines how state policies construct the meanings and boundaries of citizenship. Most commonly, people habitually act out such "already written scripts" (Isin, 2009, p. 381) by practicing the rights they have, for example, voting in national elections if they are formally citizens or going through immigration procedures when they are not. National citizenship is not often reflected upon and this is mostly the case for those who have an established or settled sense of belonging and position in a society (c.f. Stevenson & Muldoon, 2010). Regarding the second level, we presented some research that shows how lay citizens may engage in acts of negotiating the meanings and boundaries of citizenship. We advance here a social psychological approach to citizenship that acknowledges the interconnections between the two levels. This approach pays attention to both how policies construct citizenship and how citizens themselves, as members of minority (e.g. migrants) or majority groups (e.g. indigenous Greeks), negotiate these constructions within specific social and political contexts. The interconnection of the two levels and the processes of meaning construction regarding citizenship become particularly visible when a taken-for-granted state of affairs becomes disrupted (Kadianaki & Gillespie, 2015). Such disruption may occur, for instance, when citizenship regimes are adapted in order to accommodate migrant communities within a nation-state. Thus, we suggest, in times of tension we can study the dynamics of citizenship as an 'essentially contested concept' (Condor, 2011) and the connections between state policies and lay constructions. In the next section, we report on such an analysis in the Greek context.

An empirical analysis of Greek citizenship constructions

Changes in the Greek citizenship regime: The 2010 law

In 2010, the Greek government passed new citizenship legislation that was regarded as a turning point in Greek immigration policy. Until then, citizenship allocation arrangements were regulative rather than policy-based and they were largely reflective of a "view [of] Greek citizenship as a right to be exclusively reserved for those who ethnically belong to the cherished national community" (Anagnostou, 2011, p. 2). This ethnic conception of Greek citizenship is also reflected in the term '*ithagenia*', which is used in Greek citizenship legislation. This term is synthesised by the words *ithis* meaning 'directly', and *genos* meaning 'descent' or 'generation' (Christopoulos, 2013), alluding to an entitlement of those of the same descent or generation. Analyses of lay discourses of citizenship in the Greek context (Kadianaki & Andreouli, 2015; Triandafyllidou & Veikou, 2002) also reflect this dominance of an ethnic conception of citizenship.

The 2010 law included *jus soli* criteria that disrupted the domination of *jus sanguinis* for the first time since the nation building process of the 19th century (Anagnostou, 2011). According to the law, the children of migrants born in Greece could acquire the Greek citizenship if their parents completed five years of legal residence in the country. Children of migrants not born in Greece could also acquire Greek citizenship upon successful completion of six years of Greek school provided that their parents completed the required five years of legal residence. In addition, the law provided for the right to elect and be elected to holders of long-term residence permits and foreign citizens of Greek descent.

The new law emerged after years of public discontent with the existing naturalisation procedures and criteria, consecutive protests and campaigning developed primarily by migrant communities and organisations who asked for necessary reforms. It was developed by a team of lawyers of the NGO Hellenic League for Human Rights (Christropoulos, 2012) and, though modified in various ways, was passed in parliament in March 2010. The run up to the law also included an online public deliberation that gathered thousands of comments from both migrants and Greek citizens.

The 2010 law, however, evoked intense public debates that revolved around the meaning and the boundaries of citizenship and Greek national identity (Kadianaki & Andreouli, 2015). Parliamentary debates were also heated and reflected a divided political arena concerning the issue (Figgou, under review). Political debates centred around symbolic issues, such as 'who we are', rather than around practical matters (Christropoulos, 2012). It can be argued that the heated public and political debates that accompanied the 2010 citizenship law are indicative of a disruption of conventionalised understandings of Greek citizenship.

In February 2011, following an appeal and several counterappeals, the State Council, through judicial decision, declared that the law violated the Greek constitution. According to the decision, the criteria of six years of schooling and the five years of legal residence of parents – for the children born in Greece – could not sufficiently ensure that second-generation immigrants had developed strong bonds with the Greek nation. Further, it was argued that the right to vote and be elected should be reserved for Greek citizens but not foreign citizens of Greek descent, on the grounds that the criteria by which their status was granted were dubious and could result in the decomposition of the electoral basis.[1] In other words, the debate rested on the tension between the new (more) civic and the long-standing ethnic definition of citizenship that had dominated both state policy and lay discourses up to that point.

Lay perspectives on the new citizenship law

In order to explore lay perspectives on the 2010 Greek citizenship law, we present data from a study on the relationship between lay and social scientific discourses on identity, citizenship and migration (see Xenitidou & Greco-Morasso, 2014).[2] For the purposes of the study, the third author conducted one-to-one and group interviews with indigenous and nonindigenous residents in Thessaloniki, the second largest city in Greece. The researcher invited participants to talk about issues at the forefront of public attention around the time of the interview (2013–2014), such as the trajectory of the new citizenship law and the rise of the extreme right. The analysis that follows draws on thirty-two group and individual interviews with twenty-five indigenous Greek citizens and twenty-five nonindigenous migrants living in Thessaloniki. Our analysis here focuses on exploring the claims-making processes that the aforementioned institutional change incited for Greek citizens and for migrants, paying particular attention to the ways in which participants negotiated the meanings and boundaries of citizenship. In what follows, we present our findings in terms of three key themes that participants, both Greek citizens and migrants, drew upon to construct citizenship in this context: ethnicity (extracts 1–2), feelings of national belonging (extracts 3–4) and civic participation (extracts 5–6).

As anticipated, ethnicity was central in our data. This reflects the history of Greek citizenship and Greek identity in general, which have been predominantly defined in ethnic terms. Indigenous Greeks in the sample drew on ethnic understandings of Greekness to argue against citizenship for migrants, thus seeking to maintain an 'us (Greeks)/them (foreigners)' system of social relations that privileges ethnic Greeks. Migrants too oriented towards such prevalent majoritarian discourses by distinguishing between ethnic belonging and citizenship. This allowed them to both argue for more rights and avoid disrupting these hegemonic representations of Greekness. The following two extracts illustrate these points.

Extract 1

Lakis: Now, it doesn't have to do who, it doesn't have to do with where you've been born and the rest, you are Albanian, you are Albanian that's that. And I don't

> say it at all in a racist way, right? All of these happened in order also for them to become acclimatised the best possible to the Greek country, isn't that right? For this [reason] they want to give citizenship to some of other nationality. I focus on that you will take Greek citizenship with whatever way and with whatever law will come out, you personally as a person should never renounce your country. (Group interview, indigenous Greek)

Lakis, in this extract, is drawing on an ethnic representation of citizenship to make a claim against the new legislation that gives citizenship rights to migrants. While Lakis negotiates the criteria for citizenship acquisition with reference to origin, his point that origin is fixed and irreversible is treated as amenable to the stigma of racism, which he disclaims, a common rhetorical strategy in discussions of citizenship and immigration (e.g. Augoustinos & Every, 2007). The grounds for this disclaimer seem to be that while integration is important, it should not be sought at all costs nor should it be sought instrumentally or opportunistically. Citizenship acquisition by migrants is therefore treated as selling out and betraying their country of origin, and on these grounds, Lakis 'advises' migrants not to be 'trapped' into doing it. In this extract, citizenship is equated to nationality – Greekness – and, as such, reserved for ethnic Greeks, corroborating thus a socially prevalent ethnic representation of citizenship based on descent.

In the following extract, Debora, a second-generation migrant from Southern Albania, orients to such prevalent ethnic understandings of Greekness by making a distinction between feelings of national belonging and citizenship rights.

Extract 2

> *Debora:* If it was up to me, if it were in my hand I want to stay in the future, to live the rest of my life here and it would be easier for me in essence to have the Greek citizenship. Not just to show off and you know that I live in Greece and I have the Greek identity card or anything like this, but more for what it offers. Because it offers things and services and various [other things] that it offers only to the Greeks whereas to the others not. Mainly for this reason I want the Greek citizenship and not for some other reason. For the services basically. For the rights, for these.
> *Soula:* That is, you don't feel it?
> *Debora:* OK I don't believe that a paper let's say can tell you that "ok because you have Greek citizenship you are Greek". In essence, in practice, I wanted just and only just for the things it offers you, that is rights, for the services but theoretically, I don't need the paper to tell me "you know now ok you can feel Greek because you have the identity card, you have this blue identity card". (Group interview, second generation migrants from southern Albania)

Debora orients to citizenship acquisition as a practical matter related to state bureaucracy and access to rights, a seemingly civic representation of citizenship. Citizenship acquisition is constructed as a formal recognition of rights and is to be used as a functional tool to deal with bureaucratic aspects of everyday life. This construction makes the distinction between rights and feelings relevant in the negotiation of citizenship. Feelings are dissociated from citizenship on the grounds that the bureaucratic granting of the latter is not a proof of feeling. By disassociating 'belonging-proper' from citizenship, Debora is able to make a claim to Greek citizenship whilst simultaneously avoiding claiming a Greek identity. While feeling Greek is not denied, claiming a Greek identity based on feeling would potentially open this kind of talk to criticism as it would question ethnic representations of Greekness. In other words, Debora is able to claim citizenship on the basis of functionality while leaving Greekness intact.

While some migrants in the sample treated citizenship as a 'practical' matter of acquiring more rights and access to services, for other migrants as well as for some Greeks in the sample, citizenship was constructed in terms of feelings of national belonging from which rights emanate (see also Kadianaki & Andreouli, 2015). As we show, this way of bringing closer together Greek identification and Greek citizenship worked in similar ways for Greeks and migrants in our data: for the former, it helped construct another layer of assessing migrants' entitlement to citizenship, and for the latter, it provided a way of claiming citizenship through declarations of national commitment. In both cases, however, the dominant essentialised understanding of Greekness, as an internal state that cannot easily be altered, was maintained.

Extract 3

Virginia: I don't disagree with this law. That is, I believe that it should give a right to these people, whoever feels Greek and has certain preconditions, and these, it goes without saying that these preconditions someone has to define right? We can't say who feels Greek in a general way. Those preconditions that were prescribed I think, that the second generation of immigrants if they wish to they can acquire the citizenship, does not find me in opposition. That is, I believe that they have to, since they are integrated into Greek society, for what reason would they deny these people? Since they meet the legal preconditions the right to acquire the citizenship has to be given to them, if they wish to, I repeat. (Individual interview, indigenous Greek)

Virginia positions herself favourably towards the law through the use of negations – 'I don't disagree with the law', 'does not find me in opposition' – a response which assumes that a negative take on the law could have been expected as normal. While Virginia sees the new law in a positive light in principle, she considers the difficulty of pinning down the requirements that would make someone a Greek citizen in practice. The problem arises due to the difficulty of assessing feelings of being Greek. The problem of measuring feelings – that would make someone Greek 'truly' and without question (see Verkuyten & de Wolf, 2002) – is managed by Virginia with reference to second generation migrants by putting forward the criteria of legality, integration and choice. Whoever meets the stream of these criteria is entitled to Greek citizenship 'in principle', while feeling Greek is retained as a key criterion. References to feelings and cultural assimilation were prevalent in Greek participants' discourse and were also part of the state discourse. As we noted earlier, the State Council discussed amendments to the 2010 law on the basis of securing migrants' bonds with the Greek nation. The 2015 revision of the law responded to this by constituting education – schooling – as the means through which this may be achieved (measured and proven). Thus, while indigenous Greeks' feelings of national belonging are taken as a given, migrants are under the obligation to prove their commitment. This is also shown in the following extract from Kostas, a second-generation migrant from Albania.

Extract 4

Kostas: I don't know now how they are thinking about it, the others, but in my mind let's say I feel Greek citizen because from the first years we came here I took part [in] the celebrations, we learned Greek dances, at the parade, the excursions, the games, in the sad moments, the troubles, in all of these that is. That is, I felt, I felt from the beginning that I was part of this place. That is, I never had that, let's say I never had this, let's say that others had felt. Simply now when I have reached adulthood, it is not that I don't feel it, but I feel that I am outside, I don't know, from things because let's say after the age of eighteen you vote. Yes, let's say I don't vote due to citizenship, due to a lot of things. I think the most important thing is in the future. That is, whatever political move happens in Greece it doesn't interest me in essence, because I know that I am not part of this process nor am I going to be. Unless something changes, let's say with ithageneia, citizenship and the likes. I think this is the basic thing.
(Individual interview, second generation immigrant from Albania)

Kostas makes reference to his subjective feelings of being Greek, which serves to suggest that he is 'truly' Greek as private feelings cannot be easily disputed (Kadianaki & Andreouli, 2015; Verkuyten & de Wolf, 2002). Kostas also makes reference to participation in mundane, everyday life (e.g. playing) and ritualised Greek culture (e.g. celebrations) as the ways through which he came to feel Greek. In other words, cultural assimilation is constructed as the basis for belonging and feeling like a Greek citizen. Indeed, Kostas notes that he never felt out of place like other migrants in Greece. However, this 'banal' (c.f. Billig, 1995) sense of belonging was disrupted when he turned eighteen, the age when young people acquire full citizenship rights in Greece. What we see here is a rupture between 'feeling like' and 'being' a Greek citizen – the former being subjective, the latter being formally recognised by the state. Having built up this rupture as paradoxical, Kostas associates formal recognition to feelings of belonging, on the basis of which he makes a claim for Greek citizenship. Appeals to feelings as the basis of being 'truly' Greek was common across the dataset, as was the appeal to cultural assimilation. By putting forward a cultural and feelings-based conception of citizenship, migrants were able to make a claim for belonging on the basis of assimilation, therefore retaining some elements of the prevalent ethnocultural representation of Greekness.

Civic understandings of citizenship were also present in the data, albeit much less compared to ethnic and feelings-based understandings. In the following extract, Milli, a second-generation migrant from Albania, talks about citizenship in terms of a social contract between citizens and state.

Extract 5

Milli: I think, that whoever person is considered citizen of Greece, and I imagine that citizen is considered also an alien who is legal in the country, should have the right to participate in the social life of the place where he/she lives. I want, I have the need to vote, since I switch on my television and watch the parliament, since the laws concern me, the taxation that is voted concerns me. It concerns me how much you will pay tax because in this country I pay, it concerns me how much, how many hours children have lessons in the schools, because my children may be here, I am giving you an example now. The laws concern me. I if I steal something I will steal it here. According to the Greek court I will be evaluated in any case. So yes, I think that it is necessary that people vote. Anyone who lives legally in Greece I think that it is necessary to vote. (Individual interview, second generation immigrant from Albania)

Milli treats voting as an individual right directly impinging upon people's everyday lives, on which grounds she makes claims for access to this right. In her argument above, the condition for the right to vote is being a Greek citizen, which is constructed in terms of legal residence, active participation and contribution to society. This is presented as a social contract with civic rather than ethnic or cultural criteria. On these grounds, Milli claims that all legally residing 'aliens' should be entitled to acquire Greek citizenship. Such inclusive civic understandings of citizenship also featured in some of the interviews with native Greeks. However, even in its inclusionary civic sense, citizenship was at times only allowed within limits by Greeks in the sample, manifesting a dilemma between extension of citizenship as a matter of principle versus preserving or minimising the impact to the dominant culture 'in practice', as the following extract shows.

Extract 6

Melli: Look sure, sure it concerns the, the resident of [x y] municipality who is either, as we said, an alien or Greek. It concerns him because he lives there. It is just, maybe it is something deeper, the political issue that affects all our lives and its culture, our history? That is to say it has to do with all these and many foreigners, and I have experienced this first hand, don't know Greek history. Maybe, how should I put this? Their view on the issue of election would affect negatively the Greeks who live here, who live more with these people, they know what it is about, they have a clearer view. (Individual interview, indigenous Greek)

Melli's account above seems torn between voting in local elections as a right of all local residents 'in principle' and the interests of Greeks 'in practice'. The importance of the issue of voting is heightened with extreme case formulations from the local level to 'all our lives' and 'all the rest of Greeks'. She argues against an extension of the voting right in national elections to non-Greeks on the grounds that they lack knowledge of Greek history and politics. In this way, granting voting rights to non-Greeks is constructed as problematic, not on the grounds of ethnicity per se, but on the grounds that they lack the historical knowledge which is assumed to grant them with appropriate political views. This is a condition which could be seen as accompanying their status of being foreign, but which Melli supports through reference to her personal experience, thus managing the consequences of essentialising it as a trait. In this account, Greeks and foreigners are constructed as two distinct groups and voting is treated as a privilege of the political connoisseurs, namely the native Greeks due to their longer-term residence in the country.

Conclusions

In this chapter, we advanced a social psychological approach to citizenship that takes under consideration the institutional level of formal policy and practice and the bottom-up level of lay citizens' perspectives. We argued, in particular, that if social psychologists are interested in studying the politics of representation in debates about citizenship, then exploring both citizenship regimes and how people and social groups negotiate these regimes of citizenship provides a fruitful way forward. To illustrate our approach, we first presented an overview of the citizenship regime in the Greek context, followed by a more extended analysis of lay debates in the context of a recent immigration law in Greece which opened up citizenship to second-generation migrants, thus disrupting ethnic representations of Greek citizenship.

Our data show that for many native Greek citizens, the new law introduced a discrepancy between the established ethnic view of Greekness and the more civic criteria put forward by the law. Greek participants responded by negotiating the meanings and boundaries of citizenship in different ways: by restricting the scope of citizenship to ethnic Greeks, by differentiating between ethnic and civic membership, by putting forward an argument for 'true' Greekness on the basis of feelings and cultural assimilation, and by putting forward a more inclusive civic conception of Greek citizenship on the basis of a give-and-take social contract, although often with caveats which privileged ethnic Greeks. On the other hand, for migrants, the new law represented an opportunity to renegotiate the boundaries of citizenship in line with their own stakes after many years of being excluded from citizenship debates. Our data show that migrants responded to the new law by making claims for rights-based citizenship as different from 'belonging-proper' by claiming that they are Greeks 'truly' because they are culturally assimilated or because they 'feel' Greek and by claiming citizenship on the basis that they are already active members of the society. Their arguments, being centred on cultural and civic criteria, contrasted with the dominant ethnic conception of citizenship that was disrupted through the introduction of the new law.

Despite their different stakes, there are clearly overlaps in how Greek and migrant participants negotiate the meanings of citizenship in light of the new law. A key common theme is the distinction between belonging-proper and civic membership of a polity. The distinction between the two points precisely to the disjuncture between, on the one hand, prevalent ethnic lay representations of Greekness and, on the other hand, institutional arrangements that introduce civic elements to the definition of the nation. On the part of Greek citizens, this distinction serves to maintain an ethnic representation of Greekness and construct a hierarchy of belonging that constrains migrants' abilities to make claims that they are 'truly' Greek. On the part of migrants, this distinction serves to allow them to make claims for citizenship either because they can argue that they fulfil the conditions of 'true' Greekness or by disclaiming 'true' Greekness and seeking civic inclusion instead.

In light of these findings, we suggest that social psychological analyses of citizenship should unravel the different and competing constructions of citizenship within the lay realm and examine the different ways they connect with a variety of institutional discourses, particularly at times of social change. As suggested previously, citizenship may not be reflected upon but it may simply be practiced as a well-established habitus (Isin, 2009). Ethnic representations of Greek citizenship are such habitual ways of understanding citizenship in the Greek context. On the other hand, social change, such as new citizenship laws that become heavily debated in the public sphere, can disrupt such prevalent constructions. While such disruption may provide the ground for a renegotiation of the meanings and boundaries of citizenship in a way that is more inclusive, it may also elicit strong resistance in order to maintain existing representations of citizenship.

To conclude, we suggest that the social psychology of citizenship studies such points of disruption and the processes of representational change and resistance from the perspectives of both lay and official political actors. Examination of the connections between policy making and everyday life is an important social psychological endeavour with sociopolitical implications. It permits us to respond to questions such as: What are the lived realities that citizenship policies create for citizens? How do policies demarcate inclusion or exclusion of different social groups, and how is this inclusion/exclusion negotiated at the level of everyday experience? What power relations does the institutional discourse create, and how are these legitimised or contested in the social arena? These are questions that we feel a social psychology of citizenship can explore in future research.

Notes

1 In May 2015, the Greek government submitted a revision to the code of citizenship which emphasised schooling as a key criterion for citizenship for second generation migrants, thus seeking to ensure that new Greek citizens would have sufficient bonds to the Greek nation. The revision received sufficient support and was passed in parliament,

overshadowed by a heated climate about the Greek 'bail out' which monopolized public discourse in the summer of 2015.

2 The data were collected as part of the 294227 MC-GIG project "LSSDMIC – Lay and Social Science Discourses on Identity, Migration and Citizenship" awarded to the third author.

References

Anagnostou, D. (2011). *Citizenship policy making in Mediterranean EU states: Greece*. EUDO Citizenship Observatory, European University Institute, Florence and Robert Schuman Centre for Advanced Studies. Retrieved from http://eudo-citizenship.eu/docs/EUDOComp-Greece.pdf

Andreouli, E., & Chryssochoou, X. (2015). Social representations of national identity in culturally diverse societies. In G. Sammut, E. Andreouli, G. Gaskell & J. Valsiner (Eds.), *The Cambridge handbook of social representations* (pp. 309–322). Cambridge: Cambridge University Press.

Andreouli, E., & Dashtipour, P. (2014). British citizenship and the 'other': An analysis of the earned citizenship discourse. *Journal of Community & Applied Social Psychology, 24*(2), 100–110.

Andreouli, E., & Howarth, C. (2013). National identity, citizenship and immigration: Putting identity in context. *Journal for the Theory of Social Behaviour, 43*(3), 361–382.

Augoustinos, M., & Every, D. (2007). The language of 'race' and prejudice. *Journal of Language and Social Psychology, 26*(2), 123–141.

Barnes, R., Auburn, T., & Lea, S. (2004). Citizenship in practice. *British Journal of Social Psychology, 43*, 187–206.

Billig, M. (1995). *Banal nationalism*. London: Sage.

Billig, M., Condor, S., Edwards, D., Gane, M., Middleton, D., & Radley, A. (1988). *Ideological dilemmas: A social psychology of everyday thinking*. London: Sage.

Brubaker, R. (1992). *Citizenship and nationhood in France and Germany*. Cambridge, MA: Harvard University Press.

Castro, P. (2012). Legal innovation for social change: Exploring change and resistance to different types of sustainability laws. *Political Psychology, 33*(1), 105–121.

Christropoulos, D. (2012). *Who is Greek citizen? Citizenship status from the founding of the Greek state until the beginning of the 21st century*. Athens: Vivliorama.

Christopoulos, D. (2013). *Country report: Greece*. European union democracy observatory. Florence: European University Institute. Retrieved from http://cadmus.eui.eu/bitstream/handle/1814/29784/NPR_2013_09-Greece.pdf?sequence=1

Condor, S. (2011). Towards a social psychology of citizenship? Introduction to the Special Issue. *Journal of Community & Applied Social Psychology, 21*, 193–201.

Condor, S., & Gibson, S. (2007). 'Everybody's entitled to their own opinion': Ideological dilemmas of liberal individualism and active citizenship. *Journal of Community and Applied Social Psychology, 17*, 115–140.

Farr, R. M. (1996). *The roots of modern social psychology*. Oxford: Blackwell Publishers.

Favell, A. (2001). *Philosophies of integration. Immigration and the idea of citizenship in France and Britain* (2nd ed.). New York: Palgrave in association with Centre for Research in Ethnic Relations, University of Warwick.

Figgou, L. (under review). Constructions of 'illegal' immigration and entitlement to citizenship in political discourse against a recent Immigration Law in Greece.

Gibson, S. (2015). From representations to representing: On social representations and discursive-rhetorical psychology. In G. Sammut, E. Andreouli, G. Gaskell & J. Valsiner (Eds.),

The Cambridge handbook of social representations (pp. 210–223). Cambridge: Cambridge University Press.

Gibson, S., & Hamilton, L. (2011). The rhetorical construction of polity membership: Identity, culture and citizenship in young people's discussions of immigration in Northern Ireland. *Journal of Community & Applied Social Psychology, 21*, 228–242.

Gray, D., & Griffin, C. (2014). A journey to citizenship: Constructions of citizenship and identity in the British citizenship test. *British Journal of Social Psychology, 53*, 299–314.

Haste, H. (2004). Constructing the citizen. *Political Psychology, 25*(3), 413–439.

Hopkins, N., & Blackwood, L. (2011). Everyday citizenship: Identity and recognition. *Journal of Community & Applied Social Psychology, 21*, 215–227.

Howarth, C., Andreouli, E., & Kessi, S. (2014). Social representations and the politics of participation. In P. Nesbitt-Larking, C. Kinnvall, T. Kapelos & H. Dekker (Eds.), *The Palgrave handbook of global political psychology* (pp. 21–42). London: Palgrave.

Isin, E. F. (2009). Citizenship in flux: The figure of the activist citizen. *Subjectivity, 29*, 367–388.

Isin, E. F., & Nielsen, G. M. (2008). *Acts of citizenship*. London: Zed Books.

Joppke, C. (2010). The concept of citizenship. In C. Joppke (Ed.), *Citizenship and immigration* (pp. 1–33). Cambridge: Polity Press.

Jovchelovitch, S. (2007). *Knowledge in context: Representations, community and culture*. London: Routledge.

Kadianaki, I., & Andreouli, E. (2015). Essentialism in social representations of citizenship: An analysis of Greeks' and migrants' discourse. *Political Psychology*. doi:10.1111/pops.12271

Kadianaki, I., & Gillespie, A. (2015). Alterity and the transformation of social representations: A sociocultural account. *Integrative Psychological and Behavioral Science*. Advance publication online. doi:10.1007/s12124–014–9285-z

Klandermans, P. G. (2014). Identity politics and politicised identities: Identity processes and the dynamics of protest. *Political Psychology, 35*(1), 1–22.

Kymlicka, W. (1995). *Multicultural citizenship*. Oxford: Clarendon Press.

Marshall, T. H. (1964). *Class, citizenship and social development*. New York: Doubleday.

Moscovici, S. (1998). The history and actuality of social representations. In U. Flick (Ed.), *The psychology of the social* (pp. 209–247). Cambridge: Cambridge University Press.

Reicher, S., & Hopkins, N. (2001). *Self and nation*. London: Sage.

Shotter, J. (1993). *Cultural politics of everyday life: Social constructionism, rhetoric and knowing of the third kind*. Buckingham: Open University Press.

Soysal, Y. (1994). *Limits of citizenship: Migrants and postnational membership in Europe*. Chicago: University of Chicago Press.

Stevenson, C., & Muldoon, O. T. (2010). Socio-political context and accounts of national identity in adolescence. *British Journal of Social Psychology, 49*, 583–599.

Triandafyllidou, A., & Veikou, M. (2002). The hierarchy of Greekness. Ethnic and national identity considerations in Greek immigration policy. *Ethnicities, 2*, 189–208.

Verkuyten, M., & de Wolf, A. (2002). Being, feeling and doing: Discourses and ethnic self definitions among minority group members. *Culture & Psychology, 8*, 371–399.

Voelklein, C., & Howarth, C. (2005). A review of controversies about social representations theory: A British debate. *Culture and psychology, 11*(4), 431–454.

Xenitidou, M., & Greco-Morasso, S. (2014). Parental discourse and identity management in the talk of indigenous and migrant speakers in Greece and the UK. *Discourse & Society, 25*(1), 100–121.

7

IDENTITY, EMOTION AND MOBILISATION

Stephen Reicher and Yashpal Jogdand

As we write, we are in the final days of the Scottish referendum campaign. We are surrounded by a cacophony of voices telling us what to think. The campaigns are unrelenting in their attempts to mobilise our support. Which do we heed, and which do we ignore? Whose information do we trust? How do we manoeuvre our way through this unendingly multivocal world? And what does psychology have to tell us about the way in which we deal with these dilemmas?

One might respond by saying that the referendum is a once-in-a-generation event. So it is unfair to demand that academic psychology should centre its attention on exceptional phenomena. But that misses the point. The referendum itself may be exceptional. But the questions are relevant every day. Whenever it comes to the significant issues in our lives, we are always assailed by multiple voices advocating different responses. Long ago, Billig (1987) made the point that we only have an attitude on something to the extent that it is disputed.

To underline the point, consider the topic which has dominated the imagination of social psychologists for at least the last 70 years – the topic of intergroup relations in general and of racism in particular. In our contemporary world, these issues are encapsulated through debates around immigration and around so-called Islamic extremism. We can hardly open a newspaper or turn on the television news without someone telling us that immigrants dilute 'our' culture and take 'our' jobs, or that immigrants generate economic growth. We are immersed in a raucous debate, and our personal positions depend upon how we orient to the various voices that seek to mobilise us one way or another. So, even in relation to its core concerns, it is reasonable to ask how psychology addresses this process.

But, in contrast to the cacophony of everyday life, psychology remains silent – and the silence is getting stronger. This is illustrated by the fact that Gordon Allport's seminal 1954 text on prejudice, which reoriented the whole field to problematise the psyche of the perpetrator, at least contained a chapter on what he termed 'demagogues' and on 'demagoguery'. Fifty years later, a 'tribute volume' (Dovidio, Glick & Rudman, 2005) ignored the topic entirely and did not even include cognate terms like 'leadership' in the index.

Not only is psychology silent, but it conceptualises the human condition in terms of silence. We are dominated by a paradigm which assumes that human beings look at the world rather than act in the world and that we come to an understanding of our world through a process of solitary contemplation. In the world of our experimentation, that is certainly true. For the purposes of control and the independence of data provided by each participant, we sit alone, we are not allowed to speak, we are increasingly prohibited from all interaction with others, we are presented with stimuli on paper or on screen and we are asked to respond (cf. Haslam & McGarty, 2001).

In effect, psychology has reversed the proper relationship between theory and method. It is often observed that method is the practice of theory: the way we study something is a reflection of the way in which we conceptualise that thing. But contemporary (social) psychology starts from the adoption of a specific method (the experimental study, seen as the mark of scientific credibility) and conceptualises the thing we study (the human subject) in terms of the prerequisites of that method. Human life becomes a reflection of the atomised world of the psychological laboratory – a world in which it is impossible to capture the complex, slippery and noisy process through which humans, sometimes consensually and sometimes combatively, collectively make meaning.

Over four decades ago, Serge Moscovici summarised the problem concisely and eloquently when he observed that "at present, we respect the maxim that methodology makes a science instead of remembering that science should choose its methods" (1972, p. 65). He went on to argue that social psychology will not be successful science unless it abandons its fetishisation of method. All these years later, we are still waiting.

Once again, though, it might be objected that we are being unfair and that we have simply been looking in the wrong place for work that addresses our concerns. It may be that social psychologists don't include mobilisation as a dimension in all that they study. But they certainly are interested in how people are mobilised for or against different causes. Indeed there has recently been a considerable growth in work devoted to the issue of collective participation (see, for instance, Becker, 2012, van Zomeren & Iyer, 2009).

There are several models (e.g. Simon & Klandermans, 2001; van Zomeren, Leach & Spears, 2012; van Zomeren, Postmes & Spears, 2008) which all address issues of instrumentality, of identity and emotion. But they all ignore where these come from. How do people get the information and make the calculations about cost and benefit? How do they come to define themselves in terms of a given group membership? How do they come to see themselves as slighted and feel anger or outrage at this slight? In practice, people are simply surveyed and these are treated as perceptions, beliefs and feelings which people either have or don't have. As ever, there is no trace here of the voices which tell us what sort of action is in our interests, which construe how we are being treated and which tell us how to feel.

To return to the Scottish referendum, the economic impact of Union or Independence is at the heart of the controversy. Each side gives me different information and questions the information given by the other. I cannot make any calculation without addressing the question of which voice, and hence which information, I trust and believe. Moreover, what one side construes as a simple issue of information and of economic calculation (with independence the oil reserves will be insufficient, banks will move to England and the Scottish supermarket prices will rise) is treated as an issue of identity, of autonomy and of values by the other. Scotland, says Alex Salmond, is "not going to be bullied by big oil, big supermarkets, and big London government" (www.huffingtonpost.co.uk/2014/09/12/alex-salmond-scotland-is-not-going-to-bullied-by-big-oil-big-supermarkets-and-big-london-government_n_5812192.html). In other words, we Scots are being mistreated by big powerful outsiders and we should stand up against them, not against independence.

In sum, models of collective mobilisation may specify the elements which go into my decisions about whether (and how) to act. But they don't address the dynamics through which those elements are shaped and hence help us understand how people actually decide. They are models of mobilisation without any mobilisers; models of collective action entirely devoid of activists.

While the omission of mobilisers may seem a serious enough issue on its own, the problem goes deeper. For if the construction of self, of interest and of emotion is a dynamic process in which different activists offer different models and people seek to orient themselves between these different offerings, then any attempt to build a general and deterministic model of the interrelationship between elements (as the existing research seeks to do) is necessarily forlorn. The activist can enter into the system at any point, working on one of the elements in order to reconfigure the others. By arguing about our interests, he or she can implicitly define our identities and values. So, by stressing the impact of independence in terms of reducing inequality in Scotland, we are positioned as Scots who value equality. But equally, by arguing about our identities and values, the activist defines our interests. So, as Scots who intone 'a man's a man for a' that and cherish equality, our interest lies in challenging structures and policies which increase inequality.

Our aim in this chapter is to argue that we ignore the active process of mobilisation at our peril. To do so does not just render our work incomplete, it invalidates the work we have already completed. In the next section, we shall look at some of the most iconic studies in all of psychology; we shall show how leadership and mobilisation are at their core, and how the traditional understandings of these studies are misconceived precisely because leadership and mobilisation have been ignored. Then, we shall go on to look at some examples of mobilisation in real-world settings. We shall examine how arguments around identity, interest and emotion are employed in order to shape our understandings, feelings and actions in everyday life.

The lost leaders of classic social psychology

If, as Banyard and Grayson (2000) have done, you ask students of psychology to name the most significant studies ever conducted in psychology (note: psychology, not just social psychology), they will regularly name Milgram's Yale Obedience studies (Milgram, 1974) and Zimbardo's Stanford Prison Experiment (SPE; Haney, Banks & Zimbardo, 1973). In the former, participants were instructed to apply an escalating series of seemingly real electric shocks to a learner each time he made an error on a memory task. Fully 65% of people continued all the way to the maximum 450 volt shock in the best-known variant of the study. In the latter, young men were randomly allocated to the role of either prisoner or guard in a simulated prison. The guards rapidly became so brutal and the prisoners so disturbed that the study, scheduled for two weeks, had to be terminated after only six days.

If, as we have done, you ask students to explain the key messages of these studies, they will draw from Milgram the lesson that people are predisposed to follow orders, no matter how toxic. From Zimbardo they draw the lesson that you don't even need an authority figure present to tell people what to do. Simply put us in a uniform, assign us a role and we will, almost naturally, act out the requirements of that role.

These accounts are compellingly simple. But as soon as one begins to look at the respective studies in more detail, both the received account of what happened and the received explanation of why it happened begin to fall apart. Let us examine the SPE first and then turn to the obedience studies.

Consider, first, Zimbardo's claim about the behaviour of the guards in his study: "Participants had no prior training in how to play the randomly assigned roles. Each subject's prior societal learning of the meaning of prisons and the behavioural scripts associated with the oppositional roles of prisoner and guard was the sole source of guidance" (Zimbardo, 2004, p. 39). Next, consider the words (taken from the video of the study, *Quiet Rage*) which Zimbardo used when briefing these guards at the start of his study: "You can create in the prisoners feelings of boredom, a sense of fear to some degree. You can create a notion of arbitrariness that their life is totally controlled by us, by the system, you, me ... that they'll have no privacy at all. ... They have no freedom of action they can do nothing, or say nothing that we don't permit" (Zimbardo, 1989).

What is striking about this latter quote is not only that Zimbardo tells the guards what to do (in terms of general approach rather than specific instructions) but also the way that he positions himself amongst the guards and against the prisoners ("*their* life is totally controlled by *us*"). Far from being the neutral scientist holding the ring between participants, Zimbardo positions himself as head guard, the guards' leader. As we intimated earlier, any explanation of events which ignores this leadership is evidently deficient.

To argue that the SPE involves leadership is only the start, not the end of the matter. For, despite the textbook accounts, the guards did not become uniformly brutal (Griggs, 2014). Only a minority followed Zimbardo's lead, others either seeking to be fair or else actually siding with the prisoners. And of that minority, one in particular stands out – the guard dubbed 'John Wayne' for his arrogant swagger. But it would be wrong to think of him as a mere cipher who mechanically carried out Zimbardo's wishes. There is a telling passage in *Quiet Rage*, filmed after the end of the study, where 'John Wayne' (real name, Dave Eshelman) is interviewed along with one of the prisoners he abused. Guard Wayne explains that he was carrying out his own study, seeing how far he could go in mistreating others and how they would react. And when he asks the prisoner what he would have done, had he been a guard, the prisoner replies "I don't believe I would have been as inventive as you. I don't believe I would have applied as much imagination to what I was doing. Do you understand? I think, if I would have been a guard – I don't think it would have been such a masterpiece".

The point here is that Zimbardo's leadership enabled rather than constrained the guards. He created a context in which, *if they so chose*, they were able to be brutal. 'John Wayne' did so choose. He was also able to choose how to be brutal. He was allowed to create his own masterpiece. In sum, then, both Zimbardo and his guards had agency in determining the outcome of the Stanford Prison Experiment. Both made their own choices in creating a theatre of cruelty: Zimbardo, a choice to shape the stage; the guards a choice of whether and how to act upon it. Both are therefore accountable for their choices. This is far removed from the traditional account in which both Zimbardo and his participants fell naturally into their roles and could not help what they did.

Turning now to Milgram's obedience studies, it might seem that such an analysis is largely irrelevant. After all, in these studies the whole point is that participants don't act alone, but are led to apply extreme electric shocks. And yet, perversely, while the paradigm centres on the role of the authority/leader, Milgram's 'agentic state' account precludes any analysis of the role of leadership. This account (Milgram, 1974) proposes that, in the presence of authority, people become so fixated on doing the bidding of that authority that they lose sight of all else, including the fate of their victims. From this perspective, it doesn't make sense to ask what leaders have to do in order to secure compliance. They don't have to do anything in particular. Just being there is sufficient.

As with the SPE, a close look at Milgram's studies reveals the flaws in his explanation. Most obviously, the presence of an authority is far from sufficient to secure compliance. Even in the best-known variant of his studies – the so-called 'baseline' or 'voice-feedback' condition that appears in all the textbooks – under two-thirds of people (65% to be exact) do go all the way to 450 volts, while over a third (35%) withdraw at some point. What is more, in different variants of the study, the proportion of people who go all the way varies from 100% to 0%. Summing across all the variants the proportion is *less* than half – 42% (see Reicher, Haslam & Smith, 2012). So, as many have noted over the years, Milgram's studies are not just about obedience, they are about disobedience as well (for a recent compendium of relevant scholarship, see the special issue of the *Journal of Social Issues* from September 2014, 'Milgram at 50'; for a review of the literature, see the introduction to this special issue: Reicher, Haslam & Miller, 2014).

The reason why participants don't always obey is that they don't just attend to the experimenter. To appreciate this one only has to look at the famous Prozi sequence from Milgram's film *Obedience*. Fred Prozi, a 50-year-old man pleads with the experimenter: "I can't stand it. I'm not going to kill that man in there. You hear him hollering? . . . he's hollering. He can't stand it. What's going to happen to him. . . . I'm not going to get that man sick in there. . . ." and on and on (Milgram, 1965a). Prozi continues to administer shocks but it cannot be claimed that he isn't aware of the plight of the learner. If systematic evidence is needed to confirm the point, then Dominic Packer (2008) supplies it: the points at which people are most likely to disobey the experimenter are the points at which the learner makes his most impassioned pleas for the study to end. Inside Milgram's lab, as well as outside it (Cesarani, 2004), those who inflict suffering are not deaf to their victims' voices.

The irony here is that Milgram's attempt to analyse his studies as if they were a univocal exchange between experimenter and participant, with the learner going unheard, obscures the fact that the obedience studies are one of the very few examples where participants are placed in a multivocal world – where they are placed between different voices telling them to do incompatible things: the experimenter urging them to continue applying electric shocks, the learner pleading with them to stop. As we have argued, this is the situation we generally find ourselves in when, in our everyday lives, we have to decide on matters of substance. So Milgram's studies – almost uniquely – put those critical questions about how we choose between voices on the agenda, just as his analysis then takes them off again.

Actually, when we refer to Milgram's analysis, we should more accurately say 'Milgram's published analysis', especially his 1974 book. Because both in his earlier writings (e.g. Milgram, 1963, 1965b) and even more in his unpublished experimental notes (which are kept in Yale University's Sterling Library), his ideas are much richer and they do address the multivocal nature of the studies. Moreover, Milgram addresses the psychological processes which determine which voices will have more or less weight. He observes:

> the subjects have come to the laboratory to form a relationship with the experimenter. . . . They have not come to form a relationship with the subject, and it is this lack of relationship in the one direction and the real relationship in the other that produces the results. . . . Only a genuine relationship between the Victim and the Subject, based on identification, or marriage etc. could reverse the results.
>
> *(Milgram, box 46, Yale archive, cited in Haslam, Reicher, Millard & McDonald, 2014, p. 7)*

Milgram uses the term 'relationship' at two different levels in this passage. On the one hand, he equates it to an intimate interpersonal relationship, such as marriage. And he addresses this empirically in a hitherto unpublished variant of the studies (the so-called bring-a-friend condition – see Rochat & Blass, 2014) which confirms that people shock less when the victim is a close personal acquaintance of the participant. On the other hand, Milgram equates 'relationship' to a common category membership (that is, to use different terms, a shared social identity). While Milgram didn't actually conduct any studies to address this issue, he does propose a design for such a study in his notes – one in which the racial group membership of each party (experimenter, participant, learner) is systematically varied so as to cover all possible permutations.

We have taken up Milgram's suggestion and, in a series of studies using a variety of methods, have sought to demonstrate that shock level is a function of identification with science and with the experimenter as a scientific authority (e.g. Haslam, Reicher & Birney, 2014; Haslam, Reicher & Millard, 2014; Haslam et al., 2014; Reicher & Haslam, 2011; Reicher, Haslam & Smith, 2012). We therefore characterise obedient participants as 'engaged followers' who apply shocks not because they are unaware of the consequences, but because they consider that they are involved in a worthwhile cause, the success of which trumps concerns about the victim.

We further argue that this engagement is not spontaneous, but rather that Milgram (and his experimenter) worked hard to get participants to identify with the science and the scientist in his studies. Once framed in this way, relevant evidence is not hard to find. Milgram worked hard to shape participant identities both in the way that the study was set up (Russell, 2011), in the way that the study was conducted (Gibson, 2011) and also in the way that he communicated with participants after the study was completed (Haslam et al., 2014).

So, putting all the evidence together, we can see core commonalities between Zimbardo's SPE and Milgram's obedience studies – but ones which challenge rather than confirm received wisdom. This work does not show that people are somehow inherently inclined to assume roles or obey orders (and thereby harm others). They cannot attribute toxic behaviour to fixed characteristics of the individual psyche. Rather, in both cases, such behaviour is inscribed in a process of mobilisation which has three elements. First, people make active choices as to whether to engage with any given cause, role or authority figure. They are always aware of alternatives and therefore have to make conscious decisions as to what and whom they will heed. Second, leaders and authorities work hard to affect these decisions and to secure the engagement of potential followers. Third, the way they seek to ensure engagement is through the construction of inclusive identities which create a 'we' relationship between the leader/authority and their audience.

Let us now move outside the psychological laboratory to see whether and how this works in everyday life.

Entrepreneurs of identity, entrepreneurs of emotion

We are not the first to recognise that psychology is a *weird* subject: one that studies participants who are Western; educated; from industrialised, rich and democratic countries (e.g. Henrich, Heine & Norenzayan, 2010); and who constitute little more than a tenth of the world's population. Consequently, when we refer to psychology in everyday life, we are in danger of restricting ourselves to the lives of an unrepresentative and privileged few. In looking at the process of mobilisation – of how leaders seek to engage and energise people to take action – we therefore focus on one of the most ignored and most oppressed groups on the planet – the so-called untouchables (or, as those who have been mobilised to contest such categorisation term themselves, '*dalits*') of India.

Untouchables comprise some one-sixth of the Indian population – roughly 150 million people. They are at the bottom of the caste system – a structure of graded inequality which has been described as the central feature of Indian society (Gupta, 2000). Untouchables are generally those who are exploited economically and politically (Omvedt, 2006). One stark figure summarises and symbolises the extent of this exclusion. Astill (2014, p. vii) writes that "nothing unites Indians, in all their legions and diversity than their love" of cricket. And yet, since Indian independence, only one dalit is known to have played for the country.

But dalits are not only poor, they are not only subject to social exclusion (apart from cricket, being forbidden to draw water from public wells, being barred from entering temples, being banned from the use of public roads and burial grounds), they are also subject to constant public humiliations. As recounted through an emergent literature of untouchable autobiography, poetry and short stories (e.g. Dangale, 1992), the untouchable experience is one of having their humanity constantly denied, of being reduced to scavengers feeding, like dogs, on scraps. If anyone should dare to challenge such belittlement, they could be subject to extreme violence. Still today there are accounts of untouchables being brutalised for the most trivial acts: wearing smart clothes, demanding to be treated with dignity, seeking a good education (Teltumbde, 2011).

One might think that such humiliation would provoke a furious response. There is a literature to suggest that humiliation leads to violent retaliation, aggression and vengefulness (e.g. Lindner, 2006; Scheff, 1994). But centuries of humiliation did not, in and of themselves, lead untouchables to respond, to contest their subordination – in short, to become dalits. Rather, protest was dependent on explicit acts of mobilisation.

The origins of untouchable self-mobilisation lie in the caste *sabhas* (associations) of the late 19th and early 20th centuries (Hardtmann, 2009). However, from early on up to the present day, there have been two distinct traditions of protest. On the one hand, the Hindu reform movement has been concerned with changing the status of untouchables within the Hindu fold. On the other, starting with the Adi movements of the 1920s and developing into the dalit movement during the 1930s, an alternative approach has been to valorise untouchables as a separate people, distinct from the Hindus (Hardtmann, 2009; Omvedt, 1994; Srinivas, 1952).

Whereas Gandhi is often seen as the leader of the former tradition, Dr Bhimrao Ramji Ambedkar was and still is seen as the leading light of the latter (Hardtmann, 2009; see Jaffrelot, 2005, for details of his life). Yet, while his role in founding and shaping the dalit movement is undisputed, what is less known is that Ambedkar started out as a Hindu reformer.

In 1927, Ambedkar launched the 'Mahad Satyagraha', a mass protest rooted in a specific demand for the right of untouchables to drink from the public water tank in the small town of Mahad in Western India, but which more broadly aimed at improving the position of untouchables within Hinduism. Over the ensuing years, however, Ambedkar became increasingly convinced that Hinduism could not reform itself and that the leadership of Hindu India would always put the national question (i.e. relations to the British outgroup) before the social question (i.e. relations within the ingroup). Accordingly, in 1936, Ambedkar launched another initiative, the Dharmantar (or conversion) movement, which aimed at taking untouchables out of the Hindu fold by joining another religion. This culminated in 1956, just before Ambedkar's death, when he and a million followers moved over to Buddhism.

Let us look at how Ambedkar sought to mobilise untouchables in support of these two different campaigns. Our analysis is based on Jogdand (2015), which in turn draws upon Jadhav's (2013) compendium of all remaining texts and reports of Ambedkar's speeches. These speeches are replete with mention of humiliation. Consider, for instance, the following passage from 1936 (Jadhav, 2013, Vol. 1, p. 41):

> What is the sense in living in a society which is devoid of humanity, which does not respect you, protect you or treat you as a human being? Instead it insults you, humiliates you and never misses an opportunity to hurt you.

Does Ambedkar invoke humiliation in order to drive people to rage, to 'bloody revenge' (as the title of Scheff's book would suggest)? Certainly, his humiliation rhetoric involves an injunction to act. He consistently argues that those who accept such constant humiliation are themselves diminished and are (to some degree) responsible for their plight. Thus, the previous passage is followed by assertions that "any person with an iota of self-respect and decency" would reject the existing situation and that "only those who love to be slaves" would accept it (Jadhav, 2013, Vol. 1, p. 41).

Ambedkar makes similar arguments in his 1927 speeches. Thus he describes how the Mahars (a specific group of untouchables) have accepted the constant humiliation of begging for leftover food. He describes how they have lost all "self respect and dignity" and he concludes: "it is most shameful to sell your humanity for a few stale crumbs". Shame, then, is not a function of what the oppressor has done to the oppressed but of what the oppressed has failed to do in response.

But if, during both the Mahad Satyagraha and the Dharmantar movement, Ambedkar uses humiliation in order to invoke action, the way he characterises humiliation and the type of action he invokes are profoundly different in 1927 and 1936. What is more, the two are integrally linked. To start with, consider this from 1927 (Jadhav, 2013, Vol. 1, p. 93):

> Touchable Hindus are so kind and peace loving people that they never do any violence and never harm anybody. . . . They worship and protect the harmless animals like cow and also harmful serpents etc. with equal respect.

"One soul pervades all creatures," is their principle! But these same noble Touchable Hindus prevent people of their own religion from drawing water from (a) lake.

There are three critical elements involved in this passage. The first concerns the social relations of humiliation: who is demeaning whom? In other words, what are the identities involved in these humiliating encounters? Here, and throughout his 1927 speeches, Ambedkar characterises what is going on in terms of touchable Hindus mistreating untouchable Hindus. It is one subgroup within the broad Hindu category acting against another subgroup. What is more, the perpetrators violate the prescriptions of Hinduism (their own prescriptions) in the way they treat the victims.

The second element concerns who should respond. Precisely because humiliation is a violation of core Hindu values, then all Hindus – touchables as well as untouchables – suffer from it and should act against it. Many of Ambedkar's 1927 speeches were attempts to mobilise those of high caste. In one, he insists that caste practices have caused loss to touchables as well as untouchables. They have diminished the practical ability of the latter to act for the general good and the moral ability of the former to represent the general good. Overall, then, "this movement for removal of untouchability is in a true sense a movement for nation building and fraternity" (Jadhav, 2013, Vol. 1, p. 85).

The third and last element concerns how people should respond. If untouchability is a violation of Hinduism which harms all Hindus, the obvious response is to make sure Hinduism does live up to its true identity by changing its discrepant practices – that is by abolishing untouchability. Again, Ambedkar makes this explicit throughout his speeches. The work of reform, he argues, "is not only in our self-interest but it is in the interest of the nation.... Hindu society cannot survive unless the discrimination is eliminated" (Jadhav, 2013, Vol. 1, p. 98).

Now consider this from 1936:

We practice Casteism; we observe untouchability, because we are asked to do it by the Hindu religion in which we live. A bitter thing can be made sweet. The taste of anything can be changed. However, poison cannot be made Amrit (nectar). To talk of annihilating castes is like talking of changing poison into Amrit.

Again, three key elements are involved. First, as concerns the social relations of humiliation, this is no longer an intragroup phenomenon – touchable Hindus mistreating untouchable Hindus. Rather, it is an intergroup phenomenon – Hindus mistreating untouchables. So while untouchables might live in a Hindu religious world, they are not of it. In fact, throughout his 1936 speeches, Ambedkar rarely if ever refers to touchable Hindus; he refers to Hindus full stop and insists that "Hindus have not the slightest affinity towards you" (Jadhav, 2013, Vol. 1, p. 184). What is more, their brutal acts are no longer portrayed as a violation of the values of a shared identity. They express the very essence of the (outgroup) Hindu identity. Hinduism is poison. Poison cannot be made into nectar.

Second, if it is in essence of Hindus to oppress untouchables, they clearly cannot be mobilised in the cause of untouchability. In 1936, Ambedkar never addresses higher caste Hindus or tries to recruit them to his cause. To the contrary, he tells untouchables that they would be fools to expect any outside help: "if you yourself have to rise, if no-one else is to come to your aid, if this be the situation, what is the purpose in listening to the advice of the Hindus? There is no other motive in such advice but to misguide you" (Jadhav, 2013, Vol. 1, p. 195).

Third, if Hinduism is essentially oppressive, it is equally pointless to try to reform Hinduism. The only possibility is to give up on it and to leave it:

> In view of the fact that the Hindu religion which forced your forefathers to lead a life of degradation, and heaped all sorts of indignities on them, kept them poor and ignorant, why should you remain within the fold of such a diabolical creed?
>
> (Jadhav, 2013, Vol. 1, p. 42)

So, in both 1927 and 1936, there is a clear consonance between the way in which Ambedkar constitutes the experience of humiliation and the forms of collective mobilisation that he promotes. But, given that the mobilisations are very different, the way that humiliation is construed is very different. The important point here is that humiliation does not just generate heat and a propensity to act. Rather, it invokes a rich representation of the social world which has implications for precisely what forms of action are appropriate. To be more precise, in describing humiliation, one necessarily defines what categories are involved and hence constitutes the identities of one's audience. One defines the relations between categories; who is one's ally, who is one's foe and hence who can or cannot be mobilised on one's side. From this in turn flows a determination of what forms of action are fruitful or fruitless.

More generally, and returning to our discussion of the nature of collective action at the start of this chapter, our analysis of Ambedkar's speeches confirms that issues of social identity and emotion are at the heart of the way that people are mobilised to address their disadvantage. He addresses people in terms of their own category memberships and on the basis of the category interest. He gets them to care and to act on the basis of the way that their group – and not just they personally – are positioned. He gets people to engage with his cause and accept his influence on the basis of an act of common identification, as Hindus in the earlier period and as untouchables in the latter.

But our analysis also departs profoundly from earlier analyses in two key respects. First, we don't see identities and emotions as the outcomes of individual contemplation and appraisal. We see them as actively construed by mobilising agents. More simply, we reintroduce leadership to the equation. Second, we do not draw simple distinctions between identity and emotion such that one is more analytic and the other is more energetic, or that one comes before the other in a causal chain. Rather, we see them as interlinked elements in a representational system which says who we are, where we stand in the world and what we could or should do given this position (cf. Elcheroth, Doise & Reicher, 2011). Given the interdependency of elements in this system, reconfiguring any one necessarily impinges on the others. In terms of affecting the system, it really makes little odds where one operates. One can define how people feel and how they act by defining identity. Equally, one can define identity and action through the ways that one defines emotion.

What we learn from Ambedkar (and, we would argue, the lesson gains added weight for the fact that it comes from beyond the normal heartlands of psychology) is not only that identity and emotion are mobilised in the service of action but also that neither identity nor emotion has precedence over the other in determining action. What matters instead is the coherence of all three elements in the discourse of mobilisation.

Conclusion

The Scottish referendum is now done and the vote was to preserve the Union. Even so, the voices have not fallen silent. We are still assailed from all sides each time we read a newspaper, turn on the radio or watch the TV. Was it a clear victory for the 'Better Together' campaign or a stunning achievement by the 'Yes' campaign in getting so close despite the frenzied mobilisation of the British establishment and their allies in business and finance? Was the result a fair democratic choice or were people tricked by disingenuous last-minute promises? Should we feel pride and pleasure at the massive and peaceful exercise of democracy or anger and disillusion at the illegitimate tactics of the other?

As ever, we determine what to make of the result, what to feel about the result and what to do about the result in the context of these various voices, and these various voices work to engage us by purporting to speak for us in terms of various identities – Scots, ordinary people, the dispossessed and powerless or whatever. They tell us what to feel by telling us who we are. They tell us who we are by telling us what to feel (if we are angry it is because we, the powerless, having been mistreated by a powerful other). In short, what is going on all around us in everyday life as we write exemplifies what we have been writing about.

There are four core points that we want to reader to consider in reading this chapter.

1 Human understanding is a matter of mobilisation as much as perception. We don't come to our conclusions unaided but rather in a context where we receive multiple and sometimes contradictory pieces of advice.
2 Ultimately our decisions depend upon who we engage with and hence which voice we attend to. When analysts tell us the contrary – that is, decisions were driven by some internal and often inherent tendency – it is generally because the role of mobilising voices has been hidden and ignored.

3   Engagement is a matter of identification. We listen to those who we consider to represent the categories in terms of which we define ourselves and hence able to speak for us.
4   At the same time, those who seek to influence us seek actively to define who we are (whether directly or indirectly through invoking emotions) in such a way that they personally represent us and their proposals advance our interests.

References

Astill, T. (2014) *The great Tamasha*. London: Bloomsbury.
Banyard, P., & Grayson, A. (2000). *Introducing psychological research: Seventy studies that shape psychology*. London: Palgrave.
Becker, J. C. (2012). Virtual special issue on theory and research on collective action in the European journal of social psychology. *European Journal of Social Psychology, 42*, 19–23.
Billig, M. (1987). *Arguing and thinking*. Cambridge: Cambridge University Press.
Cesarani, D. (2004). *Eichmann: His life and crimes*. London: Heinemann.
Dangale, A. (1992). *Poisoned bread: Translations from modern Marathi dalit literature*. Mumbai: Orient Blackswan.
Dovidio, J. F., Glick, P., & Rudman, L. A. (2005). *On the nature of prejudice*. Oxford: Blackwell.
Elcheroth, G., Doise, W., & Reicher, S. D. (2011). On the knowledge of politics and the politics of knowledge: How a social representations approach helps us rethink the subject of political psychology. *Political Psychology, 32*, 729–758.
Gibson, S. (2011). Milgram's obedience experiments: A rhetorical analysis. *British Journal of Social Psychology, 2*, 290–309.
Griggs, R. (2014). Coverage of the Stanford prison experiment in introductory psychology textbooks. *Teaching of Psychology, 41*, 195–203.
Gupta, D. (2000). *Interrogating caste: Understanding hierarchy and difference in Indian society*. New Delhi: Penguin.
Haney, C., Banks, C., & Zimbardo, P. (1973). A study of prisoners and guards in a simulated prison. In *Naval Research Reviews: September* (pp. 1–17). Washington, DC: Office of Naval Research.
Hardtmann, E.-M. (2009). *The dalit movement in India*. New Delhi: Oxford University Press.
Haslam, S. A., & McGarty, C. (2001). A hundred years of certitude? Social psychology, the experimental method and the management of scientific uncertainty. *British Journal of Social Psychology, 40*, 1–21. doi:10.1111/bjso.12074
Haslam, S. A., Reicher, S. D., & Birney, M. (2014). Nothing by mere authority: Evidence that in an experimental analogue of the Milgram paradigm participants are motivated not by orders but by appeals to science. *Journal of Social Issues, 70*, 473–488.
Haslam, S. A., Reicher, S. D., & Millard, K. (2014). Shock treatment: Using immersive digital realism to restage and re-examine Milgram's 'Obedience to Authority' research. *PLoS One, 10*(3), e109015.
Haslam, S. A., Reicher, S. D., Millard, K., & McDonald, R. (2014). 'Happy to have been of service': The Yale archive as a window into the engaged followership of participants in Milgram's 'obedience' experiments. *British Journal of Social Psychology, 54*(1), 55–83.
Henrich, J., Heine, S. J., & Norenzayan, A. (2010). The weirdest people in the world. *Behavioural and Brain Sciences, 33*, 61–83.
Jadhav, N. (2013). *Ambedkar speaks* (3 vols.) New Delhi: Konark Publications.
Jaffrelot, C. (2005). *Dr. Ambedkar and untouchability: Fighting the Indian caste system*. New York: Columbia University Press.

Jogdand, Y. (2015). *Humiliation: Understanding its nature, experience and consequences* (Unpublished Ph.D thesis). St. Andrews, UK: University of St. Andrews.
Lindner, E. (2006). *Making enemies: Humiliation and international conflict*. Westport, CT: Greenwood.
Milgram, S. (1963). Behavioral study of obedience. *Journal of Abnormal and Social Psychology*, 67, 371–378.
Milgram S. (1965a). *Obedience* [Motion picture]. United States: Penn State University Audio-Visual.
Milgram, S. (1965b). Some conditions of obedience and disobedience to authority. *Human Relations*, 18, 57–76.
Milgram, S. (1974). *Obedience to authority*. New York: Harper & Row.
Moscovici, S. (1972). Theory and Society in Social Psychology. In J. Isreal & H. Tajfel (Eds.), *The context of social psychology: A critical assessment*. London: Academic Press.
Omvedt, G. (1994). *Dalits and the democratic revolution: Dr. Ambedkar and the dalit movement in colonial India*. New Delhi: Sage.
Omvedt, G. (2006). *Dalit visions: The anti-caste movement and the construction of an Indian identity*. Mumbai: Orient Blackswan.
Packer, D. (2008). Identifying systematic disobedience in Milgram's obedience experiments: A meta-analytic review. *Perspectives on Psychological Science*, 3, 301–304.
Reicher, S. D., & Haslam, S. A. (2011). After shock? Towards a social identity explanation of the Milgram 'obedience' studies. *British Journal of Social Psychology*, 50, 163–169.
Reicher, S. D., Haslam, S. A., & Miller, A. G. (2014). What makes a person a perpetrator? The intellectual, moral and methodological arguments for revisiting Milgram's research on the influence of authority. *Journal of Social Issues*, 70, 393–408.
Reicher, S. D., Haslam, S. A., & Smith, J. (2012). Working toward the experimenter: Reconceptualizing obedience within the Milgram paradigm as identification-based followership. *Perspectives on Psychological Science*, 7, 315–324.
Rochat, F., & Blass, T. (2014). Milgram's unpublished obedience variation and its historical relevance. *Journal of Social Issues*, 70, 456–472.
Russell, N. J. C. (2011). Milgram's obedience to authority experiments: Origins and early evolution. *British Journal of Social Psychology*, 50, 146–162.
Scheff, T. J. (1994). *Bloody revenge: Emotions, nationalism and war*. Boulder, CO: Westview Press.
Simon, B., & Klandermans, B. (2001). Politicized collective identity: A social psychological analysis. *American Psychologist*, 56, 319–331.
Srinivas, M. N. (1952). *Religion and society among the Coorgs of South India*. Oxford: Clarendon Press.
Teltumbde, A. (2011). *The persistence of caste: The Khairlanii murders and India's hidden apartheid*. London: Zed Books.
van Zomeren, M., & Iyer, A. (2009). Introduction to the social and psychological dynamics of collective action. *Journal of Social Issues*, 65, 645–660.
van Zomeren, M., Leach, C. W., & Spears, R. (2012). Protestors as 'passionate economists': A dynamic dual pathway model of approach coping with collective disadvantage. *Personality and Social Psychology Review*, 16, 180–199.
van Zomeren, M., Postmes, T., & Spears, R. (2008). Toward an integrative social identity model of collective action: A quantitative research synthesis of three socio-psychological perspectives. *Psychological Bulletin*, 134, 504–535.
Zimbardo, P. (1989). *Quiet rage* (video). Stanford, CA: Stanford University.
Zimbardo, P. (2004). A situationist perspective on the psychology of evil: Understanding how good people are transformed into perpetrators. In A. Miller (Ed.), *The social psychology of good and evil* (pp. 21–50). New York: Guilford.

8
RESISTANCE AND TRANSFORMATION IN POSTCOLONIAL CONTEXTS

Shose Kessi and Floretta Boonzaier

Introduction

Examining everyday life in postcolonial contexts is a complex undertaking. We live in societies characterized by vast differences in access to resources, where competition and conflict are pervasive and palpable. Economic poverty, health concerns such as HIV/AIDS and Ebola outbreaks, gender-based violence, xenophobia, and racism are all manifestations of the power dynamics that have given rise to social inequalities and that have created the contexts for poverty, discrimination, and violence to flourish. In the midst of such hardship, people are also driven to change their circumstances, engage in various forms of resistance, and claim access to resources and social justice. In this chapter, we explore the social psychological factors that contribute to this situation and the ideas and actions toward resistance and social change that emerge from communities in these contexts. Specifically, we ask about the kinds of theories and methods relevant to postcolonial contexts and how these might provide a challenge to mainstream psychology with a tendency to dehumanize and objectify its 'subjects'.

The postcolonial in the context of everyday politics

A *postcolonial context* refers to a period of economic, social, and political changes for nations previously under western rule. The term 'postcolonial' acknowledges the persistence of an informal and less visible western involvement in the affairs of previously colonized states in spite of their 'formal' political independence (Mosse & Lewis, 2005; Rodney, 1972). The rise of neoliberalism, accompanied by privatization and liberalization policies (Mkandawire, 2004), and the institutionalization of poverty through the development imperative (Escobar, 1995; Kothari, 2006) have maintained divisions and control between the global north and the global south. Just as the colonial project was legitimized through the racialization and feminization of colonized populations, beliefs in the backwardness and inferiority of black people and women in postcolonial contexts continue to influence North-South relations (Escobar, 1995; Esteva, 1992; Goudge, 2003; Munck & O'Hearn, 1999; Said, 1978). These images are often fueled through the media (Nederveen Pieterse, 1992) and international development discourses (Dogra, 2012; Escobar, 1995) and have become part of our commonsense understanding of postcolonial realities (Kessi, 2011). They serve to produce a system of knowledge about people from different parts of the world that is relative and hierarchical (Watkins & Shulman, 2008). Hence, powerful political and economic systems, such as neoliberalism, capitalism, racism, and heterosexism, through various channels, create the culturally shared knowledge or commonsense that prevails in postcolonial society. They impose particular beliefs, values, rights, and responsibilities, and they affect the sense of belonging of individuals and groups who espouse alternative lifestyles and worldviews.

Everyday politics in postcolonial contexts are driven by these economic, social, and identity dynamics. They determine our ability to participate in the economic, social, and political activities that are recognized and valued by society, and they also determine our likelihood of being marginalized or excluded from access to these same resources. People's abilities to participate in activities that promote their interests as citizens and forge a sense of belonging in the postcolonial nation depend on their power to be recognized for their lifestyles and worldviews (Howarth, Andreouli, & Kessi, 2014). Indeed, access to basic resources such as education, employment, and healthcare and the freedom to participate in social and political groupings – all of which create society's political culture – are not only dependent on state priorities and provision but are also negotiated through everyday interactions between people. It is often through relationships with significant others or within families and communities that the politics of belonging and exclusion are acted out. Social psychological research into everyday politics in postcolonial contexts should therefore explore the encounters between its various social actors. A postcolonial lens on everyday politics is thus one that explores the linkages between North-South relations and the daily realities of people in postcolonial spaces, their complicity in maintaining colonial structures and influence, and their ability to enact change, a task that is largely mediated by intersecting identities that derive from this historical and political landscape. This chapter focuses on the theoretical and methodological resources that can engage individuals and communities in their local contexts to challenge their situations and mobilize around social change, and this is illustrated through empirical examples drawn from the South African context.

The postcolonial and psychology

Locating this endeavor within a social psychology approach is not without some reservations. The historical Eurocentric focus of psychological approaches to human behavior has often undermined the ways of life of people from postcolonial societies and served to justify the rationale for colonization and apartheid (Foster,

1991; Nicholas & Cooper, 1990; Richards, 1997). Psychology as a discipline and psychological knowledge and the production thereof have historically served the interests of dominant groups. Studies of intelligence and other forms of psychometric testing labored to show hierarchies between populations on the basis of racial difference (Duncan & Bowman, 2009; Louw & Danzinger, 2000; Owusu-Bempah & Howitt, 2000; Richards, 1997), illustrating complicity with oppressive regimes such as apartheid and colonization. Providing scientific proof that black populations were less intelligent meant that they could be excluded from participating in economic, social, and political life and that they needed to be regulated by European forces. Psychological research has also had a historical focus on the behaviors of men, casting the white, middle class, heterosexual male experience as the norm (Macleod, 2004). In psychological research where women's experiences are included, the topics tend to reflect the "scientific gaze that regulates the female body" (Duncan & Bowman, 2009, p. 621) through concerns with reproductive and health issues and sexual relationships.

In the current postcolonial era, these orientations of the discipline continue to have an impact on the experiences of marginalized groups and contribute to ideas about people who live in postcolonial contexts. Much psychological research continues to be located within philosophical underpinnings that espouse racialized, classed, and gendered ideas of postcoloniality (Foster, 1999; Macleod, 2004). There is a need for a more radical and politicized psychology that can restore a critical approach to researching human behavior (Hook et al., 2004; Kessi et al., n.d.). Engaging with postcolonial thought emerging from different parts of the globe would equip contemporary social psychologists with important tools that shed light on how global forms of power operate and influence everyday politics in postcolonial contexts and the role that social psychology can have in exposing and disrupting these dynamics.

Decolonizing psychologies: Postcolonial and black feminist psychology

For social psychology to have an important role in social change, in particular in improving the lives of the oppressed (Jiménez-Domínguez, 2009), it requires a 'de-ideologization' (Freire, 1970) or indigenization (Long, 2014; Owusu-Bempah & Howitt, 2000; Smith, 1999) of the discipline – meaning an acknowledgment that psychologists, like all scientists, work within a political perspective and an ideological agenda (Montero & Sonn, 2009) and a recognition that what, in contemporary times, has come to be seen as 'the psychological' has been shaped historically, politically, and ideologically (Hook et al., 2004). Indeed, psychologists have produced particular types of knowledge about people living in postcolonial contexts, knowledge that was imposed upon 'indigenous' populations for the purpose of subjugation and domination. Western science has produced knowledge about people in the global South as emotional beings in contrast to the rationality of westerners (Said, 1978) through images that revolve around racialized, classist, and gendered ideas of ignorance, laziness, and irresponsibility (Kessi, 2011). People in the South, particularly women and children from underresourced contexts, are depicted as passive (Dogra, 2012) rather than active participants in transforming their communities and societies. These images serve to depoliticize poverty and violence and legitimize global forms of exploitation (Dogra, 2012, 2007). Postcolonial and black feminist psychology reject these conceptions of postcolonial realities and highlight the intersections between global politics, science, and everyday life. Indeed, they provide a more politicized approach to the scientific investigation of postcolonial societies and reflect a type of scholarship that represents more accurately the experiences of the oppressed.

There are a number of examples of decolonizing psychologies that have emerged across the globe. Liberation psychology in Latin America (Jiménez-Domínguez, 2009), African psychology (Mkhize, 2004), Filipino psychology in the Phillipines (San Juan, 2006), and a range of other indigenous psychologies in the Australasian region (see Groot, Rua, Masters-Awatere, Dungeon, & Garvey, 2012) are some examples. The psychology of racial oppression (Biko, 1978; Buhlan, 1985; Fanon, 1967; Manganyi, 1973) provides critical insights on the impact of racism in communities and the ensuing difficulties in forging positive social identities and community and interpersonal relations. These postcolonial writers use psychological theories to make the link between a globalized racial climate and people's everyday experiences. They describe how individuals in postcolonial contexts (and the diaspora) navigate negative representations of blackness and the complex identity dynamics and behavioral challenges that ensue. The work of psychiatrist and revolutionary Frantz Fanon (1967) has been pivotal in examining the impact of racialized violence on the psychological well being of people in postcolonial contexts. He describes how colonial and, by extension, apartheid violence, as racialized forms of oppression, have been internalized by the oppressed who, as a result, reproduce acts of violence against one another. Referring to the psyche of the oppressed, Buhlan (1985, p. 143) states:

> If he cannot defend his personality in the larger social arena, he must defend what is left of it in his last refuge, in the circle of his family and friends. That is why the slightest challenge, rejection, or offence by those worthy of his love or respect ... pushes him to a volcanic eruption of repressed aggression.

This argument points to the lack of symbolic resources available in postcolonial communities to create positive social identities and relationships (Campbell, 2003). Incidents of violence between members of a family and/or a community are often the most visible manifestations of oppressive structures. However, when researchers restrict their investigations of social phenomena occurring within communities to explanations that have to do with the community itself, the results can lead to victim-blaming and limit the possibilities for change. Working with communities with theoretical tools that favor the examination of broader structural, political, and representational dynamics can provide a deeper understanding of the causes of their realities and the multiple and intersecting dimensions of everyday life that need to be addressed. South African psychological research demonstrates that conflict and violence within communities must be politicized and theorized as the result of oppressive structural and political forces rather than simply as the product of internal competition over a lack of resources, the characteristics of the communities involved, or individualized psychological deficits.

Much South African work on gender-based violence, for example, has specifically made meaning of the high levels of violence against women by linking it to sociocultural and structural factors such as widespread poverty, gendered and racialized inequalities, and a long history of violence as a result of colonialism and apartheid, alongside the almost normative use of violence as a means of conflict resolution (Gopal & Chetty, 2006; Jewkes & Morrell, 2010; Morrell, 2001). A key explanatory framework for men's violence against women globally and in South Africa is the performance of masculinity, specifically, the idea that the enactment of violence is consistent with hegemonic masculinity which involves the display of power and control over women (Jewkes & Morrell, 2010). However, these performances of masculinity also need to be located in a historical and structural context. Ratele (2013), for example, has argued that there are important connections between the violence that black men perpetrate against women and other men; racialized fear, which has deep colonial roots; white male privilege; and the subordination of black people. While black and poor men are often constructed as 'the problem' in discourses of violence against women (Shefer, in press), Ratele's work has also shown that they themselves are the group most at risk of male violence (Ratele, 2008), a fact that demands a more complex understanding of the roots of violence.

Kessi's (2013a, 2011) work with young people in postcolonial contexts has demonstrated how black populations internalize negative images of themselves through a racializing and postcolonial discourse of laziness, ignorance, and irresponsibility, which manifests itself through relational forms of violence within communities. Young people often reassign negative stereotypes of themselves as being 'up to no good' onto other young people in their communities. Young women, in particular, are blamed and stigmatized for getting pregnant or selling sex. Without an analysis of the social and historical origins of relational violence, psychologists can explain these away as manifestations of the personalities and characteristics of people in postcolonial contexts.

In other contexts, the manifestation of racialized violence is much more subtle. For example, the backlash to affirmative action policies in higher education in South Africa have created the conditions for black students to internalize lower self-esteem through the dissemination of beliefs about lowering standards and performance (Kessi, 2013b; Kessi & Cornell, 2015). These experiences result in complex identity dynamics between black students who protect themselves through a discourse of blame. More privileged black students blame lower income black students for the stereotypes of underperformance, and lower income black students blame their more privileged counterparts for taking on white identities in order to fit into the culture of the establishments and in attempts to deny their racial identities. All of these examples demonstrate how racialized oppression is internalized and reenacted and how people's immediate need for power, status, and control over their lives is misdirected into acts of violence most often perpetrated toward members of their networks or communities who are weaker or closest to them.

However, victims of oppression also navigate between a discourse of resistance and blame. In the previously mentioned studies (Kessi, 2013a, 2011; Kessi & Cornell, 2015), young people also demonstrated deep levels of awareness of the precarious social and political conditions they found themselves in and displayed critical acts of resistance and change. Boonzaier's (2014b) work on intimate partner violence (IPV) highlights these tensions between complicity and resistance. She illustrates how women talk against a dominant and stigmatizing, but popular, narrative about their positioning as 'victims' in abusive relationships. They at times resist and at times position themselves within hegemonic stories about abusive relationships that involve the construction of victimized women as passively accepting the abuse, as psychologically trapped in abusive relationships, and as somehow deserving of the abuse through the shame and stigma associated with their identities as abused women.

All of these examples point to a cycle of oppression and resistance in postcolonial contexts that can develop and manifest itself at personal, interpersonal, and political levels (Moane, 2009). They highlight not only the deep, persistent, and insidious impact of racial oppression but also how race, class, and gender oppression are complicated by other intersecting markers of identity. Intersectionality, a concept emerging from black and postcolonial feminists and critical race theorists, promotes the idea that social identities or social divisions such as race, class, and gender intersect and interact to produce substantively different experiences (Collins, 2000; Warner, 2008).

Intersectionality has been heralded as one of the most important developments in feminist theorizing, generating interdisciplinary and global engagement, and it has been described as "a method and a disposition, a heuristic and analytic tool" (Carbado, Crenshaw, Mays, & Tomlinson, 2013, p. 303). Intersectionality hinges on the idea that multiple identities and experiences are interconnected and are related to power and sociostructural oppressions. Emergent from feminist debates on 'difference', the black feminist critique of the notion of 'universal sisterhood' and the varying experiences of gender oppression and its interconnections with racism and classism (for black women specifically) are key early developments of the theory. These intersecting identities and experiences of oppression (which may be based upon race, gender, class, sexuality, ability, religion, and so on) result in what Collins (2000) has described as a matrix of domination, being the "overall social organization within which intersecting oppressions originate, develop, and are contained" (p. 228). Collins's delineation of the matrix of domination compels us to consider how, within any inequitable social system, the multiple forms of oppression shape and influence each other and work not independently but as a *system of oppression*.

Kimberlé Crenshaw, who coined the term *intersectionality* in 1989, argues that separate analyses of forms of oppression deny the validity of others such that if feminists do not interrogate race, they may be complicit in reproducing the marginalization of black women, and if antiracist scholars do not interrogate gender, they may reproduce the marginalization of women. 'Either/or' approaches, while potentially contributing to forms of representational or symbolic exclusion, also have damaging implications for the empowerment of marginalized groups and for a social justice agenda.

One clue to the 'movement' of the concept and theory of intersectionality may be its utility as a tool for facilitating social change. Intersectionality was conceptualized from within feminism and critical race studies not only as a tool to understand relations of power and systems of oppression, but to transform them (Carbado et al., 2013). Thinking and organizing through the mode of intersectionality may enable social movements to begin to see their commonalities and may facilitate strategic alliances toward a social justice agenda.

These theoretical developments illustrate some of the obstacles in individualized approaches that deny the complexity of postcolonial contexts. Individuals and groups possess different levels of access to the resources required to resist experiences of oppression because of the complexity of intersecting forms of oppression. Research shows that women's experiences of violence in postcolonial contexts are complicated by a number of intersecting forms of oppression, including culture (Abraham, 2000), race (Mama, 1996), class (Gonzales de Olarte & Gavilano Llosa, 1999), and sexuality (Wilkinson & Kitzinger, 1993). Bhavnani (1993) argues that women have different interests based upon their social and cultural locations. For women who have been subjected to violence from an intimate partner, the context in which this occurs should be an important site of analysis. Women who find themselves in conditions of poverty are faced with particular challenges that intersect in important ways with their other experiences of partner abuse. Financial dependence on a partner and a lack of access to shelter, food, and other resources makes it difficult for women to successfully leave abusive partners (Boonzaier & van Schalkwyk, 2011). In South Africa, as in most postcolonial societies, poverty has racialized dimensions so that poor women, who are also likely to be black, are already subjected to oppressive material conditions that intersect with their experiences of IPV.

In the US, Crenshaw's (1994) work has been illustrative in showing the intersections of structural oppressions faced by poor black women, showing that black women are frequently burdened with child care and domestic responsibilities and the associated burdens of poverty, and they find it difficult to leave abusive partners. Crenshaw's work has resonated in a South African study in an impoverished community in Cape Town, showing how, as a result of their particular location in this community (one that had been created as a result of apartheid's Group Areas Act and that continues to be devastated by very high levels of gang violence), women face challenges in seeking help from the police, who are often uncooperative and frequently display patriarchal attitudes that ensure they 'side' with the abusers (van

Niekerk & Boonzaier, in press). A further complicating factor for poor women who attempt to obtain police intervention to stop the abuse is that the police station is located outside of the community, requiring women to have the resources to use public transport to pay a visit to the police station; telephone calls frequently result in either no intervention or the police arriving many hours after the domestic violence incident has taken place.

These experiences expose how power relations based upon the intersecting categories of race, class, economic privilege, and geographical location become central. These differing interests are also epitomized in current global North-South relations, where foreign policies and the interests of global capital continue to reflect exploitative relations and have an impact on the daily lives of people in the South (Campbell, 2006).

The different levels of analysis point to the utility and complexity of the theory of intersectionality in postcolonial contexts. The theory allows us to analyze how social divisions operate at intersubjective, institutional, experiential, and representational levels and to theorize the connections between these, as well as the important symbolic and material effects they produce and maintain (Yuval-Davis, 2006). Postcolonial and feminist research have long questioned the assumed expertise of western and male-dominated science and instead consider that people living in oppressive conditions are the experts of their own lives and are most knowledgeable about the challenges they face and the aspects of their daily lives that need to change (Bhabha, 1994; Phoenix, 1990). Cannella and Manuelito (2008) speak of revisioning an anticolonial social science (including a feminist agenda) which "would privilege research goals/purposes that no longer accept the Eurocentric assumption (error) that some human beings have the power to 'know' others (whether cognitively or through personal stories) but would rather acknowledge and focus on the complexities of our contemporary sociopolitical condition(s)" (p. 49).

These goals have important implications for a theoretical perspective located within the discipline of psychology, a discipline concerned with the study of the human condition, but with a long history of inattention to the complexities of our social and political contexts. Oppressive power operates through structural, political, and representational modes (Crenshaw, 1991) within families and communities and on a global platform. Developing theoretical concepts with the potential to challenge, resist, and overcome these processes is central.

Research methods for decolonizing psychologies

In this part of the chapter, we explore the types of methodological approaches that might espouse what we see as a more politicized approach to research in postcolonial settings. Social psychologists cannot deliver solutions to the problems of the oppressed, but they can point to the manifestations of these problems and assist people in achieving the changes that they seek. Under such conditions, the psychologist acts as a facilitator of social change (Jiménez-Domínguez, 2009) – this means, for example, making the linkages between people's daily realities of oppression and the broader and globalized institutional precepts and ideologies that perpetuate their oppression. Political-psychological research then becomes a dialogical process of consciousness and action in which the oppressed *participate* in imagining and creating solutions to improve their lives, and social psychologists use their knowledge to encourage, assist, and support that process. It is the daily lives, experiences, and activities of people, which are contextual, that inform researchers on what actions can be effective in disrupting their oppression. From this perspective, an anticolonial science is an evolving practice of knowledge production that cannot be separated from everyday life and that constantly grows through the contributions that people make based on their lived experiences.

This politicization of academic practices also puts into question the taken-for-granted assumptions of objectivity and truth in scientific reasoning (Gergen, 2009). When conducting social psychological research from postcolonial and black feminist perspectives, objectivity is not measured through the level of distance maintained between the researcher and the subject or the people under study (often a precondition of quantitative or experimental methods) but through methods that reflect the political intention and motivation of the research and their logic in responding to the theoretical questions (Bauer & Gaskell, 1999). Research processes are always encounters between actors with potentially different ideas, motivations, and access to power, and often research findings are a reflection of the dialectics of power between researchers and those who are researched (Boonzaier, 2014a). In such a process, objectivity is not about reaching *consensus*, which could reflect the dominant view (Bauer & Gaskell, 1999), but rather how effective the chosen methods are in revealing the different perspectives of the participants, in disrupting power dynamics, and instituting social change. Therefore, in studies that attempt to destabilize the workings of power, objectivity should be concerned with the alternative ways and meanings attributed to social phenomena that derive from the research process. They should provide spaces for disruption and contradiction through praxis that encourage resistance and/or that conceive of alternative ways of seeing and doing (Hook & Howarth, 2005). This is not a straightforward process, and it is often dependent on differences in the material, social, and cognitive resources available to the various actors (Jovchelovitch, 2008) and the knowledge, skills, and motivations of the researcher/facilitator (Braden & Mayo, 1999; Campbell, 2003).

Narrative and participatory action research (PAR) methods

Participatory action research methods (PAR) and narrative methods are some of the proposed methods for social psychologists in postcolonial contexts. Both narrative methods (such as life histories) and PAR place particular emphasis on agency or the capacity of participants to frame and tell stories in ways that make sense to them. These are potentially empowering tools that promote critical consciousness and communication in social relations, all of which address the social psychological questions under investigation.

The importance of a narrative lens for a social (political) psychology of the postcolonial cannot be overemphasized, particularly within a broader psychological project that has favored individualized understandings of complex lives. While narratives have personal individual elements, they are not only that; they allow us to think in new ways about individual engagement within broader political and ideological processes. Narrative research attends to power dynamics and the political by asking about the social arrangements that may facilitate or constrain the telling of particular kinds of stories (Riessman, 2008). It asks about the social context of the story and about the cultural resources that are available and make the story possible. A focus on narrative allows for the understanding of participants' lives in relation to broader categories of power and subordination (Riessman, 2008). Relatedly, a focus on narrative also allows one to consider whose perspectives are privileged in the stories being constructed and whose are marginalized or left out (Parker, 2005). Traditional psychological research has a long history of dehumanizing research participants, as Walker (cited in Banister et al., 2011, p. 138) has argued: "rarely do people emerge from our studies as people with their dignity intact. Worse still the report may read as though the evaluator was the most intelligent person present." The restoration of the agency of the teller, through the presentation of the self (and others) in a narrative, is a key political concern for narrative researchers and important too in postcolonial contexts in which the stories of dominant groups continue to hold sway.

Furthermore, through storytelling and representation, narratives engage the observer by creating emotional understandings (Laszlo, 1997; Rappaport, 1995) that challenge the unconscious feelings in social relations (Laszlo, 1997). Hence, narratives not only describe situations but also expose the consciousness and affect of the respondents (ibid). In doing so, narratives provide a powerful means through which psychological empowerment may be facilitated and through which dignity may be restored to those who are on the margins of society. Through the construction and contestation of narratives, participants are engaged to think critically about relationships between each other and their relationships with members of their communities and the broader society. In that sense, the narratives developed by the participants of a research project form part of an emancipatory and consciousness-raising process of defining themselves rather than being defined by others. Narratives are said to be emancipatory as "the process of creating a narrative enables the person to give meaning to the constant change in his or her life, to bring order to disorder" (Murray, 2000, p. 338). This process of emancipation unlocks the consciousness of individuals who can begin to reflect on the intersecting forms of oppression they experience and the resulting dialectics of complicity and resistance. This process will raise questions of how, on the one hand, their narratives are produced by power and how they reproduce power and how, on the other hand, they can develop counternarratives as a means of challenging dominant discourses (Murray, 2000).

Participatory action research (PAR) has proven to be an effective mechanism for producing counternarratives. PAR engages research participants in collaborative activities with an explicit agenda of social justice and social change (Brydon-Miller, 1997), in other words, in activities that seek to challenge and disrupt relations of power. In that engagement, participants produce narratives about their lives that emerge from their experiences of participating with others in these political activities. Participation therefore enriches the component of consciousness in the narrative project when it engages participants in concrete experiences of political engagement; participation is the "activity that locates individuals and social groups in their socio-political world" (Howarth et al., 2014, p. 21). PAR is often said to have empowering effects on participants who experience, often for the first time, their own potential (or agency) in contributing toward change in their communities and the recognition that they gain from others in that process (Strack, Magill, & McDonagh, 2004). Focusing on empowerment also emphasizes power as central to social and political change.

Social psychological studies focusing on consciousness, empowerment, participation, and social action in postcolonial contexts (Cornish, 2006; Kessi, 2013b; Kessi & Cornell, 2015; Kessi et al., n.d.; Skovdal, Ogutu, Aoro, & Campbell, 2009; Vaughan, 2010) have gained some traction in challenging oppressive structures through voicing the concerns and priorities of marginalized groups and developing strategies and tactics to alleviate and challenge material and symbolic constraints. These advantages of PAR highlight the need for psychological research in postcolonial contexts to address the interface between people's everyday realities of oppressive contexts and the institutional, political, and historical dynamics that produce experiences of violence and exclusion. It also gives those who are most marginalized by the workings of power a central role in producing the knowledge necessary for change (Campbell & Jovchelovitch, 2000), challenging the assumed neutrality of mainstream research and the traditional roles of researchers and participants.

By encouraging the development of narratives, participatory skills, and political understandings (Foster-Fishman et al., 2005), politically oriented research methods create spaces for producing new forms of knowledge that can become part of a process of historization and emancipation "moving from silence into speech as a revolutionary gesture" (hooks, 1989, p. 12).

Conclusion

Everyday realities in contemporary postcolonial contexts are marked by complex and uneven patterns of complicity and resistance to institutional and relational forms of violence and oppression. This situation calls not only for a politicization of everyday lives in postcolonial settings, but also a politicization of psychology as a discipline that can broaden our understandings of complex social identities and contexts and expand the creativity of our theories and methodologies. Adopting postcolonial and black feminist perspectives enriches social psychological research in these contexts by highlighting the multiple and intersecting workings of power that impact marginalized individuals and communities in different ways and that seek to locate the origins of violence and oppression in historical contexts of colonization, racism, gender, and economic exploitation. These perspectives thus provide a historical lens through which researchers can find alternative and more critical explanations to everyday realities that challenge institutional frameworks, ideological beliefs, and interpersonal relations. We have argued that the theory of intersectionality, coupled with narrative and PAR methods, can contribute to the beginnings of more politicized approaches to science and specifically the discipline of social psychology which itself needs to transform and rearticulate a scholarship focused on social change and social justice if it is to be relevant to the lives of marginalized people in postcolonial contexts.

References

Abraham, M. (2000). *Speaking the unspeakable: Marital violence among South Asian immigrants in the United States*. New Brunswick: Rutgers University Press.

Banister, P., Bunn, G., Burman, E., Daniels, J., Duckett, P., Goodley, D., ...Whelan, P. (2011). *Qualitative methods in psychology: A research guide* (2nd ed.). Berkshire: Open University Press.

Bauer, M.W., & Gaskell, G. (1999). Towards a paradigm for research on social representations. *Journal for the Theory of Social Behaviour, 29*(2), 163–186.

Bhabha, H. (1994). *The location of culture*. London and New York: Routledge.

Bhavnani, K. (1993). Talking racism and the editing of women's studies. In D. Richardson & V. Robinson (Eds.), *Thinking feminist: Key concepts in women's studies* (pp. 27–48). New York: The Guilford Press.

Biko, S. (1978). *I write what I like*. London: Bowerdean.

Boonzaier, F. (2014a). Methodological disruptions: Interviewing domestically violent men across a 'gender divide'. *NORMA: International Journal for Masculinity Studies, 4*, 232–248.

Boonzaier, F. (2014b). Talking against dominance: South African women resisting dominant discourse in narratives of violence. In M. N. Lafrance & S. McKenzie-Mohr (Eds.), *Creating counter-stories: Women voicing resistance* (pp. 102–120). London: Routledge Press.

Boonzaier, F. A., & van Schalkwyk, S. (2011). Narrative possibilities: Poor women of color and the complexities of intimate partner violence. *Violence Against Women, 17*(2), 267–286.

Braden, S., & Mayo, M. (1999). Culture, community development and representation. *Community Development Journal, 34*(3), 191–204.

Brydon-Miller, M. (1997). Participatory action research: Psychology and social change. *Journal of Social Issues, 35*(4), 657–666.

Buhlan, H. A. (1985). *Frantz fanon and the psychology of oppression*. New York: Plenum.

Campbell, C. (2003). *Letting them die: Why HIV/AIDS prevention programmes fail*. US and Canada: African Issues: Indiana University Press.

Campbell, C. (2006). HIV/AIDS: Politics and inter-group relations. In K. Ratele (Ed.), *Intergroup relations: South African perspectives* (pp. 171–192). Cape Town: Juta Press.

Campbell, C., & Jovchelovitch, S. (2000). Health, community and development: Towards a social psychology of development. *Journal of Community and Applied Social Psychology, 10*, 255–270.

Cannella, G. S., & Manuelito, K. D. (2008). Feminisms from unthought locations. Indigenous worldviews, marginalized feminisms, and revisioning anticolonial social science. In N. K. Denzin, Y. S. Lincoln & L. T. Smith (Eds.), *Handbook of critical and indigenous methodologies* (pp. 45–59). Los Angeles: Sage.

Carbado, D. W., Crenshaw, K. W., Mays, V. M., & Tomlinson, B. (2013). Intersectionality. Mapping the movements of a theory. *Du Bois Review*, *10*(2), 303–312.

Collins, P. H. (2000). *Black feminist thought: Knowledge, consciousness, and the politics of empowerment* (2nd ed.). New York: Routledge.

Cornish, F. (2006). Challenging the stigma of sex work in Calcutta: Material context and symbolic change. *Journal of Community and Applied Social Psychology*, *16*(6), 462–471.

Crenshaw, K. W. (1991). Mapping the margins: Intersectionality, identity politics, and violence against women of color. *Stanford Law Review*, *43*, 1241–1299.

Crenshaw, K. W. (1994). Mapping the margins: Intersectionality, identity politics, and violence against women of color. In M. A. Fineman & R. Mykitiuk (Eds.), *The public nature of private violence* (pp. 93–118). New York: Routledge.

Dogra, N. (2007). Reading NGOs visually—implications of visual images for NGO management. *Journal of International Development*, *19*, 161–171.

Dogra, N. (2012). *Representations of global poverty: Aid, development and international NGOs*. New York: I.B. Taurus.

Duncan, N., & Bowman, B. (2009). Liberating South African psychology: The legacy of racism and the pursuit of representative knowledge production. In M. Montero & C. Sonn (Eds.), *Psychology of liberation: Theory and applications* (pp. 93–113). New York: Springer Science+Business Media.

Escobar, A. (1995). *Encountering development: The making and unmaking of the third world*. Princeton, NJ: Princeton University Press.

Esteva, G. (1992). Development. In W. Sachs (Ed.), *The development dictionary* (pp. 1–23). London: Zed.

Fanon, F. (1967) [1952]. *Black skin, White masks*. London: Pluto.

Foster, D. (1991). 'Race' and racism in South African psychology. *South African Journal of Psychology*, *12*(4), 203–209.

Foster, D. (1999). Racism, Marxism, psychology. *Theory & Psychology*, *9*(3), 331–352.

Foster-Fishman, P., Nowell, B., Deacon, Z., Nievar, M. A., & McCann, P. (2005). Using methods that matter: The impact of reflection, dialogue and voice. *American Journal of Community Psychology*, *36*(3/4), 275–291.

Freire, P. (1970). *Pedagogy of the oppressed*. London: Penguin.

Gergen, K. (2009). *An invitation to social constructionism: Second edition*. London: Sage.

Gonzales de Olarte, E., & Gavilano Llosa, P. (1999). Does poverty cause domestic violence? Some answers from Lima. In A. R. Morrison & M. L. Biehl (Eds.), *Too close to home: Domestic violence in the Americas* (pp. 35–49). Washington: Inter-American Development Bank.

Gopal, N., & Chetty, V. (2006). No women left behind: Examining public perspectives on South African police services' handling of violence against South African women. *Alternation*, *13*(2), 117–133.

Goudge, P. (2003). *The whiteness of power: Racism in third world development aid*. London: Lawrence & Wishart.

Groot, S., Rua, M., Masters-Awatere, B., Dudgeon, P., & Garvey, D. (2012). Editorial special issue. Indigenous psychologies. *The Australian Community Psychologist*, *24*(1), 5–10.

Hook, D., & Howarth, C. (2005). Future directions for a critical social psychology of racism/anti-racism. *Journal of Community and Applied Social Psychology*, *15*(6), 506–512.

Hook, D., Mkhize, N., Kiguwa, P., Collins, A., Burman, E., & Parker, I. (2004). *Critical psychology*. Cape Town: UCT Press.

hooks, b. (1989). *Talking back: Thinking feminist thinking black*. Boston MA: South End Press.

Howarth, C., Andreouli, E., & Kessi, S. (2014). Social representations and the politics of participation. In C. Kinnvall, T. Capelos, P. Nesbitt-Larking (Eds.), *Palgrave handbook of global and political psychology* (pp. 19–38). Basingstoke: Palgrave Macmillan UK.

Jewkes, R., & Morrell, R. (2010). Gender and sexuality: Emerging perspectives from the heterosexual epidemic in South Africa and implications for HIV risk and prevention. *Journal of International AIDS Society*, *13*(6), 1–11.

Jiménez-Domínguez, B. (2009). Ignacio Martín-Baró's social psychology of liberation: Situated knowledge and critical commitment against objectivism. In M. Montero & C. Sonn (Eds.), *Psychology of liberation: Theory and applications* (pp. 37–50). New York: Springer Science+Business Media.

Jovchelovitch, S. (2008). Reflections on the diversity of knowledge: Power and dialogue in representational fields. In T. Sugiman, K. J. Gergen, W. Wagner & Y. Yamada (Eds.), *Meaning in action: Constructions, narrations and representations* (pp. 23–37). Japan: Springer.

Kessi, S. (2011). Photovoice as a practice of re-presentation and social solidarity: Experiences from a youth empowerment project in Dar es Salaam and Soweto. *Papers on Social Representations*, *20*(1), 7.1–7.27.

Kessi, S. (2013a). Re-politicizing race in community development: Using postcolonial psychology and photovoice methods for social change. *PINS*, *45*, 17–35.

Kessi, S. (2013b). Transforming previously white universities: Students and the politics of race representation. *New Agenda: South African Journal of Social and Economic Policy*, *50*, 53–56.

Kessi, S., & Cornell, J. (2015). Coming to UCT: Black students, transformation, and discourses of race. *Journal of Student Affairs in Africa*, *3*(2), 1-16.

Kessi, S. Learmonth, D., & Boonzaier, F. (n.d.). Through the lens of marginalised women in Cape Town: Photovoice, empowerment and community-based change. Unpublished manuscript.

Kothari, U. (2006). Critiquing 'race' and racism on development discourse and practice. *Progress in Development Studies*, *6*(1), 1–7.

Laszlo, J. (1997). Narrative organisation of social representations. *Papers on Social Representations*, *6*(2), 155–172.

Long, W. (2014). Understanding 'relevance' in psychology. *New Ideas in Psychology*, *35*, 28–35.

Louw, J., & Danziger, K. (2000). Psychological practica and ideology: The South African case. *Psychologie en Maatchappij*, *90*, 50–61.

Macleod, C. (2004). South African psychology and 'relevance': Continuing challenges. *South African Journal of Psychology*, *34*(4), 613–629.

Mama, A. (1996). *The hidden struggle: Statutory and voluntary sector responses to violence against black women in the home*. London: Whiting & Birch Ltd.

Manganyi, N. C. (1973). *Being black in the world*. Johannesburg: Ravan Press.

Mkandawire, T. (2004). *The spread of economic doctrines in postcolonial Africa*. Geneva: UNRISD.

Mkhize, N. (2004). Psychology: An African perspective. In D. Hook, N. Mkhize, P. Kiguwa, A. Collins, E. Burman & I. Parker (Eds.), *Critical psychology* (pp. 24–52). Cape Town: UCT Press.

Moane, G. (2009). Reflections on liberation psychology in action in an Irish context. In M. Montero & C. Sonn (Eds.), *Psychology of liberation: Theory and applications* (pp. 135–153). New York: Springer Science+Business Media.

Montero, M., & Sonn, C. (2009). *Psychology of liberation: Theory and applications*. New York: Springer Science+Business Media.

Morrell, R. (2001). *Changing men in Southern Africa*. London: University of Natal Press.

Mosse, D., & Lewis, D. (2005). *The aid effect: Giving and governing in international development*. London and Ann Arbor, MI: Pluto Press.

Munck, R., & O'Hearn, D. (1999). *Critical development theory: Contributions to a new paradigm*. New York: Zed Books.

Murray, M. (2000). Levels of narrative analysis in health psychology. *Journal of Health Psychology*, *5*(2), 337–347.

Nederveen Pieterse, J. (1992). *White on black: Images of Africa and blacks in western popular culture*. New Haven, CT: Yale University Press.
Nicholas, L. J., & Cooper, S. (1990), *Psychology & apartheid*. Johannesburg: Vision Publications.
Owusu-Bempah, J., & Howitt, D. (2000). *Psychology beyond western perspectives*. Leicester: BPS Books.
Parker, I. (2005). *Qualitative psychology: Introducing radical research*. New York: Open University Press.
Phoenix, A. (1990). Social research in the context of feminist psychology. In E. Burman (Ed.), *Feminists and psychological practice* (pp. 89–103). London: Sage.
Rappaport, J. (1995). Empowerment meets narrative: Listening to stories and creating settings. *American Journal of Community Psychology, 23*(5), 795–807.
Ratele, K. (2008). Masculinity and male mortality in South Africa. *African Safety Promotion: A Journal of Injury and Violence Prevention, 6*(2), 19–41.
Ratele, K. (2013). Subordinate black South African men without fear. *Cahiers d'Études Africaines, LIII*(1–2), 247–268.
Richards, G. (1997). *'Race' racism and psychology: Towards a reflexive history*. London: Routledge.
Riessman, C. K. (2008). *Narrative methods for the human sciences*. Los Angeles: Sage.
Rodney, W. (1972) *How Europe underdeveloped Africa*. London: Bogle-L'Ouverture Publications.
Said, E. (1978). *Orientalism*. New York and London: Routledge & Kegan Paul.
San Juan Jr., E. (2006). Toward a decolonizing indigenous psychology in the Philippines: Introducing sikolohiyang pilipino. *Journal for Cultural Research, 10*(1), 47–67. doi:10.1080/14797580500422018
Shefer, T. (in press). Resisting the binarism of victim and agent: Critical reflections on 20 years of scholarship on young women and heterosexual practices in South African contexts. *Global Health Promotion*.
Skovdal, M., Ogutu, V. O., Aoro, C., & Campbell, C. (2009). Young carers as social actors: Coping strategies of children caring for ailing or ageing guardians in Western Kenya. *Social Science & Medicine, 69*(4), 587–595.
Smith, L. T. (1999). *Decolonizing methodologies: Research and indigenous peoples*. London: Zed.
Strack, R. W., Magill, C., & McDonagh, K. (2004). Engaging youth through photovoice. *Health Promotion Practice, 5*(1), 49–58.
Van Niekerk, T., & Boonzaier, F. (in press). Rules and representations: Social networks' responses to men's violence against women in South Africa. In M. Hydén, D. Gadd & A. Wade (Eds.), *Response-based approaches to the study of interpersonal violence*. Hampshire: Palgrave Macmillan.
Vaughan, C. (2010). 'When the road is full of potholes, I wonder why they are bringing condoms?' Social spaces for understanding young Papua New Guineans' health-related knowledge and health-promoting action. *Aids Care, 22*(Supplement 2), 1644–1651.
Warner, L. R. (2008). A best practices guide to intersectional approaches in psychological research. *Sex Roles, 59*, 454–463.
Watkins, M., & Shulman, H. (2008). *Towards psychologies of liberation*. New York/London: Palgrave Macmillan.
Wilkinson, S., & Kitzinger, C. (Eds.). (1993). *Heterosexuality: A 'feminism & psychology' reader*. London: Sage.
Yuval-Davis, N. (2006). Intersectionality and feminist politics. *European Journal of Women's Studies, 13*(3), 193–209.

9
EVERYDAY RECONCILIATION

Sandra Obradović and Caroline Howarth

When we turn on the TV after a long day at the office, at school or wherever else we might have spent our day, we are overwhelmed with stories of conflict. These can be large-scale conflicts like wars between nations, medium-scaled conflicts like those between political parties or small-scaled conflicts like the stories we hear about neighbours quarrelling over property and students fighting in classrooms.

We are surrounded by conflict. However, conflict tends to coexist with cooperation. Even during a war between two nations, for example, there is intranational cooperation while the international conflict occurs. Cooperation creates solidarity among members; it creates a sense of 'mutualism' and, in many cases, a sense of shared identity. Conflicts, on the other hand, tend to highlight differences and intergroup tensions. So how do we go from conflict to cooperation? Or, reversely, how do we go from cooperation to conflict?

The focus of this chapter is to consider different approaches to reconciliation and offer insights into intragroup reconciliation within the context of intergroup conflict, an area that is somewhat undertheorised in the reconciliation literature to date. We argue that we must examine the role of 'everyday reconciliation' in promoting intergroup peace-building not just among local communities but also among politicians and policymakers. By 'everyday reconciliation' we mean the ways in which our daily encounters with social and political representations of the past can be reinterpreted to create more nuanced images of conflicts and foster more critical and aware future generations. While theories of intergroup conflict resolution tend to draw clear boundaries between victims and perpetrators, reality is usually messier. Thus, we argue that it is important in theorising about conflict to take into account not only what occurs, but also how it is understood and talked about within local contexts or, to be more precise, how it is *socially represented*. We do so by exploring the ways in which education, intergenerational dialogue and identity politics promote or inhibit the ways in which individuals can critically reflect on their nation's past.

The chapter is divided into three sections where we examine different processes intended to promote reconciliation: (1) top-down approaches that focus on justice, (2) bottom-up approaches that focus on socioemotional aspects and (3) a more multilayered approach that examines the connections between intragroup processes and intergroup relations.

Top down: Promoting reconciliation through justice and punishment

In conflicts, an imbalance is created between individuals, groups or societies that might be material, through inequalities in geopolitical space, resources or number of casualties. It can also be symbolic, where a conflict creates an inequality in social status or social identity recognition. Top-down approaches tend to focus on the former imbalances rather than the latter. This section focuses on three different top-down approaches to conflict resolution as a process leading to reconciliation, including procedural justice, retributive justice and restorative justice, and discusses their relevance for peace-building.

Procedural justice: Fairness and legitimacy of the decision-making process

A procedural justice approach to reconciliation emphasises that the actual process of conflict resolution should be perceived as fair. The argument behind this approach is that if the procedure is considered fair, the institutions distributing punishment become legitimate and therefore people will be more likely to comply with the outcomes (Jackson et al., 2012). Two aspects of this are particularly significant here: (1) the symbolic value conveyed through process and (2) the role of voice in decision making.

Procedure and identity

According to the group-value model proposed by Lind and Tyler (1988), a procedural justice approach to punishment communicates to individuals their value as members of specific groups to society at large. As Murphy (2011) explains, "fair procedures communicate respect and value, while unfair procedures communicate disrespect, marginality or even exclusion from a valued group" (p. 212). This argument is evident in studies examining the role of identity on perceptions of fairness, legitimacy and attitudes towards procedural decision-making processes (e.g., Bradford et al., 2014). Thus, identity has implications for our perceptions of what is just. Yet these perceptions are not simply subjective beliefs; they can also be reflections of social reality. Take the example of undocumented immigrants. They fall out of the category of 'legal citizens' and are therefore not afforded the same rights by authorities as 'ingroup members' are. This lack of recognition of minority groups "has implications for people's abilities to participate in the public sphere" (Hopkins & Blackwood, 2011, p. 215). In line with this, studies have shown that minorities indeed tend to perceive political institutions like the police as less legitimate compared to majority members (Factor et al., 2014), partly because systems of minoritisation are associated with bodies like the police and instances of institutional discrimination. These issues also tie closely to the lack of representation, or voice, in political institutions.

Procedural voice

Tyler (2000) highlights that having a 'voice' is a key element of procedural justice. Individuals "feel more fairly treated if they are allowed to participate ... by presenting their suggestions about what should be done" (p. 121). Maoz (2001), examining the role of voice in dialogue between Israelis and Palestinians, found that participants of majority group status tended to dominate dialogue; however, with time and frequency of meetings, this tended to move towards a greater symmetry. Further, he flags up that this does not necessarily mean that minorities feel powerless and voiceless when faced with majorities, but rather that their choice of silence can function as a form of resistance. Thus, voice and silence can both function to convey or challenge political power. What this kind of work emphasises is the need to understand that some forms of reconciliation may not necessarily lead to justice for minoritised groups, and hence are sometimes resisted. As Dixon, Levine, Reicher and Durrheim (2012) have argued, attempts to improve intergroup relations and reduce prejudice, in particular, may very well end up bolstering structural inequalities between groups. Hence, reconciliation programmes may also sometimes inadvertently support conditions of inequality and injustice. What is important to examine is the perception of justice and legitimacy and the ways in which these may connect to real possibility for agency and social change (Howarth, Wagner, Kessi & Sen, 2012). In sum, when tackling an intergroup conflict, perceived fairness and legitimacy are not only a matter of institutional processes, but are intrinsically linked to our social identities and membership in various social groups.

Retributive justice: 'Just desert' and restoration of equality

Retributive justice "refers to the repair of justice through unilateral imposition of punishment" (Wenzel et al., 2008, p. 375). The emphasis, unlike with procedural justice, is on the end result rather than process as justice is found in the symbolic outcome that punishment brings. When considering retribution, we look at the importance of two issues: (1) the rationale behind punishment and (2) the individualisation of guilt.

Why punish?

Retributive justice has been heavily criticised for conceptualising crime through a Westernised ideology, where an offense is considered not a violation of an individual but rather a violation of the law and the institutions that uphold it (Clark, 2008). Nevertheless, identity plays a role in shaping the motives behind punishment as "people's notion of justice following a transgression depends on how they construe their relationship to the offender and interpret the incident" (Wenzel et al., 2008, p. 376). For example, if the victim considers the perpetrator an outgroup member, motives behind retribution may focus on status and power restoration. This motive functions to safeguard the positive self-image of the ingroup members by distancing them from any similarities to the offender. In contrast, when the goal is to restore a social consensus to the importance of norms and rules, offenders are usually considered as part of the ingroup, and restoration of norms allows for a restoration of the offender back into their community.

Individualising guilt

In a context of intergroup conflict, international crime courts are set up with the hope that individualising guilt will remove "blame from entire ethnic, religious or political groups and therefore negates collective guilt" (Clark, 2008, p. 336) and reduce the likelihood of revenge (Stover & Weinstein, 2004, p. 14). A problem with this approach is that it is often done in isolation from the affected parties. For example, the twin Criminal Tribunals set up in former Yugoslavia (ICTY) and Rwanda (ICTR) have been criticised for their geographical distance from the regions in question (Stover & Weinstein, 2004). In the case of Former Yugoslavia (FY), it is believed that the actual work of the ICTY has had little influence on public opinion and that this has instead been shaped by local elites and "by the manner in which the local media depicts proceedings at The Hague" (Klarin, 2009, p. 90).

In addition to problems of location, cultural and community knowledge are sometimes not adequately accounted for in the setup of international courts. For instance, in the TRC in Sierra Leone, the dichotomous divide between perpetrators and victims did not resonate among locals, as 'perpetrators' of crimes were considered family and/or friends rather than outsiders (Millar, 2012). Thus, in the context of a collectivist culture like Sierra Leone, the imposition of individualised understandings of justice can actually be more harmful than helpful by creating divides between people that were not initially there. Indeed, one of the dangers with retributive justice is that it treats offenders and victims as two separate categories, often seen in isolation from one another.

Restorative justice: Local involvement, restoration and healing

An alternative for reconciliation beyond the punishment paradigms of procedural and retributive justice is restorative justice, "a process whereby parties with a stake in a specific offense resolve collectively how to deal with the aftermath of the offense and its implications for the future" (Marshall, 2003, p. 28). The emphasis is on repair and healing of victims, offenders and the local communities affected by conflict. Unlike retributive justice, which conceptualises crime as a violation of the law, restorative justice understands crime as a violation against individuals and their relations (Clark, 2008). Thus, this approach highlights social context, social relations and communities in a top-down reconciliation process.

Restorative justice as a second chance

The literature on restorative justice has focused on how to repair relations between victims and offenders through various programs such as family group conferences, community boards and victim-offender mediation programs. These programs centre on interaction between affected parties with specific goals for each. For the victims, the programs allow an input in the process and an ability to have voice; for the community, they allow for reaffirmation of social values and norms; and for the perpetrators, they offer an opportunity to apologise for their crimes and get the counselling and rehabilitation they need to become a part of the community again. Thus, the focus is on giving people a second chance and mending relations with the community as a whole.

Reconciliation through local restorative justice

Unlike procedural and retributive approaches to justice, restorative justice is connected most directly to the reconciliation literature where scholars have focused on how institutions and authorities can promote social restoration without resorting to punishment. However, it is not only third-party actors or governmental institutions who initiate peace-building processes in postconflict societies but rather, when it comes to restorative justice measures, civic society members come to play a crucial role. For example, in Rwanda, individualised notions of conflict resolution set up by international actors have been coupled with local *gacaca* courts allowing communities to be directly involved in the process (Clark, 2008).

In other contexts, like East Timor, local communities have focused on innovatively adapting traditional practices to reintegrate refugees and rebuild social relationships (Babo-Soares, 2004), and in Serbia, several NGOs have been set up to deal with issues including returning refugees home, reconciling different versions of the past through dialogue and offering creative spaces like theatres to promote intergroup dialogue (Clark, 2008). There are benefits to these 'local' programs that international justice courts do not have, including (1) their embeddedness in the local context, (2) their involvement and engagement with affected individuals and communities and (3) their attunement and ability to narrow in on specific intergroup problems (ibid). Such international and local approaches should be considered as complimentary aspects promoting reconciliation on different levels of a conflict.

Bottom-up reconciliation

For reconciliation to be meaningful and lasting, it is necessary to reconstruct previously disrupted interpersonal and intergroup relations. There is an extensive literature available on bottom-up reconciliation focusing on the different preconditions for peace-building to start; the different expectations, needs and wants of victims versus perpetrators; as well as the different ways in which reconciliation can be achieved, depending on if the final goal is integration or separation. Though bottom-up reconciliation focuses on the everyday community level, politics and institutions nevertheless play an important role in providing a public space for promoting peace-building but also giving individuals the means with which to do this. By participation we do not mean simply exercising citizenship rights, but also having the ability to politically engage in constructing and shaping representations of reality and possibilities for change (Howarth, Andreouli & Kessi, 2014).

This section will begin by exploring the role that memory has in shaping ingroup identities as well as intergroup relations. Following this, we look specifically at the ways in which identity politics work in contexts of conflict, discussing how both concepts can be used to mobilise social action for conflict but equally to mobilise action for intergroup cooperation and reconciliation.

Memory

Gillis (1994, p. 3) wrote that "memories and identities are not fixed things, but representations or constructions of reality, subjective rather than objective phenomena". After a war, collective memories of a past become key components in justifying the continuation of conflict or supporting its resolution. Recently, literature has discussed the similarities between *collective memories* and *social representations* of the past (Wagoner, 2015), and within this section we will use the two terms interchangeably.

The past, seen as a social construct, is dynamic and constantly being reshaped by the concerns of the present (Halbwachs, 1992). Collective memories of past conflicts or group divisions are kept alive through their association (or anchoring) into new events (Schuman & Rodgers, 2004). In this way, memory can come to play a role in not only hindering reconciliation, but also in justifying a continuation of conflict through a narrative of defence against a potential outgroup threat. Indeed, Monroe (2012), in her discussion on the different 'types' of people in Nazi Germany, showed that supporters of the Nazi regime justified their actions as exercising defensive action against a growing and threatening outgroup, the Jews. Similarly, in the Israel-Palestine conflict, memory serves to connect Israelis "historically to the territory and region" while delegitimising the outgroup in the process (Hammack, 2009, p. 52).

Politicians and authorities also hold a stake in what we consider historical facts as specific historical narratives become 'official' through their institutionalisation in history textbooks, commemoration events and other cultural symbols. As Wilmer (2002) argues, "historical narratives, as a consequence of publicizing education, have become instruments of political agency . . . [they] are routinely appropriated to legitimate political acts" (pp. 80–81).

So what can be done to reverse this process? Much the same as politicians can use negative memories to legitimate political acts, they can also do the opposite.

Social representations of the past can promote reconciliation by allowing for mutual recognition of different 'truths'. However, while confronting the past is important, creating a shared version of the past it not necessarily the end goal, nor is it always possible. Rather, it may suffice to acknowledge and accept the existence of different collective memories and official 'truths' (Kelman, 2008). Thus, memories can function to promote positive intergroup relations by the use of 'positive propaganda' (Hartmann, 2014) that emphasises the heterogeneity of ingroups and creates shared identity dimensions across groups.

Identity

We have argued that social representations of history function as building blocks of social identities. For example, in former Yugoslavia, the revival of ethnic identities prior to the outbreak of war led to a strong emphasis on differences in language, religion and culture, creating a widening gap between the coexisting national groups (Stover & Weinstein, 2004, p. 146). This emphasis on differences that were prior seen as unproblematic was a way for political leaders to gain power and mobilise people for action (Elcheroth et al., 2011). As Wilmer (1998) explains "the process of constructing a 'state' identity is often implicitly nothing more than the articulation of a hegemonic group's identity *as the civic identity*" (p. 107). In former Yugoslavia, this was evident as groups like Serbs and Croats, who had been seen as equals within each nation, suddenly turned into minorities and foreigners in their supposed own country. Thus, we need to understand how politics play a role in shaping our sense of belonging and how the boundaries of our ingroup are shaped by the political goals of elites.

So again we ask, what can be done to reverse this process? Some propose making identities complex, highlighting within-group diversities and outgroup heterogeneity, going beyond the us/them distinction (Maalouf, 2000), while others advocate the promotion of dual identities where a superordinate identification becomes the uniting factor (Kelman, 2004). The rationale behind both arguments is that creating an awareness of the differences among outgroup members, as well as creating mutualities across groups, will allow for a 'humanisation' of the other as well as an increased perspective-taking (Čehajić & Brown, 2010). Superordinate identification, in particular, has been linked to increased across-group helping behaviour (Monroe, 2012) and willingness to forgive perpetrator groups (Wohl & Branscombe, 2005).

Thus, there are a number of different ways to promote more inclusive identities, create commonalities across groups and increase cooperation between groups. One of the most important things to consider, however, is the role of fear and threat in keeping conflicts alive and hindering reconciliation. Conflicts that extend over time can sometimes become 'intractable', leading to zero-sum identities. In other words, a negative interdependence becomes created between my ingroup and your outgroup, and this negative relationship is maintained by fears of future conflict. These fears, in turn, function to legitimise a sense of threat to the ingroup and the need to act defensively before the other strikes (Sapountzis & Condor, 2013).

Several studies have shown how majority groups and/or perpetrator groups position themselves as victims under threat, justifying their actions from a position of defence rather than aggression (Monroe, 2012; Reicher et al., 2005). Thus, we see the need for identities to be renegotiated in order for intergroup reconciliation to be successful. How exactly this can be done is the topic of the next section, as we argue that overcoming identity threats and fears is only possible by first acknowledging the wrong-doing of one's own ingroup, which in turn allows for a more nuanced understanding of past conflicts and intergroup relations.

Everyday reconciliation

There is a problem, or rather a gap, in the current literature on intergroup reconciliation. Theories focusing on the various requirements, stages and sides involved in reconciliation tend to do so in a binary way. However, as Hammack's (2009) work on the reproduction of conflict through narratives shows, these theories at times prove to be problematic when the question of peace-initiation is considered. Although individuals can come to accept some of the preconditions for reconciliation, such as recognition of the outgroup and acknowledgment of their rights to territory or other claims, who is responsible for initiating peace is not always clear because ingroups do not consider themselves responsible for that part. Herein lies the core issue and the focus of this last section – *who* is to begin the peace process, and *how* do we get them to do it?

Much of the literature discusses the various needs of victims vis-a-vis perpetrators when it comes to psychological, emotional and social changes. However, in conflicts that have been prolonged over time, how can we really say that there is a clear division between the victim and the perpetrator group? Further, if we hypothetically manage to do so, we are faced with yet another problem. Do these groups themselves accept these labels? As is well known, there is a tendency in intergroup conflicts for both sides to claim victimhood at the hands of the other. Thus, how do we get to the point where one group accepts its wrongdoings and acknowledges itself as the perpetrator group, or at least *one* of the groups of perpetrators, that needs to take the first step towards reparations? We will argue in what remains of this chapter that this can emerge from everyday, intragroup reconciliation.

Everyday reconciliation refers to the daily encounters with past conflicts and how these are managed within the ingroup. This approach starts with looking at the definition of 'us' and how this in turn has consequences for how we see 'them'. It is common to find that in intergroup conflicts, the atrocities performed by the ingroup are often silenced or minimised both within institutional contexts, like schools and the governments, as well as culturally, through symbolism and 'selective' memory in everyday encounters and debates. Thus, everyday reconciliation aims to explain how an ingroup accounts for and comes to terms with its past transgressions. Therefore, we argue that we need to place greater attention on processes of intragroup reconciliation, where the focus becomes on overcoming the ingroup's past and hopefully furthering more tolerant, critical and open future generations.

Rarity of self-criticism

It is expected of perpetrator groups that they acknowledge their transgressions against other groups and ask for forgiveness in order to initiate a process of intergroup reconciliation. However, how much evidence is there that this actually occurs? Though there has been an increased use of political apology for past atrocities, this top-level acknowledgement may not reflect the opinions or beliefs of the everyday citizen, but rather be seen as an attempt to better the public image of a nation. Unfortunately, even in this case, where an elite apology is offered, it is usually for events of great temporal distance. In a meta-analysis of studies on self-criticism within nations concerning their 'shameful' pasts, Leach, Zeineddine and Čehajić-Clancy (2013) found that acknowledgement and criticism was rare. Their meta-analysis shows a great absence of guilt, shame and responsibility for the past in studies relating to diverse historical periods, geographical locations and with various temporal distances to the present. This finding is rather telling and ironic as those nations that are involved in setting up international tribunals, demanding other nations to acknowledge their wrong-doings, are in turn not willing to practice what they preach. In Britain and the Netherlands, for example, little agreement was voiced with criticism of their colonial actions and compensation was not considered necessary (Leach et al., 2013). We then ask, in situations where 'perpetrators' are expected to initiate reconciliation but no one is willing to acknowledge that they fit the bill, how do we move on?

Education

There is an existing debate within the education literature as to the purpose of history education in schools. Should history be seen as a body of unquestioned knowledge which creates belonging and cohesion, or should it function to teach young generations the skills to be critical and aware of the multiple perspectives and interpretations through which history can be narrated? Educating students about their country's past helps to create and define what it means to be a citizen, and yet in relation to peace-building efforts and managing intergroup relations, history education tends to be pushed to the margins (Van Ommering, 2015). In contrast, Marko-Stöckl (2007/2008) argues that the foundation for reconciliation is in schools. It is in this context that conflicts and differences are kept alive as new generations are taught to understand the 'other' as an enemy and as different from the self.

However, and most importantly, it is also in this context that a national consciousness and identification with a nation's past, present and future occurs (Van Ommering, 2015). In other words, teaching history is a way of learning about 'us' and 'our' past. In doing so, a dominant perspective on the past is enforced and criticism may be limited. Indeed, the rarity of self-criticism in history education has been studied and confirmed, and postconflict textbooks have been shown to emphasise a sense of victimhood within groups emerging from conflict (Dutceac Segesten, 2011). Thus, the way history is being taught is critical for the prevention of future conflicts and the creation of a stable peace. This is because "the young must learn critical thinking about the causes of the recent wars, and the nature of stereotyping, tolerance and human rights" (Elcheroth et al., 2014, p. 324).

Further support for this argument can be found in Licata and Klein (2010), discussed in Leach et al.'s (2013) meta-analysis. Their study showed that across generations in Belgium, young students and parents tended to report more feelings of guilt about their colonial past than did grandparents. This was explained as an outcome of the recent institutional switch towards a more negative framing of Belgian colonisation. In other words, schools were influential in creating a rise in self-criticism as the institutional 'facts' were teaching Belgians that they had a negative past which needed to be acknowledged. In addition, studies have shown that narratives of the past that offered more explicit and detailed accounts of events tended to increase feelings of self-criticism and anger towards one's ingroup's actions in the past (Leone & Sarrica, 2014). Thus, rarity of self-criticism might be an outcome of uninformedness rather than indifference. In other words, there are more factors that need to be considered when judging the ability with which young people are able to be critical of their ingroup's past, one of which is family socialisation.

Intergenerational dialogue

When approaching intergenerational transmission of knowledge, specifically knowledge of past atrocities, the literature tends to be divided on the traumatic versus healing outcomes of this process. Though this debate is outside of the scope of the current topic and chapter, the point we wish to discuss is the social role that intergenerational dialogue can play in allowing future generations to become more open citizens. When looking at the role of intergenerational dialogue and trauma, research on children of Holocaust survivors in Brazil found that the transmission of trauma was more common in families that silence the past compared to those with more open styles of communication (Braga et al., 2012). Silencing the past is often justified through arguments of protection, not wishing to burden their children with stories of what they suffered through themselves (Obradović, forthcoming). In addition, silencing of history can become harmful to the intergenerational transmission of not only history, but also culture and traditions (Wallace et al., 2014). In other words, silencing the past can have consequences for identity as the inability to know one's past the same way as one's parents can create differences in how history is incorporated into one's sense of self and membership in a wider community. In turn, this can lead to a sense of discontinuity as younger generations become unable to share their (critical) feelings about the past with older generations, while older generations in turn are unable to pass on their stories and memories to younger family members.

In their research on intergenerational dialogue in Rwanda, Wallace et al. (2014) found that the positive outcomes of dialogue for youth included the emergence of critical thinking, greater positivity towards the future and possibilities of reconciliation as well as a removal of fears of discussing the past and initiating dialogues with other community members. Thus, there are benefits to this kind of dialogue as it not only opens up space for more community-wide dialogue, but also teaches younger individuals that the past is not necessarily a shameful topic to be avoided. Rather, this kind of dialogue creates possibilities for stories of *positive* intergroup cooperation and relations to be told, giving the past a more nuanced image. Furthermore, it allows young people to be a part of the debate about reconciliation. Research in Northern Ireland and Bosnia showed that younger people felt that their potential as peacemakers or troublemakers in the future was largely shaped by the behaviour of politicians and older generations, a process being negatively influenced by the lack of intergenerational dialogue (Magill & Hamber, 2011).

Ingroup identity matters

A study carried out in Serbia by the first author (Obradović, forthcoming) exploring the relationship between social representations of the past and identity found that there was a close link between remembering and ingroup belonging. Forgetting the past was equated with self-blaming and the perspective of the 'other', thus limiting the extent to which younger generations could be critical of the past without simultaneously feeling a sense of betrayal of their ingroup. In this context, echoing Braga et al.'s study (2012), though participants were not part of the same families, there was a noticeable lack of familial dialogue on the past, contradicting the great emphasis both generations placed on remembering. In addition, the dialogues people have about the past and the identities derived from it are not only shaped by their social groups and environments, but also by which discourses afforded legitimacy on a political level (Penic, Elcheroth & Reicher, 2015).

Thus, we need to consider the role that everyday reconciliation has for promoting more inclusive and open identities, but also how this use of everyday dialogue, imagery and social representing functions to create just the opposite of inclusive identities. For example, the political manipulation of social representations of identity can function to justify social exclusion of specific groups, a strategy used in many countries such as the UK, France and Greece, where the rise in support for nationalistic political parties is linked to an increased sense of outgroup hostility. This is precisely what everyday reconciliation can challenge. By promoting intergenerational dialogue and intergroup cooperation, creating more critical education and allowing people to ask questions without being positioned as other, we can work to overcome identity fears by nuancing representations of the past. Here, politicians and policymakers can help by emphasising the contextual difficulties and issues that led to conflict, creating awareness of the circumstances that caused war. This will (hopefully) lead to an understanding of ingroup and outgroup members as humans acting in difficult situations, creating more understanding and acceptance of what was done by and to one's ingroup.

Conclusion

The present chapter has mapped out several different approaches to reconciliation, drawing on both legal, top-down approaches as well as more bottom-up or mixed approaches. While the discussion has highlighted the importance of bottom-up theories and practices of reconciliation, it is important to note that we do not ignore the significance of third-party members in promoting peace. These actors can play crucial roles in promoting effective contact, dialogue and cooperation between groups as well as in regulating this process as it occurs. In addition, communal practices like the work of NGOs, grassroots movements, school projects and community activities should be promoted and funded. Here, political leaders play important roles as authorities within a nation whose support of reconciliation will have a tremendous influence on the progress of peace-building. However, this support needs to be genuine, not to be confused with a strategic political goal or motive to enhance one's own power, and it needs to be connected to the perspectives of those 'on the ground'. Hence we need to be critically reflective about reconciliation – who proposes it, for whom and to what end.

In other words, we need to be critical about what reconciliation means to the various actors involved in the processes. The three distinct sections give us an insight into the various ways in which not only conflict but also the peace process itself can be conceptualised differently depending on whose interests are being met. In other words, the different parties involved may represent the same reconciliation initiative differently. Thus, the normative assumptions around what is considered 'successful' reconciliation need to be explored and debated. Policymakers are in a unique position to join in on this debate with social psychologists, peace psychologists, educators and NGOs to draw on their extensive research and knowledge in creating the best-fit practices for their own particular contexts. This literature should not be read as generalizable but rather as different approaches that worked in different context. Thus, more emphasis should be placed on contextual sensitivity when employing different peace-building strategies.

Last, but not least, it is important to note that reconciliation is not only a process of mending relations with outside groups but also relations with inside groups – those in the past and those in the future. Without accepting and knowing history as a story filled with both the good and the bad of a nation, future generations will not learn to be critical and open to different narratives of history. Rather, the future will be shaped by the concerns of the past and the historical drama in which an ingroup is trapped, with a focus on intergroup conflict and outgroup blame, making it impossible to rid the group of the burden of seeking protection, security and safety from the 'imagined' threats of tomorrow.

This focus on everyday reconciliation should be an important step to develop in examining how we can move from contexts of intergroup conflict to contexts of cooperation and intergenerational, intergroup and international dialogue.

References

Babo-Soares, D. (2004). Nahe biti: The philosophy and process of grassroots reconciliation (and justice) in East Timor. *The Asia Pacific Journal of Anthropology*, 5(1), 15–33.
Bradford, B., Murphy, K., & Jackson, J. (2014). Officers as mirrors: Policing, procedural justice and the (re)production of social identity. *British Journal of Criminology*, 54(4), 527–550.

Braga, L., Mello, M., & Fiks, J. (2012). Transgenerational transmission of trauma and resilience: A qualitative study with Brazilian offspring of Holocaust survivors. *BMC Psychiatry*, *12*(1), 134–145.

Čehajić, S., & Brown, R. (2010). Silencing the past: Effect of intergroup contact on acknowledgment of ingroup atrocities. *Social Psychological and Personality Science*, *1*(2), 190–196.

Clark, J. (2008). The three Rs: Retributive justice, restorative justice, and reconciliation. *Contemporary Justice Review: Issues in Criminal, Social, and Restorative Justice*, *11*(4), 331–350.

Dixon, J., Levine, M., Reicher, S., & Durrheim, K. (2012). Beyond prejudice: Are negative evaluations the problem and is getting us to like one another more the solution? *Behavioural and Brain Sciences*, *35*(6), 411–466.

Dutceac Segesten, A. (2011). *Myth, identity, and conflict: A comparative analysis of Romanian and Serbian textbooks*. Lanham, MD: Lexington Books.

Elcheroth, G., Corkalo Biruski, D., & Spini, D. (2014). Conclusion: War and community: What have we learned about their relationship? In D. Spini, D. Corkalo-Biruski & G. Elcheroth (Eds.), *War, community and social change: Collective experiences in the former Yugoslavia* (2013th ed., pp. 227–236). New York: Springer.

Elcheroth, G., Doise, W., & Reicher, S. (2011). On the knowledge of politics and the politics of knowledge: How a social representations approach helps us rethink the subject of political psychology. *Political Psychology*, *32*(5), 729–758.

Factor, R., Castilo, J., & Rattner, A. (2014). Procedural justice, minorities, and religiosity. *Police Practice and Research*, *15*(2), 130–142.

Gillis, J. R. (1994). Memory and identity: The history of a relationship. In J. R. Gillis (Ed.), *Commemorations: The politics of national identity* (pp. 3–24). Princeton, NJ: Princeton University Press.

Halbwachs, M. (1992 [1952]). *On collective memory* (translated and edited by L. A. Coser). Chicago: University of Chicago Press.

Hammack, P. (2009). Exploring the reproduction of conflict through narrative: Israeli youth motivated to participate in a coexistence program. *Peace and Conflict: Journal of Peace Psychology*, *15*(1), 49–74.

Hartmann, F. (2014). A slipping memory: Can the international criminal tribunal be a bulwark against oblivion? (Invited voice). In D. Spini, D. Corkalo-Biruski & G. Elcheroth (Eds.), *War, Community and social change: Collective experiences in the Former Yugoslavia* (2013 ed., pp. 199–204). New York: Springer.

Hopkins, N., & Blackwood, L. (2011). Everyday citizenship: Identity and recognition. *Journal of Community & Applied Social Psychology*, *21*(3), 215–227.

Howarth, C., Andreouli, E., & Kessi, A. (2014). Social representations and the politics of participation. In K. Kinnvall, T. Capelos, H. Dekker & P. Nesbitt-Larking (Eds.), *The Palgrave handbook of global political psychology* (pp. 19–38). London: Palgrave.

Howarth, C., Wagner, W., Kessi, S., & Sen, R. (2012). The politics of moving beyond prejudice. *Behavioural and Brain Sciences*, *35*(6), 437–438.

Jackson, J., Bradford, B., Hough, M., Myhill, A., Quinton, P., & Tyler, T. R. (2012). Why do people comply with the law? Legitimacy and the influence of legal institutions. *British Journal of Criminology*, *52*, 1051–1071.

Kelman, H. C. (2004). Reconciliation as identity change: A social psychological perspective. In Y. Bart-Siman-Tov (Ed.), *From conflict resolution to reconciliation* (pp. 111–124). Oxford: Oxford University Press.

Kelman H. C. (2008). Reconciliation from a social-psychological perspective. In A. Nadler, T. Malloy & J. D. Fisher (Eds.), *Social psychology of intergroup reconciliation* (pp. 15–32). Oxford and New York: Oxford University Press.

Klarin, M. (2009). The impact of the ICTY trials on public opinion in the former Yugoslavia. *Journal of International Criminal Justice, 7*(1), 89–96.

Leach, C., Zeineddine, F., & Čehajić-Clancy, S. (2013). Moral immemorial: The rarity of self-criticism for previous generations' genocide or mass violence. *Journal of Social Issues, 69*(1), 34–53.

Leone, G., & Sarrica, M. (2014). Making room for negative emotions about the national past: An explorative study of effects of parrhesia on Italian colonial crimes. *International Journal of Intercultural Relations, 43*(Part A), 126–138.

Licata, L., & Klein, O. (2010). Holocaust or benevolent paternalism? Intergenerational comparisons on collective memories and emotions about Belgium's colonial past. *International Journal of Conflict and Violence, 4*(1), 45–57.

Lind, E. A., & Tyler, T. R. (1988). *The social psychology of procedural justice.* New York: Plenum Press.

Maalouf, A. (2000). *On identity.* London: Harvill Press.

Magill, C., & Hamber, B. (2011). 'If they don't start listening to us, the future is going to look the same as the past': Young people and reconciliation in Northern Ireland and Bosnia and Herzegovina. *Youth Society, 43*(2), 509–527.

Maoz, I. (2001). Participation, control, and dominance in communication between groups in conflict: Analysis of dialogues between Jews and Palestinians in Israel. *Social Justice Research, 14*(2), 189–208.

Marko-Stöckl, E. (2007/2008). My truth, your truth – our truth? The role of history teaching and truth commissions for reconciliation in former Yugoslavia. *European Yearbook of Minority Issues, 7,* 327–352.

Marshall, T. F. (2003). Restorative justice: An overview. In G. Johnstone (Ed.), *A restorative justice reader: Texts, sources, context* (pp. 28–45). Cullompton, UK: Willan Publishing.

Millar, G. (2012). 'Our brothers who went to the bush': Post-identity conflict and the experience of reconciliation in Sierra Leone. *Journal of Peace Research, 49*(5), 717–729.

Monroe, K. (2012). *Ethics in an age of terror and genocide: Identity and moral choice.* Princeton, NJ: Princeton University Press.

Murphy, K. (2011). The relationship between procedural justice, emotions and resistance to authority: An empirical study. In S. Karstedt, I. Loader & H. Strang (Eds.), *Emotions, crime and justice* (pp. 211–234). Oxford, UK: Hart Publications.

Obradović, S. (forthcoming). Don't forget to remember: Collective memory of the Yugoslav wars in present-day Serbia. *Journal of Peace Psychology.*

Penic, S., Elcheroth, G., & Reicher, S. (2015). Can patriots be critical after a nationalist war? The struggle between recognition and marginalization of dissenting voices. *Political Psychology,* doi: 10.1111/pops.12262

Reicher, S., Hopkins, N., Levine, M., & Rath, R. (2005). Entrepreneurs of hate and entrepreneurs of solidarity. *International Review of the Red Cross, 87*(860), 621–637.

Sapountzis, A., & Condor, S. (2013). Conspiracy accounts as intergroup theories: Challenging dominant understandings of social power and political legitimacy. *Political Psychology, 34*(5), 731–752.

Schuman, H., & Rodgers, W. L. (2004). Cohorts, chronology, and collective memories. *Public Opinion Quarterly, 68*(2), 217–254.

Stover, E., & Weinstein, H. M. (2004). *My neighbor, my enemy: Justice and community in the aftermath of mass atrocity.* Cambridge: Cambridge University Press.

Tyler, T. R. (2000). Social justice: Outcome and procedure. *International Journal of Psychology, 35*(2), 117–125.

Van Ommering, E. (2015). Formal history education in Lebanon: Crossroads of past conflicts and prospects for peace. *International Journal of Educational Development, 41,* 200–207.

Wagoner, B. (2015). Collective remembering as a process of social representations. In G. Sammut, E. Andreouli, G. Gaskell & J. Valsiner (Eds.), *Cambridge handbook of social representations* (pp. 143–162). Cambridge: Cambridge University Press.

Wallace, D., Pasick, A., Berman, P., & Weber, Z. (2014). Stories for Hope-Rwanda: A psychological–archival collaboration to promote healing and cultural continuity through intergenerational dialogue. *Archival Science, 14*(3), 275–306.

Wenzel, M., Okimoto, T., Feather, G., & Platow, N. (2008). Retributive and restorative justice. *Law and Human Behavior, 32*(5), 375–389.

Wilmer, F. (1998). The social construction of conflict and reconciliation in the former Yugoslavia. *Social Justice, 25*(4), 90–113.

Wilmer, F. (2002). *Social construction of man, the state and war: Identity, conflict, and violence in former Yugoslavia*. New York and London: Routledge.

Wohl, M. J. A., & Branscombe, N. R. (2005). Forgiveness and collective guilt assignment to historical perpetrator groups depend on level of social category inclusiveness. *Journal of Personality and Social Psychology, 88*(2), 288–303.

10
CLIMATE CHANGE ACTIVISM BETWEEN WEAK AND STRONG ENVIRONMENTALISM

Advocating social change with moderate argumentation strategies

Paula Castro, Mehmet ali Uzelgun and Raquel Bertoldo

Introduction

There are certain social transformations that are to a large extent socially accepted as desirable, and yet they fail to happen, or at best they progress very slowly. Today some of these transformations are supported by global governance tools, such as international protocols and treaties, signed in supranational forums and afterwards transposed to national legislative frameworks (Castro, 2012; Giddens, 2009). Climate change (CC) is a case in point, and it is perhaps the best current example of a global governance effort, that is of an issue being tackled around the world through governance tools that are developed at the global level and then passed on to the national and local levels (de Búrca et al., 2013; Uzelgun & Castro, 2015). This type of global governance requires the new meaning – that is values, norms, information – incorporated in the new policies to travel from more global to subsequently more local levels. It moreover requires the new meaning to travel from the legal/policy spheres to the consensual, everyday, national and local universes (Castro & Mouro, 2011; Uzelgun & Castro, 2015).

In this context, the role of environmental and climate activists and campaigners in advancing new policies and new meaning is a crucial one. Activists and campaigners, engaging in the public debate through going to climate demonstrations, doing NGO work or defending environmental protection in everyday conversations are placed in central positions for mediating between levels and universes. Through their formal discourses in international and national meetings, but also through their informal communicative practices, they contribute for new meaning and new actions to filter into everyday contexts and social relations.

However, in both their mundane conversations and more formal discourses, activists and campaigners can defend very different ideas and courses of action.

They can argue for *weak* or *strong* versions of sustainability, a central distinction in the environmental domain (Dobson, 1990; Dryzek, 2005; Kashima, Paladino & Margetts, 2014; Uzzell & Rathzel, 2009). The *weak* version, entailing a *moderate* type of social change, claims that market forces and technology can bring about a sustainable society (Douglas & Wildawsky, 1992), assumes production is a neutral process simply responsive to demand and assumes that achieving social change means mainly remodelling the behaviour of individuals and altering lifestyles (Castro, 2012; Uzzell & Rathzel, 2009). The *strong* sustainability version, in contrast, maintains the critical vision inherited from the environmental movement of the 1970s (see Castro, 2006; Dobson, 1990), demanding a fundamental transformation of current relations of production and consumption, contesting the workings of the free market and fully refusing the assumption that there is a power balance between producers and consumers (Mol & Spaargaren, 2000; Uzzell & Rathzel, 2009). This more *radical* version of social change thus defends *changing society* beyond simple adaptation (Dryzek, 2005).

The divide between *weak* and *strong* environmentalism opens up a wide space for debate and resignification, showing that sustainability in general, and CC adaptation in particular, are goals that, although governed by globally accepted treaties and regulations, have many areas where consensus is fragile and regarding which the "battle of ideas" (Moscovici & Markova, 2000) is constant. In turn, this opens different argumentative options for activists. At this juncture, then, a better psychosocial understanding of everyday environmental politics under conditions of global governance crucially requires exploring such aspects as (1) whether activists of the CC cause seem to argue for more moderate or more radical versions of sustainability and courses of action, and whether they are using confrontational or conciliatory arguments for that; and (2) whether those individuals who argue for strong or radical social change are more or less positively viewed than those defending more moderate options.

Studying communication and argumentation

For addressing these types of questions, we need theories offering concepts useful for linking the new meaning produced in specialized or reified universes – such as the policy ones – to the everyday contexts of communication and argumentation. The theory of social representations (TSR) (Moscovici, 1976), the rhetorical approach (Billig, 1999) and argumentation theory (van Eemeren & Grootendorst, 2004) offer some of these. Together they provide important contributions for understanding how everyday conversations take up and help shape the transformation of new political and policy meaning while they travels from global to local contexts.

Social representational analyses of how new meaning travels in society identified different communicative genres (Moscovici, 1976). The initial analyses, focusing on the mass media, showed how in the communicative genre of *propagation* a complex process of conciliation and accommodation of old and new meanings takes place, transforming both; in *propaganda*, in turn, a dichotomic world is depicted by arguments organised to highly agree with one set of beliefs and to highly disagree with another (Moscovici, 1976). These different genres are also expressed in "conversation at the interpersonal level" (Castro, 2006; Moscovici & Marková, 2000, p. 402), relying upon different small words, like conjunctions (Billig, 1999), and different formats (Castro, 2006). Propagation relies on the 'yes-but' concessive format (e.g., 'yes, CC is a serious problem, but we are already doing a lot to solve it'), instrumental for conciliation (Uzelgun et al., 2015). Propaganda uses the 'yes/no' contrasting format (e.g., *'yes, we need to act upon CC now, no, there is no time for compromises'*), closing down space for negotiation and conciliation (Castro, 2006).

Taking these concepts to empirical use in the CC debate, we present in this chapter two studies aiming to contribute to a better understanding of the everyday politics of conversations about change. The first study specifically explores the interpersonal consequences of individuals supporting more or less radical options. Recent studies about feminist and environmental activism suggest that individuals tend to associate radical or 'typical' activists with negative stereotypes, devaluing them and being less influenced by them than by moderate activists (Bashir et al., 2013). These studies fail, however, to clarify what will happen in the long run to the influence of radical activists, an important issue, since classical studies of minority influence (Moscovici, Lage & Naffrechoux, 1969) show that radical messages, although less influential in the short term, can be more influential in the long term. These studies fail also to explore another important short-term issue: whether activists describing a more radical position are more devalued on the dimension of *competence* or on the dimension of *warmth*, as these are identified by the stereotype content model (Russell & Fiske, 2008).

Study 1 specifically explores this latter question. Consequently, the study clarifies Bashir et al.'s (2013) findings by 'breaking' the stereotypes associated with activists in the two basic dimensions of the SCM, so as to examine in which of them radical and moderate activists are more negatively seen. It also extends previous research by looking at how the global divide between weak and strong environmentalism enters the everyday politics of interpersonal representations.

The second study examines the arguments of committed campaigners from environmental NGOs (ENGOs) when these respond – in the context of an interview – to the (radical) objections and critiques that a (fellow) activist poses to moderate or weak options for CC adaptation. It is explored if the activists respond by using the confrontational arguments of propaganda, or the negotiated, mitigated ones of propagation. By looking at these questions, we extend previous research by looking at how the global (political) divide between weak and strong environmentalism enters the everyday politics through the argumentation strategies of members from crucial mediating systems in CC, the ENGOs.

After presenting each study we will discuss them together.

Study 1. Defending radical change: How are environmental activists seen?

As mentioned, the variety of environmental positions is usually organised by differentiating between weak and strong sustainability, one advocating for 'radical' and another for 'moderate' change (Dobson, 1990; Dryzek, 2005; Kashima et al., 2014). The radical tendency proposes profound transformations in the economical and sociopolitical organisation of our societies, while a more moderate view proposes individualised solutions based in a managerial approach and a remodelling of individual behaviours (Uzzell & Rathzel, 2009) that some call *mundane* environmentalism (Kashima, Paladino & Margetts, 2014).

In this context, different types of environmental actions are open to individuals. Stern (2000) proposes the following systematisation of environmental actions, organised according to how public and radical their support for sustainability is: activist behaviours, nonactivist or moderate behaviours of the public sphere, and private sphere behaviours.

- **Activist behaviours:** These involve "movements to move forward in the face of inertia and active resistance" (Stern et al., 1999, p. 82) and concern those behaviours intending to alter the way society deals with environmental issues. These behaviours include the direct involvement with environmental associations and public demonstrations (Stern, 2000).
- **Moderate activist behaviours of the public sphere:** These correspond to "political activities that are less public or present less risk than engaged activism" (Stern et al., 1999, p. 82) but which still involve public displays of support for environmental causes. Examples are writing letters to political officials, signing petitions, financially contributing to environmental movements or sharing information through social media or informal conversations. They may have indirect impact "by influencing public policies" (Stern, 2000, p. 409) and can be taken as an expression of moderate activism.
- **Private sphere behaviours:** These refer to household (i.e. private) behaviours that aim to reduce the direct impact of individual activities, form part of *weak* environmentalism and are fostered by current public policies: energy saving practices, home insulation, waste recycling. Such behaviours "have environmentally significant impact *only in the aggregate*" (Stern, 2000, p. 410) and are a widely accepted, 'mundane' form of environmentalism (Kashima et al., 2014).

As mentioned, Bashir and colleagues (2013) found that individuals involved in radical activist behaviours are seen through negative stereotypes (e.g. tree-hugger, hippie). However, their study does not attempt to 'break' the evaluation of the radical activists in the two basic *competence* and *warmth* dimensions identified by the stereotype content model (SCM) (Fiske et al., 2002). These two dimensions of interpersonal (Russell & Fiske, 2008) or intergroup perception (Fiske et al., 2002) have also been seen as informative of the dimensions of *agency* and status (competence) or cooperation and altruism (warmth) (Fiske et al., 2002; Russell & Fiske, 2008). The association of these two basic dimensions with characteristics related with the relative position of social groups in society is what justifies our interest in resorting to this model to better understand social change. For example, the perception of *competence* (measured with traits like intelligence and capability), was seen to be associated with an individual or group's socioeconomic status (Fiske et al., 2002) as well as with their concrete agentic capacity to achieve an end or goal. And the perception of *warmth* (measured with traits like friendliness) was seen to be associated with an individual or group's degree of cooperation for the common good, perceived closeness or (lack of) competition (Fiske et al., 2002; Russell & Fiske, 2008; Wojciszke, Abele & Baryla, 2009). In this sense, warmth can be taken as an indicator of the extent to which an individual is prepared to cooperate for upholding a certain social order. Consequently, drawing from this model, activists expressing strong environmentalism should be socially devalued in terms of warmth but not competence.

For examining these ideas, we compared the evaluation of individuals saying that they adopted different types of proenvironmental behaviours – activist, moderate/nonactivist and private sphere behaviours (Stern, 2000) – in terms of competence and warmth (see Bertoldo, 2014). Drawing from SCM (Fiske et al., 2002), we expected: (1) all individuals to be equally perceived as competent, given that they explicitly affirm their intentions through behaviours – an *agentic* expression of their orientations (Abele & Wojciszke, 2007); (2) individuals displaying the radical activist behaviour to be perceived as *less warm* than the others, given that the goal of radical social change behind activist behaviours makes them regarded as less cooperative and less communal (Abele & Wojciszke, 2007), characteristics associated with the warmth dimension. We also examine which individuals – radical activists, moderate activists and individuals that perform the private sphere behaviours – are more valued on the dimension of competence as compared to that of warmth.

Method

Participants were 177 first-year psychology students from the Lisbon University Institute (ISCTE-IUL). They averaged 20.96 (17–42, SD = 4.2) years old and 87.5% female. They responded to an online questionnaire where vignettes describing statements of individuals reporting five different behaviours were randomly presented. The individual's gender was not specified, and the vignettes described the behaviours as offered in response to a question posed by a TV reporter in the streets on Earth Day: "And you, what do you do for the environment?" (see Table 10.1).

Participants were asked to read the response and form an image of the person who gave it. Then they were asked to *judge* this person on the traits composing the dimensions of competence (capable, intelligent, and competent, $\alpha = .84$) and warmth (good person, friendly, warm, cheerful and tolerant, $\alpha = .73$) using

TABLE 10.1 Vignettes in which individuals describe different proenvironmental behaviours.

	Type of behaviour	Response to the question "and you, what do you do for the environment?"
Public sphere	1. Activist	I am an activist in an environmental association that defends radical changes in the way our society deals with environmental protection. Whenever I can, I also take part in demonstrations aiming to change environmental politics.
	2. Moderate activist	I sign petitions related with environmental protection or with carbon reduction. Whenever I can, I pay those carbon-offset taxes.
Private sphere	3. Organic purchase	When I go shopping, I prefer buying organic fruits and vegetables to regular ones.
	4. Recycling	In my house I separate the paper, glass and packages to deposit them later in the appropriate containers.
	5. Water and energy saving	I avoid as much as I can to waste energy and water at home. I always turn domestic appliances off so that they are not left in 'stand by' mode. I also tend to always turn off the lights in the divisions where nobody is.

a scale from 1 (not characteristic at all) to 7 (very characteristic) (for details, see Bertoldo, 2014).

Results

Two one-way anovas were performed on the scores of competence and warmth. Results show that all individuals are similarly evaluated in terms of competence ($F(4,172) = 1.77, p = ns$), but differentiated in terms of warmth ($F(4,172) = 2.87, p < .05, \eta_{p2} = .06$). Posthoc tests indicate that the differences found mainly concern the person attesting an activist behaviour (seen as the least warm) and the person who recycles (seen as the warmest) (see Table 10.2). Scores of competence and warmth were also directly compared across conditions (student's t test). Individuals presenting activist ($t(33) = 4.96, p < .001$), organic purchase ($t(35) = 3.50, p < .01$) and water/energy saving behaviours ($t(34) = 3.48, p < .01$) were seen as more competent than warm. Equivalent levels of competence and warmth were attributed to the individuals describing moderate activist and recycling behaviours.

These results show then that individuals are not, as expected, differentiated in terms of competence, the dimension that is associated with agency. They are, however, differentiated in the *warmth* dimension, the one associated with degree of cooperation for the common good or with the established social norms and representations (Bertoldo, 2014). Individuals describing activist behaviours and strong

TABLE 10.2 Differences between the competence and warmth attributed to the individuals describing different types of proenvironmental behaviours.

	Activist		Moderate activist		Organic purchase		Recycling		Water & energy saving	
	M	DP	M	DP	M	DP	M	DP	M	DP
Compet.	5.03	1.57	4.36	1.36	5.05	1.43	5.08	1.60	5.18	1.30
Warmth	3.89[a]	1.17	4.34[a,b]	1.08	4.37[a,b]	1.09	4.79[b]	1.03	4.38[a,b]	1.03

a, b: difference between the means as measured by the Scheffe post-hoc test; means classified under the same letter are not statistically different.

environmentalism are seen as less warm in relation to individuals presenting recycling behaviours (private sphere, weak environmentalism), who are seen as warmer. Furthermore, and unlike moderate activists, they are seen as more competent than warm.

Discussion

This first study sought to understand in which of the two basic interpersonal evaluation dimensions (competence and warmth) radical environmental activists – that is those ostensibly calling for radical change and presenting activist behaviours – are more devalued. Results show that they are valued in the competence dimension – they are seen both as competent and as more competent than warm – and somehow devalued in the warmth dimension. We interpret this as a social penalisation for failing to uphold a certain social order and challenging established norms and social representations (see Bertoldo, 2014) and thus see this result as extending Bashir et al.'s (2013) analysis in a more social way. One limitation of the study is the fact that the gender of the individual acting was not specified. Considering that women usually display higher environmental attitudes than men (Félonneau & Becker, 2008), taking this aspect in consideration could constitute an interesting clue for future research.

Now that we have shown that radical activists are seen as less warm, although competent, and suggested a possible psychosocial justification for this pattern, let us ask whether the discourse of activists themselves avoids choosing (too) radical arguments and formats, which can be taken as a sign of an awareness of these processes. We now turn to investigating how climate activists communicate their concerns.

Study 2. Striving to be moderate? Environmental NGO activists on climate change solutions

In their emergence phase, environmental concerns were organised as a *radical* 'counter-culture' (Castro, 2006; Douglas & Wildawsky, 1982; Laessøe, 2007). However, during the 1970s and 1980s, when the growing environmental concern of the public was institutionalised through (moderate) public policies, ministries and laws, and the green movements faced a decisive moment (Castro, 2012; Laessøe, 2007). They could choose to integrate the (*moderate*) environmental policy decisions and forums (Jamison, 1996) or to stay outside, remaining more radical but excluded from most decision making. To be considered serious actors and to gain legitimacy in national and international policy processes, ENGOs then chose to become more professional, more scientific and less 'ideological' (Yearley, 1996).

In this context, concerns with how to achieve and maintain their legitimacy vis-à-vis the global social and policy norms are crucial aspects of the current communication efforts of activist organisations. Many authors suggest that an NGO's legitimacy rests upon their acknowledgement of the broader and pre-existent legitimising norms and discourses (Bernstein, 2011; Edwards & Hulme, 1996). This is also implied by the previous study. In terms of the theory of social representations (Moscovici, 1976), this means that polemic public interventions characterised by direct confrontation and dichotomic depictions of the problems – that is a propaganda type of oppositional yes/no communication – are likely to be avoided. To examine whether this is the case, this study focuses on a controversy about the utility of carbon offsetting mechanisms.

Carbon offsetting – paying a small percentage to compensate the carbon emissions created by one's consumption (for instance by financing the plantation of trees as "carbon sinks") – is presented as a moderate solution against CC from a weak sustainability perspective. For its supporters, it is a way to 'undo' one's carbon emissions. From a strong sustainability perspective, carbon offsetting is criticised for perpetuating hegemonic policy agendas that fail to engage with (unequal) relations of production (Uzzell & Rathzel, 2009) and sustainable habits (Bumpus & Liverman, 2008). In this sense, it is a nonactivist, consumer-based mechanism that depends on private sphere behaviours, as others from Study 1 presented. In this second study, we aim to examine how climate activists and committed campaigners from ENGOs argue about and represent the controversial policy of carbon offsetting when challenged and supported by the arguments of an activist arguing for radical change.

Video-elicitation interviews: Instigating argumentation

As part of a larger study on CC communication ($N = 22$), interviews with non-governmental CC campaigners from Portugal and Turkey were conducted. The participants were members of a variety of ENGOs that are active in CC communication and action in the two countries, as well as transnationally, and are thus actors of a global governance regime. They were presented with a series of short video excerpts selected so as to offer confrontational arguments. Our assumption was that the people featured in the video excerpts would be the main argumentative opponents of the interviewees (Uzelgun, 2014).

Here we focus exclusively on the video excerpt that features a climate activist who contests the usefulness of carbon-offset mechanisms.[1] In it, the climate activist endorses a strong version of social-ecological change. He argues that climate action should aim for "more profound systemic changes in the way we organise our societies and economies" and "moving away from the growth based model, reigning in the corporate self-interest". Such counterhegemonic political options are by him contrasted with carbon offsetting, "a fictitious commodity" that has been "created to exploit the rising levels of climate consciousness". Importantly, however, in arguing against "placing all of the responsibility on individual consumers" the activist uses a concessive format: "I think personal lifestyles have a role to play in how we respond to climate change, but I think our choices as individuals are still very limited in the context of climate change". Through this 'yes-but' concession, the activist both recognises the potential contributions of the changes in personal lifestyles and their limits. Following from Study 1, we expected the two oppositions that he resorts to – carbon offsetting versus collective political action, individual versus systemic changes – to instigate argumentation characterised by mitigated claims, indirect disagreements and negotiation of the available options.

In analysing the arguments that address the claims made in the video excerpt, we employed the basic tenets of argumentation theory (van Eemeren & Grootendorst, 2004; see Uzelgun et al., 2015), and the theory of social representations (Moscovici, 1976). Attention was specifically paid to the use of discourse markers (e.g. but, so, still), salient argumentative forms (e.g. yes/no, yes-but) and functions (e.g. concession, dichotomisation), which were linked to the genres of communication (e.g. propaganda, propagation). Once the salient argumentative forms were identified, about 10% of the corresponding arguments were reconstructed following the procedures described in van Eemeren and Grootendorst (2004).[2] As demonstrated with examples in the following section, this reconstruction makes it possible to see the social and dialogical functions of the argumentative moves carried out by the interviewees and the representation of the carbon offsetting controversy in the propaganda and propagation genres.

Analysis

A salient feature of the arguments used by our interviewees to address the claims made by the climate activist (henceforth, the activist) was their concessive form. This form was functional in mitigating the disagreements over the uses of carbon offsets and moderating the activist's discourse on the incompatibility of (consumer-based) private and public-political efforts. Here is a short example:

Example 1, Interview 16

I'd say that I half agree with him. We certainly need to move on to community efforts, eeh, however *we should not despise* either individual efforts, eeh, or the economics of the problem. Because that's what make most business and most people think. So, I think we have to do both.

The yes–but conceding format used here (rather than a yes/no contrasting format characteristic of propaganda) was a determining characteristic of the interviews, and it can be simplified as follows:

1   We have to pursue both community and individual efforts.

    1.1a (Yes) We certainly need to move onto community efforts.
    1.1b (However) We should not despise individual and economic efforts.

        1.1b.1 Individual and economic efforts are what make most business and most people think.

In this example, the interviewee addresses the claims made by the activist only indirectly, by employing an agreement preface (Billig, 1991; Pomerantz 1984). It shows that this initial affirmative clause (1.1a) is functional in appropriating the point made by the opponent: The interviewee represents it as "the need to move onto community efforts" in a way that conceals the claims made about the "growth-based model" and "corporate self-interest". Once such claims are reconstructed in a more easily acceptable form and acknowledged, the disagreement follows: "We should not despise" individual efforts (1.1b). Notably, the "we should not despise" argument is here a second-order claim through which the interviewee actively criticises the use of a propaganda-type, confrontational discourse in the CC debate.

In the conclusion (marked by *so*), the interviewee emphasises that "we have to do both". He thus effectively replaces the yes/no opposition of propaganda he picks out from the activist's discourse, by a yes-but propagation format. In doing this, he reconciles what was presented to him as two contradictory poles, presenting his position at equal distance to both. In sum, the conflict generated by the activist between the private sphere and public-political "efforts" is eliminated, providing reasons (1.1b.1). Notably, these reasons explicitly appeal to the majority view, that is the dominant or hegemonic meaning systems.

The next excerpt is an example of those arguments in which the position of the interviewee is slightly inclined towards one of the poles in countering the claims made in the video excerpt:

Example 2, Interview 8

As a person, I had my doubts, and I'm sceptical about carbon trading, but I don't agree with, in that sense, I . . . I think still *human lifestyle changes do matter*. Unlike him, I mean, he . . . I understand he is trying, because he is trying to make a point, and he's focusing more on the systematic, systemic changes, obviously, that part I agree. That's why I'm focused on international change, these are you know, or governmental, national levels. There has to be, you know, rules, regulations, applying big business, related to everything . . . but at the end of the day, I think, humans, I mean, as persons each of us, changing our lifestyles you know doing . . . respecting and doing more things, saving energy, changing, *these are important*.

As in the previous example, the interviewee offers an initial agreement as preface, and only then raises her counterpoint, reconstructed as 1.1b:

1 Personal lifestyle changes are important in mitigating climate change.

    1.1a (Yes) I'm (also) sceptical about carbon trading.
    1.1b (But) Still, personal lifestyle changes do matter.

Then she "understands" the point the activist is trying to make, and claims that it is what she is doing by focusing on international change. Another yes-but concessive construction follows: on the affirmative clause, she concedes that "there has to be ... rules, regulations, applying [to] big business". In the but clause, "changing our lifestyles" as persons, "respecting" and "saving energy" are defended against the claims imputed to the activist:

1 Personal lifestyle changes are important in mitigating climate change.

    1.2a (Yes) Focusing on systemic changes is important.
    1.2b (Yes) There have to be international and national level rules, regulations for big business.
    1.2c (But) Personal changes in our lifestyles are (as) important.

In order to emphasise the rhetorical aspect of the manoeuvring carried out here, it is crucial to identify the argumentative relations between the activist's and the interviewee's points. The argument conceding the need for regulations (1.2b) does not actually represent an argument raised by the activist. It rather draws on an implication of the activist's argument about "com[ing] together in communities, to start organising, to create political pressure for the bigger systemic changes that need to happen". The interviewee interprets this implication in the framework of international and national level "regulations". More critically, against the activist's criticism of carbon offsets, the interviewee argues that "changing our lifestyles" is important (1.2c). Thereby, she represents the case of the activist as being *against* changes in individual lifestyles. However, the activist's claim against carbon offsets rests upon characterising them as offering "peace of mind", an obstacle against change. By doing a not very charitable interpretation of the activist's case (see Lewiński, 2012), the interviewee cuts out the confrontational elements from the activist's discourse in a way that opens up space for arguing in a conciliatory way, in favour of the use of carbon offsets.

Let us now turn to a third example, in which the interviewee tends to agree with the activist.

Example 3, Interview 6

Yes I agree with him. Eeh, *but maybe one point*. Eeh, I wouldn't say I don't believe in carbon offsets, but, as he mentions, carbon offset is being promoted as a eeh, thing that is really tricky. And as he said it is eeh making people think

Climate change activism **157**

that ok, I will buy a plane ticket and pay 5 dollars more, and somewhere in the world a tree whatever, might be eeh put in place, oh now I'm relieved, because I paid my 5 dollars. And it's not really individual action that can save the world, that I believe. However, *carbon offsets eeh can be used as a mechanism*, if it were to be, eh used in a holistic way.

In this example, after a first signal of agreement the interviewee goes on to contend not that she believes in carbon offsets, but instead that she is *not against* carbon offsets. She endorses a series of arguments offered by the activist, specifying her points of agreement with him. Looking there, we can say she indeed agrees with him. "However", she then reprises the "one point" signalled at the beginning and arrives at the conclusion that carbon offsets can be used as a mechanism, if they are used in a *holistic way*. That is, instead of dismissing the potential utility of carbon offsetting, the interviewee strives to assign conditions for its use in a way to open space for offering conciliatory, propagation-like arguments. Her argumentation resembles that of interviewee 16 (the first example), in that it tends to raise a second-order criticism about how CC mitigation efforts are communicated ("I wouldn't say . . .").

A similar, but more implicit, evaluative component characterises also our last example:

Example 4, Interview 20

Eeh . . .he's saying that . . . well this . . . collective action is needed, it's not individual, basically. I mean basically he's saying that carbon offsetting, which eeh, which is a way supposedly to, eh, pay for neutralising your emissions, whether that's in personal or corporate level, is actually not neutralising them. And again the science is probably a little bit more grey than that. There is some neutralisation happening, I mean, carbon dioxide or other greenhouse gases . . . some of them do cycle, they are absorbed, and they are reabsorbed and reemitted. But, eh, it's, it's not complete enough, I mean it's not like . . . 99% of them getting reabsorbed and only 1% is leaking. There's probably a huge amount that aren't. . . . *So*, I think he's grossly speaking correct, eh, it's been hugely unregulated still, and even when it is regulated, the regulation structures have . . . tended towards being very permissive.

In the first sentence of this excerpt, the criticism of the activist is represented as located in the opposition between "collective" and "individual" levels of action, and as he is credited with saying that carbon offsetting does not work (does not actually neutralise) at both levels, the interviewee disagrees. Importantly, her disagreement is mitigated by the use of qualifiers: "*a bit* more grey" and "there is *some* neutralisation happening". In other words, she disagrees with the activist's claim only to some extent. As in the foregoing example, her criticism targets the way the claims are communicated, namely in yes/no (black-and-white) oppositions, instead of in a grey zone of conciliation. That she does not reject the activist's claim becomes obvious in the succeeding part of the excerpt, where she concludes that "he's grossly speaking correct", since regulation structures of offsetting mechanisms tend towards being too permissive, and there is probably a huge amount that is not neutralised. Through this shift between the contested positions and negotiating the amount that is "neutralised", she manages to convert a yes/no type of confrontation into a yes-but type of reconciliatory criticism.

After the discourse marker *so*, the interviewee announces the problem as carbon offsetting still being hugely unregulated, arguing that regulation structures tend towards being too permissive, in support of the activist's "grossly correct" position. Hence, she represents and reiterates the activist's case by removing the main confrontational element (carbon offsets do not neutralise anything) and providing more moderate reasons. As in the vast majority of the arguments that respond to the video excerpt, in her agreement with the activist's argument for radical social change, she refrains from confronting the policy norm (carbon offsets can be used to counter CC), transforming an oppositional discourse into a concessional, reconciliatory one.

Discussion

This study has explored the dialogical and social functions of the conciliatory argumentative formats that were saliently used by ENGO activists in the dispute on the utility of carbon offsets. As shown by exemplary excerpts, through yes-but conceding formats it becomes possible to recognise the views of an argumentative partner that expresses counterhegemonic views, transforming, criticising and in this case *moderating* them, while upholding one's views (Billig, 1991; Moscovici, 1976). Notably, although the discourse of argumentative partner (the climate activist) involved both confrontational (yes/no) and concessional (yes-but) elements, our interviewees have mainly focused on the confrontational, nonhegemonic ones, precisely to reinterpret and transform them into concessional forms. They strived to eliminate the conflicts and to avoid oppositions, dichotomies and disagreement both with the activist, who argued for radical social-ecological change, and with the 'milder', that is more moderate, proposals for socioeconomic change.

The organising principles of such manoeuvring were the *prefacing* of disagreements, the *restraining* of one's claims and the *mitigation* of the perceived conflict, in relation to issues of self-presentation and politeness (e.g. Holtgraves, 1997; Sifianou, 2013). It is well established that the rhetorical power of formal and expert discourse (Baber & Bartlett, 2005; Sifianou, 2013) owes to the recognition of the perspectives of others and to the balanced consideration of options. However, this is only a starting point for interpreting complex political controversies such as this one, and explanations can also be sought at the societal, not just the interactional, level.

Concerning the societal level, our focus was on whether ENGO members would go along with the radical discourse of a fellow activist in arguing against the hegemonic discourses on carbon offsetting. This was an indirect way of exploring whether their arguments might exhibit signs of awareness of the negative stereotypes attributed to activists. Seeing that our interviewees strived to avoid confrontational, all-or-nothing arguments, refraining from direct disagreements with both sides of the controversy, we can say that their communication efforts are characterised by *propagation* of alternatives rather than *propaganda* of one strongly supported choice. In many instances, instead of arguing for radical change, they argued against arguing for radical change, issuing second-order criticisms concerning the confrontational elements in the presented argument. In terms of the foregoing study, their everyday political behaviours can thus be depicted as concerned with offering a self-image (as an active minority) as warm and upholding cooperative intentions, and in view of these, as nonpartisan, reasonable parties to the global policy debate on CC.

Conclusion

In the two studies presented we brought together contributions from social and environmental psychology and first showed that individuals who are represented as wishing to radically change society are regarded with negative stereotypes affecting warmth-related traits. We took this as an indication that radical proposals for change are seen as violating cooperative expectations. Then we showed that the discourse on CC solutions of ENGO members seems to refrain from radical, confrontational, propaganda-like arguments. We interpreted this as suggesting that this discourse is possibly showing awareness of the negative stereotypes of radicals and seeks to reflect a cooperative image. Hence, the conjunction of the two studies seems to indicate that, in dealing with the 'battle of ideas' in climate policy and discourse, activists would better – and indeed do – avoid strong disagreements and oppositions.

This seems in line with Giddens's (2009) proposition that all actors of climate policy need to work with the 'geopolitical realities' and economic exigencies, rather than work against them by choosing a one-sided focus on risks and 'boundaries of nature'. However, if the option of recognising the geopolitical realities affords a certain level of legitimacy and warmth to ENGO campaigners, it also seems to make them enter the debate with the rather consensual arguments of weak change, incompetent to a certain degree in challenging the dominant policy agendas.

In summary, then, ENGOs active in the CC debate seem to be caught in the dilemma of trying to achieve radical change by using moderate arguments, avoiding being seen as uncooperative. This means that they might be placing themselves, through this strategy, in a position of also avoiding provoking the "cognitive conflict" that according to the genetic model is necessary for private "conversion in the long-term", and focusing on obtaining public "compliance in the short term" (Moscovici, Lage & Naffrechoux, 1969). This model shows that minority "individuals and groups that *innovate* exercise influence by creating or increasing conflict". In striving to establish a new norm, such a minority may choose to refuse compromises and maintain a "constant pressure" with the goal to "wring concessions from the majority" (Moscovici, 1985, p. 21). On the other hand, individuals, groups and institutions that aspire to fully generalise a new norm that already gathers some consensus tend to avoid "the prospect of conflict and its potential repercussions" (ibid, p. 19) via compromises, with a view of progressively achieving a fuller "consensus which satisfies everyone" (ibid, p. 19).

Todays' moderate options of CC campaigners, in their role as carriers of global meaning to national and local contexts, can be thus contributing "to re-absorb" the conflicts previously created by the innovating minority groups (Moscovici, 1985, p. 21). Moderate options that avoid setting the scenery for a more difficult and more prolonged debate can be seen to favour – in the organisation of their everyday politics – a debate oriented to the short term, "confined primarily to the period of social interaction" (ibid, p. 33). This orientation to the short term, together with the avoidance of open conflict and the concomitant use of hegemonic arguments in order to oppose hegemonic goals, may be one of a multiplicity of aspects that may help explain the situation we highlighted in the beginning of this chapter – that is why certain social transformations that are to a large extent socially accepted and seen as desirable continuously fail to happen, or at best progress very slowly. As authors of the present text, we would consequently argue that a more difficult debate, which does not avoid conflict and does use arguments carrying counterhegemonic meaning, is much needed regarding climate change.

Notes

1 The video excerpt used can be found at www.youtube.com/watch?v=uk9Ev91jjQ8, starting from the beginning to 02:20 (duration 2 minutes 20 seconds).
2 These procedures involve, in summary, *deletion* of those parts of the discourse that are not relevant to the difference of opinion at stake, *addition* of those parts that are relevant but are held implicit, *substitution* of ambiguous expressions by clear ones and *permutation* of parts of the discourse in a way that brings out the best of their relevance to the argumentative process.

References

Abele, A. E., & Wojciszke, B. (2007). Agency and communion from the perspective of self versus others. *Journal of Personality and Social Psychology, 93*, 751–763.
Baber, W. F., & Bartlett, R.V. (2005). *Deliberative environmental politics.* Cambridge: MIT Press.
Bashir, N. Y., Lockwood, P., Chasteen, A. L., Nadolny, D., & Noyes, I. (2013). The ironic impact of activists: Negative stereotypes reduce social change influence. *European Journal of Social Psychology, 43*, 614–626.
Bernstein, S. (2011). Legitimacy in intergovernmental and non-state global governance. *Review of International Political Economy, 18*, 17–51.
Bertoldo, R. (2014). *A Valorização social do pró-ambientalismo enquadrado por normas formais: Uma análise psicossocial comparativa entre Brasil e Portugal* (Unpublished doctoral dissertation). Lisbon University Institute, ISCTE-IUL, Lisbon. Retrieved from https://repositorio.iscte-iul.pt/handle/10071/8490
Billig, M. (1991). *Ideology and opinions: Studies in rhetorical psychology.* London: Sage.

Billig, M. (1999). *Freudian repression: Conversation creating the unconscious*. Cambridge: Cambridge University Press.
Bumpus, A. G., & Liverman, D. (2008). Accumulation by decarbonization and the governance of carbon offsets. *Economic Geography, 84*, 127–155.
Castro, P. (2006). Applying social psychology to the study of environmental concern and environmental worldviews: Contributions from the social representations approach. *Journal of Community & Applied Social Psychology, 16*, 247–266.
Castro, P. (2012). Legal innovation for social change: Exploring change and resistance to different types of sustainability laws. *Political Psychology, 33*, 105–121.
Castro, P., & Mouro, C. (2011). Psycho-social processes in dealing with legal innovation in the community: Insights from biodiversity conservation. *American Journal of Community Psychology, 47*, 362–373.
de Búrca, G., Keohane, R. O., & Sabel, C. F. (2013). *New modes of pluralist global governance*. University Public Law and Legal Theory Working Papers. Paper 386. New York. Retrieved May 22, 2014 from http://lsr.nellco.org
Dobson, A. (1990). *Green political thought*. New York: Routledge.
Douglas, M., & Wildawsky, A. (1992). *Risk and culture: An essay on the selection of technical and environmental dangers*. Berkeley, CA: University of California Press.
Dryzek, J. S. (2005). *The politics of the earth: Environmental discourses* (2nd ed.). Oxford: Oxford University Press.
Edwards, M., & Hulme, D. (1996). Too close for comfort? The impact of official aid on non-governmental organizations. *World Development, 24*, 961–973.
Félonneau, M. L., & Becker, M. (2008). Pro-environmental attitudes and behavior: Revealing perceived social desirability. *Revue Internationale de Psychologie Sociale, 21*(4), 25–53.
Fiske, S. T., Cuddy, A. J. C., & Glick, P. (2002). A model of (often mixed) stereotype content: Competence and warmth respectively follow from perceived status and competition. *Journal of Personality and Social Psychology, 82*, 878–902.
Giddens, A. (2009). *The politics of climate change*. Cambridge: Polity.
Holtgraves, T. (1997). Yes, but . . . Positive politeness in conversation arguments. *Journal of Language and Social Psychology, 16*, 222–239.
Jamison, A. (1996). The shaping of the global environmental agenda: The role of non-governmental organisations. In S. Lash, B. Szerszynski, & B. Wynne (Eds.), *Risk, environment and modernity* (pp. 224–245). London: Sage.
Kashima, Y., Paladino, A., & Margetts, E. A. (2014). Environmentalist identity and environmental striving. *Journal of Environmental Psychology, 38*, 64–75.
Læssøe, J. (2007). Participation and sustainable development: The post-ecologist transformation of citizen involvement in Denmark. *Environmental Politics, 16*, 231–250.
Lewiński, M. (2012). The paradox of charity. *Informal Logic, 32*, 403–439.
Mol, A. P. J., & Spaargaren, G. (2000). Ecological modernisation theory in debate: A review. *Environmental Politics, 9*, 17–49.
Moscovici, S. (1976). *La psychanalyse, son image et son public*. Paris: Presses Universitaires de France.
Moscovici, S. (1985). Innovation and minority influence. In S. Moscovici, G. Mugny & E. van Avermaet (Eds.), *Perspectives on minority influence* (pp. 9–51). Cambridge: Cambridge University Press.
Moscovici, S., Lage, E., & Naffrechoux, M. (1969). Influence of a consistent minority on the responses of a majority in a color perception task. *Sociometry, 32*, 365–380.
Moscovici, S. & Marková, I. (2000). Ideas and their development, a dialogue between Serge Moscovici and Ivana Marková. In G. Duveen (Ed.), *Social representations: Explorations in social psychology* (pp. 18–77). Cambridge: Polity.

Pomerantz, A. (1984). Agreeing and disagreeing with assessments: Some features of preferred/dispreferred turn shapes. In J. M. Atkinson & J. Heritage (Eds.), *Structures of social action* (pp. 57–101). Cambridge: Cambridge University Press.

Russell, A. M. T., & Fiske, S. T. (2008). It's all relative: Competition and status drive interpersonal perception. *European Journal of Social Psychology, 38*, 1193–1201.

Sifianou, M. (2013). The impact of globalisation on politeness and impoliteness. *Journal of Pragmatics, 55*, 86–102.

Stern, P. C. (2000). Toward a coherent theory of environmentally significant behavior. *Journal of Social Issues, 56*, 407–424.

Stern, P. C., Dietz, T., Abel, T., Guagnano, G. A., & Kalof, L. (1999). A value-belief-norm theory of support for social movements: The case for environmentalism. *Research in Human Ecology, 6*, 81–97.

Uzelgun, M. A. (2014). *Science and rhetoric in a globalizing public sphere: Mediating systems of climate change knowledge and action* (Unpublished doctoral dissertation). Lisbon University Institute, ISCTE-IUL, Lisbon. Retrieved from https://repositorio.iscte-iul.pt/handle/10071/8839

Uzelgun, M. A., & Castro, P. (2015). Climate change in the mainstream Turkish press: Coverage trends and meaning dimensions in the first attention cycle. Published before print in *Mass Communication and Society, 18*, 730–752. doi:10.1080/15205436.2015.1027407

Uzelgun, M. A., Mohammed, D., Lewiński, M., & Castro, P. (2015). Managing disagreement through *yes, but . . .* constructions: An argumentative analysis. *Discourse Studies, 17*, 467–484.

Uzzell, D., & Räthzel, N. (2009). Transforming environmental psychology. *Journal of Environmental Psychology, 29*, 340–350.

Van Eemeren F. H., & Grootendorst, R. (2004). *A systematic theory of argumentation: The pragma-dialectical approach*. Cambridge: Cambridge University Press.

Wojciszke, B., Abele, A., & Baryla, W. (2009). Two dimensions of interpersonal attitudes: Liking depends on communion, respect depends on agency. *European Journal of Social Psychology, 39*, 973–990.

Yearley, S. (1996). Nature's advocates: Putting science to work in environmental organizations. In A. Irwin & B. Wynne (Eds.), *Misunderstanding science* (pp. 172–190). Cambridge: Cambridge University.

COMMENTARY ON PART II

Culture, narrative and the everyday dynamics of identity

Helen Haste

The arguments of the previous five chapters capture some of the core strivings of social psychologists since their earliest days. There has always been a tension between extracting core features of behaviour and believing that such extraction is inevitably and misleadingly selective, or that behaviour does not exist in isolation and extraction per se is a meaningless activity. This distinction is useful and predicates very different approaches to research design, and indeed within each there is scope for much epistemological variation. There can be positivism within extraction models and within contextualising models, just as there can be critical perspectives in both qualitative and quantitative methods. Fetishising methodology, to use Moscovici's phrase, can happen anywhere, as can the fallacy, first pointed out by Pliny the Elder, that we only define as worthy of study what it is that we have the tools to measure.

The five chapters focus on diverse versions of critiquing extraction, and they attempt to develop models and methods that take account of context. I will first summarise the critiques of extraction models, then I will consider the emergent models, theory-building and methodological issues which take account of context.

Laboratory experimentation iconically 'extracts', because by definition it is designed to isolate what are perceived to be the core elements of the phenomenon. Questionnaire-based attitude research also may do this, as the pursuit of 'pure' item wording in questionnaire design inherently assumes that a single thing is being measured. Attitude work then typically involves methods to establish that a cluster of items measure a unitary phenomenon, further refining the process of extraction. This is also true of many methods of personality typology. These methods reflect an assumption that the phenomenon in question is static unless modified by substantial events or forces. Further, they are largely enduring attributes of the *individual person*. People 'have traits', they 'have dispositions' to obey authority, they 'hold attitudes'. Laboratory experimentation explores first what the static phenomenon is (and whether it is universal or distributed according to different person typologies), and second, it explores what kinds of conditions might destabilise the stasis – including whether this is a temporary or long-term change.

These general critiques of extraction models are reflected in different ways in all five chapters, but Reicher and Jogdand point out something more extensive, that in fact the originators of many classic studies in social psychology did not pursue a purely extractive model; they saw their experiments as part of a much larger canvas and were fully aware of the dangers of selection and reduction. The problem lies in how these classic studies, especially the dramatic work of Milgram, Zimbardo, Festinger and Asch, which touches on issues that appeal to topical or popular concerns, enter into the canon of psychological science – and perpetuate an overly simplistic model of what an 'experiment' is and does. (I must personally admit to reading Asch more thoroughly only some three decades after I first encountered [and later taught] his experiments on group pressure, and only then realising the rich complexity of his ideas and how they fitted into broader theory.)

Bowdlerising subtle theorists for the consumption of the young (and the public) contributes considerably to the fetishising of method; this is one critique. However, another critique concerns the social environment of the experiment; what are the social desirability or situational expectations of the experimental situation? In many social psychology experiments, including both Zimbardo's and Milgram's as Reicher and Jogdand note, a crucial aspect is the effect of different forms of instruction, and the data show how important this linguistic context is. However as they and other chapters in different ways note, there are many other cues about the situation and its expectations. These can be the physical isolation of 'subjects' and the deliberate overt exclusion of social contact. They can also be 'isolation' in attitude or belief studies which by focusing only on specific topics or on specific ways to address material frame the exercise and limit access to 'everyday' ways for responding. When researchers look closely at (often informal) material on the social context of experiments – whether in a laboratory or a real-life context – they can see the multiple overt and covert cues, plus the multiple ways of interpreting them open to the respondents, as Reicher and Jogdand describe.

What model of the human?

One of the aspects of such framing is the tendency, throughout psychology, to treat human beings primarily as 'puzzle solvers', engaged in individualised cognitive tasks involving logic and the arrival at 'solutions' – often unique 'right' answers. This is unsurprising in a field dominated for so long by the study of the processes of learning and the route to resolving uncertainty and ambiguity whether in perception, cognition or decision making. There is also the overarching meta-question of 'what makes for "good" performance?' (which many observers have also pointed out is a particularly 'American' question). Puzzle-solving also lends itself to the neat construction of experimental tasks, and their analysis. Drawing heavily on the ideas of Jerome Bruner (who, at the time of this writing, is still a magnificently active thinker at 100 years old), I have explored three implicit models of the human that we find in psychology: the puzzle-solver, the story-teller and the tool-user (Bruner, 1990; Haste, 2008, 2009). They make very different assumptions about what processes are important and what is the relationship between the individual and the social and linguistic environment. The five chapters in different ways reflect departure from the dominant puzzle-solver model.

Puzzle-solving, as noted, emphasises cognition and logic and is essentially individualistic. Affect is ignored or treated as either interference or possibly as a motivating factor-enhancing performance – it is peripheral to the main process. The story-teller model has a quite different focus, treating humans as essentially social beings and meaning-making as a socially constructed dialogic process. Narrative, rather than logic, is central not only because it is a core linguistic form, necessarily social and interactive, but because the form of thinking, and of communication, is different from logic.

As the five chapters illustrate in different ways, narrative is effective first because it *contextualises* both meaning and value. The chapter by Kessi and Boonzaier particularly describes how narratives work. An event is described, a theme or argument is presented, and this is done in a way that includes, either by allusion or explicit description, a causal explanation for its origins or purpose and the likely consequences or effects. The allusions made are culturally familiar to the audience (or explicitly explained if not) and engage the audience through factual common ground but also with an appeal to affect. Shared values, whether to enhance common ground or as a means to persuade, are reflected in the examples chosen by using explicit adjectives and nouns and the positioning of the protagonists (Davies & Harré, 1990; Harré & Moghaddam, 2003). Another feature of narrative, as Bruner points out, is that very young children can follow a story and understand its meaning long before they can engage in logical functioning; narrative is a foundational feature of interpreting the world and of communication. A major implication is also that communication is about argumentation and persuasion and the negotiation of co-constructed meaning (Billig, 1995).

The tool-user model derives much from Vygotsky and Bakhtin (Bakhtin, 1986; Vygotsky, 1978; Wertsch, 1998). It incorporates a role for the individual agent, actively constructing meaning 'inside the head' but constantly in dialogue with a wide range of tools and experiences in interaction with the social and physical environments, as well as narrative and dialogic construction of meaning in linguistic interaction. The experience of interacting physically with the world and being able to modify it as well as master it shapes and frames ways of thinking, such as in metaphors we invoke to make meaning. An example is how new technologies change our social practices and also how they alter the metaphors we use to describe and explain. New media have dramatically expanded the social practices of communication (Allen & Light, 2015; Gosling, 2012; Haste, 2009; Haste & Hogan, 2012). Models of mind, for both scientists and laypersons, were profoundly changed by the development of computers (Gardner, 1987; Gigerenzer, 2000).

Metaphors frame not only how we explain things, but also the values we assign to them. Andreouli, Kadianaki and Xenitidou show how Greek identity, inclusion and exclusion derive from the strong and powerfully validated experiences of family ties and allegiances. Obradović and Howarth show how in many situations of long-standing conflict, appeals to retribution or punishment are not useful because acts of violence are seen and experienced as acts between groups of persons that damage relationships rather than acts in which an individual agent breaks a law and should be held accountable to those who administer the law. The social structures which define the nature of the transgression and how it should be governed are very differently conceptualised and experienced. The *experience* of the violence is not one of law-breaking but of relationship-breaking. Therefore, the narratives of the remedy for intractable conflict, and likely effective strategy, emphasise reconciliation and the restoration of social consensus between the groups themselves, not 'top-down' justice.

The tool-user model may also be useful for addressing a critique that pervades the five chapters: that experience is not taken into account in many social psychological studies. First, the investigation assumes a 'here and now' snapshot that is isolated from what respondents might bring to it. But also, meaning-making, attitudes and values are the *products* of action and interaction with the social and physical environments rather than just their antecedent determinants.

Meaning-making as a core process

A shift to narrative analysis, reflected in the five chapters, is profound not only because of the emphasis on language but because it is a shift to treating humans as 'meaning-makers'. Meaning-making is more than information processing. First, it assumes that information and experience do not come in a prepackaged form to be passively ingested. If people do take in information, it is because it is familiar and fits their existing framing. To make meaning is to construct, select and modify. The construction of meaning first takes place within a social and cultural context – the narratives and discourses that are available. Second, a great deal of meaning-making takes place in dialogic interaction, including linguistic dialogue and finding common ground face to face and also dialogue with other aspects of the environment, including manipulating physical objects and space. The five chapters give us different examples of these processes. Investigating meaning-making therefore manifestly requires that we take account of local and contextual factors, not just those that might operate as situational cues at the time of the study. Cultural narratives, cultural practices and the cultural norms of relationships have until recently rarely been considered in psychology, as much focus has been on the presumed isolated individual wrestling with a problem-solving or value-assessing task.

The five chapters illustrate powerfully that context is not just a background variable but a core to the process of meaning-making. As Andreouli, Kadianaki and Xenitidou point out, narratives of Greek national identity contain core criteria around ethnicity and also the concept that migration implies betrayal of one's country and identity of origin. Defining one's own and others' Greek civic identities requires manipulation of ethnicity in conjunction with the civic criteria of citizenship. Castro, Uzelgun and Bertoldo note that there are two quite distinct narratives of sustainability with very different implications for civic action. 'Weak' forms of sustainability are consistent with modification of individual action or tweaks of existing social or economic practices. 'Strong' forms of sustainability require challenging economic and political structures; individual action is at best palliative, at most a dangerous distraction, and the outlook is pessimistic if radical change is not implemented.

A key aspect of narrative is the way that cultural and individual change are effected. Social change requires the creation of counternarratives. It is not enough to deny or declare invalid a dominant narrative that informs meaning-making, positioning and identity, though these may be first steps. Effective change requires counternarratives which enable the reframing of power relations, positioning of groups, identity and the actions and agency available for resistance and reconstruction. As noted previously, Obradović and Howarth spell out the implications of very different narratives of accountability within retributive and restorative justice after periods of intractable conflict. Reicher and Jogdand explore the narratives both of the tradition of untouchable status within Hinduism and the counternarratives that have emerged to challenge this in order to transform both dalit identity and perceptions of other Hindus.

We see this in the discourses reported by Andreouli, Kadianaki and Xenitidou regarding the construction of possible Greek identities. Kessi and Boonzaier powerfully describe two dimensions of counternarrative. First is the pressing need for researchers to become aware of, and counter, the postcolonial narratives that too often frame the research questions which perpetuate versions of difference, inequality and entitlement. Second, they emphasise the way that talking about or reflecting upon current narratives brings to consciousness the underlying dynamics of power, relationships and also potential sites of empowerment and emancipation. Third, they describe how counternarratives emerge in periods of resistance and change, deconstructing the dominant narratives. Kessi and Boonzaier also explicate in detail the intersectionality of narratives and the need to recognise that there are different narratives for race, gender and class and it is at the interaction of these narratives in particular contexts, and the necessary counternarratives, where change is needed.

Context and culture matter

The critique around cultural context therefore is far more than even a matter of dominant values which may differ and be salient diversely for different groups. The critique requires that we start from the assumption that exploring the cultural narratives and the representations of social and ethical institutions and of identity are prerequisites of any social psychological research on how people make meaning (Haste, 2013). Arguably, this implies methods that go beyond thematic analysis, which categorises content only and fails to consider what discursive analysis offers – what people are doing with words, what are the illocutionary processes. It would be unreasonable to require all social psychological studies to use the time-consuming in-depth methods of discourse analysis, but it is salutary to bear in mind the basic principles that meaning-making is about positioning of the self, the interlocutor and any groups referenced; that meaning-making is a communicative act relying on common ground; and that it reflects both identity and implications for what is possible action (Willig, 2013; Wodak & Meyer, 2009).

Consider for example the vegetarian who refuses a Big Mac. Does she object morally to killing animals for food, or does she object to the necessarily inhumane ways that meat production treats animals? Does she object to the wasteful use of land in rearing animals rather than crops, or does she, as some young children do, object to eating animals because they are one's friends? Each of these reasons, although having a common action implication regarding the Big Mac, has very different action implications regarding making a moral stance. Each also implies different identity elements, including cultural factors such as religious beliefs or local taboos and tastes, such as the different reasons for not eating dogs in different cultures (unclean pollutants versus beloved pets). At the very least, social psychology needs always to ask the meta-question, 'why is this belief held, and what purpose does it serve?' even if that question is not addressed in depth in a specific project. This is implied in all five of the chapters.

Emergent critical perspectives

Let us consider what is emergent from the critical analysis reflected in the five chapters. First, it is evident that it is not enough to study attitudes as traditionally conceptualised and studied in social psychology, nor is the habit of mapping attitudes as if they were fixed and static structures that determined reactions and actions. Our values and beliefs may predispose us to respond to concepts, communications and actions, but they are dynamic, flexible and, in particular, selectively employed according to context and salience. They are snapshots within a larger meaning-making process in which narratives provide a story of origins and causes, outcomes or consequences. 'Attitudes' are made transparent in expressed or implicit values, in how people and groups are positioned and in who and what are included or excluded from the story. But without the narrative, the attitude is superficial and one-dimensional. They may predict (some) action – 'vegetarians' don't accept Big Macs – but without knowing the narrative we do not understand the attitude.

As the five chapters in different ways show, this is also important for change. To persuasively impact another's worldview, there must be argumentation which addresses the meaning-making process, not just the superficial attitude statement. Michael Billig (1995), echoing Bakhtin (1986), drew attention to the essentially dialogic nature of conversation, in which any utterance we make is a response to another utterance (which could include an 'internal' thought), and we can only understand any statement by seeing what it is being argued against. Statements do not exist in isolation from a persuasive purpose, even if the 'persuasion' is affirmation of the previous statement. This is a profound shift from treating attitudes as static properties or attributes of mental structure. Billig also argues, as Reicher and

Jogdand note, that attitudes actually only become evident in dialogue or argumentation. Therefore, attitude change needs to be considered within a framework of what prompts a particular attitudinal response and which aspect of the underlying narrative is accessible to modification. In active persuasion, interlocutors often draw on a series of possible narratives. Castro, Uzelgun and Bertoldo demonstrate how different argumentation styles work to expose the underlying narrative as well as provide different kinds of effectiveness in managing dialogue and persuasion. Their subtle analysis shows how the 'concessive' mode permits not only a broader range of narratives being invoked, but also more discursive negotiation of possible narratives and counternarratives.

These five chapters address a wide spectrum of 'everyday' psychology and the plea to take it more seriously. I see two particular themes. One is to focus on the messy and complex aspects of real life rather than the sanitised and stripped down selection of targets or variables. This at the very least might make social psychology more 'useful' for public policy and for general lay understanding, but it is also arguably more scientific, because the phenomena in question are part of a larger and more complex picture. A second theme concerns the implications for methodology; many traditional methods in the field are not equipped for either dynamic approaches or multifaceted approaches. To generate appropriate methods requires rethinking about what processes are seen to be key to the phenomena in question; these five chapters give us some insights.

A major emergent factor evident in the five papers is the importance of identity. Social identity theory, as it developed in the 1970s, focused on categorisation processes and how these framed the identities of self and others. Subjective identity is, however, a consequence of positioning and is quite fluid; how one defines oneself and what categories are salient at any particular contextual moment depend on the cues from others' positioning of oneself or one's own location of oneself for the positioning of others. Social categories and representations drawn upon often rapidly change in salience. Identity is social and cultural and highly context dependent (Hall, 1997; Hammack, 2011; Haste & Bermudez, 2016; Hermans & Gieser, 2012). Dialogue, both as the self vis-a-vis others' direct positioning and as the self as a member of a group that is being positioned by the argumentation of others, manifestly is a site of negotiated current identity – how one feels subjectively, how one projects a desired identity in that context and how others accept, reject or ignore this. However, available identities derive from the vast range of cultural narratives to which we are exposed. Identities are defined and represented through extensively available but circumscribed cultural narratives and social practices which define appropriate interpersonal actions and styles. This seems to me to be a core message of, and agenda for, 'everyday psychology'.

References

Allen, D. S., & Light, J. S. (Eds.) (2015). *From voice to influence: Understanding citizenship in the digital age.* Chicago: University of Chicago Press.

Bakhtin, M. M. (1986). *Speech genres and other late essays.* Austin: University of Texas Press.

Billig, M. (1995). *Arguing and thinking: A theoretical approach to social psychology* (2nd ed.). Cambridge: Cambridge University Press.

Bruner, J. S. (1990). *Acts of meaning*. Cambridge, MA: Harvard University Press

Davies, B., & Harré, R. (1990). Positioning: The discursive production of selves. *Journal of Theory of Social Behaviour, 20*(1), 43–63.

Gardner, H. (1987). *The mind's new science: A history of the cognitive revolution*. New York: Basic Books.

Gigerenzer, G. (2000). *Adaptive thinking: Rationality in the real world*. Oxford: Oxford University Press.

Gosling, W. (2012). *Helmsmen and heroes* (2nd ed.). London: Weidenfeld & Nicolson.

Hall, S. (1997). *Representation: Cultural representations and signifying practices*. Thousand Oaks, CA: Sage.

Hammack, P. (2011). *Narrative and the politics of identity*. New York: Oxford University Press.

Harré, R., & Moghaddam, A. (2003). *The self and others: Positioning individuals and groups in personal, political and cultural contexts*. Westport, CT: Praeger.

Haste, H. (2008). Constructing competence: Discourse, identity and culture In I. Plath (Ed.), *Kultur – Handlung – Demokratie. Diskurse ihrer Kontextbedingungen* (pp. 109–134). Wiesbaden: Verlag für Sozialwissenschaften.

Haste, H. (2009). What is 'competence' and how should education incorporate new technology's tools to generate 'competent civic agents'? *The Curriculum Journal, 20*(3), 207–223.

Haste, H. (2013). Deconstructing the elephant and the flag in the lavatory: Promises and problems of moral foundations research. *Journal of Moral Education, 42*(3), 316–329.

Haste, H., & Bermudez, A. (2016). The power of story: History, narrative and civic identity. In M. Carretero, S. Berger & M. Grever (Eds.), *International handbook of research in historical culture and education: Hybrid ways of learning history*. London: Palgrave Macmillan.

Haste, H., & Hogan, A. (2012). The future shapes the present: Scenarios, metaphors and civic action. In. M. Carretero (Ed.), *History education and the construction of identities* (pp. 311–326). Charlotte, NC: Information Age Publishers.

Hermans, H., & Gieser, T. (Eds.). (2012). *Handbook of dialogical self theory*. Cambridge: Cambridge University Press.

Vygotsky, L. (1978). *Mind in society*. Cambridge, MA: Harvard University Press.

Wertsch, J. (1998). *Mind as action*. Oxford: Oxford University Press.

Willig, C. (2013). *Introducing qualitative research in psychology* (3rd ed.). New York: McGraw Hill.

Wodak, R., & Meyer, M. (Eds.) (2009). *Methods of critical discourse analysis* (2nd ed.). Thousand Oaks, CA: Sage.

PART III
Political discourse and practice

11
THE PRECARIAT, EVERYDAY LIFE AND OBJECTS OF DESPAIR

Darrin Hodgetts, Shiloh Groot, Emily Garden and Kerry Chamberlain

The monetary subjugation of civil society by speculative capital has been linked to societal unrest and increased disparities in income between 'the haves' and the 'have nots' for millennia (Graeber, 2011; Hodgetts et al., 2014; Standing, 2011). Countries, including New Zealand and the United Kingdom, are experiencing an epoch of neoliberalism characterized by the coordination of economic and social life that is being shifted increasingly from the state to private interests. In line with the neoliberal worldview – cultivated by the political right over recent decades – almost all domains of life have been subordinated to market rationality and economic liberalization. Welfare and healthcare supports that were established to reduce, or at least buffer people against, the harshest consequences of poverty caused by social hierarchies and inequalities are being systematically dismantled (Hodgetts et al., 2014). Recently, increased austerity for the poor has exacerbated the dilemmas faced by families already living stressful and inadequately resourced lives, characterized by social exclusion and income, food and housing insecurities (Boon & Farnsworth, 2011; Green, 2012). Neoliberal politics of austerity are played out in the lives of socioeconomically vulnerable groups and have sparked renewed interest in concepts such as social class (Hodgetts & Griffin, 2015).

This chapter draws on the everyday experiences of adversity of 100 families who live particularly austere lives in Auckland. We focus on the materiality of these lives and consider how particular objects of despair, such as empty food cupboards and lunchboxes, prepaid power meters and urine soaked blankets, metonymise frustrations, anxieties and injustices in the lives of impoverished people. These objects render income, housing and food insecurities 'real'. Our analysis demonstrates the consequences of sociopolitical hierarchies and associated inequalities for the everyday and precarious lives of families in need. A focus on material objects reveals the human agency, practices and ways of being that emerge as families work materially to make sense of austerity and survive.

Contemporary re-engagements with the concept of social class in psychology (Hodgetts & Griffin, 2015; Tyler, 2008) reflect a long-standing, politicized tradition in community psychology of documenting how socioeconomic upheavals are played out in the everyday lives of communities in need (Hodgetts et al., 2010a; Jahoda, Lazarsfeld & Zeisel, 1933/1971). Although the concept of class remains polysemic, it is useful for opening up explorations of how the personal is interwoven with the sociopolitical (Hodgetts & Griffin, 2015). Attention is given to the impacts of economic and sociopolitical positioning of groups within social hierarchies and their differential access to power, employment, money, housing, food, education, healthcare, opportunities in life and goods and services (Bourdieu, 1987; Hodgetts & Griffin, 2015; Standing, 2011). Many contemporary approaches to class focus on networks of inequalities that manifest both economic and sociocultural processes (Hodgetts & Griffin, 2015). A central concern is the ways in which class intersects with interrelated social formations of oppression, including gender, ethnicity, race, disability and sexuality. These work in concert in the constitution of lives, social relations, discrimination and inequalities. Although shaped by local, societal and global politics, social classes are also co-constructed by people through daily practices. Broader landscapes of power operate through everyday practices and relationships to reproduce social hierarchies and to produce various dynamic 'social locations' for ordinary people at the intersections between these social formations.

Social class remains a useful concept for unravelling the complexities surrounding the reproduction of privilege and power and the subordination that is perpetuated by the inequitable distribution of social, cultural and economic resources between groups (Bourdieu, 1987). We approach social class as comprised of a dynamic set of social and material relations based around power and the operation of economic, political, cultural and ideological relations of domination and subordination (Hodgetts & Griffin, 2015). Rather than simply comprising an economic group, a given social class can be read as a dynamic and evolving social space. Here, social space refers to a sense of place shared among human beings from, or currently living within, similar cultural, social psychological and material circumstances. The concept of habitus is central to understanding social class as a social space through which people come to experience sameness and difference and attraction and revulsion, depending on the class status of those around them (Bourdieu, 1987). We use the concept of habitus to invoke a network of dispositions, material practices, ways of being and tastes through which a people come to understand and engage with the world and other people. We will consider how the social space of families living austere and precarious lives due to their class positioning, and their associated habitus, becomes embodied and intertwined with their everyday lives, practices and experiences.

In terms of conceptual work on new class formations that span various intersections, the rise of the precariat (Standing, 2011) is directly relevant to this chapter. The precariat reflects the entrenching of neoliberalism and undermining of work conditions and securities for the traditional working and middle classes (Standing, 2011). The precariat comprises an emerging social class of 'denizens' whose rights and being are brought into question; they are people who live insecure lives with limited economic and social capital and very constrained hope of social mobility. The precariat is made up of people with insecure and highly casualized employment and reduced employment rights. Their lives are characterized by the dynamics of underemployment, a revolving door between work and unemployment, unliveable wages and a raft of insecurities that are played out in everyday life. Such precariat lifeworlds feature uncertainty, despair, limitations of agency and resistance and insecurities in housing and food (Standing, 2011).

In exploring the psychopolitical aspects of urban poverty for the precariat, it is important that we do not lose site of the materiality of everyday experience. In focusing on material and cultural aspects of adversity, psychologists have explored how material objects provide personal anchorage points within everyday landscapes. For example, Hodgetts and colleagues (2010a, 2010b) document how homeless people talk about MP3 players, books and other possessions when recounting how they cope with adversity and seek to preserve their humanity. Such objects are used to preserve a sense of self and provide some ontological security within insecure lives. Retelling the significance of an object can also invoke a nexus of politicized social practices that exceeds the materiality of the specific thing (Miller, 2010). Through the use of material objects, members of the precariat can cultivate agentive strategies for escaping aspects of adversity and for exploring the larger existential issues of life, one's place within it and who one might become (Cohen & Taylor, 1973). Objects serve a purpose in enabling people to make sense of and communicate the inequalities they face – their situations, frustrations and despairs – and to invoke the inequities they face daily. We can see a dialogical relationship between members of the precariat and the basic commodities of life, through which objects and the people involved with them are remade and take on new meanings in signifying an inequitable social system (Miller, 2010). Precarious lives are signified by precarious access to a place to belong and to food, bedding, clothing and utilities.

Such lives are hard and feel hard. As researchers, we need to respond by engaging with the emotional and material nature of everyday experiences of hardship. We need to consider how, in trying to explain what it is like to live unstable, precarious, stressful, draining and hard lives, members of the precariat often do so with reference to material objects. This chapter explores how certain 'objects of despair' become focal points for the dilemmas of the precariat, their frustrations and hardships, and their emotional and agentive responses to austerity. Complementing the sporadic research into emotionality and social class (Tyler, 2008), we consider ways in which class is felt through the despair associated with being trapped in austerity, guilt in not being able to provide for one's family and anger in being surveilled by institutions that are essentially disinterested. To do so, we draw eclectically from scholarship on materiality (Miller, 2010), actor networks (Latour, 2005), social practices (Reckwitz, 2002), interobjectivity (Moghaddam, 2003), everyday life (de Certeau, 1984), being (Heidegger, 1927/1962) and the precariat (Standing, 2011).

Theory, focus and approach

Actor network theory (Latour, 2005) provides a useful starting point for orientating us towards the materiality of austere lives, directing us towards the political, material and relational aspects of everyday austerity. As a theory of social interaction, actor network theory considers the material objects that populate everyday lifeworlds to be actors indisputably connected to the relational networks of human beings. The ontology of objects is active rather than passive and is implicated in the performance of social life because objects do things to the lifeworlds in which they are situated. Also reflecting discussions within psychology on interobjective relations (Daanen & Sammut, 2012; Moghaddam, 2003), divisions between active human beings and passive material objects become blurred as material objects are worked upon, enacted and re-enacted within everyday lives (Jóhannesson & Bærenholdt, 2009). As we will show, people constantly use material objects to signify and solidify social orders, relationships, shared practices and identities. This blending of distinctions between people and things is particularly salient, given the precarious relationship between families experiencing poverty and the various goods that many of us take for granted, such as food, clothing and bedding. Through engagements with everyday objects, peoples' experiences, desires and frustrations become anchored to particular items, giving these things sociocultural and political significance within sociopolitical geometries (Latour, 2005).

Further insights into these processes can be gained from philosophical considerations on the nature of being. Following Heidegger (1927/1962) we consider how, through the use of mundane objects, people can realize themselves as interconnected beings in the world. For Heidegger, being is fundamentally relational and an ongoing process that involves the use of things in the world. Human beings extend out into the world through affective connections to everyday objects that present to us as meaningful in their own right and through which social formations are lived and reproduced (Heidegger, 1927/1962). Through processes of socialization within social groups, human beings obtain taken-for-granted knowledge of themselves, familiar objects and how the world works. This knowledge is embodied, emplaced and enacted. It rarely requires conscious awareness or reflection. It is when relationships with familiar things are problematized or disrupted that people have to forge new understandings through conscious deliberations (Daanen & Sammut, 2012). As we will demonstrate, objects that are rendered problematic for members of the precariat due to austerity come to manifest frustrations and anchor personal desires for a better life. Accounts of these material objects enable members of the precariat to locate themselves within broader social-political landscapes and social policies and in relation to austerity measures.

Also informed by the work of scholars such as Latour (2005), Heidegger (1927/1962) and Bourdieu (1987), social practice theories offer insights into the complexities surrounding objects in everyday life (Reckwitz, 2002). As Halkier and Jensen (2011, p. 104) note, "the most basic theoretical assumption is that activities of social life continuously have to be carried out and carried through, and that this mundane performativity is organized through a multiplicity of collectively shared practices". A dynamic nexus of social practices makes up lifeworlds and constitutes the everyday conduct of life (Hodgetts et al., 2010a). These practices comprise activity structures and can be understood as routine forms of human action that involve bodies and physical acts, knowing how to get by, the use of material objects, the conduct of relationships both interpersonal and structural and emotional experiences (Reckwitz, 2002). Objects are central to social practices because they enable the performance of physical acts and the reproduction of social structures and personal innovations upon these (Latour, 2005; Reckwitz, 2002). A social constructionist approach to social practice theory (Reckwitz, 2002) also aids our exploration of the sociocultural and economic relationships and inequalities that are embedded in, reproduced and resisted through various social practices involving the use of 'things'. By focusing on the use of material objects and associated practices, we are able to explore responses to adversity as ongoing, contingent, relational and material accomplishments in everyday life.

The concept of phronesis (Flyvbjerg et al., 2012), practically orientated knowledge regarding how to respond to life events, is central to our analytic approach. People experiencing hardships develop a stock of intimate, practical, experiential knowledge about their particular situations that other people lack. Such experiential wisdom is not simply cognitive in nature; it is embodied through stress, humiliation, frustration, fear, despair, anxiety and anger. It also materializes through the involvement of particular objects (cf. Daanen & Sammut, 2012). We explore the ways in which reference to such objects conveyed more felt and personally experienced accounts of adversity, relationships and agency as participants in our research worked to construct and convey their experiences. A key consideration is how general (societal) structures and relationships are reproduced via particular (personal) situations and the use of material objects. In this regard, our work is informed by Simmel's (1903/1964) *principle of emergence* of social phenomenon and his orientation towards looking locally in order to understand systemic elements of the sociocultural world within which people reside and make do. Asserting that the specific resembles the general, but is not reducible to it, Simmel worked as an impressionist to extract general arguments out of detailed considerations of local urban practices. Likewise, our analysis moves from the local social practices of our participants in broad brush strokes to the social universe at play in situated happenstance. We work to bridge the gap between philosophical abstractions and detailed empirical engagements with actual everyday lives, which are typically written out of history. The importance of objects of despair in informing knowledge of the politics of precariat lives emerges from the analytic dialectics between theoretical abstraction and everyday experience.

Everyday things in precarious lives

We draw on insights from the Family100 project, which is located within the Auckland City Mission (ACM) and seeks to develop alternative understandings of families in need and to promote initiatives that better meet their needs (Hodgetts et al., 2014). The research was designed and conducted by the authors of this chapter with funding from the Auckland City Mission. Participating families were selected to be representative of families regularly accessing the ACM food-bank; the cohort consisted of 40% Māori, 25% Pacific Islander, 22% European, and 13% Asian and other minority groups. The sample of families reflects the intersection of issues of ethnicity, gender and disability within precariat households. Specifically, 100 householders spoke frankly with social workers about their experiences every two weeks over one year using a range of drawing exercises and interviews. We met with the social workers every week to conduct training, collaboratively develop research materials, review participant responses and ensure continuity over the project. Drawing exercises involved asking participants to think about and diagram service networks, social relationships, health, food, finance, education and other such issues. Such visual exercises increase reflection and engagement on the part of participants in the interview process, give form to issues that can be difficult to discuss in the abstract, and enable participants to set part of the agenda for discussion by highlighting elements we did not expect. Materials for analysis consisted of discussion notes from the fortnightly interactions, participant drawings and bimonthly recorded interviews.

This chapter focuses on particular objects – including houses, kitchen furniture, food and lunchboxes, power meters and cords, blankets and slippers – which provide focal points for participant frustrations, stress and conflict. We consider these objects as focal points for their ability to expose related practices of what poverty is really like and how people work materially to make sense of it. We explore how 'making do' implicates these objects in a variety of practices, such as obtaining electricity from one's neighbors when one's own power has been disconnected, sleeping as a household in a single room to retain warmth and escaping into dreams of a better life (cf. Cohen & Taylor, 1973). A focus on things and practices enables us to invoke human agency in conveying the implications of austerity for these families. Our interpretation also moves beyond particular objects, situating these in terms of broader insecurities around housing, income and food, and the political paternalism of authorities that impact our participants' everyday lives.

Food-related examples are particularly striking in highlighting the implications of material objects in broader relational and social practices that shape precarious lives. These include accounts of empty cupboards that produce shame; lunchboxes that materialize anger and conflicts around the provision of food for children; and a kitchen table and chairs that disrupt the commensality of a family's dwelling and eating. A disconnect between self and place is often raised in relation to food and food-related objects. Kitchen cupboards invoke feelings of shame through not having food to share with visitors. As Pirihira notes:

> I stress over having no food in the cupboards. I feel embarrassed when people come to my house. Even for coffee. I hate the thought of opening up my cupboards, "I haven't done the shopping yet." It's always that stress. . . . I've

had a lot of embarrassing situations where I've had to make excuses, "Sorry, there's nothing there." To me, it's embarrassing all the time. I hardly have anyone come to my house.

(Pirihira, Māori, 62 years)

Making excuses, such as having not done the shopping yet, for not being able to host and feed a visitor constitute a strategy or social practice through which food insecurity and scarcity are positioned (Halkier & Jensen, 2011). The situation conveyed in the quotation also invokes the transgression of important cultural norms for these families around hospitality that emerge for Pirihira at the intersection of ethnicity, gender and socioeconomic status. Culturally, this Māori, precariat woman expresses a sense of *whakama* (shame and humiliation) at not being able to provide *kai* (food) to *manuhiri* (visitors) as part of her obligations to *manaaki* (host and care for visitors). Empty cupboards prevent such families from meeting their cultural and gendered obligations to respect and show kindness to visitors due to limited economic resources. Over time, this can reduce social ties that buffer people against adversity.

Also surfacing in relation to accounts of food and food-related objects are clashes in class-based habitus (Bourdieu, 1987) between the precariat families and middle-class professionals. For example, these families are pressured by schools and welfare agencies to provide their children with the 'right kind of foods' and healthy options. Several families mentioned having to send their children to school with lunches in clear bags or lunchboxes so that the contents could be viewed and vetted by teachers. Through such practices, food becomes a point of distinction between groups in society where power relations are reproduced, and middle-class taste is imposed on precariat families (Bourdieu, 1987) who have limited options with regard to what their children eat. In one such example, our fieldnotes state that Peta "lives with constant worry that her kids are being singled out by teachers and fellow pupils alike for being poor". These tensions manifest in their lifeworlds in relation to school lunches and the stigma that comes with a lack of food, let alone the 'healthy options':

> I can't send my kids to school with a tin of beans. If I could I would. . . . If I keep them home cos I haven't got the right foods to send them to school with, it's, "Why aren't you sending them to school?" And then when I do send them . . . it's, "Where's their lunches? Why did you send them to school with basically nothing?" And I think, well, either way I can't win.
>
> (Peta, Māori, 45 years)

Amelia makes a similar point, elaborating on how lunchboxes that do not contain the right types of food become objects of judgment and contestation between parent and school:

> I think they're getting a wee bit too picky about what kind of foods. There's a lot of kids don't have what they [teachers] want in their lunches. I make sure

> my kids' lunchboxes are always full. Now the school's saying that you're not allowed this, not allowed that.... At least they're fed. At least if the kid's got a full lunchbox .... I put my kids first no matter if it's not the healthiest of food.... Whatever parents wanna put in their lunchboxes they should be able to put in.... But, no. Letters get sent home with them, have them confiscated and everything. To this day I'd still like to know where the confiscated food's gone.... I told them to get fucked. I did.... Look at society today, half the kids go to school with no lunches.
>
> *(Amelia, Māori, 44 years)*

Here, we see a clash of habitus associated with the different class positions of these parents and teachers take form in relation to children's lunches (cf. Daanen & Sammut, 2012). The dominant middle-class worldview, which comes from a place of food security and ability to engage in healthy dietary practices, is morally sanctioned in society. It presents members of the precariat as consumers of 'junk food' and parents as incompetent in making appropriate choices for their children and, therefore, in need of scrutiny. Junk food is an object of scorn for teachers, but a reward for many families who have limited options for treating children. These parents resist the imposition of teacher's objectification of children's lunches by reasserting their own meanings that reflect their lived realities. Food becomes an object for expressing austerity and a mismatch between the expectations of schools and the resources of precariat parents, leading to conflict, anger, stress and, in some cases, truancy as a means of avoiding stigma. In such accounts, we witness the manifestation of broader relations in society through particular objects. Contestation over the contents of lunchboxes binds these families into the present social order and hierarchy (cf. Heidegger, 1927/1973; Latour, 2005).

Food insecurities challenge and disrupt parents' engagements with their children's education and position them as 'bad parents'. Such accounts deflect understandings of self as responsible parents who do what they can for their children, but who are often frustrated in the process by external agents. Next, another participant discusses how the kitchen table is a constant reminder of her precarious situation characterized by limited personal control over her immediate environment. Angel foregrounds her frustrations with the family's situation and the scrutiny they endure from authorities who are unresponsive to the family's needs:

> The way we eat, they [welfare authorities] should butt out. What I think is they shouldn't come in the house concerned that my children don't eat healthy food.... I've been asking them [housing authority] to remove the chairs that are fixed against the table in the kitchen ... for us to sit properly and eat. The kids, they can't sit down and eat, they have to stand up and grab their food. If they sit the chair is too low and the table is high up to their chest here.... You don't feel like you're enjoying your food.... I'm sick of seeing the kids feel awkward at the table ... I hate it. Sometimes I walk in the kitchen with a hammer, I tell my husband, "I'm not gonna

call them [housing NZ], I'm gonna do it myself" [destroy the table]. My husband said, "No, don't do it. This is not our house, they're gonna charge us if you do that." . . . And one time the case manager came over and I showed her. I said, "Can you help me with this table?" She said, "Oh, sorry, there's nothing we can do about it. That belongs to the house and you can't do nothing." I was sitting down myself, I said, "Look". . . . She doesn't wanna look at me, she looks like she's not interested in what I'm explaining to her!

(Angel, Tongan, 36 years)

In this account, a table and chairs provide a metonym for the state housing and welfare systems, which do not fit the family. They are positioned as being out of place and frustrated with public housing and a lack of response from authorities to what they see as their needs. Such members of the precariat often feel out of place because their ways of being are disrupted by their lack of control over such issues as housing and food. The account of a case manager that does not want to look reflects a phronetic understanding of an unresponsive system which does not want to witness the hardships and frustrations people face. Such case managers try to avoid taking such families interobjective understandings of their material environments into account when these differ from, and require critical reflection on, the institutional perspective (Daanen & Sammut, 2012). Angel's account also conveys her alienation from such things and what it is like to feel out of place within one's surroundings. Angel goes on to recount how she vented her frustration and anger by taking the hammer to and removing the chairs from the table. The hammer provides a related metonym; one that offers agency and a means of resistance to external control and assertion of the right to dwell and belong.

Issues of disruption and the constant struggle to create a place that feels like home where the family can gain a sense of stability, warmth and well being in the face of unresponsive organizations were central to participant social practices and accounts of the use of things in everyday life. In one example, Greg recounts his precariousness in relation to access to basic utilities such as electricity. He uses a GLO-BUG (pay-as-you-go electricity meter), which restrains his efforts to heat a damp house. His account invokes vigilance, restraint and rationing as everyday social practices:

It's just too expensive with running a 2,000 watt heater for a few hours. You're paying near to 30 bucks a week. . . . If you're not keeping an eye on it, it could be 35 bucks a week. . . . Make sure you don't have the heater on because you can use a 2,000 watt heater for an hour and that will be all your light usage for 24 hours. . . . You know that you can't deal with it on GLO-BUG. . . . It's just a pre-pay phone card type of thing. . . . And you put a minimum of 20 bucks, it costs $1.50 to put in every time. . . . If you get below $11.00 they cut you off. . . . They'll give you a warning and some stupid lights. . . . When it's green, it's fine. When it's orange, you're power's low. It's going to be off in two days. When it turns red your power's going to be cut off at 12 o'clock . . . . It drives you a little bit nutty.

(Greg, Pakeha, 42 years)

Constantly monitoring the lights on the power meter reminds participants, such as Greg, of their precarious access to electricity and other such basic utilities that other members of society often take for granted. Such accounts remind us of the constant stress of being poor and show how the meter has become an active agent in the lives of the precariat. When the meter light goes orange, families go to bed to save power; the power meter regulates lighting and determines bedtime and other interactions in the household. Rationing power also comes at a cost; it is linked to an inability to keep the house warm and dry and to ill health. As Amelia states:

> I have mold in my rooms. There's nothing you can do about it. . . . Just wipe it down again. I'm a bad asthmatic, so that doesn't help. I've got a dehumidifier, but that just eats out the power so what do you choose? An extra blanket or an extra day's power? No doubt it sacrifices my own health.

Through accounts of material objects, such as the GLO-BUG meter, we witness the implications of inequity for people's health. In these objects reside the ramifications of austerity measures that restrict the ability of families to pay for electricity and produce exploitative relationships in social hierarchies. Investor demands for high returns from privatized power companies[1] are linked to the precariat living in cold and damp houses unable to afford increasing electricity prices. Identifying such links constitutes an engagement with aspects of the 'referential whole' of material objects (Heidegger, 1927/1973). This is to invoke what Heidegger referred to as the network of involvements contained within material objects. At a micro level, we have regulation and restraint, but this has broader ramifications in the reproduction of social hierarchies and exploitative relationships. In monitoring lights on a GLO-BUG power meter, our participants resituate and enmesh themselves in broader intergroup relationships in society and reveal themselves as living insecure lives in poverty (Heidegger, 1927/1973). Their humiliated lives and selves are realized and situated systemically through the use of such things.

Power meters and power cords (discussed later) are not isolated things but are part of a larger whole that carries relationships in society. These objects become intelligible in relation to lives of scarcity and the exploitation of power companies and investors. Monitoring the meter is a form of rationing that characterizes such households as members of the precariat who are being exploited by those further up the social hierarchy. In line with theoretical work on interobject relations, we propose that our participants become consciously aware of the GLO-BUG due to the rupturing of the 'taken-for-grantedness' of electricity supply (Daanen & Sammut, 2012). They are forced to keep an eye on this prepaid meter and to develop particular practices for managing their limited access to electricity. In the process, these participants become estranged from the GLO-BUG as a foreign object in their dwellings, and they are able to consciously reflect on the function of this object within their lifeworlds, which they associate with austerity, hardship, anxiety and inequality.

Several of our participants stated that they avoided the GLO-BUG power meters. In doing so they invoke a perverse system in which the precariat pay the most for electricity (highest wattage rate). For those unwilling to use GLO-BUG meters or unable to pay their conventional power bills because they prioritize 'eating over heating', their electricity is disconnected. Shelley (Māori, 43) lives in a public housing unit with her four children, the youngest of whom has bronchiolitis. The unit is cold and uninsulated and, as a result, Shelley accumulated a large power bill in an attempt to keep her children warm and healthy. In recounting the situation, Shelley summons issues of housing, power, heating, illness and neighborly relationships in reference to social practices she has developed in response to her power being disconnected:

> My neighbors are drinkers and they drink out in their shed. At 7:30 you can hear them popping their first can, in the morning. . . . We race out and hang out our washing and go back inside because there's a lot of men and they all sit and drink and it's not very nice. It's not nice for the kids. . . . They're really good neighbors. It's just their lifestyle is different to mine. . . . They helped us out with a cord running next door. My power's running through them at the moment. . . . I take the kids down to the pools in the afternoon and then they have a swim and then shower. No, it's not ideal at all. . . . A few months now, but there's still nothing I can do about it because I don't have the money to pay it [outstanding power bill]. . . . I'd rather have the hot water than the power. You can survive without power.

Part of Shelley's response to austerity involves the development of phronetic knowledge of how to get by, including the strategy of running a power cord next door to a 'gang house' and taking the children to local swimming pools for showers. Her account exemplifies collaboration and resistance among the precariat through the use of a power cord that reduces her costs. The situation is not ideal, and in recounting it, Shelley invokes power relations and complexities in such cooperative strategies that render the situation even more precarious.

Tina (Māori, 42) also talks in a manner that weaves objects such as her house, electricity, a dryer, blankets and other objects into the conduct and hardships of her everyday life. Of particular note in this account are the ramifications of unresponsive and uncaring institutions in society in necessitating that our participants develop innovative and unorthodox practices for obtaining basic utilities. Tina spoke repeatedly of approaching welfare and health authorities for resources to meet the extra costs associated with managing her son's health needs that arose from him being hit by a car:

> It's very cold and damp around the windows and the shower. . . . Sometimes the water comes, sometimes it doesn't and we have to limit our showers

> to keep the hot water going. . . . The condition of the house is freezing – no carpets. . . . My kids and myself have been sick now because of the conditions at home. The main thing is, because my son – 14 and a half – he was involved in a hit and run accident, so he started to bed wet a lot. It's just costing when its winter and it's raining, I can't afford to dry his blankets and he gets frustrated, so I have to give him my blanket. . . . We don't tend to sleep in our own rooms cos it's so cold in there. . . . I get all my kids together, even my eight-month-old baby, and put her in the middle and put my son on the other side and my daughter on the other side, even though he bed wets, but I don't want him to be cold, so I just sit on top of their mattress. . . . I gave birth to a premature baby again, cos I stressed out, what my kids are gonna eat and how to dry his bedclothes, his blankets. . . . We will get lucky, the sun will come out on one of those days.

Through such accounts we can witness the dilemmas parents face for keeping themselves and their children warm, clean and healthy. These dilemmas are rendered material and tangible through reference to windows, heaters and blankets in a manner that brings forth the hardships and frustrations that characterize such precarious lives. Tina brings into view her immediate situation in a manner that implicates the denial of support to meet the family's practical needs. Here we can see how lives already rendered undignified are further dehumanized by being literally soaked in urine, the result of restraints on welfare spending that means that blankets shared by householders cannot be cleaned and dried. Such accounts demonstrate how a local nexus of material objects involved in enacting particular social practices is used to articulate austerity in a manner that implicates unresponsive welfare agencies in structurally violent relationships with precariat clients (Hodgetts et al., 2014).

Participant references to specific objects also foreground their aspirations for a better life for themselves and their children. For example, accounts of footwear, clothing and bedding communicate how these families live through disrupted relationships with the little things in life that many people take for granted and which can mean a lot in terms of expressing inequalities and disparities across ethnic groups. Tiare (Samoan, 37) talks about her children needing slippers:

> My kids don't have slippers like the Pakehas [European New Zealanders]. . . . My kids don't have those. I go to a Pakeha's house and I see their kids with slippers, so warm. I dream. Oh, my gosh, I wish my kids had those. They could sleep in it. But no, there's no carpet. . . . I can't go to the toilet because I can't put my baby down and if I give it to an older one of my children, it's not fair on her to wake her up or keep her up till 10 o'clock at night just to help me with this baby screaming and screaming. Why? It's freezing. It's freezing. . . . I've sacrificed. Everything I use for this house is a sacrifice because I could use it on my kids. I have sacrificed a nice quilt from the Auckland City Mission for my baby. I've sacrificed it to cover those holes. . . . And

I swear, when God pours that blessing upon me my kids will wear slippers. They'll have five pairs in their own cupboards.

This account asserts Tiare's subjectivity as a responsible parent who cares. The slippers function as a metonym for comfort and a warm, secure childhood watched over by a caring mother willing to make sacrifices. We should not overlook the function of imagination and dreams of a better life in such accounts. Such imaginative work aids coping, gives members of the precariat something to look forward to and constitutes 'escape attempts' that offer instances of respite, hope and normality that open up and keep alive possibilities for 'genuine escapes' from austere lives (Cohen & Taylor, 1973).

Our analysis speaks to how the precariat takes form through engagements with material objects in everyday life. Objects deliberated upon play a constitutive role in such lives. These objects are woven into a lived everyday nexus (Heidegger, 1927/1973) that comes to stand for austerity and the precariat. These participants come to understand themselves, their situations and their [dis]placements in society through particular things. Their accounts reflect how networks of relations between social actors are not always intrinsically coherent and may indeed contain conflicts (Latour, 2005). Scarcity or the absence of essential items creates dilemmas for the precariat. Noble (2004) has noted that the accumulation of things is associated with the 'accumulation of being'. Objects tether people to and help recreate particular ways of being. For our participants, such accumulation and tethering of being is particularly complex. The scarcity of, and inequities in, access to basic material resources of daily living is associated for them with the dissipation of being. Responses involve the development of social practices through which participants struggle to maintain access to basic necessities and to recreate a place to belong in an alienating world. Our participants become people who do not fit ideals for healthy eating, the design of public housing, and neoliberal subjectivities. When problematized in households, mundane objects become 'objects of despair' that are assimilated into the subjectivities of participants, marking them as people who lack things. A lack of the basics restricts their ability to be full members of society and to take part in cultural and communal practices.

Discussion

This chapter demonstrates the utility of psychologists attending to the material world of objects and everyday practices in extending understandings of lived experiences of austerity. We have documented how objects of despair are used as anchor points when people convey experiences of austerity. By problematizing dominant taken-for-granted associations with everyday objects, our participants are able to show what it is like to live their lives and the emotional impacts of hardship. In their accounts of objects of despair, we can see how human beings come to reflect upon and grasp themselves materially in everyday life and render poverty tangible to outsiders. We can see how insecurities in housing, food, electricity and autonomy intersect in everyday life. Poverty is rendered perceptible to us through despairing accounts around children's lunchboxes, kitchen furnishings, power meters, urine-soaked blankets and children's slippers. Our participants can articulate the implications of their class positions on their very existence. Participants' relationships with everyday objects resituate them within social hierarchies that characterize the intersectionality of social class today (Hodgetts & Griffin, 2015). Accounts of material objects reveal how these lives have to fit around unresponsive institutional structures that 'manage the poor' and comprise a structurally violent social field (Hodgetts et al., 2014). More than this, through their relationships with everyday things, our participants come to understand their situations, selves and the injustices of their situations and themselves (Heidegger, 1927/1973).

Many of our participants' accounts of things are made against highly politicized symbolic contexts in which precariat parents are often presented as incompetent and neglectful (Tyler, 2008). Classist and prejudicial tendencies are particularly directed at people who depend on welfare provision resulting in reduced care, compassion and communal responsibility towards people in need (Hodgetts et al., 2014). The prominence of moral disdain towards the precariat comes with an objectifying reification of negative traits around a lack of parenting skills and motivation among the 'under class', a perspective that has been carefully cultivated by the political right over recent decades (Michels, 2013). Our analysis paints a very different portrait of the precariat than is evident in dominant neoliberal and victim-blaming 'underclass' narratives. Our participants problematize public caricatures that objectify people living austere lives and pressure people in need to feel defective, dirty and ashamed. These are people who do their best despite precarious access to basic things that make contemporary lives habitable.

Finally, psychological research often misses the implications of broader political debates and policies on the everyday lives of vulnerable people, such as our participants (Tileagă, 2014). Striking omissions include detailed engagements with the material and emplaced practices through which everyday politics take place. Psychological research has all but failed to recognize the sociocultural and political significance of everyday objects, social practices and the mundane (cf. Hodgetts et al., 2010b). Our analysis exemplifies how psychological research needs to document how societal structures and power relations are reproduced through everyday social practices. Central here is an engagement with material and emplaced experiences of austerity that moves out from participant accounts and the local setting to the broader sociopolitical forces that provide much of the situated context for these experiences (Simmel, 1903/1997). In exploring everyday objects of despair, we aim to contribute to a wider understanding of the role of things in everyday experiences of adversity in an increasingly inequitable society (Hodgetts et al., 2014). This chapter demonstrates how political analyses of everyday life can benefit from an interpretive shift beyond specific objects and social practices into the broader social structures that shape the everyday situations of austerity and the lives of families in need. Such engagements with participant knowledge of poverty in everyday life and the development of daily practices are centrally important in challenging neoliberal structures in contemporary society.

Note

1 In the last year, the New Zealand government partially privatized several power companies, arguing that this provided an important investment opportunity for 'mum and dad investors'.

References

Boon, B., & Farnsworth, J. (2011). Social exclusion and poverty: Translating social capital into accessible resources. *Social Policy & Administration, 45*, 507–524.

Bourdieu, P. (1987). What makes a social class? On the theoretical and practical existence of groups. *Berkeley Journal of Sociology: A Critical Review, XXXII*, 1–17.

Cohen, S., & Taylor, L. (1973). *Escape attempts: The theory and practice of resistance to everyday life*. London: Penguin.

Daanen, P., & Sammut, G. (2012). G.H. Mead and knowing how to act: Practical meaning, routine interaction, and the theory of interobjectivity. *Theory & Psychology, 22*, 556–571.

de Certeau, M. (1984). *The practice of everyday life* (trans. S. Rendall). Berkeley: University of California.

Flyvbjerg, B., Landman, T., & Schram, S. (2012). *Real social science: Applied phronesis*. Cambridge: Cambridge University Press.

Graeber, D. (2011). *Debt: The first 5000 years*. New York: Melville.

Green, K. (2012). *Life on a low income*. London: Resolution Foundation.

Halkier, B., & Jensen, I. (2011). Methodological challenges in using practice theory in consumption research. *Journal of Consumer Culture, 11*, 101–123.

Heidegger, M. (1927/1962). *Being and time* (trans. J. Macquarrie & E. Robinson). London: SCM Press.

Hodgetts, D., Chamberlain, K., Groot, S., & Tankel, Y. (2014). Urban poverty, structural violence and welfare provision for 100 families in Auckland. *Urban Studies, 51*(10), 2036–2051.

Hodgetts, D., Drew, N., Stoltie, O., Sonn, C., Nikora, N., & Curtis, C. (2010a). *Social psychology and everyday life*. Basingstoke: Palgrave/MacMillan.

Hodgetts, D., & Griffin, C. (2015). The place of class: Considerations for psychology. *Theory & Psychology*. doi:10.1177/0959354315576381

Hodgetts, D., Stolte, O., Radley, A., Chamberlain, K., & Groot, S. (2010b). The mobile hermit and the city: Places, objects and sounds for a social psychology of homelessness. *British Journal of Social Psychology, 49*, 285–303.

Jahoda, M., Lazarsfeld, P., & Zeisel, H. (1933/1971). *Marienthal: A sociography of an unemployed community*. London: Tavistock.

Jóhannesson, G., & Bærenholdt, J. O. (2009). Actor-network theory/network geographies. In K. Rob & T. Nigel (Eds.), *International encyclopaedia of human geography* (pp. 15–19). Oxford: Elsevier.

Latour, B. (2005). *Reassembling the social*. Oxford: Oxford University Press.

Michels, H. (2013). The 'underclass' debate – A discourse that maligns people living in poverty. *Social Change Review, 11*, 45–57.

Miller, D. (2010). *Stuff*. Cambridge: Polity Press.

Moghaddam, F. (2003). Interobjectivity and culture. *Culture & Psychology, 9*, 221–232.

Noble, G. (2004). Accumulating being. *International Journal of Cultural Studies*, 7: 233–256.
Reckwitz, A. (2002). Toward a theory of social practices: A development in culturalist theorizing. *European Journal of Social Theory*, 5, 243–263.
Simmel, G. (1903/1997). The metropolis and mental life. In D. Frisby & M. Featherstone (Eds.), *Simmel on culture* (pp. 174–185). London: Sage.
Standing, G. (2011). *The precariat – The new dangerous class*. New York: Bloomsbury.
Tileagă, C. (2014). *Political psychology: Critical perspectives*. Cambridge: Cambridge University Press.
Tyler, I. (2008). 'Chav mum, chav scum': Class disgust in contemporary Britain. *Feminist Media Studies*, *8*, 17–34.

12
PUBLIC OPINION AND THE PROBLEM OF INFORMATION

Susan Condor

The term *public opinion* first gained popularity the 18th century European enlightenment. Today, because of its centrality to the rationale of advanced liberal democracies, public opinion constitutes a nexus between the worlds of formal and everyday politics. This chapter outlines a tension between two competing assumptions about the relationship between public opinion and rational democratic governance. On the one hand, public opinion is treated as the ultimate source of political authority. On the other hand, the everyday opinion of mass publics is understood to be too heavily motivated by personal self-interest and too deficient in factual understanding to ever serve as a legitimate basis for the governance of complex modern societies. In the second part of the chapter, I present a case study from my own research on vernacular political reasoning, focusing on the phenomenon of *empty attitudes*: sincere opinions on matters of public debate which can be satisfactorily justified without recourse to detailed factual information.

Public opinion as an ambiguous concept

In his 1965 text, *Public Opinion*, Harwood Childs famously listed 50 definitions of the term. Since that time, it has become almost obligatory for authors to start out by reflecting on the polyvalence of the composite term and of each of its subcomponents. These different theoretical understandings underlie a dilemmatic orientation to the status of public opinion in relation to strategies of rational and reasonable governance. On the one hand, public opinion is understood as the mechanism by which thick political communities are formed and through which citizens realize their potential as active political subjects. On the other hand, public opinion is viewed as a mechanism for, and an object of, political surveillance and regulation.[1]

For social scientists, precision is generally regarded as a *sine qua non* of academic life (Billig, 2013), and since the 1920s, authors have suggested that difficulties in reaching a consensual definition might preclude the adoption of public opinion as a technical concept (see Palmer, 1936). However, as the topic of intellectual or political debate, the ambiguity of the term *public opinion* may also have positive affordances. Sociologists of science have shown how vague constructs facilitate academic innovation and interdisciplinary cooperation. Psychologists, linguists and students of organizational culture emphasize the role of fuzzy logic in everyday cognition and communication. Studies of political communication have noted the advantages of strategic ambiguity for communicators wishing to future-proof their rhetoric or to appeal simultaneously to diverse audiences.

As an example, we may consider how politicians invoke public opinion in the course of political debate. Perhaps the most straightforward cases involve what Drury (2014) calls *ad populum* arguments, in which speakers align themselves with existing public opinion. In terms of theories of democratic representation (e.g. Rehfeld, 2006), we might gloss these as situations in which politicians adopt – in appearance at least – a *delegate* footing. *Ad populum* arguments need not entail simple appeals to common category membership (cf. Haslam et al., 2011). Rather, they often involve a speaker simultaneously identifying with an immediate audience, whilst at the same time excluding that audience from the public with whose opinions they are aligning. In the following example, taken from a UK House of Commons debate over EU immigration in 2013, the speaker represents the political landscape in terms of two opposing camps: "public opinion" (elided with "British citizens", "the British people" and "constituents"), versus "this esteemed House of Commons" of whom those of "our colleagues" who are absent "this Chamber this morning" are treated as category prototypes:

> British citizens are concerned that immigration from the European Union is on far too large a scale. It is not about the colour of somebody's skin or the skills that they can bring, but about the numbers of people. . . . That is the concern of the British people. I am afraid that this esteemed House of Commons is out of step with public opinion. The fact that fewer than 15 out of 650 hon. Members are in this Chamber this morning suggests to me that far too many of our colleagues are not listening closely enough to their constituents. The big issue in the country, about which people are talking every day of the week, is immigration.[2]

In other situations, politicians may employ what Drury terms *contra populum* arguments, establishing the rationality of their own political judgment through contrast with the ill-informed, unreliable or antisocial forces of public opinion. In the following extract, taken from a UK Justice Committee Report, the author is adopting a *trustee* model of democratic representation in which elected ministers have a duty to exercise their own expert judgment to protect the interests of their constituents and the state.

> Wider factors, such as the media, public opinion and political rhetoric, contribute to risk averse court, probation and parole decisions and hence play a

role in unnecessary system expansion. If Ministers wish the system to become sustainable within existing resources, they must recognize the distorting effect which these pressures have on the pursuit of a rational strategy.³

Formal political rhetoric does not simply embed contemporary publics and their current opinions, but also enlists the public in projections of the future. Politicians often appeal to *latent public opinion* (Key, 1961): future reactions on the part of a public. The following example comes from the Second Reading of the Scotland Bill in the UK House of Commons in 1998:⁴

> Far too many people seem to have forgotten what English nationalism is capable of. Even the briefest scanning of the history of the United Kingdom should be enough to remind us all: rape, pillage and mayhem leap from virtually every page of that history. Throughout Scotland, Wales and Ireland there are countless monuments to the local heroes who were slain in a vain attempt to stem a relentless tide of English domination. It is worth looking back at what history has to teach us.

UK Parliamentary debates concerning the Scotland Bill typically displayed a nonsymmetrical stance towards public opinion. On the one hand, the population of Scotland, who had voted in favour of a separate Scottish Parliament in a referendum, was generally represented as a unitary citizenry with rights to political voice. In contrast, the population of England typically entered Parliamentary debate through *contra populum* arguments. This asymmetric representation was particularly evident among MPs representing constituencies in England, who often presented themselves as trustees of the British State, defending the minority national publics from the impeding threat of popular English ochlocracy. Speakers regularly added literary embellishment to these representations through quotation from G.K. Chesterton's poem "The Secret People", as illustrated by following example from a House of Commons debate in 1998:

> The ugly ogre of English nationalism, which I detest, will begin to march soon unless it is forestalled. The Government have lit a camp fire of concern in England, which will soon burn into a forest fire unless we address it speedily. As G. K. Chesterton wrote in 1915,
> "Smile at us, pay us, pass us: but do not quite forget. For we are the people of England, that have never spoken yet" – and they will speak soon.⁵

Technologies of representation

In 1921, Lord Bryce answered his own rhetorical question, "How is the drift of public opinion to be ascertained?" as follows:

> The best way in which the tendencies at work in any community can be discovered and estimated is by moving freely about among all sorts and

> conditions of men.... In every neighborhood [sic] there are unbiased persons with good opportunities for observing, and plenty of skill in "sizing up" the attitude and proclivities of their fellow citizens.
>
> *(p. 156)*

This example reminds us that until the 1930s, if one wished to monitor public opinion, the only available options were a census, the kind of informal ethnography advocated by Bryce (and exemplified in the UK by Mass Observation) or straw polls such as those regularly conducted by US newspapers. Since this time, of course, the study of public opinion has become almost synonymous with the polling method popularized by George Gallop, which combines standardized, closed-ended questioning with representative sampling (Osborne & Rose, 1999).

As the title of their text, *The Pulse of Democracy*, suggests, Gallop and Rae (1940) promoted opinion polling as a practical technology for conveying citizens' views to their political representatives. The new technology was not, however, without its critics. As early as 1948, Blumer noted that, "those trying to study public opinion by polling are so wedded to their technique and so preoccupied with the improvement of their technique that they shunt aside the vital question of whether their technique is suited to the study of what they are ostensibly seeking to study. Their work is largely merely making application of their technique" (p. 542). One consequence of what Blumer called the "operationalist position", according to which "public opinion consists of what public opinion polls poll" (p. 543), was that research on public opinion rapidly became disconnected from academic theory in social psychology (Allport, 1937), political science (Price, 1992) and sociology (Manza & Brooks, 2012). This is not to say that polling methods were conceptually neutral. On the contrary, this technology constructed public opinion in a way that reinforced dominant understanding of democratic participation in the mid-20th century USA (Herbst, 1993). Polling methods resemble the private ballot, one-man-one-vote method of democratic participation. Reports of opinion polls present an image of the public sphere as an undifferentiated mass society comprised of essentially disconnected individuals thinking and (re)acting in parallel. In principle, pollsters could draw attention to the range of opinions existing within their target populations. In practice, public opinion tends to be equated with majority-preferred response options in a manner analogous to majority rule decision-making. Channeled through the polls, the voice of the people is heard simply reacting to policy options rather than engaging in constructive public deliberation.

The problem of information

Promoting opinion polling as the technology of choice for democratic governance during World War II, Gallop and Rae (1940) emphasized that political "ignorance, stupidity and apathy are the exception, not the rule" (p. 287). A quarter of a century later, under different political circumstances, Philip Converse (1964) famously argued that the majority of the US electorate did not possess "meaningful beliefs, even on issues that have formed the basis for intense political controversy among elites for substantive periods of time" (p. 245). He argued that poll responses were rarely informed by politically sophisticated, internally consistent, abstract (*ideological*) reasoning. On the contrary, they often took the form of *non-attitudes*: answers produced by individuals who had no meaningful understanding of the topics on which their views were solicited. Converse's account of the rational shortcomings of mass publics resonated with deficit models of public opinion that had been popular since Lippmann's (1922) seminal treatise and generated a heated debate that continues to the present day.

Converse was not the first to question the epistemological status of the "opinions" revealed through polling methods. In one early critique, Riesman and Glazer (1949) argued that a "real understanding" of public opinion "will only come . . . when polling moves away from an emphasis on set answers to set questions to an emphasis on the 'latent' meaning of answers, understood in terms of an entire interview and a grasp of what went on in the interpersonal situation of the interview" (p. 633). Similarly, social psychologists often challenged polling technologies, advocating "full discussion" as a preferable method for studying public opinions (e.g. Likert, 1947; Murphy & Likert, 1938; see Converse, 1987; Lazarsfeld, 1944), a position summarized by Asch (1952):

> Perhaps we ought to take the bull by the horns and insist that an interview should approximate to a genuine conversation, in which one person explores a problem with another; perhaps the interviewer's optimum role is not that of a camera or a ballot box. It may even be of value to observe how the person deals with facts and arguments that are new to him, to confront him with problems. . . . Such procedures would approximate more closely to the requirements of psychological investigation and might prove fruitful for theory.
>
> *(pp. 559–560)*

Prefiguring Converse's critique, Asch noted "the problem of information": the "danger of polling on matters about which there is little information and in which people are not interested is that the data will spuriously support the assumption that a public opinion exists" (p. 550). Unlike Converse, however, Asch regarded the problem of information as but one instance of a more general problem of interpreting poll data:

> the information obtained from [closed ended opinion poll] questions is the distribution of the number of people who say "yes" or "no"; the rest is interpretation. For interpretation one must rely upon a knowledge of . . . ideas that the data has neither produced nor is capable of checking. The data make sense to us only because we have . . . some idea of the "why" of the answers.
>
> *(pp. 546–547)*

Opinionation without information: A case study of everyday political reasoning

For the past 15 years, my colleagues and I have been studying not only the "whats" and the "whys", but also the "hows" of everyday political reasoning using the kinds of methods advocated by the early social psychologists. In particular, we have considered how an analytic focus on the ways in which people formulate political arguments in conversational contexts can enable us to appreciate the rationale behind those kinds of opinions (or non-opinions) that survey researchers are inclined to treat as *prima facie* evidence of citizen ignorance, irrationality and democratic incompetence (e.g. Condor 2010; 2011; 2012; Condor & Gibson, 2007; Sapountzis & Condor, 2013).

For the purposes of this chapter, I will focus on what Asch termed the "problem of information". First, I will consider how an analysis of the rhetorical construction of opinion can enable us to appreciate the extent and kinds of factual information that people actually use when they discuss political issues. Second, I will demonstrate how conversational data can provide us with insights into the *rhetorical heuristics* that people employ in situations where they are unable to justify a particular political stance with detailed factual information or claims to epistemic authority (cf. Heritage, 1995).

Background to the research

In the late 1990s, the UK government initiated a process of political decentralization that included the establishment of a new Scottish Parliament. As we have already seen, the spectre of latent English public opinion featured heavily in subsequent parliamentary debates. The Earl of Onslow summed up the concerns of many when, during the second reading of the Scotland Bill in the UK House of Lords in June 1998, he asserted that, "The English simply will not put up with it". The polls, however, generally failed to substantiate these pessimistic predictions. In 2001, Curtice and Seyd argued that the poll data indicated that "a Scottish parliament appears not only to be the settled will[6] of Scots but also of the English" (p. 163). This gloss illustrates Bourdieu's (1973) argument concerning the "consensus effect" of polling. Granted, none of the polls had indicated a groundswell of opposition to the new constitutional settlement. However, neither did they point to a consensus in favour. The depiction of English public opinion as settled was – in the absence of longitudinal evidence – clearly speculative and overlooked the susceptibility of the survey findings to question wording and ordering effects (Bryant, 2008). The interpretation of the poll data as evidence of a definitive national will also involve, to echo Asch, ideas that the data had neither produced nor was capable of checking.

One possibility overlooked by the pollsters was that these survey responses might not reflect genuine attitudes at all. Did people in England actually possess the necessary information to answer questions about the new Scottish Parliament in any meaningful way? On the face of it, there were grounds for skepticism. There had been little press coverage of the devolution debates in England (Rosie et al., 2006), and the poll data (characterized by a disproportionate use of "don't know" and non-extreme response options) was consistent with the possibility that the respondents were using satisficing strategies (cf. Krosnick et al., 1996).[7]

In the absence of information concerning everyday understandings of the devolution process in England, my colleagues and I explored this issue through an interviewing strategy designed to elicit accounts that would, as far as possible, reflect the vocabulary and lines of argument that people might use in their everyday lives.[8] Respondents were recruited using maximum diversity sampling, and the eventual data corpus comprised 1,928 recordings of informal "chats" with individuals and groups of friends or family members.[9] A subset of panel data involved repeat interviews with the same individuals, designed to monitor change over time.[10]

Empty attitudes and rhetorical heuristics

Opinions towards the Scottish Parliament expressed in our studies paralleled trends identified by the polls, with about 70% of participants claiming neutral or positive attitudes. Basic content analysis was sufficient to discount the possibility that these were simply spurious responses (Goldsmith, 2001) to questions that the respondent had not understood. The interviews were conducted in such a way as to enable respondents to raise issues spontaneously. Under these circumstances, more than 90% of our participants demonstrated prior awareness of the new Scottish Parliament. However, this was not to say that they displayed much specific information concerning the devolution process. In fact, 60% of our respondents discussed the changes to the UK constitution at some length without mobilizing any factual information other than general background knowledge (e.g. "Scotland's always had its own legal system") or information which could be inferred from a mere awareness of the Scottish Parliament's existence (e.g. "they make their own decisions").

Respondents sometimes mentioned their lack of knowledge in the course of justifying neutral opinions (see Extract 1). However, most respondents who argued in favour of the new Scottish Parliament did so without mobilizing any topic-specific information. As we shall see shortly, these *empty attitudes* (Condor, 2012) could be warranted in a range of ways and could prove to be surprisingly reliable over time and across conversational contexts.

Everyday political talk tends to be formulated with a view to norms of public reason: that is, assumptions about the kinds of positions, and forms of intervention, that are (and are not) typical, expected or appropriate for members of particular communities. Interestingly, our respondents commonly treated a lack of information about the Scottish Parliament as typical of, and as uncontroversial within, their opinion community:

Extract 1[11]

I:	So, going back to what you said about the Scottish Parliament. Um. What were your thoughts on that at the time?
Karen:	Err. I'm not sure. I'm not sure.
I:	What about now? Do you think it was a good idea? Or [1.5]
Karen:	I don't think I have an opinion one way or the other [1]
I:	So it's not something that interests you?
Karen:	Well, I wouldn't say that. I think you know it's interesting but I just don't know that much about it. You don't hear much about it down here do you? So it's difficult to have an opinion one way or the other.

Respondents could also treat ignorance as normative in a prescriptive sense, suggesting that the English public lacked category entitlement to factual information on the devolution debates or process. In the following extract, the respondent characterizes the English public as a latent mob in a manner that parallels the forms of representations employed by MPs in Parliamentary debates:

Extract 2

I:	Did you think that was the right decision?
Mark:	Well yeah. Of course. They had a referendum and that's what they decided.
I:	And it was the right decision?
Mark:	Well, it's hardly for us to say, is it? It's up to them. And that's what they voted for. That's democracy.
I:	Some people have been saying that it wasn't a very good decision.
Mark:	I wouldn't know about that. I have not heard much about it. You don't really hear anything in the newspapers, or on the Today programme of whatever you know.
I:	Do you think that maybe there should be more information in the media?
Mark:	Well:: not really. I don't really see it as being any of our business.
I:	Some people I think say that people in England should at least know what is going on in other parts of the United Kingdom (2) that they have a a right-
Mark:	Yeah they probably do [laugh] well of course there will always be troublemakers. People out for a fight. People who are going to be like, "What about the English?" And that's I dunno but I wouldn't be surprised if that's what Scotland wanted a different umm parliament to get away from all of that so they could just make the decisions for themselves without all of that nonsense that they've always had to put up with across (.) history.

Respondents were also inclined to attribute the English public with limited rights to hold, or to publicly express, negative opinions towards the Scottish Parliament. Heritage (1984) has noted that contranormative statements are liable to be *accounted for*, *delayed* within a turn and *prefaced* or *qualified*. These features were always present when English people voiced negative views of the new Scottish Parliament (see e.g. Extract 6). In contrast, the expression of positive opinions was typically treated as normatively unaccountable, an orientation which could be discursively marked through argumentative elision and the use of the generic *you* and the rhetorical *just*.

Respondents could treat simple affirmation (*yes; of course*) or default arguments (*why not?*)[12] as sufficient justification for positive opinions:

Extract 3

I: Mm. Okay. Do you think places like, countries like Scotland, and like Wales, and like Northern Ireland, are entitled to have their own parliaments?
Joyce: Yes.
I: Why? (2)
Joyce: Now then, actually, I can't express it, positively ((laughter))
at all, but I can't see any reason why not.

Gigerenzer (2015) defines one-reason decisions as "a class of heuristics that bases judgments on one good reason only" (p. 124). The rhetorical parallel, often apparent in our respondents' arguments in favour of the Scottish Parliament, was the use of a single bottom-line (cf. Potter et al., 1994) consideration. This could involve a bald allusion to the legitimacy of Scottish public opinion (*If that's what they want*) possibly coupled with references to procedural justice (*that's democracy; fair enough*). One common rhetorical heuristic involved generic assertions of Scottish difference formulated as a matter of political needs:

Extract 4

Dan: Yeah, it [the Scottish parliament] was a good idea.
I: It was a good idea. Why was it a good idea?
Dan: Because, it was. I think they're different from us and therefore they need different things. I think there should be collaboration between the two but I think giving them the parliament was a good idea.
I: How are they different from us?
Dan: Different lifestyles.
I: What's different about them?
Dan: I don't know. Perhaps their principles, the way they live, their lifestyles. Erm, I don't know, it's really hard to say, I think, but just an impression you get.

Alternatively, this generic difference would be formulated as a matter of distinctive *identity*:

Extract 5

Jerry: [. . .] And especially now with Britain breaking up. We need to know which bit we are. It's like it can't just be "we're all British" you know, because the Scots

> have their own identity, they're "We're not British, we're Scottish" and the Welsh too they've always been really Welsh. And now with the new Parliaments I suppose it's really only some people in Northern Ireland who are really like, "wahh we're British".
>
> *I:* Is that something you were in favour of? The new parliaments?
>
> *Jerry:* Oh yes. Why not? It just makes sense. [. . .]

In his account of non-attitudes, Converse (1964) depicted ideological thinking as involving explicit awareness of elite perspectives on the connection between various political ideas ("what goes with what"). In contrast, studies of political rhetoric suggest that absence of an explicitly worked-through political argument need not necessarily indicate the absence of an underlying ideological rationale. On the contrary, the existence of commonplace or orthodox beliefs within a particular speech community may be discursively signalled by rhetorical elision. In the case of our data set, it was evident that minimal lines of argument in favour of the Scottish Parliament tended to rest on an implicit bedrock of shared assumptions about political legitimacy, including banal (Billig, 1995) assumptions concerning rights to national self-determination.

What distinguished our more politically sophisticated respondents was not their *use* of ideological reasoning, but their tendency to explicitly *mention* the core political values that informed their opinions (cf. Sperber & Wilson, 1981). In the stretch of talk reported in Extract 6, Vicky is voicing a negative opinion of the Scottish Parliament. She reflexively orients to the fact that her views deviate from the dominant orthodoxy and, as such, require detailed explanation and justification. Vicky's warrant for her opinion involves an explicit appeal to core political values, specifically a left-wing internationalist opposition to all forms of political nationalism:

Extract 6

> *Vicky:* Well, (2) *I'm not sure how to put it (.) It sounds terrible and I- I can sort of see it from their point of view.* You know, I, I, I understand wh- why they want it or think they want it. (.) So erm I do understand how they feel and (.) at one level I hope it all works out. But another part of me is thinking (.) and it's not (.) I'm not (.) you know it sounds a bit racist ((laugh)) but as I said my Dad's from Scotland so I'm half Scottish myself and (2) I dunno (.) eh (3) cos one of my most vivid childhood memories is visiting my cousins in Scotland and how they kept bullying me for being English and I remember being sort of surprised that the grown-ups never said anything about it, it was in fact like it was "ha ha" something funny you know. Obviously, that's different but at the same time I would have thought that maybe people should perhaps be working trying to prevent that sort of mindset. And as a Socialist and someone who works a lot with international organizations I don't like nationalism full stop. And I'm inclined to think that whatever the problems the Scots think

they have with the Union nationalism isn't the solution (3) This current obsession with national identity and divisions isn't healthy. You just have to look at what's happened in the Balkans. And I know it probably sounds terrible but I seriously think that to establish a new national parliament just at a time when with Europe there's some sort of chance that we could really be moving forward (.) looking towards the larger picture (.) well it all seems rather counterproductive.

In this exchange, Vicky displays her understanding of a range of political issues. However, viewed in the context of the interview discussion as a whole, it is clear that these references were effectively substituting for domain-specific political information concerning the Scottish Parliament per se. At no stage in the extract, or the three-hour interview from which it was drawn, did Vicky ever refer to any specific factual information pertaining to UK constitutional change.

Opinion consistency: Empty attitudes as rhetorical constraint

In his seminal account of non-attitudes, Converse (1964) famously argued that uninformed opinions lack ideological *constraint* and are therefore subject to random variation over time and across contexts. Consequently, it was interesting to note that in the panel study element of our research, individuals' empty attitudes concerning the Scottish Parliament were not inclined to vary in response to changes in the conversational context, and they displayed a remarkable degree of consistency over time. This stability was not simply confined to attitude valence. Commonly, people justified their opinions on different occasions by drawing from the same stock of considerations, lines of argument, exemplary narratives, tropes and clichés.

For illustrative purposes, let us consider how one particular respondent – Jerry – discussed the Scottish Parliament on three separate occasions over a seven-year period. In his first interview (Extract 5), Jerry claimed a positive opinion towards the new Scottish Parliament, a position which we warranted with a reference to the existence of a distinctive Scottish identity relayed through the use of active voicing ("We're not British, we're Scottish"). Twenty-two months later, Jerry participated in a group discussion in which the topic of the Scottish Parliament arose spontaneously:

Extract 7

Jerry: What's the matter with Scotland?
Vicky: Nothing's the matter with Scotland. I'm half Scottish myself. It's a beautiful place. I just wouldn't want to live there.
I: Because?
Vicky: It's that, "we're Scottish, you're English" mentality.
Jerry: I like that though. If they think of themselves as Scottish, why not?
Vicky: Obviously I don't mind them thinking of themselves as Scottish. I think of myself as English. But it's one thing having a sense of identity, and another to be nationalistic.

Jerry: So do you not think there should be a Scottish Parliament, then?
Vicky: I dunno. On the one hand there's part of me that thinks obviously they voted for it and so I can't turn round and say to them, as an English person, "no you can't have it". But personally I just don't like nationalism. And I think recently we've seen what a dangerous thing nationalism can be and you'd think that it might have made everyone think before just jumping on the bandwagon.
Jerry: But doesn't that make sense for every nation to rule themselves.
Vicky: Er (.) I suppose one reason I do feel so strongly about this is I used to visit my Dad's family in Scotland as a child, and I HATED it (.) cos my cousins were always at me about being English. They'd mock my accent and say "English go home" and my Aunt and Uncle were like "Ha isn't that sweet". And I think that sort of nationalism can easily come come out in other ways. And in terms of politics I think that at the start of the twenty first century we should be thinking about how to make the world more inclusive how to have more cooperation between people not go back to that nineteenth century idea of every little separate nation for itself. So no, a Scottish Parliament, Welsh whatever I think it's a backward step.
(3)
I: Do you agree?
Dan: I dunno. I don't have strong views but I think it's probably a good thing. A good thing. Scottish people have always had a different way of life to us and so I can understand why they would want to have their own parliament. They want different things and we want different things because it's a completely different culture.
Jerry: I agree and, I mean they they themselves (.) the Scots have their own identity (.) And if it was like they said "yes we are UK" and everyone got on and was happy with it, then I'd be all for y'know. But it's not like that (.) as you say they've got their own culture and they say "we're Scottish". So if that means they want their own parliament and their own independence fair enough. It just makes sense for every country to just have it's own separate parliament.

In this extract we see Jerry again expressing a positive view towards the Scottish Parliament and justifying this opinion with turns of phrase ("have their own identity", "fair enough", "it just makes sense") and rhetorical tropes, including the use of active voicing to convey a sense of Scottish claims to national identity, which are markedly similar to those that he employed in his original interview.

Similarly, Dan is justifying his opinion through the same non-specific reference to lifestyle differences between England and Scotland that he had used in a one-to-one interview two years earlier (Extract 4), and Vicky is again justifying a negative stance with reference to her principled opposition to political nationalism and employing the same anecdote concerning her childhood experiences as we saw her use in Extract 6.

Jerry's third interview was conducted seven years after his original research chat. Extract 8 records the stretch of talk that followed after the interviewer had directly solicited Jerry's views on devolution and the Scottish Parliament.

Extract 8

I: I was just wondering, like we're interested in what people think about some of the current erm events that have been going on since we last spoke to them

Jerry: Right. OK.

I: One thing is like devolution, and the Scottish Parliament. Do you have maybe any views on that?

Jerry: Yeah well I think it's right that they should have their own parliament because they they don't say they are British, they have their own identity. Britain isn't like Scotland, Wales, England, Northern Ireland all getting on, and if they want their own parliament, they are separate countries, then yeah it makes sense? Y'know it's fair enough.

I: Do you think that England should have its own parliament?

Jerry: Yes. If you have a Scottish Parliament, then why not?
(2)

I: Do you think that's- things to do with the Scottish Parliament and whether there should be an English parliament, is that something you've maybe changed your mind about at all, over the past few years (.) or not really?

Jerry: I dunno. Um (.) Until you mentioned it just now (.) I don't know if I've thought of it to be honest with you. Um that it's- it's not, know what I mean? It's not something you really hear a lot about, is it? It's not something you know about. You know, it doesn't exactly crop up in conversation, does it? "Hello how's things and by the way you know that thing about devolution-?" ((laughter))

I: So how often would you say you discussed this sort of thing?

Jerry: I dunno (2) I'm not sure I ever have to be honest with you.

Years after his first interview, and in a very different kind of research context,[13] Jerry is still claiming positive attitudes towards the Scottish Parliament; he is still warranting this stance with reference to the fact that "they ... have their own identity", and he is still treating national political self-determination as an incontrovertible political value.

This kind of consistency over time and across contexts was typical of empty-attitude formulations and seemed to be a consequence of the fact that respondents' abilities to conceptualize and articulate views was effectively constrained by their reliance on a limited set of political considerations and rhetorical heuristics.[14] This observation points to the possibility that there may exist more than one causal route to the accomplishment of attitude reliability. On the one hand, the articulation of coherent, stable and robust opinions may represent a function of political knowledge and active engagement, combined with the capacity to locate a particular issue within a more general system of political events, beliefs and values (the process that

Converse called "ideological constraint"). On the other hand, insofar as instability in political attitude avowals may stem from variations in the situational salience of particular political considerations (Zaller, 1992), it would follow that attitude *in*consistency may also depend upon social actors possessing a reasonably extensive repertoire of relevant considerations to apply to a political event or process.

Concluding comments

In this chapter I have noted a deep-rooted cultural ambivalence in discussions of public opinion. On the one hand, public opinion is treated as the ultimate source of political authority in direct or representative democracies. On the other hand, the irrational tendencies ascribed to public opinion can be regarded as the antithesis of the reasonable judgments required for political decision making. Survey researchers often reify this conceptual ambivalence by distinguishing between two forms of political common sense, exemplified by Converse's "black and white" model. On the one hand, politically sophisticated individuals' responses to opinion polls reflect genuine opinions. Their attitudes are highly crystalized, stable over time and derived from an active engagement with factual information. These "genuine" opinions possess internal consistency and are integrated within a general, abstract, ideological frame of reference. On the other hand, the poll responses of less sophisticated individuals often take the form of non-attitudes: verbal responses which are not based on factual knowledge or are integrated into an abstract system of ideology and which are subject to quasi-random variation depending on question wording and context.

By exploring the ways in which political opinions are expressed in everyday talk, it becomes easier to examine how people actually mobilize political information. In this chapter I have focused on a particular class of opinionation, which I termed *empty attitudes*. Superficially, empty attitudes look rather like non-attitudes: they involve a speaker adopting a stance for or against a political policy without reference to any domain-specific information. However, once we start to examine the ways in which empty attitudes are expressed, we become aware of some notable points of similarity with survey researchers' notions of sophisticated, crystalized opinions.

In the data corpus that I have been considering, there were some cases in which respondents' attitude claims involved ("spurious") verbal responses to questions that they did not appear to understand. More often, however, empty attitudes comprised sincere (if not especially salient, central or strongly held) evaluative stances.[15] When respondents were unable to mobilize domain-specific information to support their views, they were nevertheless able to draw upon a stock of ideological values and knowledge concerning political rights, responsibilities and social justice to enable them to formulate their opinions as justifiable and acceptable interventions in a current public controversy. Individuals who were more actively engaged in political life could explicitly mention the political principles on which their views were based. However, less politically sophisticated respondents could still employ rhetorical heuristics that drew implicitly upon general ideological principles. Notwithstanding, or more precisely because of, their lack of issue content, empty attitudes could be highly internally coherent and consistent over time and tended to be justified in highly abstract terms. And, in common with many abstract forms of social reasoning, empty attitude formulations tended to prioritize deontic issues rather than "rational" concerns over personal or group self-interest (Condor, 2012). Cognitive psychology perspectives on heuristic political reasoning often adopt a deficit model of public opinion. Starting from the assumption that "information is critical for citizens to perform their democratic duties", authors emphasize the "shortfalls of shortcuts" (Rogowski, 2013, p. 1). However, were we to extend Gigerenzer's (2015) perspective on the ecological rationality of heuristic judgments to the field of political opinionation, we might start to appreciate some of the ways in which rhetorical heuristics may function to enable social actors to enact the role of reasonable democratic citizens in complex modern societies.

Notes

1 Although I am focussing on modern debates about public opinion, similar concerns can be identified in classical debates concerning *episteme* versus *doxa* (Barilli, 1989).
2 Mr Hollobone (Kettering) (Con) *Hansard* 11 Dec 2013: Column 80WH.
3 Justice Committee – First Report *Cutting crime: The case for justice reinvestment*. House of Commons, 1 December 2009.
4 Mr Wilshire (Spelthorne) (Con) *Hansard* 12 Jan 1998: Columns 89–90.
5 Mr. Luff (Con) *Hansard* 16 Jan 1998: Column 63.
6 The phrase "settled will of the Scottish people" is a conventionalized formulation first introduced by the Labour Party leader John Smith.
7 The 2003 British Social Attitudes survey included a four-item test of knowledge. Secondary analysis by the present author indicated a lower than chance level of correct response to the four knowledge questions: in England, 72% of respondents answered one or no questions correctly.
8 This research was conducted with Jackie Abell, Clifford Stevenson and Stephen Gibson. For details of the methodology, see Condor (2010, 2012).
9 This method was chosen to reflect the kinds of situations in which everyday discussion of political issues might normally occur (Scheufele, 1999).
10 Collected for the project: Migrants and Nationals, conducted with Frank Bechhofer, David McCrone and Richard Kiely at Edinburgh University, funded within the Leverhulme Trust Constitutional Change and Identity programme.
11 Transcription symbols:
    dash -   Abrupt cut off
    question mark ?   Rising inflection
    [2.5]   Pause measured to the nearest second
    (.)   Pause of less than one second
    [...]   Omitted material
12 *Why not* arguments also point to the operation of just world beliefs (Lerner, 1980).
13 This was a telephone interview, taking the form of a direct question-and-answer exchange, and it was directed by a different interviewer.
14 This may, of course, have been the result of the respondents' attempts to appear consistent. However, the interviews were deigned to be nonreactive with respect to the core topics of our research. Respondents often failed to display any memory of earlier conversations (see e.g. Extract 8), and it was notable that their views on issues on which they possessed more factual knowledge tended to be far less consistent.

15 Although public opinion researchers typically assume that people develop genuine attitudes only through active engagement with relevant information, social psychologists argue that people may not require detailed information to develop sincere attitudes (e.g. Zajonc, 1980). As Thurstone noted, "the important point for the purpose of attitude measurement is that . . . vagueness in supplying cognitive detail does not in the least invalidate [an individual's] expression of attitude" (1931, p. 267).

References

Allport, F. (1937). Toward a science of public opinion. *The Public Opinion Quarterly, 1*, 7–23.
Asch, S. (1952). *Social psychology*. Englewood Cliffs, NJ: Prentice-Hall.
Barilli, R. (1989). *Rhetoric*. Minneapolis: University of Minnesota Press.
Billig, M. (1987). *Arguing and thinking*. Cambridge: Cambridge University Press.
Billig, M. (1995). *Banal nationalism*. London: Sage.
Billig, M. (2013). *Learn to write badly*. Cambridge, UK: Cambridge University Press.
Blumer, H. (1948). Public opinion and public opinion polling. *American Sociological Review, 13*, 542–549.
Bourdieu, P. (1993). Public opinion does not exist. In *Sociology in question* (trans. R. Nice) (pp. 149–157). Newbury Park, CA: Sage.
Bryant, C. (2008). Devolution, equity and the English question. *Nations and Nationalism, 14*, 664–683.
Bryce, J.V. (1921). *Modern democracies* (Vol. 1) New York: Macmillan.
Childs, H. (1965). *Public opinion*. Princeton, NJ: D van Nostrand Company.
Condor, S. (2010). Devolution and national identity: The rules of English dis/engagement. *Nations & Nationalism, 16*, 525–543.
Condor, S. (2011). Sense and sensibility: The conversational etiquette of English national self-identification. In A. Aughey & C. Berbech (Eds.), *These Englands: A conversation on national identity* (pp. 29–55). Manchester: Manchester University Press.
Condor, S. (2012). Understanding English public reactions to the Scottish Parliament. *National Identities, 14*, 83–98.
Condor, S., & Gibson, S. (2007). 'Everybody's entitled to their own opinion': Ideological dilemmas of liberal individualism and active citizenship. *Journal of Community and Applied Social Psychology, 6*, 178–199.
Converse, J. (1987). *Survey research in the United States: 1890–1960*. Berkeley: University of California Press.
Converse, P. E. (1964). The nature of belief systems in mass publics. In D. E. Apter (Ed.), *Ideology and discontent* (pp. 206–261). London: Collier-Macmillan.
Curtice, J., & Seyd, B. (2001). Is devolution strengthening or weakening the UK? In A. Park, J. Curtice, K. Thomson, L. Jarvis & C. Bromley. (Eds.), *British social attitudes: The 18th report* (pp. 227–244). London: Sage.
Drury, J. P. M. (2014). *Speaking with the people's voice*. College Station: Texas A & M University Press.
Gallop, G., & Rae, S. F. (1940). *The pulse of democracy*. New York: Glen & Schuster.
Gigerenzer, G. (2015). *Simply rational*. Oxford: Oxford University Press.
Goldsmith, R. E. (2001). Reducing spurious response in a field survey. *Journal of Social Psychology, 129*, 201–212.
Haslam, S. A., Reicher, S. D., & Platow, M. J. (2011). *The new psychology of leadership*. Hove, East Sussex: Psychology Press.
Herbst, S. (1993). *Numbered voices: How opinion polling shaped American politics*. Chicago: University of Chicago Press.

Heritage, J. (1984). *Garfinkel and ethnomethodology.* Cambridge: Polity Press.
Heritage, J. (1995). The terms of agreement. *Social Psychology Quarterly, 68,* 15–38.
Key, V. O. (1961). *Public opinion and American democracy.* New York: Alfred Knopf.
Krosnick, J. A., Narayan, S. S., & Smith, W. R. (1996). Satisficing in surveys. In M. T. Braverman & J. K. Slater (Eds.), *Advances in survey research* (pp. 29–44). San Francisco: Jossey-Bass.
Lazarsfeld, P. F. (1944). The controversy over detailed interviews – an offer for negotiation. *Public Opinion Quarterly, 8,* 38–60.
Lerner, M. (1980). *The Belief in a Just World.* New York: Plenum.
Likert, R. (1947). The sample interview survey. In W. Dennis (Ed.), *Current trends in psychology* (pp. 427–434). Pittsburgh: University of Pittsburgh Press.
Lippmann, W. (1922). *Public Opinion.* New York: Harcourt, Brace and Company.
Manza, J., & Brooks, C. (2012). How sociology lost public opinion. *Sociological Theory, 30,* 89–113.
Murphy, G., & Likert, R. (1938). *Public opinion and the individual.* Oxford: Harper.
Osborne, T., & Rose, N. (1999). Do the social sciences create phenomena? The example of public opinion research. *British Journal of Sociology, 3,* 367–396.
Palmer, P. A. (1936). Public opinion in political theory. In C. Wittke (Ed.), *Essays in history and political theory* (pp. 230–257). Cambridge MA: Harvard University Press.
Potter, J., Edwards, D., & Ashmore, M. (1994). The bottom line. *Configurations, 2,* 1–14.
Price, V. (1992). *Public opinion* (pp. 7–24). Thousand Oaks, CA: Sage.
Rehfeld, A. (2006). Towards a general theory of political representation. *The Journal of Politics, 68,* 1–21.
Riesman, D., & Glazer, N. (1949). The meaning of opinion. *The Public Opinion Quarterly, 12,* 633–648.
Rogowski J. (2013). The shortfalls of shortcuts: Elections, heuristics, and vote choice. Retrieved from http://pages.wustl.edu/files/pages/imce/rogowski/shortfalls_shortcuts.pdf
Rosie, M., Peterson, P., MacInnes, J., Condor, S., & Kennedy, J. (2006). Mediating which nation? National identities in the British Press. *Semiotica, 16,* 327–344.
Sapountzis, A., & Condor, S. (2013). Conspiracy accounting as intergroup theory. *Political Psychology, 34,* 731–745.
Scheufele, D. (1999). Deliberation or dispute? *International Journal of Public Opinion Research, 11,* 25–58.
Sperber, D., & Wilson, D. (1981). Irony and the use-mention distinction. In P. Cole (Ed.), *Radical pragmatics* (pp. 295–318). New York: Academic Press.
Thurstone, L. (1931). The measurement of social attitudes. *Journal of Abnormal and Social Psychology, 27,* 249-269.
Zajonc, R. (1980). Feeling and thinking: Preferences need no inferences. *American Psychologist, 35,* 151–175.
Zaller, J. R. (1992). *The nature and origins of mass opinion.* New York: Cambridge University Albany Law Review.

13
EVERYDAY POLITICS AND THE EXTREME RIGHT

Lay explanations of the electoral performance of the neo-Nazi political party Golden Dawn in Greece

Lia Figgou

Introduction

Political life in many European countries has recently witnessed the dramatic rise of the voting rates of extreme right political parties, a phenomenon that has naturally provoked social scientific research. In order to explain the electoral success of the extreme right, social and political scientists have paid attention to various factors. First, they have turned their attention to those conditions that restructured the political spectrum and reorganized political alliances in various countries. Studies have explored the sociopolitical changes that paved the way for extreme right parties to appear as important political agents in particular contexts and have identified similarities, but also striking differences, between the far right camps across Europe (Arzheimer, 2009; Mammone, Godin & Jenkins, 2012; Pauwels, 2014).

Party organization, leadership and communication strategies have been considered to have an impact on the extent to which extreme right parties attract – and sustain – electoral success (Harrison & Bruter, 2011). Most authors have identified a duplicitous communication policy adopted by extreme right leaders, according to which they tend to circulate extreme messages in private, when they address their hard core supporters, but they tend to use a moderate, nonpolarized language in their public rhetoric (Billig, 1978, 2001; Goodman & Johnson, 2013; Richardson & Wodak, 2009). A cyclical communication strategy has been identified by Harrison and Bruter (2011), according to which populist references tend to be dominant in extreme right-wing discourse during electoral campaigns, while extreme xenophobic messages come to the fore during noncampaign periods. Research has also paid attention to the strategic management of party status in order to mobilize support (Figgou, Mylopoulou & Birmbili-Karaleka, 2013; Rooyackers & Verkuyten, 2011; Sapountzis, in press), showing that while in terms of access to power extreme right parties are represented to have a minority status, in terms of popular interests they are constructed as par excellence representatives of the majority.

Existing studies have also attempted to cast light on the motives and the profiles of right-wing extremist voters and to provide answers to a double question. The first refers to the extent to which voter decision is mainly influenced by the way in which specific issues have been emphasized and handled in the pre-electoral campaign (issue voting) or reflects voters' attitudes and derives from congruence with the general ideological agenda of extreme right-wing parties (party voting). A second puzzlement concerns the extent to which voting decision reflects tangible or symbolic interests of voters or constitutes a protest vote, the drives of which are not necessarily 'rational' (Billiet & De Witte, 2008; Rydgren, 2008).

Political psychology has fundamentally contributed to the exploration of attitudes and motives that determine the electorate's receptivity of extreme right ideological positions. The assumption that ideological commitments spring – at least partly – from underlying psychological needs and motives has guided highly influential projects in social and political psychology. Authoritarianism (as a complex mixture of personality conflicts, socialization pressures and prejudiced orientations), coined by Adorno and his colleagues more than six decades ago, remains compelling (e.g., Altemeyer, 1988; Stenner, 2005) and has been used to predict extreme right-wing voting (Billiet & De Witte, 2008; Lubbers & Güveli, 2007). Social dominance orientation – identified as one's degree of preference for inequality among social groups – has been related to right-wing political party preferences (Pratto, Stallworth & Sidanius, 1997; Sidanius, Pratto & Bobo, 1996) and extreme right-wing voting in particular (Cornelis & Van Hiel, 2014). Political psychologists have also put forward that although attitudes may constitute valid explanatory factors of the extreme right ideological orientations of advantaged social groups, the disadvantaged may embrace far right-wing ideologies motivated by psychological efforts to cope with economic insecurity and threat (Napier & Jost, 2008).

The attempt to study politics through the lens of individual attitudes, personality dynamics and motivated cognition has recently attracted critique by a number of scholars who aim to transplant concepts and tools from critical social psychology to political psychology (Haste, 2004; Tileagă, 2013; Weltman & Billig, 2001). These scholars' visions of political psychology involve a focus on the *thinking society* (Moscovici, 1984b) and an approach to language, communication and interaction as the arenas in which political ideologies are – intersubjectively – produced and reproduced and political issues are defined and explained. By shifting the interest of political psychology from individual differences and universal cognition to the historically specific common sense of particular communities, critical political psychological perspectives also underscore the need to put everyday politics in the centre of our attention.

This chapter constitutes an attempt to study extreme right politics by paying attention to lay explanations. It is based on the assumption that the interest to explain the rising popularity of the extreme right is not confined to social and political scientists or to the protagonists of institutional politics. It also constitutes an important topic of everyday debates and a concern for lay people. But although the attempts to explain the phenomenon by political and social scientists proliferate, its lay explanations remain fairly unexplored. The particular focus of the chapter is on the common sense explanations of the surprisingly strong electoral performance of Golden Dawn, a political party with an overtly Nazi ideological agenda and practices, in recent elections in Greece. Before proceeding to consider the sociopolitical context of the study, however, let me sketch the theoretical approach to social explanations that it has adopted.

Studying social explanations as social representations situated in argumentative contexts

In his attempt to provide a unifying meta-theoretical framework and to construct bridges between the *lonely paradigms* that are dispersed in the archipelagos of social psychology, Moscovici (1984a) argued that explanations – largely approached in terms of individualistic attribution schemata – should be studied within the context of the *social representations* that vindicate them, within the context of lay theories about politics and morality, culture and society, personality and psychology.

The theory of social representations has been criticized that it overemphasized consistency and consensus in the social representations of certain communities or groups (Potter & Wetherell, 1987). Nevertheless, according to authors working within this tradition, the fact that they constitute consensual ways of making sense of social reality does not prevent social representations from containing contradictory elements (Howarth, 2014; Provencher, 2011). As Wagner and Hayes (2005) maintained, from the early stages of research on social representations, it was apparent that representations with conflicting meanings were part of everyday thinking and the concept of 'cognitive polyphasia' was coined by Moscovici (1984b) to depict these incompatible representations. Focusing on the commonsense explanations of health-related issues, Jovchelovitch and Gervais (1999), for example, paradigmatically showed how members of the Chinese community in England applied contradictory explanations in their talk, depending on the audience and the particular situation.

Billig et al. (1988), in their seminal account of the ideology of everyday life, shared with the theory of social representations the interest to study the thinking society and emphasized the contradictory aspects of everyday ideology, including everyday explanations. Nevertheless, they did not consider dilemmas and contradictions as a possibility, but as a *sine qua non* characteristic of everyday ideology. The availability of contrary themes, according to their approach, is a necessary condition, in order for social actors to think and argue about the issues that dominate their everyday lives. Social explanations, as particular lines of arguing, take their full meaning from the argumentative context, from those explanations that they aim to criticize (see also Billig, 1987).

By emphasizing the rhetorical aspects of common sense explanations, the approach of Billig et al. (1988) entailed also a focus on the rhetorical formulation of accounts and on language as social practice. By the same token, it paved the way for a combination between the focus on the micro-interactional with social representations theorists' attention to the diffuse cultural-historical processes that shape the availability of social explanations (Gibson, forthcoming). An approach to explanations as context-specific social practices has also been elaborated in the writings of discursive psychologists. According to them, social actors are routinely engaged in managing issues of agency and responsibility and explanations are bound up with issues of accountability (Edwards & Potter, 1992; see also Antaki, 1994).

Central in the way in which speakers attend to accountability issues is, according to Potter (1996), the management of *footing* (Goffman, 1981). Footing practices that present the speaker as both *animator* and *origin* of the talk increase accountability vis-a-vis distanced footing practices (e.g. careful quotation). Related to the topic of 'footing' is the 'mention and use distinction' in the formulation of social explanations put forward by Potter and Litton (1985; see also McKinlay, Potter & Wetherell, 1993). According to these authors, when we study social explanations as social representations in action situated in specific rhetorical-argumentative contexts, we need to pay attention to the distinction between social explanations that are 'mentioned' but not necessarily used to account for specific phenomena, explanations that are espoused 'in theory' and explanations that are developed with a very specific application and are used 'in practice'. Similarly, Howarth (2006) pointed to the distinction between representations which are 'used' to defend a particular construction of reality and representations that are 'mentioned' in resistance to other versions of reality considered to be in conflict with a speaker's stake, position and self-identity. These alternative versions of reality, usually attributed to other people, are *altered*, according to Gillespie (2008), by being simplified and stereotyped and by being located as dialogical shadows (as 'straw men') in polemical representations.

In this chapter, in line with the premises of the theory of social representations, I am interested to study my participants' explanations of the rise of Golden Dawn within the context of commonplace theories about politics and societies that maintain them. In line with Billig's (1987) rhetorical psychology, explanations are approached as rhetoric situated in particular argumentative contexts. Finally, in line with discursive psychologists, my approach also takes into account the rhetorical formulation of particular explanations and considers explanations as social practices oriented to moral accountability issues.

Background to the study: Golden Dawn and its electoral performance

Together with one of the deepest postwar recessions, Greece has recently also witnessed the electoral breakthrough of Golden Dawn (Χρυσή Αυγή, *Chrysi Avgi*), a political party with an overtly Nazi ideological agenda, emblems and practices. Golden Dawn was founded in early 1980s by its current leader, Nikos Michaloliakos. It has been identified with National-Socialist Germany through its publications, symbols and contacts with other European neo-Nazi organizations (Psarras, 2012). What brings Golden Dawn close to the political action of the historic German Nazi party (NSDAP) are, according to other commentators, its leading model, in which the absolute authority of the head is recognized; its paramilitary organization; and its use of violence (Ellinas, 2010, 2013; Georgiadou, 2013).

The party remained relatively inactive until the 1990s. In the beginning of the 1990s, in a climate influenced by the nationalistic eagerness which followed the clash between Greece and the Former Yugoslav Republic of Macedonia over the name Macedonia, Golden Dawn started its public appearances, and throughout the 1990s it gained notoriety for incidents of violence and Nazi propaganda. After the 1990s, it made an effort to avoid explicit reference to National Socialism and to present itself as a Greek nationalist party (Psarras, 2012). Nevertheless, the position of the party on the political scene of the country remained rather marginal until 2010. The first signs of change appeared in the municipal elections of November 2010 in which Golden Dawn got 5.29% of votes in the municipality of Athens. The big change, though, occurred in the national elections of June 2012 when, Golden Dawn won about 7% and managed to elect 18 representatives.

The strong electoral performance of Golden Dawn was followed by revelations about the involvement of its leader, MPs and executive members in murders and dozens of racist assaults. In fact, the reactions caused by the murder of a Greek antifascist rapper, Pavlos Fyssas, by a Golden Dawn member in September 2013 opened Pandora's box and hastened the judicial investigation of cases of racist violence that had been mostly left unexplored. Nevertheless, and despite the fact that its leadership was in prison, in the local elections of May 2014, Golden Dawn's mayoral candidate in Athens won 16.1% of the vote. Golden Dawn also won 6.28% of the total vote and elected 17 representatives in the last national elections of January 2015.

The study

Participants, procedure and analytic priorities

Data were derived from 12 interviews and 4 focus group discussions conducted in Athens and Thessaloniki (Northern Greece). They all took place in the period between September 2012 and February 2013. Participants were 22 men and 20 women aged between 19 and 65 years and of different political affiliations, none of which – according to their self reports – had voted for Golden Dawn. The interview plan (used both in individual interviews and focus group discussions) involved questions on the reasons of Golden Dawn's electoral success (in the 2012 national elections), its relations to other Greek political parties, the ways in which the media coped with its electoral performance and potential ways of restraining the rise of Golden Dawn. Interviews were conducted on a one-to-one basis. In each focus group discussion, two moderators were present. Interviews and focus group discussions were fully transcribed. For the purposes of the present chapter, extracts have been translated from Greek to English. Needless to say that translation unavoidably involves the danger of losing subtleties of meaning.

Analysis used tools and concepts from rhetorical psychology (Billig, 1987) and discursive (Edwards & Potter, 1992) and critical discursive psychology (Wetherell, 1998). At a first stage, analytic focus was on the identification of recurrent topics/themes and commonplace resources mobilized in participants' explanatory accounts. At a second stage, analytic focus shifted to the rhetorical formulation of accounts and to issues of footing (Goffman, 1981) and accountability. Finally, an attempt was made to link participants' accounts with the broader argumentative context, treating them as fragments of broader historically and culturally specific social representations.

Analysis indicated a number of commonplace resources used or mentioned in order to explain the rise of Golden Dawn. A complex mosaic, comprising a series of multifaceted relationships between the rise of Golden Dawn and aspects of social and political life, was constructed in participants' discourse. There is no room to refer to all sorts of accounting in this chapter. I will rather focus on those mobilized in all individual interviews and group discussions without exception, albeit constructed and formulated in two ways: (1) the construction of voting for Golden Dawn as a response to the 'immigration problem' and (2) the representation of votes for Golden Dawn as protest votes aiming to penalize the political system and its representatives.

Constructing voting for Golden Dawn as a response to the (illegal) immigration problem

Rather unsurprisingly, given the emphasis put on immigration in its pre-electoral campaign, one of the commonplace explanations articulated by my participants associated the electoral success of Golden Dawn with immigration in Greece. Extract 1 constitutes a paradigmatic example mentioning such an explanation.

Extract 1

```
 1   Int/er:   Why do you think people voted for Golden Dawn in the last
 2             elections? How come (.) I mean why Golden Dawn has suddenly
 3             acquired so [much support?
 4   Alexis:   [How? I would say (...) people believe that immigration
 5             is responsible (.) that Golden Dawn has been voted to solve (.) let's
 6             put it this way (.) to solve the immigration problem. In recent years
 7             there has been an enormous increase of illegal immigration in the
 8             country
 9   Int/er:   Mmm (.) So IT IS immigration [that
10   Alexis:   [immigration IS a problem (.) it is a
11             fact I can't doubt. I can't deny that some areas of Greece have indeed
12             a problem with the accumulation of immigrants (.) for me of course
```

13		things are not as the Golden Dawn people and the media present
14		them. Their propaganda that immigrants are responsible for ALL the
15		ills of our country (. . .) It is their way to manipulate the masses and to
16		create enemies. Unfortunately there are people who think this way.

(Man, 38, Thessaloniki)

Extract 1 comes from the opening part of an interview with a man in Thessaloniki, Alexis. Although he starts by adopting the footing of the principle of the talk, he shifts to the footing of the animator (Goffman, 1981) in order to mention (Potter & Litton, 1985) immigration as a potential explanation of the electoral performance of Golden Dawn (ll. 3–5). The speaker distances himself from the assumption that Golden Dawn could indeed provide a solution to the immigration problem (ll. 5–6) and from the irrationally generalized representation of immigrants as responsible for all the ills of the country (ll. 10–14) (cf. Figgou & Condor, 2006). This representation, attributed to the Golden Dawn people and the media, constitutes, according to Alexis, a means of manipulation exerted on other Greek people. People who adopt the anti-immigrant agenda of Golden Dawn are pejoratively constructed as the masses (l. 13). Such a construction has important implications both for the speaker's own accountability as well as for the agency attributed to Golden Dawn supporters. The participant represents himself as immune from improper influence. He also depicts Golden Dawn supporters, however, as not having full responsibility for their actions. The masses are not regarded to be acting rationally and autonomously (Reicher, 2001; see also Figgou, 2013).

Despite his rhetorical distance from the representation of voting for Golden Dawn as a potential response to immigration, Alexis adopts the footing of the principle of the talk, in order to construct immigration as a real problem. The problematic nature of immigration in Greece is portrayed both as a fact (ll. 6–7) as well as a personal belief (ll. 11–12). Hence, Alexis seems to manage his accountability by formulating a balanced account. He distances himself from the victims of Golden Dawn's anti-immigration propaganda. He avoids denying, however, that immigration in Greece is a real problem. Immigration is also considered to be a serious problem by the participant quoted in Extract 2.

Extract 2

1	Int/er:	I want to look at how people explain the electoral success of Golden
2		Dawn (.) what are the reasons for the fact that (.) at least as the polls
3		indicate (.) it continues to attract potential voters and supporters.
4	Lina:	I see. You have to look at the situation in Athens in order to get the
5		answer. It is there that Golden Dawn got many votes (.) and the
6		main problem there is immigration
7	Int/er:	So you think it is immigration
8	Lina:	Illegal immigration (.) I am not talking about legal immigrants (.)
9		illegal immigration is the most important concern in Greece at the
10		moment (.) the most serious problem that the country faces. Those

11		who deny it they simply try to hide themselves behind their finger.
12		They just beat about the bush.
13	Int/er:	Erm (...) and ...
14	Lina:	And here comes Golden Dawn and says let's (.) let's throw them all
15		out of the country. Extreme (.) of course (...) but it is a solution in
16		people's eyes. For me this is the reason for them being popular,
17		being supported.

(Woman, 47, Thessaloniki)

Extract 2 constitutes a paradigmatic example of explicitly using (Potter & Litton, 1985) an explanation in terms of immigration. According to Lina, the electoral success of Golden Dawn can indeed be attributed to the expectation of some Greek people that it could provide a solution to the immigration problem (ll. 16–17). The validity of such an explanation becomes evident, the speaker maintains, if someone considers the situation in Athens, where the increased polling rate of Golden Dawn goes hand in hand with the increased accumulation of immigrants (ll. 4–6).

Despite their differences regarding the extent to which an explanation of the rise of Golden Dawn in terms of immigration is mentioned or used, there are also apparent similarities between Extracts 1 and 2. In common with Alexis in Extract 1, Lina constructs immigration as a serious concern. Her focus is on illegal immigration, a category which, according to other commentators (O'Doherty & Le Couteur, 2007), can function to legitimate social exclusionary practices by explicitly evoking associations of immigration with unlawfulness. The speaker explicitly distances herself from those who refute the 'immigration problem' in Greece, representing their stance as hypocritical, as a tendency to "beat about the bush". Her account seems to echo voices that attribute the success of Golden dawn to activists and antiracists and to be in line with findings documented in recent discursive studies on immigration and race talk (Augoustinos & Every, 2010). According to these studies, social actors are not only concerned to comply with the norm against prejudice; they are also cautious to deny the problematic aspects of immigration and to attribute opposition to it to some form of racism.

Lina – also in common with the participant in Extract 1 – is concerned with protecting herself from the stigma of extremity and keeping a distance from Golden Dawn's 'solution' to the immigration 'problem'. To recognize the problematic aspects of immigration does not mean to adhere to the extreme anti-immigrant agenda of Golden Dawn. Even if immigration is, indeed, the most serious problem, throwing them all out of the country, according to Lina, is an "extreme" act.

Constructing votes for Golden Dawn as votes against politicians and politics

According to another commonly identified way of accounting in my data, votes for Golden Dawn were constructed as protest votes, aiming to express the indignation of large sections of the Greek society towards politicians and the Greek political system in general.

Extract 3

1	*Moderator:*	Why so many people voted for Golden Dawn in your
2		opinion?
3	*Dimitris:*	I think that (...) let's say (...) I've heard many times (.) this is
4		of course an example (.) but I think it's representative.
5		When (.) when I go home by taxi, taxi drivers (.) because I
6		often talk about politics with them you see
7	*Moderator:*	Yes [they are keen to
8	*Dimitris:*	[they say "I have been voting for PASOK for thirty years
9		and this time I voted for Golden Dawn (.) and the reason why
10		I voted for them is that I want someone to be there to scare
11		them, to punish them for bringing us into this mess. Just did
12		it for this reason"
13	*Moderator:*	Who are the ones to be scared?
14	*Dimitris:*	[Politicians
15	*Philipos:*	[The government
16	*Moderator:*	So you think that's the way they think? Erm (.) the Golden
17		Dawn [voters
18	*Dimitris:*	[Yes, I mean they are not all of them skinhead
19		fascists (.) These are no more than 1% out of the 500,000
20		votes.
21	*Philipos:*	Less than that (.) the fascists ...

(Focus group 2, Athens)

Extract 3 constitutes an exchange between the moderator and two young men in Athens. Prior to the exchange, Dimitris referred to the remarkably high rates of voting for Golden Dawn in Athens, and the moderator's invitation to provide an explanation has been prompted by this reference. The explanation mentioned by the speaker represents Golden Dawn's electoral performance as the result of people's indignation against the politicians in Greece. False starts and pauses (ll. 2–5), but also footing shifts and the use of active voicing (Wooffitt, 1992) (ll. 7–11), work rhetorically to distance the speaker from the explanation mentioned. Nevertheless, at the same time, its commonplace nature is emphasized. It is represented as widely held, representative of how 'people in the street' think and act (ll. 3–4), as part and parcel of everyday politics. According to this commonplace explanation, people just did it in order to punish those who brought Greece into the messy situation of the current economic crisis. They did it in order to scare politicians and the government.

The narrative of Dimitris is encouraged by the moderator's intervention and reinforced by the contribution of Philippos. Two categorical distinctions are collaboratively constructed (Condor & Figgou, 2012) by the participants in the interaction. The first is between Golden Dawn and the political system. By arguing that people voted for Golden Dawn, in order to punish politicians for the mess in which they have brought Greece, they construct Golden Dawn as against the political establishment and above politics. The second is between the hard-core supporters of Golden Dawn (the "skinhead fascists") and those who – like the taxi driver who has been voting for the center-left party PASOK for 30 years – are not driven by their political ideology.

This second distinction has been widely identified in both individual interviews and focus group discussions. Participants put forward elaborated accounts on the profile of Golden Dawn members and its hard-core supporters, described as dogmatic, uneducated and psychologically unstable. These lay authoritarian personality accounts (Adorno et al., 1950) put forward by the participants serve to psychologize and to discredit through 'psychologization' (Papastamou, 1986) the extreme fascist members and hard-core supporters of Golden Dawn. At the same time, though, they constitute – explicitly or by implication – another category of voters whose votes constitute the result of indignation, and this is at least understandable. These non-ideology-driven voters are, according to the participants, the majority, while irrational fascists constitute less than 1% of the voters.

In the following extract, Stella and Andreas mobilize similar assumptions to those put forward in the previous extract constructing voting for Golden Dawn as the result of people's indignation and despair.

Extract 4

1	Moderator:	So what do you think of the fact that these people have been
2		elected in the [Parliament
3	Stella:	[This was a protest vote, I mean it is not that
4		people suddenly acquired neo-Nazi beliefs (.) it is not
5		ideological, it is a sign of (.) it is a complaint for our current
6		[situation
7	Andreas:	[Yeah things can't
8	Stella:	Can't get worse.
9	Andreas:	People have reached (.) our standard of living (. . .) it can't be
10		lower (.) so people say 'I don't vote for anybody. Things
11		can't be worse for me'
12	Stella:	This is the main reason

(Focus group 4, Thessaloniki)

According to contributors in Extract 4, votes for Golden Dawn are represented as reflecting despair and expressing Greek people's complaints for their current situation. They are also explicitly constructed as non-ideology-driven votes. Such an explanation is not only used by the speakers but it is also constructed – by various rhetorical means – as a fact out there in the world (Edwards & Potter, 1992). The credibility of the assumption that voting for Golden Dawn is not ideology driven is further grounded on the implausibility of the premise that people suddenly acquired Nazi beliefs. Since it is not sensible to suggest that all of a sudden people acquired neo-Nazi beliefs, as Stella puts it, then it is sensible to assume that this is not an ideological vote.

According to Billig et al. (1988, p. 151), words like *ideological* and *political* are often used in everyday discourse to refer to arguments and judgments that are characterized by bias and duplicity instead of being derived from an examination of the facts of evidence, and they are deduced from principles or, even worse, from dogmas. The account quoted in Extract 4 – as well as others similar to this one in my corpus of data – seems to presuppose an understanding of ideology in terms of a dogmatic and inflexible party line (see also Weltman & Billig, 2001). According to the line of arguing mobilized in Extract 4, people who have voted for Golden Dawn are non-ideology-driven voters since they do not endorse its extremist neo-Nazi agenda and do not follow a party line. In contrast, they voted for Golden Dawn because they "decided not to vote for anybody". Hence, apart from not being an ideology-driven vote, this was also an anti-political vote, a vote for nobody.

The argument that Golden Dawn voters were not driven by their political beliefs is also put forward in the following exchange.

Extract 5

```
1   Vassilis:   I don't think that this is true (...) I mean both young and older voters
2               did not vote based on their political beliefs. They wanted to send
3               some people (.) mainly politicians into a panic of fear (...) they
4               wanted something to happen, to change a change to come out of
5               this.
6   Spyros:     Have you seen anything to change?
7   Vassilis:   You can't say nothing happened.
8   Spyros:     Has anything changed?
9   Vassilis:   And how often have you seen things to change dramatically?
```

(Focus group 3, Thessaloniki)

Prior to the exchange quoted in Extract 5, Spyros drew a comparison between Golden Dawn's ideology and that of the leaders of the fairly recent military junta in Greece and argued that young people, who ignore Greek political history and who are largely indifferent in politics, constitute the majority of Golden Dawn voters. In Extract 5 Vassilis starts out his talk by expressing his disagreement with such an explanation. According to him, support to Golden Dawn should not be considered to derive either from political ignorance or from political beliefs. Following the line of arguing put forward by participants in the Extracts 3 and 4, Vassilis constructs votes for Golden Dawn as punitive votes, aiming to send some people – mainly politicians – into a panic of fear (ll. 2–3). He maintains, however, that voting for Golden Dawn is also a reaction against stagnation and inertia. By voting for Golden Dawn, people aimed at changing things. In the rest of the exchange, participants leave behind their concerns on the intentions of Golden Dawn supporters and keep on by disagreeing on whether anything has really changed in Greece as a result of the electoral result. Interestingly, the content and the political direction of change is not a matter to argue over. Change is treated as an *a priori* desirable and positive end.

Concluding remarks

My focus in this chapter was on the lay explanations of the recent strong electoral performance of the neo-Nazi political party Golden Dawn, as articulated in interviews and focus group discourse by Greek people. Analysis concentrated on two widely identified and variously articulated explanatory resources. According to the first, a vote for Golden Dawn constituted a response to the immigration issue, while according to the second, it was a protest vote aiming to punish politicians for the current situation in Greece. The first explanation was predicated upon a construction of immigration in Greece as a *par excellence* problem. Although participants in most cases kept distance from the anti-immigrant agenda of Golden Dawn, they themselves emphasized the problematic implications of immigration. The second was grounded upon a categorical distinction between the political system and Golden Dawn, portraying Golden Dawn as being against politicians and above politics. Widely shared was also a categorical distinction between ideology-driven and non-ideology-driven voters. The former, the bearers of fascist or neo-Nazi ideology, were considered to constitute a small minority, while the latter, the vast majority of voters, were portrayed as everyday people who are either driven by despair and indignation or victims of improper influence and propaganda.

Considering the role of the interactional context in affording these particular sorts of accounts/categorizations, I argued that my participants seemed to be oriented to a double accountability concern. On the one hand, they seem to position themselves as rational subjects, distanced from the extreme racist and fascist ideological agenda of Golden Dawn and from those who adopt it. On the other hand, they avoid casting the stigma of fascism on others. Condor et al. (2006) have maintained that social actors are interested not only in saving their own face but also in protecting others from charges of racism. Moreover, there is growing empirical evidence that apart from the widely identified taboo against racism (Augoustinos & Every, 2007; van Dijk, 1992), there is also a taboo against making accusations of racism (Goodman & Burke, 2010). My findings indicate that accusing others of fascism and ideological extremity may be related to similar concerns and may be constituted as equally problematic.

Nevertheless, apart from being coproduced in certain interactional contexts, the lay explanations put forward by my participants are also situated within broader argumentative, social and historical contexts. Hence, I would also like to consider the assumptions that votes for Golden Dawn were anti-immigration, protest and non-ideology-driven votes within the context of the broader, mainstream political dialogue in crisis-ridden Greece. Needless to say, the construction of immigration as a problem was prominent in the pre-electoral rhetoric of mainstream political parties in Greece which, in their attempt to win over voters, took over a great part of Golden Dawn's anti-immigrant rhetoric (Ellinas, 2010). Furthermore, an approach to politics as consensual and pragmatic is promoted both in Greece and in Europe, in general, as institutions led by technocrats and coalition governments, who are supposed to make important political decisions above or despite ideological differences between political parties, are represented as the ideal vehicles for governing and managing the economic crisis.

By way of conclusion and in the light of these findings, I would like to reflect upon the ways in which political psychology could benefit from a focus on the everyday, in general, and on lay accounts of extreme right politics, in particular. First, as indicated previously, parallels can be drawn between the explanations of lay actors and their implications in concrete contexts, on the one hand, and those of political psychologists, on the other, enabling the latter to estimate the potential but also the limitations of their concepts and tools. Second, an attempt to study extreme right politics through the 'kaleidoscope of common sense' (Billig et al., 1988), instead of studying the ideological profile and the attitudes of extreme voters alone, can broaden our view and understanding of the dissemination of extreme right ideologies. As my findings show, there is room to criticize but also to understand and legitimize support for the extreme right in the discourse of the same participants. Moreover, as other commentators have suggested, extreme right-wing ideologies and practices may be quite widespread even in contexts where right-wing extremism or populism as party phenomena or as crystallized attitudes and voting intentions remain relatively weak (Minkenberg, 2013).

References

Adorno, T.W., Frenkel-Brunswik, E., Levinson, D. J., & Sanford, R. N. (1950). *The authoritarian personality*. New York: Harper and Row.

Altemeyer, B. (1988). *Enemies of freedom: Understanding right-wing authoritarianism*. San Francisco: Jossey Bass.

Antaki, C. (1994). *Explaining and arguing: The social organization of accounts*. London: Sage.

Arzheimer, K. (2009). Contextual factors and the extreme right vote in Western Europe, 1980–2002. *American Journal of Political Science, 53*(2), 259–275.

Augoustinos, M., & Every, D. (2007). The language of 'race' and prejudice – A discourse of denial, reason, and liberal-practical politics. *Journal of Language and Social Psychology, 26*(2), 123–141.

Augoustinos, M., & Every, D. (2010). Accusations and denials of racism: Managing moral accountability in public discourse. *Discourse & Society, 21*(3), 251–256.

Billiet, J., & De Witte, H. (2008). Everyday racism as predictor of political racism in Flemish Belgium. *Journal of Social Issues, 64*(2), 253–267.

Billig, M. (1978). *Fascists: A social psychological view of the national front*. London: Academic Press.

Billig, M. (1987). *Arguing and thinking: A rhetorical approach to social psychology*. Cambridge: Cambridge University Press.

Billig, M. (2001). Humor and hatred: The racist jokes of the Ku Klux Klan. *Discourse & Society, 12*(3), 267–289.

Billig, M., Condor, S., Edwards, D., Gane, M., Middleton, D., & Radley, A. (1988). *Ideological dilemmas: A social psychology of everyday thinking*. London: Sage.

Condor, S., & Figgou, L. (2012). Rethinking the prejudice problematic: A collaborative cognition approach. In J. Dixon & M. Levine (Eds.), *Beyond prejudice: Extending the social psychology of conflict, inequality and social change* (pp. 200–222). Cambridge: Cambridge University Press.

Condor, S., Figgou, L., Abell, J., Gibson, S., & Stevenson, C. (2006). 'They're not racist. . . . ' Prejudice denial, mitigation and suppression in dialogue. *British Journal of Social Psychology*, *45*(3), 441–462.

Cornelis, I., & Van Hiel, A. (2014). Extreme-right voting in Western Europe: The role of social-cultural and antiegalitarian attitudes. *Political Psychology*. Advance online publication. doi:10.1111/pops.12187.x

Edwards, D., & Potter, J. (1992). *Discursive psychology*. London: Sage.

Ellinas, A. (2010). *The media and the far right in Western Europe: Playing the nationalist card*. Cambridge: Cambridge University Press.

Ellinas, A. (2013). The rise of the Golden Dawn: The new face of the far right in Greece. *South European Society and Politics*, *18*(4), 543–565.

Figgou, L. (2013). Essentialism, historical construction, and social influence: Representations of Pomakness in majority talk in Western Thrace (Greece). *British Journal of Social Psychology*, *52*(4), 686–702.

Figgou, L., & Condor, S. (2006). Irrational categorization, natural intolerance and reasonable discrimination: Lay representations of prejudice and racism. *British Journal of Social Psychology*, *45*(2), 219–243.

Figgou, L., Mylopoulou, I., & Birmbili-Karaleka, A. (2013). Construction of ideological extremity and 'minoritization' in the pre-electoral rhetoric of the far right party 'Golden Dawn'. *Scientific Annals of Aristotle University of Thessaloniki School of Psychology*, *10*, 499–527 (in Greek).

Georgiadou, V. (2013). Right-wing populism and extremism: The rapid rise of 'Golden Dawn' in crisis-ridden Greece. In R. Melzer & S. Serafin (Eds.), *Right-wing extremism in Europe: Country analyses, counter-strategies and labor-market oriented exit strategies* (pp. 75–102). Berlin: Friedrich-Ebert-Stiftung.

Gibson, S. (forthcoming). From representations to representing: On social representations and discursive-rhetorical psychology. In G. Sammut, E. Andreouli, G. Gaskell & J. Valsiner (Eds.), *The Cambridge handbook of social representations*. Cambridge: Cambridge University Press.

Gillespie, A. (2008). Social representations, alternative representations and semantic barriers. *Journal for the Theory of Social Behaviour*, *38*(4), 375–391.

Goffman, E. (1981). *Forms of talk*. Oxford: Basil Blackwell.

Goodman, S., & Burke, S. (2010). 'Oh you don't want asylum seekers, oh you're just racist': A discursive analysis of discussions about whether it's racist to oppose asylum seeking. *Discourse and Society*, *21*(3), 325–340.

Goodman, S., & Johnson, A. (2013). Strategies used by the far right to counter accusations of racism. *Critical Approaches to Discourse Analysis across Disciplines*, *6*(2), 97–113.

Harrison, S., & Bruter, M. (2011). *Mapping extreme right ideology: An empirical geography of the European extreme right*. Basingstoke: Palgrave.

Haste, H. (2004). Constructing the citizen. *Political Psychology*, *25*(3), 413–439.

Howarth, C. (2006). A social representation is not a quiet thing: Exploring the critical potential of social representations theory. *British Journal of Social Psychology*, *45*(1), 65–86.

Howarth, C. (2014). Connecting social representation, identity and ideology: Reflections on a London 'riot'. *Papers on Social Representations*, *23*(4), 4.1–4.30.

Jovchelovitch, S., & Gervais, M.-C. (1999). Social representations of health and illness: The case of the Chinese community in England. *Journal of Community and Applied Social Psychology*, *9*(4), 247–260.

Lubbers, M., & Güveli, A. (2007). Voting LPF: Stratification and the varying importance of attitudes. *Journal of Elections, Public Opinion and Parties*, *17*(1), 21–47.

Mammone, A., Godin, E., & Jenkins, B. (Eds.). (2012). *Mapping the extreme right in contemporary Europe: From local to transnational*. London and New York: Routledge.

McKinlay, A., Potter, J., & Wetherell, M. (1993). Discourse analysis and social representations. In G. M. Breakwell & D. V. Canter (Eds.), *Empirical approaches to social representations* (pp. 134–153). Oxford: Oxford University Press.

Minkenberg, M. (2013). The European radical right and xenophobia in west and east: Trends, patterns and challenges. In R. Melzer & S. Serafin (Eds.), *Right-wing extremism in Europe: Country analyses, counter-strategies and labor-market oriented exit strategies* (pp. 9–35). Berlin: Friedrich Ebert Stiftung.

Moscovici, S. (1984a). The Myth of the Lonely Paradigm: A rejoinder. *Social Research, 51*, 939–967.

Moscovici, S. (1984b). The phenomenon of social representations. In R. Farr & S. Moscovici (Eds.), *Social Representations* (pp. 3–69). Cambridge: Cambridge University Press.

Napier, J. L., & Jost, J. T. (2008). Why are conservatives happier than liberals? *Psychological Science, 19*(6), 565–572.

O'Doherty, K., & Le Couteur, A. (2007). 'Asylum seekers', 'boat people' and 'illegal immigrants': Social categorization in the media. *Australian Journal of Psychology, 59*(1), 1–12.

Papastamou, S. (1986). Psychologization and processes of minority and majority influence. *European Journal of Social Psychology, 16*(2), 165–180.

Pauwels, T. (2014). *Populism in Western Europe: Comparing Belgium, Germany and the Netherlands.* London and New York: Routledge.

Potter, J. (1996). *Representing reality: Discourse, rhetoric and social construction.* London: Sage.

Potter, J., & Litton, I. (1985). Some problems underlying the theory of social representations. *British Journal of Social Psychology, 24*(2), 81–90.

Potter, J., & Wetherell, M. (1987). *Discourse and social psychology.* London: Sage.

Pratto, F., Stallworth, L., & Sidanius, J. (1997). The gender gap: Differences in political attitudes and social dominance orientation. *British Journal of Social Psychology, 36*(1), 49–68.

Provencher, C. (2011). Towards a better understanding of cognitive polyphasia. *Journal for the Theory of Social Behaviour, 41*(4), 377–395.

Psarras, D. (2012). *The black book of Golden Dawn.* Athens: Polis (in Greek).

Reicher, S. (2001). The psychology of crowd dynamics. In M. A. Hogg & R. S. Tindale (Eds.), *Blackwell handbook of social psychology: Group processes* (pp. 182–208). Oxford: Blackwell.

Richardson, E. J., & Wodak, R. (2009). Recontextualising fascist ideologies of the past: Right-wing discourses on employment and nativism in Austria and the United Kingdom. *Critical Discourse Studies, 6*(4), 251–267.

Rooyackers, I. N., & Verkuyten, M. (2011). Mobilizing support for the extreme right: A discursive analysis of minority leadership. *British Journal of Social Psychology, 51*(1), 130–148.

Rydgren, J. (2008). Immigration sceptics, xenophobes or racists? Radical right-wing voting in six West European countries. *European Journal of Political Research, 47*(6), 737–765.

Sapountzis, A. (in press). Citizenship as rhetorical resource against immigration: The case of A1 newspaper. *Psychology: The Journal of the Greek Psychological Society* (in Greek).

Sidanius, J., Pratto, F., & Bobo, L. (1996). Racism, conservatism, affirmative action and intellectual sophistication: A matter of principled conservatism or group dominance? *Journal of Personality and Social Psychology, 70*, 476–490.

Stenner, K. (2005). *The authoritarian dynamic.* New York: Cambridge University Press.

Tileagă, C. (2013). *Political psychology: Critical perspectives.* Cambridge: Cambridge University Press.

van Dijk, T. A. (1992). Discourse and the denial of racism. *Discourse and Society, 3*(1), 87–118.

Wagner, W., & Hayes, N. (2005). *Everyday discourse and common sense: The theory of social representations.* London: Palgrave Macmillan.

Weltman, D., & Billig, M. (2001). The political psychology of contemporary anti-politics: A discursive approach to the end-of-ideology era. *Political Psychology, 22*(2), 367–382.

Wetherell, M. (1998). Positioning and interpretative repertoires: Conversation analysis and post-structuralism in dialogue. *Discourse and Society, 9*(3), 387–412.

Wooffitt, R. (1992). *Telling tales of the unexpected: The organisation of factual discourse.* Hemel Hempstead: Harvester.

14

POLITICAL BELIEFS AND POLITICAL BEHAVIOUR

Isabelle Goncalves-Portelinha, Christian Staerklé, and Guy Elcheroth

Even though our everyday lives are imbued with political meaning, politics is commonly alluded to with reference to governmental affairs, political figures and parties, elections, and voting. In its broadest acceptation, political behaviour refers to any action that participates (directly or indirectly) in the maintenance or the transformation of a given social system. Accordingly, political behaviour can take a vast array of forms. While voting in local or national elections or joining a public protest march are obvious examples of explicit political behaviour, they constitute only the easily discernible tip of the iceberg. Below the surface, in their everyday lives, people engage in a variety of practices that can be considered "banal" in the sense of Billig (1995): normally unspectacular, often dispassionate, but typically essential for the constant spinning and respinning of a web of political beliefs on the backdrop of which political action becomes meaningful and political struggle appears worthwhile. Choosing a newspaper at the kiosk, talking with neighbours about yesterday's TV program, posting a "like" in the social media, but also sanctioning an employee, buying certain types of goods, or using public transportation are but a few examples of the diverse activities that can be coloured by inconspicuous political statements communicated through words, deeds, or gestures. This chapter focuses on the processes through which people share (or refrain from sharing) their political stances in everyday life and how these processes generate fluid political climates that facilitate or hinder explicit political behaviours such as voting or protesting.

Specifically, this chapter examines the underpinnings of political opinion formation and expression by focusing on the role of the beliefs people hold as to what others think, value, or do – namely, on meta-representations. More broadly, it is concerned with highlighting the sociopsychological processes at play in political shifts. It intends to spell out an approach to these processes that engages with a number of intriguing real-world puzzles. For instance, how has the European far right managed to secure a series of political successes after decades of marginalisation? When do war opponents come to reveal their positions in the context of international conflicts? What enables voters to form opinions and express their stances on a national referendum?

With this in mind, we will first provide a brief overview of research on political behaviour; then we will draw on the social representations approach (e.g., Elcheroth, Doise, & Reicher, 2011; Staerklé, Clémence, & Spini, 2011) to consider meta-representations and the critical role that these beliefs play in the emergence of social change. We will argue that understanding political opinion formation and expression as functions of meta-representations allows us to encompass the individual, social, and power-related processes in which political behaviours are embedded, and, by so doing, to move beyond explanatory frameworks to focus on the psychology of individuals. Finally, case study research examining the spread of nationalist movements on the rise in Europe will be presented to illustrate the role of meta-representations in the processes enabling political minorities to develop into majorities.

Overview of research on political behaviour

In its general meaning, political behaviour has been at the core of social psychological research since the inception of the field (see Doise & Staerklé, 2002). Suffice it to mention the seminal work of Kurt Lewin, Stanley Milgram, or Henri Tajfel to grasp the influence of societal political events on the development of the discipline. Different research traditions on social psychological analyses of political behaviour arose from the pioneering works of Carl Hovland's Yale Communication Program and Lewin's Research Center for Group Dynamics (e.g., Hovland, Lumsdaine, & Sheffield, 1949; Lewin, 1951). Since then, a vast array of studies on attitude change and social influence has accumulated, illustrating the centrality of political behaviour in the field of social psychology. Political behaviour, in particular voting behaviour, has also been an important topic for research in political science that finds its origin in the work of Lazarsfeld and colleagues on American voting behaviour (e.g., Lazarsfeld, Berelson, & Gaudet, 1948).

Over the last several decades, scholars have produced a remarkable number of findings that have sought to enlighten the underpinnings of political behaviour, notably within the social cognition paradigm that has defined the field of political psychology since the 1970s (McGraw, 2000). As an example, research focusing on affective responses and automatic processes has brought evidence that voters' decisions can be altered by emotions such as anxiety or driven by implicit (i.e., unconscious) political attitudes towards candidates (Arcuri, Castelli, Galdi, Zogmaister, & Amadori, 2008; Marcus, MacKuen, & Neuman, 2011). Yet, most of this research apprehends individuals as isolated figures and in abstraction from the social contexts in which their behaviours are embedded. Accordingly, the source of social change is to be found at the individual level (Staerklé, 2006).

Reflecting the more recent trend towards a societal political psychology (see Staerklé, 2015a), political psychologists now address how political behaviour is entrenched in groups, institutions, and power relationships and how processes of political opinion formation are dependent on socially defined contents (see Elcheroth et al., 2011; Nesbitt-Larking, Kinnvall, Capelos, & Dekker, 2014; Sammut, Andreouli, Gaskell, & Valsiner, 2015). Consistent with this trend, Paluck (2009a, 2009b, 2012; Paluck & Shepherd, 2012) has criticised individualistic and cognitive approaches, highlighting their limited predictive power and scope for intervention along with their inability to explain rapid social change. We shall now turn to an alternative approach that, to circumvent the latter shortcomings, emphasises the role of social norms and group influence on political behaviour.

Social norms and behaviour

In comparison to the different individualistic approaches in classical analyses of political behaviour, research on the role of social norms and group influence on political behaviour has lagged behind. Both classic and recent research has nevertheless evidenced the power of social norms over behaviour (e.g., Cialdini, Reno, & Kallgren, 1990; Paluck, 2009a; Sherif, 1936). Here, norms are understood as "socially shared definitions of the way group members should or do behave" (Paluck, 2009a, p. 575).

Research on the influence of social norms has usually focused on its effects on attitudes and behaviour (e.g., Newcomb, 1943). Scholars have also examined how well people perceive social norms and how the resulting norm perception affects individuals' attitudes and behaviours. For example, research on pluralistic ignorance[1] has shown that misperception of the normative use of alcohol on a college campus was predictive of students' alcohol-related attitudes and behaviours (Prentice & Miller, 1993).

In public opinion research, the latter line of thought is represented by the spiral of silence theory (Noelle-Neumann, 1984/1993), which suggests that the perceived evaluation of the political climate affects individuals' willingness to express their views. This leads them to form opinions and behave in ways consistent with what they perceive as being the majority opinion, that is, silencing their opinions when they believe they hold a minority position. Eventually, political outcomes end up mirroring people's beliefs about the majority opinion rather than prior political preferences. Recent research has confirmed the dynamic nature of the theory, showing that individuals who feel they are in the majority become more dominant and louder over time, while the minority camp becomes increasingly silent (Matthes, 2015).

Even though there is converging evidence about the impact of perceived social norms over behaviour, research has only recently started to investigate how such beliefs as to what others think are construed (Paluck, 2009a; Paluck & Shepherd, 2012). Indeed, research has predominantly focused on the effect of norms unambiguously provided by an experimental procedure, that is, by exposing participants either to descriptive statistical information or to experimental confederates (e.g., Cialdini et al., 1990). Much in contrast to people's everyday experiences, this approach creates social norms that are salient and transparent in a particular setting.

Recent research has thus started to document how individuals infer social norms in everyday life. When discerning what others think, they find their beliefs influenced by salient individuals (Paluck & Shepherd, 2012), the media (Davis, Bowers, & Memon, 2011; Elcheroth & Reicher, 2014; Paluck, 2009a), and the public behaviours displayed by others (e.g., Falasca-Zamponi, 1997; Fein, Goethals, & Kugler, 2007). More needs to be done though to understand the underpinnings of political behaviour and, with it, social change. Indeed, while research has investigated the way people make up their minds about what is socially normative, it has left unexamined the social context that constrains the formation of these beliefs. Pragmatically, this refers, for instance, to the in-depth examination of aspects related to the social group to which norms relate. This, we believe, would allow us to better apprehend the circumstances under which the identification of a new norm becomes not only relevant but plausible. Such considerations also require us to take into account the wider societal context in which the group finds itself, for example, with respect to power relationships within and between groups. Accordingly, when investigating how beliefs come to be perceived as shared, more attention is to be given to communication (direct and mass mediated, implicit and explicit; see, e.g., Elcheroth & Reicher, 2014; Paluck, 2009a; Paluck & Shepherd, 2012) and in particular to the way processes of communication converge to shape political climates wherein definitions of issues restrain the range of conceivable solutions (Elcheroth et al., 2011; Staerklé, 2011).

The social representations approach

From a theoretical perspective, the latter considerations are best encompassed by the social representations approach (SRA; Bauer & Gaskell, 1999, 2008; Duveen, 2001; Elcheroth et al., 2011; Howarth, 2006; Moscovici, 1961/1976; Staerklé et al., 2011) that conceives intergroup communication as a means to understanding the way groups, characterised by unequal positions in the social hierarchy, mobilise representations to achieve or to resist social change (Staerklé, 2015b). Representations are understood as particular kinds of knowledge that permit communication and organise social relations (Doise, 1985; Moscovici, 1961/1976). Critically, the SRA conceptualises social categories as the organising principles for the representation process and representations of social categories as fundamental to group relations (see Elcheroth et al., 2011). Accordingly, this approach emphasises the need to consider both the process by which social categories are constructed and integrated and the role of social identification in structuring the world.

Consistent with the line of research on social norms and behaviour reviewed previously, the SRA stresses group influence by proposing that political behaviours are directly shaped by the beliefs people hold as to what other group members think (Elcheroth et al., 2011). In comparison to much of the work carried out on social norms and normative beliefs, the social representations approach brings to the fore the functions of both identity and representational processes and hence the role of communication within power structures and social hierarchies. This theoretical framework thereby provides a holistic approach to the influence of normative beliefs on political behaviour.

Acknowledging this theoretical orientation and highlighting the previously mentioned social parameters, we shall now refer to the beliefs individuals hold as to what other group members think, value, or do as "meta-representations". This view not only reasserts the need to embrace the intricacy of the social context in which the formation of these beliefs occurs, but it also spells out the distinction between two concepts that come often undifferentiated in the social influence literature, namely what the social norm actually is and what people perceive the norm to be. This terminology further encapsulates the idea that normative beliefs, as objects of systematic influence in contexts of power struggle, fluctuate over time and space and are constantly reassessed through instances of communication.

The SRA opposes everyday communication directed towards common understanding and stability to strategic communication aimed at achieving social change through the shaping of others' thoughts and behaviours (Sammut & Bauer, 2011). Communication modes (Moscovici, 1961/1976) are associated with influence processes taking place between groups qualified by unequal status and power. Specifically, *diffusion* concerns the emergence and spread of beliefs as undifferentiated influence of various representations unrolls. Information disseminated with no distinguishable sources or targets of communication provides the "raw material" that allows individuals to make sense of the issue at stake, to identify the importance attributed to distinct values in a society, and to engage in societal debates (Staerklé, 2015b). In contrast, the communication mode of *propagation* is associated with majority influence and strategic attempts to secure support for the views of the majority; propagation thus focuses on purposeful production of consent destined to maintain or extend the majority dominant position in society (Staerklé, 2015b). Majority attempts to persuade others of a specific point of view often take the form of sophisticated communication strategies aimed at imposing a representation to make it hegemonic, subjectively valid and normal. In propagation, a source of influence exerts pressure to normative conformity through the use of meta-representations by highlighting symbolic benefits of conformism ("true citizens believe X") and pointing out negative effects of rejecting the majority point of view ("the country is doomed if too many people believe Y"). Meta-representations are therefore instrumentalised by interest groups and individuals exhorted to conform to the majority in order to be accepted as group members by other majority members and to receive social validation of their views. This is particularly patent in research derived from the spiral of silence theory (Noelle-Neumann, 1984/1993). Since, as will be illustrated in the final part of this chapter, meta-representations can be highly malleable and easy to manipulate, they may be strategically used to shape opinion expression and ultimately political outcomes (see Falasca-Zamponi, 1997).

In propagation mode, the source of influence, in an attempt to convince others of the validity of its worldview, may strategically self-categorise itself as the legitimate representative of a superordinate social category (for an illustration, see Marine Le Pen's speech following the 2014 French elections for the European parliament). "Majority" is thus a flexible and ambiguous concept that may be purposefully invoked to validate representations. Asserting that one's view represents a majority position is a strategic and rhetorical construction in itself that seeks to provide the source of influence with legitimacy (Stevenson, Condor, & Abell, 2007; Staerklé, 2015b).

The third mode of communication, *propaganda*, is associated with minority influence directed at resisting dominant representations and fostering dissent and social change. Minorities and subordinate groups need to resort to a different communication strategy than majorities given the more limited resources at their disposal. In particular, minority groups advance more forcefully and with less compromise a given claim that not only challenges hegemonic majority positions but also provides an alternative to dominant social arrangements (see Moscovici, 1980). The critical function of meta-representations is fully realised in such processes of social change and resistance to change where opposing stances, in particular with respect to contested ideological and political opinions, are debated in the public arena (Elcheroth et al., 2011). Here, meta-representations play an important role in shifts of opinion prevalence, for example when minority stances become progressively perceived as normatively acceptable, or when majority opinions are challenged by minorities.

The nature of meta-representations

Meta-representations are fluid and malleable because of the nature of social identities defining the groups individuals belong to. Indeed, people have at their disposal a vast array of identities and they act on the basis of the group norms (i.e., meta-representations) they associate with the group they identify with (Reicher, 2004). Thus, the way individuals categorise the world and themselves determines the relevance of the meta-representations they hold. Put differently, meta-representations affect behaviours only to the extent that these representations relate to a social identity that is meaningful to them, that is, that they speak to the way people experience social reality and organise their social practices. Social identity therefore constrains the extent to which meta-representations both influence behaviour (i.e., relevance) and are influenced by what individuals encounter in their everyday life (i.e., plausibility). Importantly, when social behaviour is politicised, the definition of group identity is subject to an active process of influence from those who seek to shape social reality (see Reicher, 2004; Reicher, Hopkins, Levine, & Rath, 2005).

Novel social occurrences thus alter meta-representations only insofar as these are deemed consistent with the content of the social identity at stake. Behaviours mirror what individuals believe other ingroup members think as much as they are shaped by the normative beliefs attributed to outgroup members. Communication within the group also confers substantiality to the understanding of social reality. This is illustrated by research in the self-categorisation tradition describing the critical role of social interactions on ingroup communication: not so much for allowing group members to share information per se, but rather for enabling an awareness of a shared understanding to emerge (i.e., consensualisation; Haslam, Turner, Oakes, McGarty, & Reynolds, 1997).

It is worth stressing here that malleability is not a stable feature of meta-representations, but that it certainly varies over time and sometimes may even be confined to rather short-lived temporal windows. Transient shifts in political climates and the lack of transparency and predictability inherent to volatile contexts are likely to facilitate temporary disjuncture between what most people believe in private, what they express in public, and how others perceive their beliefs (see Bodor, 2012). Such contexts can therefore provide fertile grounds for political entrepreneurs to manipulate public perceptions of where the majority stands, to marginalise political competitors, or to transform a political minority into a majority. In other words, they can open windows of opportunity for political agency by creating the conditions for rapid social change in which small actions can produce large effects and result in new social facts.

More specifically, in instances where mass media swiftly turn their focus toward a new political outcome, mass communications have the potential to lead people to question their prior beliefs as to what others think on that precise issue. In line with the spiral of silence theory, this dynamic, in turn, is likely to undermine people's willingness to publicly affirm their stances and speak out on polemical issues, as opposed to cases in which individuals are more convinced of relevant others' views and assured about available social validation for their own stance.

Before moving on to the presentation of research examining the recent rise of nationalist movements in Europe, two final points require our attention. First, the assertion that meta-representations directly influence political opinion expression (see Paluck, 2009a) entails pragmatic consequences: for social change to occur, the Dantesque task of changing the attitudes of the mass is not required (see Bem, 1970); rather, altering meta-representations may prove to be an efficient and effective means to achieve social change.

Second, the importance given to meta-representations in the shaping of political behaviours is also to be explored in light of individual agency. Indeed, the social representations approach makes clear that "resistance is simultaneously a social and a psychological possibility" (Howarth, 2006, p. 23). Instances of emerging social change when social norms are perceived as ambiguous and uncertain leave space for debate, conflict, and resistance; here, (meta)representations are at the centre of strategic communication aiming at persuading others of a specific understanding of things (Staerklé, 2015b). When societal agents seek to actively shape (meta)representations (see Reicher et al., 2005), individuals might either endorse the alleged new (meta)representations or on the contrary resist their dissemination (see Hornsey, Majkut, Terry, & McKimmie, 2003; Packer, 2009). These potentialities are limited though by instances of influence (e.g., mass media) that may constrain, if not stifle, them. In other words, individuals are not seen as passive recipients of (meta)representations imposed upon them from external agents. Instead, individuals are actively involved in the construction, contestation, and dissemination of meta-representations and thus also in shaping political behaviours of others.

Meta-representations in shifting contexts: The rise of the European far right

Meta-representations are an efficient tool to better understand not only political behaviours, but also rapid social change. We shall now illustrate how meta-representations affect political opinion expression and how they participate in enabling political minorities to develop into majorities by presenting a study carried out in the context of the 2012 French presidential elections (see Goncalves-Portelinha & Elcheroth, 2013). This research aimed at shedding light on the sociopsychological processes leading the National Front (NF), a previously marginalised far-right party, to become a mainstream political party.[2] To this end, the study, divided into longitudinal and experimental parts, was implemented at Nanterre University, a French campus traditionally hostile to the NF.

First-year social sciences students from Nanterre University were asked to complete two questionnaires: one shortly before the French presidential election first round (T1) and a second one during the week following the election second round (T2). The experimental manipulation of meta-representations was introduced in the T2 survey. Inspired by real-world practice (e.g., Le Monde, 2012), it consisted of varying information about the alleged results of a bogus opinion poll regarding French/Nanterre students' support for Marine Le Pen (MLP), presidential candidate for the NF.

Participants in the "French students favourable to MLP" condition were exposed to information stating that a recent opinion poll revealed that the majority of French social sciences students "understood" people who voted for MLP. Participants in the "Nanterre students as exception" condition read the same information followed by a statement recalling that Nanterre University was among the exceptions as the majority of its social sciences students reported not understanding people who voted for MLP. Finally, participants in the control condition were not provided with any information regarding the opinion poll.

At both T1 and T2, participants indicated their personal attitudes towards MLP and the meta-representations they held as to what other Nanterre students thought of MLP. At the end of T2, participants were given the opportunity to register for a campus workshop to discuss NF politics with other students.

Results showed that a concise piece of information reflecting common media practice was sufficient to modify participants' beliefs regarding the support of fellow university students for MLP. Specifically, participants in the "French students favourable to MLP" condition perceived Nanterre students to be more positive towards MLP than participants in the remaining conditions. This appears all the more compelling given the well-known reputation for Nanterre University to be a left-wing stronghold. Furthermore, normative beliefs changed throughout the electoral period: participants in the control condition thought other Nanterre students to be more positive towards the NF after as compared to before the election. Importantly, the study also revealed a major shift during the electoral campaign among left-wing students: before the election, left-wing students in the control condition perceived their own position as corresponding to the average position on campus. However, after the election they thought other students to be on average more positive towards MLP than themselves. That is, in only a few weeks' time, left-wing students moved from perceiving their own position as a majority view to perceiving it as a minority view.

Contrary to change in personal attitudes, change in meta-representations had behavioural repercussions as participants registered to a lesser extent to participate in discussion workshops on the NF politics after being exposed to the information that the majority of French students were positive towards the party candidate. Consistent with Falasca-Zamponi's research (1997), these results enlighten the processes implicated in the shift of political climates. Indeed, in a context where minority opinions are increasingly voiced, not speaking up against the minority is likely to lead others to *erroneously* believe most people to agree with what is still the actual minority and in turn to discourage even further the voicing of dissent against that minority.

In the previous sections, we mentioned the importance of taking into account the specificities of the social context to better understand how and when meta-representations affect political behaviours. We therefore discuss some characteristics of the Nanterre study context that allowed for the experimental manipulation of meta-representations to alter political behaviours.

First, the credibility of the information provided to participants in the "Nanterre students as exception" was most certainly permitted by the long-term reputation that the university gained during the May 1968 uprisings to be a stronghold of left-wing ideologies and resistance to the far right. Second, the plausibility of the second experimental condition, that is, of the "French students favourable to MLP", might have been reinforced by the surprisingly high electoral score obtained by the NF in the first round. Surely, this electoral shock led people to doubt their former beliefs as to French population's "true" opinions vis-à-vis the NF (see Bodor, 2012). Moreover, the NF banalisation efforts and important first-round scores were massively mediatised during the inter-round period. When combined with an inclination to view other individuals as more vulnerable to mass communications influence (Davison, 1983), this specific context is likely to have potentiated the malleable nature of meta-representations.

In addition, the findings provide an indication regarding Nanterre students' group identity. The fact that the experimental manipulation had an impact on participants' meta-representations suggests that a strong left-wing standpoint and opposition to the far right do not lie at the core of the group representation and that they are no longer the defining features of the group for identified members.

These findings call for an obvious question: would these effects hold in a different societal context or in a context wherein the group identity content would be very much tied in with a specific political stance? This is what a second study examined.

This mixed-method research was implemented in the context of a 2012 Swiss referendum. Each year, Swiss citizens vote to make decisions about governance, and in June 2012, a populist right-wing party, the Swiss People's Party (SPP), launched an initiative to impose mandatory referenda for all international agreements. Again with the aim of understanding how marginalised political positions can become mainstream, the study was carried out in a context traditionally hostile to the SPP, that is, the faculty of Social and Political Sciences at the University of Lausanne.

Shortly before the vote, first-year psychology students were asked to complete a brief survey in which the experimental manipulation was introduced. The text used for the experimental manipulation was based on actual findings from an opinion poll previously conducted among Swiss voters. Participants in the "Young Swiss favourable to the SPP initiative" condition read the results of an opinion poll according to which a majority of young Swiss were favourable to the initiative. Participants in the "Lausanne students unfavourable to the SPP initiative" condition were exposed to the same information followed by a paragraph recalling that Lausanne University social science students were known for differentiating themselves from the SPP positions. Participants in the control condition were not given any information regarding the opinion poll. All participants were asked to report the extent to which they identified with fellow students of the University of Lausanne. At the end of the survey, they indicated whether they would agree to participate in a focus group to discuss the vote outcome and, if so, to report a date when they would be available to do so.

Much in contrast with what was observed in the Nanterre study, the results showed that highly identified participants were less willing to participate in the focus group when reminded of the anti-SPP position of fellow students. Participants were more inclined to put effort to defend their group political view when perceiving themselves as the only representatives of the group. When surrounded by like-minded individuals, however, they would adopt more passive attitudes.

Importantly, the discussions that took place during the actual running of the focus groups made clear that participants held firm meta-representations regarding what other social sciences thought, as there was no doubt that they strongly opposed the SPP positions. Put differently, the societal context in which this experiment was situated did not provide cues susceptible to disrupt students' meta-representations. This political perspective emerged as central when the group identity was mobilised. Ultimately, the study suggests that the unwavering nature of the meta-representations held by social science students prevents the SPP from reaching majority status in the specific context of the faculty campus.

As a whole, the Nanterre and Lausanne studies stress the necessity of considering the characteristics of the social context when examining how meta-representations affect political behaviour. Certainly, meta-representations can influence political opinion expression. This influence though is far from invariable; rather, its form and effectiveness depend on a number of social factors such as, for instance, the representation of group identity, the way people categorise themselves and others, or the uncertainty associated with the group norm. In this respect, the malleability of meta-representations is to be understood as a variable, not as a given. While research seeking to identify the sources of meta-representations (e.g., Paluck,

2009a; Paluck & Shepherd, 2012) remains crucial, we believe the field would gain much insight into the processes leading political minorities to become majorities if researchers explore the conditions under which meta-representations can indeed be altered. In this line, recent research suggests that specific points of time during tight and controversial electoral campaigns are more opportune than other moments to instil changes in meta-representations (Bodor, 2012).

Moreover, the specific limitations of both the Nanterre and Lausanne research to samples from WEIRD populations (i.e., Western, educated, and from industrialised, rich, and democratic countries; Henrich, Heine, & Norenzayan, 2010) calls for a brief consideration as to whether the meta-representations account of political behaviour provided here would hold across other contexts. To the extent that research on social influence suggests that motivations for conformity are often stronger among non-WEIRD populations (e.g., Kim & Markus, 1999), it is reasonable to believe that meta-representations would similarly affect political behaviour in the form of expression of one's opinion in different contexts (see Paluck, 2009a). However, in environments especially prone to violence as a retribution for deviance (e.g., Falasca-Zamponi, 1997), one might expect the relationship between political behaviour and novel, alternative meta-representations to be less straightforward. That is, people might require firmer and more tangible evidence of the raising validity of a new meta-representation or of the ongoing validity of an old meta-representation before taking the step of implementing an otherwise risky behaviour.

On a related note, research carried out in universities benefits from a context in which a specific social category (i.e., student identity) with rather clear boundaries is readily identifiable and salient. Outside universities, though, the identification of the social categories people resort to to ponder their behaviour becomes more challenging. It is, for instance, somewhat doubtful (at least in the current French and Swiss electoral contexts) that a given 20-year-old citizen would uniquely mobilise her general university-related identity when deciding for which policy to cast her vote. As emphasised earlier, social categories and thus meta-representations are contingent upon the context in which individuals find themselves. Social category content is moreover subject to influence from *entrepreneurs of identity* (Reicher et al., 2005) who actively attempt to mould their representations to reach specific political outcomes, thereby illustrating the status of social identities and representations as strategic and paramount means to political success. The context-bound nature of social categories, meta-representations, and of the influence of the latter on political behaviour thus implies that varied methodological approaches – combining ecological case studies, network analyses, media studies, multilevel research designs, and mixed methods studies – are required to investigate social influence processes occurring throughout diversified contexts and populations.

Conclusion

This chapter provided an overview of research examining the underpinnings of political behaviour from the perspective of a social representations approach. We first reviewed classic and recent research in political science and political psychology and discussed the limitations of predominantly individualistic and cognitive accounts of opinion formation. In the second section of the chapter, we focused on the influence of meta-representations on political behaviour. We drew on the social representations approach to consider the crucial role of group members' beliefs as to what other group members think in the emergence of social change. With the final section featuring recent research examining the rise of the far right in Europe, we contrasted two case studies to illustrate how meta-representations participate in the process of allowing political minorities to become majorities. We also emphasised the need for considering the social context when studying the influence of meta-representations on political behaviour.

A first goal of the chapter was to highlight the social constructivist character of political beliefs and political behaviour, as well as of meta-representations as the vehicles through which patterns of beliefs and behaviour are often consolidated and sometimes abruptly altered. Normative beliefs are not fixed; they fluctuate over time and space and are subject to strategic attempts to influence or remould them. A second aim of the chapter was to show how understanding political behaviour as a function of meta-representations permits us to conceptually integrate individual, social, and power-related processes on producing political behaviours. Let us recall, for example, that social groups diverge in the possibilities they have to act upon meta-representations, if only by their access to the material and symbolic means to channel such influence.

Examining the role of meta-representations in social change further requires us to look at the timing and location of qualitative shifts in public opinion, the social structures through which the diffusion process operates, and the sources, channels, and recipients of mass mobilisation. These goals require embracing and creatively combining a diversity of methodological approaches that articulate the study of psychopolitical dynamics at the levels of political entrepreneurs and their constituencies. By providing an account of how groups remain or become powerful by influencing political opinion formation and expression through the shaping of meta-representations, this chapter eventually sheds light on sociopsychological processes that enable and constrain political agency, understood as the capacity to intervene in the political sphere and bring about social stability or social change through collective action (see Ratner, 2000).

Notes

1 Pluralistic ignorance suggests that individuals overestimate public support for a prevailing norm while holding themselves in a divergent view.
2 In the first round of the election, the NF candidate gathered 18% of the votes, thus situating the NF as the third force in the French political spectrum.

References

Arcuri, L., Castelli, L., Galdi, S., Zogmaister, C., & Amadori, A. (2008). Predicting the vote: Implicit attitudes as predictors of the future behavior of decided and undecided voters. *Political Psychology, 29*, 369–387.

Bauer, M. W., & Gaskell, G. (1999). Towards a paradigm for research on social representations. *Journal for the Theory of Social Behaviour, 29,* 163–186.

Bauer, M. W., & Gaskell, G. (2008). Social representations theory: A progressive research programme for social psychology. *Journal for the Theory of Social Behaviour, 38,* 335–353.

Bem, D. (1970). *Beliefs, attitudes, and human affairs.* Belmont: Brooks/Cole.

Billig, M. (1995). *Banal nationalism.* London: Sage.

Bodor, T. (2012). The issue of timing and opinion congruity in spiral of silence research: Why does research suggest limited empirical support for the theory? *International Journal of Public Opinion Research, 24,* 269–286.

Cialdini, R. B., Reno, R. R., & Kallgren, C. A. (1990). A focus theory of normative conduct: Recycling the concept of norms to reduce littering in public places. *Journal of Personality and Social Psychology, 58,* 1015–1026.

Davis, C. J., Bowers, J. S., & Memon, A. (2011). Social influence in televised election debates: A potential distortion of democracy. *PLoS ONE, 6,* e18154.

Davison, W. P. (1983). The third-person effect in communication. *Public Opinion Quarterly, 47,* 1–15.

Doise, W. (1985). Les représentations sociales. Definition d'un concept. *Connexions, 45,* 243–253.

Doise, W., & Staerklé, C. (2002). From social to political psychology: The societal approach. In K. Monroe (Ed.), *Political psychology* (pp. 151–172). Hillsdale: Lawrence Erlbaum.

Duveen, G. (2001). Representations, identities, resistance. In K. Deaux & G. Philogene (Eds.), *Representations of the social: Bridging theoretical tradition* (pp. 257–270). Oxford: Blackwell.

Elcheroth, G., Doise, W., & Reicher, S. (2011). On the knowledge of politics and the politics of knowledge: How a social representations approach helps us rethink the subject of political psychology. *Political Psychology, 32,* 729–758.

Elcheroth, G., & Reicher, S. (2014). 'Not our war, not our country': Contents and contexts of Scottish political rhetoric and popular understandings during the invasion of Iraq. *British Journal of Social Psychology, 53,* 112–133.

Falasca-Zamponi, S. (1997). *Fascist spectacle: The aesthetics of power in Mussolini's Italy.* Berkeley: University of California Press.

Fein, S., Goethals, G. R., & Kugler, M. B. (2007). Social influence on political judgments: The case of presidential debates. *Political Psychology, 28,* 165–192.

Goncalves-Portelinha, I., & Elcheroth, G. (2013). *Does it matter whether I believe that other students support Marine Le Pen? The role of meta-representations in the French presidential elections.* Unpublished manuscript.

Haslam, S. A., Turner, J. C., Oakes, P. J., McGarty, C., & Reynolds, K. J. (1997). The group as a basis for emergent stereotype consensus. *European Review of Social Psychology, 8,* 203–239.

Henrich, J., Heine, S. J., & Norenzayan, A. (2010). The weirdest people in the world? *Behavioral and Brain Sciences, 33,* 61–83.

Hornsey, M. J., Majkut, L., Terry, D. J., & McKimmie, B. M. (2003). On being loud and proud: Non-conformity and counter-conformity to group norms. *British Journal of Social Psychology, 42,* 319–335.

Hovland, C., Lumsdaine, A., & Sheffield, F. (1949). *Experiments on mass communication.* Princeton: Princeton University Press.

Howarth, C. (2006). A social representation is not a quiet thing: Exploring the critical potential of social representations theory. *British Journal of Social Psychology, 45,* 65–86.

Kim, H., & Markus, H. R. (1999). Deviance or uniqueness, harmony or conformity? A cultural analysis. *Journal of Personality and Social Psychology, 77,* 785–800.

Lazarsfeld, P. F., Berelson, B., & Gaudet, H. (1948). *The people's choice.* New York: Columbia University Press.

Le Monde (2012). *Marine Le Pen arrive en tête parmi les jeunes de 18–24 ans* [*Marine Le Pen leading the way among 18–24 years old*]. Retrieved from www.lemonde.fr/a-la-une/article/2012/04/09/marine-le-pen-arrive-en-tete-parmi-les-jeunes-de-18-24-ans_1682579_3208.html?xtmc=marine_le_pen _arrive_en_tete_parmi_les_jeunes&xtcr=1

Lewin, K. (1951). *Field theory in social science*. New York: Harper.

McGraw, K. M. (2000). Contributions of the cognitive approach to political psychology. *Political Psychology, 21*, 805–832.

Marcus, G. E., MacKuen, M., & Neuman, W. R. (2011). Parsimony and complexity: Developing and testing theories of affective intelligence. *Political Psychology, 32*, 323–336.

Matthes, J. (2015). Observing the 'spiral' in the spiral of silence. *International Journal of Public Opinion Research, 27*, 155–176.

Moscovici, S. (1961/1976). *La psychanalyse, son image et son public* (2nd ed.). Paris: Presses Universitaires de France.

Moscovici, S. (1980). Toward a theory of conversion behavior. *Advances in Experimental Social Psychology, 13*, 209–239.

Nesbitt-Larking, P., Kinnvall, K., Capelos, T., & Dekker, H. (2014). *Palgrave handbook of global political psychology*. London: Palgrave.

Newcomb, T. M. (1943). *Personality and social change*. New York: Dryden.

Noelle-Neumann, E. (1984/1993). *The spiral of silence: Public opinion – our social skin* (2nd ed.). Chicago and London: University of Chicago Press.

Packer, D. J. (2009). Avoiding groupthink: Whereas weakly identified members remain silent, strongly identified members dissent about collective problems. *Psychological Science, 20*, 546–548.

Paluck, E. L. (2009a). Reducing intergroup prejudice and conflict using the media: A field experiment in Rwanda. *Journal of Personality and Social Psychology, 96*, 574–587.

Paluck, E. L. (2009b). What's in a norm? Sources and processes of norm change. *Journal of Personality and Social Psychology, 96*, 594–600.

Paluck, E. L. (2012). The dominance of the individual in intergroup relations research: Understanding social change requires psychological theories of collective and structural phenomena. *Behavioral and Brain Sciences, 35*, 451–466.

Paluck, E. L., & Shepherd, H. (2012). The salience of social referents: A field experiment on collective norms and harassment behavior in a school social network. *Journal of Personality and Social Psychology, 103*, 899–915.

Prentice, D. A., & Miller, D. T. (1993). Pluralistic ignorance and alcohol use on campus: Some consequences of misperceiving the social norm. *Journal of Personality and Social Psychology, 64*, 243–256.

Ratner, C. (2000). Agency and culture. *Journal for the Theory of Social Behaviour, 30*, 413–434.

Reicher, S. (2004). The context of social identity: Domination, resistance, and change. *Political Psychology, 25*, 921–945.

Reicher, S., Hopkins, N., Levine, M., & Rath, R. (2005). Entrepreneurs of hate and entrepreneurs of solidarity: Social identity as a basis for mass communication. *International Review of the Red Cross, 87*, 621–637.

Sammut, G., Andreouli, E., Gaskell, G., & Valsiner, J. (2015). *The Cambridge handbook of social representations*. Cambridge: Cambridge University Press.

Sammut, G., & Bauer, M. (2011). Social influence: Modes and modalities. In D. Hook, B. Franks & M. Bauer (Eds.), *The social psychology of communication* (pp. 87–106). Hampshire: Palgrave.

Sherif, M. (1936). *The psychology of social norms*. New York: Harper.

Staerklé, C. (2006). The individual as the source of progressive thinking: A comment on Liu & Sibley (2006). *Papers on Social Representations, 15*(6), 1–6.7.

Staerklé, C. (2011). Back to new roots: Societal psychology and social representations. In J. P. Valentim (Ed.), *Societal approaches in social psychology* (pp. 81–106). Bern: Peter Lang.

Staerklé, C. (2015a). Political psychology. In J. D. Wright (Ed.), *International encyclopedia of the social & behavioral sciences* (2nd ed., Vol. 18, pp. 427–433). Oxford: Elsevier.

Staerklé, C. (2015b). Social order and political legitimacy. In G. Sammut, E. Andreouli, G. Gaskell & J. Valsiner (Eds.), *The Cambridge handbook of social representations* (pp. 280–294). Cambridge: Cambridge University Press.

Staerklé, C., Clémence, A., & Spini, D. (2011). Social representations: A normative and dynamic intergroup approach. *Political Psychology, 32*, 759–768.

Stevenson, C., Condor, S., & Abell, J. (2007). The majority–minority conundrum in Northern Ireland: An orange order perspective. *Political Psychology, 28*, 107–125.

15
SOCIAL POLICY IN EVERYDAY CONTEXTS

Jenevieve Mannell

Introduction

The term 'policy' is often used to refer to a document or statement that outlines a particular action to be taken by a government or organisation. In reality, however, policy statements belong to highly complex social processes which often involve multiple stakeholders, power struggles, and conflicting ideas about the best possible solution to a particular policy issue. Social psychologists have long been interested in understanding the complex and relational aspects of the policy process, including collective decision-making, the role of shared beliefs in driving policy implementation, and the broader effects of policies on the social psychology of groups or populations.

While policy has been a common interest, social psychologists have taken vastly different approaches to studying policy processes. Critical social psychologists have largely taken an activist approach to examining the policy process, engaging in questions about *who* is involved in decision making and arguing for the involvement of affected user groups (Campbell & Burgess, 2012; Frank & Bjerge, 2011). Community psychologists have focused on the need for policy to be aligned with community perspectives on social issues (Campbell, Cornish, Gibbs, & Scott, 2010) and the ways in which both communities and community service providers can challenge the original objectives of policy through their actions (Lipsky, 1983; Mannell, 2014a; Speer & Christens, 2012). In contrast, the policy interests of organisational social psychologists have focused on the effectiveness of policy in organisational environments, with some scholars highlighting the challenges policy often faces in these environments, for instance, in attempting to appeal to different organisational discourses (Mannell, 2010; Niska & Vesala, 2013). Alternatively, political psychologists have explored the political manoeuvres that shape the policy process, as well as the effects of policy on the social and political dynamics of society (Bacqué, Fijalkow, Launay, & Vermeersch, 2011; Hammond, 1996; Kaarbo & Gruenfeld, 1998; Kawashima-Ginsberg & Levine, 2014; Larson, 1994).

While extremely fruitful, the majority of these engagements between social psychology and policy have focused on the objectives set out by the policy itself and have taken these objectives as a basis for analysis. By limiting policy analyses to the objectives outlined in policy documents (such as improving school performance or reducing smoking-related deaths), the focus becomes the potential for social psychology to improve these policies (e.g. by describing how to effectively engage user groups or contributing knowledge about the psychosocial factors that contribute to smoking behaviours). While the question of whether or not a policy has achieved its objectives is critical in helping to identify best practice, this focus also limits our understanding of how policy interacts with and shapes the social world in ways that may extend beyond these objectives. It obscured attention to the social psychological pathways through which policy may act as a mechanism for social changes that are neither linear nor predictable. At its core, the emphasis on policy making and its psychological impact assumes that the 'right' policy decision leads to positive social outcomes, often overlooking the variety of ways in which social policy is deeply embedded in the practices of our everyday lives.

In order to address this gap, I take a societal approach to psychology in this chapter, which emphasises the need to understand social psychological phenomenon as constructed within and by society (Howarth et al., 2013). The aim is to explore the potential for thinking of policy as a socially embedded practice and develop our understanding of how policy both affects and is affected by the social world. In adopting a societal approach to social psychology, the social changes that policy strives to achieve are understood as something that cannot be predicted or purposefully enacted, but as ongoing and nonlinear processes (Howarth et al., 2013). The implication of this for studies of policy is that we need to pay attention to the unintended rather than intended effects of policy as a means of identifying the social psychological pathways that connect policy to many of the changes taking place in our everyday lives. As I outline in this chapter, the work of Serge Moscovici on social representations theory (SRT) (Moscovici, 1988; Moscovici & Duveen, 2000) and others who have followed in the social representations tradition (including Gerard Duveen, Robert Farr, Sandra Jovchelovitch, Ivana Markova, Caroline Howarth, among others) provide a useful theoretical lens for exploring these unintended effects.

The remainder of this chapter begins with a discussion of how the unintended effects of policy are currently being explored by political social psychologists. Following this, I draw on the theoretical SRT literature to explore how this theory and its current developments can contribute to new understandings of policy's unintended effects, specifically through examining the role of policy in: (1) the production of new forms of knowledge, (2) the shaping of social identities, and (3) social action and resistance. I draw on a case study of how gender policy is being implemented in South Africa in order to illustrate how social representations can be used to surface the unintended effects of policy. The overall aim of this chapter is to map the ways in which SRT can create new spaces for engagement between political social psychology and policy studies.

Political social psychology and policy studies

The process of developing and implementing policy is inherently political, involving numerous stakeholders including government actors, the private sector, media, public interest groups, and affected populations (Buse, Mays, & Walt, 2005). Several political social psychologists have taken a keen interest in the political manoeuvres that occur between these various stakeholders and the implications of psychological processes of human judgment, beliefs, and attributions in policy making (Hammond, 1996; Kaarbo & Gruenfeld, 1998; Larson, 1994). Others have paid attention to the impacts of policies on the political issues that affect particular social contexts, including multiculturalism, processes of acculturation, political participation, and gender relations (see, for example, Bacqué, Fijalkow, Launay, & Vermeersch, 2010; Kawashima-Ginsberg & Levine, 2014). Following from the interest of this chapter in the unintended effects of policy in society, my focus is on this latter body of literature, and specifically the work of a small number of political social psychologists who have begun to explore how policies can impact social and political interactions that are neither predictable nor accounted for by policy itself.

An example of this interest in the unintended effects of policy by political social psychologists can be seen in a study of the effects of citizenship policies by Ariely (2012). While citizenship policies are intended to define 'who will become a member of the political community' (Ariely, 2012, p. 243), Ariely's study moves away from evaluating this objective to assess the effects of different approaches to citizenship policies on broader social norms and identities. His findings are fascinating and highlight the potential for policy to have effects far beyond its original objectives. Ariel shows how 'inclusive' citizenship policies that grant citizenship based on birth in the country rather than by the nationality of parents are associated with less xenophobic attitudes towards immigrants, drawing on data available from national surveys in 24 different countries. In another similar study that pays attention to the unintended effects of policy at a national level, Freedman (2001) examines the collection of national policies that define Malaysia's political system and points to the unintended effects these policies have on the acculturation of the minority Chinese community in Malaysia. Once again, Freedman is not interested in whether these political policies have achieved their objectives within the political system, but in the effects of these policies on a minority ethnic group. These studies by Ariely and Freedman draw explicit connections between national policies and the broader effects they can have on society.

A study by Kislev (2015) takes this interest in the unintended effects of policy one step further in highlighting how the unintended effects of policy are not always limited to national boundaries and can also extend into transnational spaces. Kislev's ambitious study explores the effects of the Israeli government's multicultural policies on Israeli migrants to the United States. He accomplishes this through tracking the key multicultural changes that have taken place within Israel over the past decade and then assessing how these changes map onto trends in the identification of US migrants from Israel. His findings suggest that a rise in migrant identification with Israel since 2000 stems not from events in the US, but rather from changes in Israeli national policy and a new approach to the integration of minority communities. Kislev's study points to the possibility of studying the transnational effects that policies can have on the social psychology of populations who are notably separated from the national political processes that produce the policies in the first place.

This literature on the unintended effects of policy opens up an exploration of the nature of policy itself and how it influences changes in society. In order to further develop this perspective within political social psychology, however, a theoretical lens is needed to frame the social psychological pathways through which these changes take place. Better understandings of these social psychological pathways can provide a basis for linking social policy and its unintended effects on society's political issues, for instance, by exploring how is it that certain policies affect national identities even across borders, as in Kislev's (2015) study of Israeli migrants to the US, or how the ideas put forward in policy inhibit the assimilation of migrant communities even when policymakers do not intend these impacts, as shown in Freeman's (2001) study of minority ethnic Chinese in Malaysia. In order to interrogate these pathways and establish a theoretical framework for thinking about the connections between political social psychology and policy, the next section turns to SRT.

Social representations and policy

Social representations theory (SRT) takes an interest in the common sense knowledge we have about the world. First conceptualised by Moscovici (1988), SRT is interested in the ways in which social knowledge about the world is formulated and reproduced through processes of communication and interaction (Jovchelovitch, 2007). This positions 'lay knowledge' about the world as valuable and not a distortion of 'truth' or as of lesser value than the 'scientific' or 'evidence-based' forms of knowledge that are thought to inform good policy. Elcheroth, Doise, and Reicher (2011) have previously outlined the value of a social representations approach for political psychology, pointing to overlapping interests between social representations and the study of political phenomena. Others have used social representations as a theoretical framework for empirical studies of policy processes (Devine-Wright & Devine-Wright, 2006; Mérand, 2006). This chapter contributes to this body of literature by exploring the ways in which policy is intimately involved in the production of social representations.

In drawing on SRT, I am positioning policy as part of a 'thinking society' (Moscovici, 1961, 1985), where thinking is a collective social act rather than something performed by an individual. As Tileagă (2013) summarises, a thinking society is the setting where social representations are 'formed, asserted, circulated and contested and where they acquire a certain autonomy in the process' (p. 65). Moving away from analysing policy as something formed by knowledgeable elites and paying attention to the role of policy within a thinking society provides a means of understanding the social psychological pathways that connect policy to its unintended effects. Policy is taken as its own social representation about a particular social issue (e.g. gender equality) that interacts with other social representations that are either similar or different from the original (e.g. multiculturalism or economic affairs) in often unpredictable ways. In a sense, policy is an actor in a thinking society rather than a plan of action formed by expert knowledge on the best approach to a particular social issue. The objects of study therefore becomes the processes through which a particular policy influences the social representations or common sense understandings circulating within society rather than whether a policy delivers on its objectives.

Since Moscovici first introduced the concept of a thinking society and the theory of social representations, others have developed aspects of the theory that help to build further on its insights for understanding the unintended effects of policy. For instance, Jovchelovitch (2007) reflects on the processes that produce and sustain social representations through posing questions about who, how, why, what, and what for. Her description of the representational processes that determine the who and what of social representations is particularly for policy studies. In asking about the who of social representations, Jovchelovitch points to the ways in which representations often reflect the identity of the 'knowers' and are deliberately formed in ways that promote or support these identities. This promotes consideration of the ways in which policy knowledge often tries to hide the identity of the knowers, or policy makers, in order to emphasise the objectivity of the knowledge being presented in policy documents. In asking what, Jovchelovitch explores what exactly is being represented and how an object is constructed through representation. The emphasis here is on processes of 'anchoring' and 'objectifying' in the formation of social representations. Together these two processes make an unfamiliar object into something familiar through anchoring the new object in a more familiar social representation and then solidifying the characteristics of the more familiar representation into the new object through objectification (Bauer & Gaskell, 1999). For Jovchelovitch, understanding this process highlights how social representations are rooted in a context and a history. The form of knowledge produced by policy also needs to be understood in this light.

In exploring the potential of social representations for political psychology, Elcheroth and colleagues (2011) argue for the importance of considering social identities 'as social representations and subject to the dynamics of representation' (p. 735). Social identities are social representations in the sense that one's social identify is interwoven with the social representation of the groups one belongs to. How we perceive ourselves depends to some extent on how we represent our social groups and how others represent us (Howarth, 2002). In examining the dynamics of social representations, Elcheroth and colleagues (2011) also point to how social representations act on meta-knowledge: we create representations not only based on what we think about an issue, but according to what we think others think. Policy therefore has a key role to play in shaping our social identities in two different ways: (1) by establishing new social representations that influence people's own representations of the groups they belong to, and (2) by framing particular groups in positive or negative ways that influence how people think others perceive them and their social groups.

In addition, social representations are not only evident in the ideas or beliefs expressed or the words used to convey ideas, but also in the actions that are taken within a particular environment (Moscovici & Duveen, 2000). This means that social representations must be understood not only as something communicated through language but also through social practices (Elcheroth et al., 2011). As such, a distinction needs to be made between the ideas or forms of social knowledge that people mention and the ways in which they act on this social knowledge, with attention drawn to what social representations actually *do* rather than what they say (Howarth, 2006). In making this argument, Howarth draws on a study of the social representations of young black students in Brixton schools to highlight the active and contested nature of social representations. She describes how black students recognise the dominant representation of themselves as 'troublesome black youth' and how many students have found ways to resist this representation within their daily activities. Social representations are therefore not static ideas, but rather open to critique and change through the dialogical processes that bring them into being in the first place. This ideas of social representations as both *active* (constructed through ongoing dialogue and open to change) and *contested* (resisted through particular actions) have a number of implications for considering the effects of policy. The active nature of social representations means that policy cannot be seen as a fixed entity that dictates a particular means of addressing a social issue, but rather as a dialogical process between policy makers, implementers, and a targeted population. In exploring the effects of policy, we therefore need to consider not only the social representations embedded in a policy document, but equally the actions that are taken by those implementing the policy and any acts of resistance that occur.

Drawing from this summary of SRT and its development as an approach within social psychology, three main aspects stand out as particularly relevant for understanding the pathways that link social policy to its unintended effects in society: (1) the role of policy in producing social representations as collective ideas about particular social issues; (2) the potential for the social representations evident in policy to influence social identities; and (3) the importance of considering social representations as changeable and potentially resisted by targeted populations in our understanding of policy effects. In the remainder of this chapter, I explore each of these aspects in light of a study on the implementations of gender policy in South Africa. I begin with an overview of this study.

Case study: Gender policy in South Africa

Since the end of apartheid in 1994, South Africa has been a breeding ground for international donor policies on gender equality. International donors have primarily been interested in addressing two main gender-related issues in South Africa: the high rate of gender-based violence, including rape, and the way in which gender inequalities contribute to the spread of HIV. Often-cited statistics tell us that women in South Africa are four times more likely to have HIV then men within certain age groups, and rates of domestic and sexual violence are among the highest in the world (Republic of South Africa, Ministry of Health, 2010). In order to capture the large influx of funding from international donors to address these issues, domestic South African organisations developed a variety of gender equality programmes, including programmes that support feminist activism, micro-credit or small enterprise activities for women, community level discussions about 'harmful' gender norms, and support for gender mainstreaming in government agencies.

This chapter draws on a multisite ethnographic study carried out in 2010 of how international donor policies on gender were being adopted by practitioners in these South African organisations (NPOs) (Mannell, 2012). This study involved an analysis at two different levels: (1) the international donor policies attempting to address gender issues in South Africa and (2) the practice of implementing these policies, including data from organisational observations of gender programmes, and in-depth interviews with 32 gender practitioners across 28 different organisations in South Africa's largest urban centres: Cape Town, Johannesburg, and Durban. A complex landscape of social representations emerged from this study, including very different representations about how to address gender inequalities by the various stakeholders involved. These social representations are described in detail in order to explore the pathways that link gender policy to its unintended effects in South African society and to highlight the value of using SRT as a means of exploring these effects.

Gender policy as a product and producer of social representations

A social representations approach to policy takes policy both as a representation of a particular issue and as part of a communication process that produces and reproduces knowledge about social issues such as gender. Rather than understanding gender policy as having a direct impact on specific objectives, such as gender-related behaviours (i.e. male violence or the role of masculinity in supporting particular sexual practices), I am interested in pointing to the multiple ways in which gender policies produce social representations about how gender inequalities should be addressed within the context of South Africa.

Three distinct social representations of how gender inequalities should be addressed are evident in policy documents developed by international donors to gender programmes in South Africa (including bilateral donors and international NGOs). These include: (1) by teaching women and/or men, (2) by ensuring women have access to the same rights as men, and (3) by addressing social rules about gender (Mannell, 2014a). Table 15.1 shows key examples of these three different social representations.

TABLE 15.1 Social representations of how to address gender inequalities in South Africa, with key examples from the policy documents of international donors

Social representation of how to address gender inequalities	Examples from the policy documents of international donors
(1) By teaching men and women about gender inequalities	'The resulting actions can target women or men as direct players or beneficiaries, and must help reduce gender inequalities. For instance, in the fight against violence, working with men or working to understand the mechanisms that lead to violence in men are relevant areas for action.' Ministère des affaires étrangères et européennes (France), 2010, p. 6
(2) By ensuring women have access to the same rights as men	'Targeting actions to empower women include women-specific approaches that are necessary in order to compensate for actual gender-specific disadvantages and discrimination. Here, the task is to reform overall conditions by empowering women to assert and exercise their rights as stakeholders and rights holders with the same rights and duties as men.' Federal Ministry of Economic Cooperation and Development of Germany, 2009, p. 7
(3) By addressing social rules about gender	'Institutions are the rules – both stated and implicit – for achieving social or economic ends; the rules that determine who gets what, what counts, who does what and who decides. These are the rules that maintain women's unequal position in society. They include values that perpetuate the gendered division of labour, devalue women's lives, restrict women's access to land and other key economic resources, restrict women's mobility and, perhaps most fundamentally, devalue reproductive work.' Gender at Work, cited from www.genderatwork.org/gender-work-framework, retrieved 26 April 2012

Exploring these policy documents and their implementation through the lens of SRT contributes key insights about how policy produces social representations about gender. The fact that there are significant differences between policy documents points to how the documents themselves are social products, developed through ongoing conversations between academics, policy makers, advocates, government officials, and so forth. The policy produced by international donors cannot be seen as representing the truth about how gender inequalities are best addressed. Despite efforts to present the rationale for policy recommendations as objective statements about best practice, the sheer diversity of the approaches put forward by different policy makers emphasises the socially constructed nature of these documents.

We can see this clearly through drawing on Jovchelovitch's question about 'what' is being represented. The three representations of how to address gender inequalities summarised in Table 15.1 can each be associated with distinct theoretical traditions in gender studies. In other words, they have both a history and a context. The first of these social representations – addressing gender inequalities through teaching both men and women – arose from a feminist interest in involving men in gender programming in order to address the historic failure of many women's programmes that had been in place during the 1970s and '80s due to men's insistence on maintaining their privilege and power. The second representation – focusing on women's rights and ensuring that they have access to the same rights as men – draws on the history of human rights frameworks established throughout the 20th century (Donnelly, 2013) and the power of these frameworks as internationally agreed conventions that governments can be held accountable to. Finally, the third representation – that gender inequalities need to be addressed through tackling the broader social rules or norms of society – draws on the poststructural view of gender that came together with the third wave of feminism prominent during the 1990s and the way in which the power relations embedded in social norms or discourses are taken as central to the construction of gendered subject positions within this perspective (Butler, 1990, 1993). The diversity of these three representations within gender policy for South Africa points to the absence of a singular notion of how gender inequalities should be approached and the role of history and context in producing different social representations. I have argued elsewhere (Mannell, 2014b) that these social representations of how gender inequalities should be addressed in South Africa have contributed to major conflicts between practitioners and the lack of a cohesive social movement for tackling gender-related issues.

The influence of policy on social identities

As mentioned, the social representations embedded in policy can also shape our social identities through: (1) establishing social representations that influence people's own representations of the groups they belong to, and (2) framing particular groups in positive or negative ways, which influences how people think others perceive them. In the context of Social Africa, gender policies have brought a host of different social identities to gender-related programming in South Africa. I focus in this section on one of these social identities in particular: men as masculine in ways that are 'harmful' to women.

In gender policies for South Africa, the international donors that focus on men as part of gender programmes tend to rationalise this focus through highlighting the role of certain masculine behaviours or 'masculinities' that perpetuate the use of violence against women, promiscuity, unsafe sexual behaviour, and so on. This presents a particular representation of these 'harmful' masculinities as part of men's roles as fathers, partners, and husbands and links them to acts of violence against women. For instance, the Swedish International Development Agency (SIDA) states in their policy document:

> SIDA will take action to . . . strengthen the role of men as fathers, and men's and boys' ability to combat negative male gender roles and stereotypical images of masculinity linked to the use of violence and a lack of respect for sexual and reproductive rights.
> *(Swedish International Development Agency, 2010, p. 26)*

Given the role of social representations in influencing people's own representations of the groups they belong to, the way in which this representation of masculinities contributes to men's own understandings of their social identities needs to be considered.

We can observe the influence of this type of policy on men's social identities by examining the programmes that implement masculinities policies, for example, programmes that attempt to address 'stereotypical masculinities' or 'negative male gender roles' that are harmful to women. A range of gender programmes across South Africa target men specifically as a means of implementing the type of policy outlined by SIDA, including programmes by Sonke Gender Justice, Engender Health, and Brothers for Life. For example, the approach taken by Sonke Gender Justice can be seen in the following quote from a manual used for its One Man Can campaign:

> Men can choose not to behave violently towards women, children, and other men. Saying that men choose to use violence, rather than that men lose control and become violent, is the first step in holding men accountable for their decisions and actions. . . . In conducting formative research for the campaign, we learned that many men and boys do worry about the safety of women and girls – their partners, sisters, mothers, girlfriends, wives, co-workers, neighbours, classmates and fellow congregants – and want to play a role in creating a safer and more just world, they often do not know what to do about it.[1]

From this quote we can see that Sonke's One Man Can campaign is intended to influence the social identities of men and to formulate positive social identities around men's concerns for the safety of women and girls. A testimonial from an interview with a man who had been involved in a similar gender programme, called Stepping Stones, shows how men do use these alternative identities to resist dominant social representations of men and masculinities:

> For me I feel it was a life-changing intervention because my thinking about women suddenly changed. Growing up I knew women as sub-human to men; I knew that we were a better 'species', if I may use that loose term, than women. Where I come from, to be a man you have to be strong, you have to flex your muscles whenever you get a chance. And you have to show this strength to other men by being violent. I have been able to use the

information that I got, use the reflection that I got from Stepping Stones to ask myself: 'Do I need to do this? What do I stand to benefit from doing this? And now I'm able to make those judgement calls on my own. Even if men from my community have started to think about me as a softie now and all that, it is ok, you know, I understand . . . I began to realise that there are different ways of being a man.

In this way, the social representation evident in policy about masculinities leads to programmes that then influence men's social identities.

However, the focus on men's concerns for the safety of women as a means of shaping new social identities may also have unintended effects on women's identities within this context, which SRT helps to highlight. As in Howarth's (2006) study of dominant representations of young black students in Brixton schools as 'troublesome black youth' and the implications this has for the social identities of these students, programmes that work with men in South Africa need to be careful not to reproduce social identities of women as constantly in need of male protection. In emphasising the concern that men hold for the women in their lives, masculinities policies and associated programmes may be contributing to representations of women as weak or unable to cope without a male partner. According to the social representations approach outlined in this chapter, these negative social representations of women have the potential to influence how women perceive themselves and how they think they are being perceived by their male partners, potentially playing a role in confirming negative social identities for women. This also needs to be taken into consideration in analysing policy and the programmes derived from it.

Social representations as active and contested

As outlined previously, analysing policy using SRT also requires attention to the act of implementing policy. This draws the analysis of policy away from a focus on documentation to consider how policy may be changed through entering dialogue with 'local' knowledge in practice. In the study from South Africa, we can see how the social representations of gender expressed in international policy are sometimes adopted while at other times being resisted by policy implementers in the context of their practice. As an act of resistance, practitioners often fail to implement gender policy in the way it is intended (Mannell, 2014a).

The participants targeted by gender programmes in the South African study draw on very different systems of knowledge than the international donors who design gender policies. The representations of gender evident in policy frequently emphasise the various ways in which gender inequalities contribute to poor health and development outcomes as rationales for intervention by international donors (Mannell, 2012). However, this representation of gender does not always resonate with local communities. Practitioners working for South African organisations funded by these international donors can become caught in the middle of these two systems of knowledge. The disparity between the social representations embedded in policy and those of communities is often recognised by practitioners, as discussed in this interview:

> [In the communities we work with] some people have more power than other people and the whole issue of gender and power, gender power relations intercepts with other forms of power relations in society, especially class and race in South Africa. And that intersection is never dealt with. Okay, so we never speak. And when we talk about gender in training or when we're doing gender mainstreaming in organisations or whatever, we never actually address class and race.

For this practitioner, social representations of inequality held by South Africans include inequalities of race and class. However, these representations do not appear in gender policy, and the result is that they are often not discussed during gender programmes.

Practitioners react in different ways to the differences in the social representations they face in gender policy and in their interactions with communities. Some practitioners adopt the representation of gender that is prevalent in policy (e.g. gender as a concern for health or for development), while others actively resist this representation. Resistance to policy representations of gender often occur when practitioners allow 'local' South African representations to enter into the discussions they have as part of their gender programmes. Many practitioners do this quite deliberately, facilitating this resistance to policy representations of gender by carrying out activities that have been designed to ask people about their own social representations and using this as a basis for social change and transformation. This approach is explained by one of the practitioner in the following way:

> For me, for real gender [transformation] to happen, I need to understand for myself how I am affected by gender, what gender is for me in the reality of my life. Then I can start to see it elsewhere and to see how I can sort of try and change or try and influence change around me. But if – I guess this is true with a whole lot of things in life, a whole lot of changes – if you don't personalise the change, the change is not sustainable.

This approach to gender programming is not about tackling the ways in which gender inequalities contribute to health or development issues. Instead, practitioners resist these representations by taking an active interest in understanding the representations of gender held by the populations they work with and focusing on personal transformation.

A social representations approach provides a framework for thinking about how these attempts to resist the policies of international donors are part of the effects of gender policy on social/political norms in society. The social representations that result from the implementation of a particular policy may be quite different from the representations embedded in the policy itself. In implementing programmes, practitioners may resist particular social representations that do not conform to the social representations of the communities they work with. They may create ways to allow 'local' representations to emerge. The broader findings from this study show that it is in these moments of asking people how they themselves define gender inequalities in their own lives that real social change has the potential to occur (Mannell, 2012). This practice of resisting the social representations found in policy therefore needs to be taken as part of the policy process and its unintended effects.

Conclusions: Researching policy in everyday contexts

The societal approach to the social psychology of policy taken in this chapter frees us from an analysis of whether policy meets its objectives to explore the interactions that take place between policy and social knowledge. As explored throughout this chapter, a social representations approach has the potential to make several unique contributions to the study of social policy. For instance, SRT provides a lens for understanding how social knowledge is produced and reproduced in everyday contexts. As such, it draws into question the ability of policy makers to identify the 'reality' of a social issue and dream up 'effective' policy solutions; rather it highlights the role policy plays in both contributing to and shaping particular representations of social issues such as gender. These representations are then seen as contributing to particular social identities for populations targeted by policy, as well as those not targeted by a specific policy. In addition, a social representation approach to policy pays attention to the representations that are embedded in the act of implementing policy and the broader consequences this can have for the unintended effects of policy.

Approaching policy through an SRT lens therefore requires a different approach to policy analysis, one that moves away from a focus on policy documents to pay attention to the series of events that is involved in developing and implementing policy. Taking account of the various events surrounding a policy issue in a particular context provides a landscape for examining how the stakeholders involved have constructed a particular social issue, the identities being formulated as part of this process, and the actions or resistances that arise. In this approach, the objects of analysis within each policy 'event' become the everyday understandings of policy held by the stakeholders involved, which include not just policy 'makers' but also practitioners involved in putting policies in place through the development and execution of programmes and the individuals targeted or otherwise affected by a particular policy. This type of approach inherently assumes that everyone can know policy and that expert knowledge on a particular social issue tells us little about how a particular policy will influence the social world.

SRT has the potential to not only expand our understanding of how policy operates within everyday contexts, but also to improve understandings of policy processes more broadly. During the 1970s, the field of policy implementation studies experienced a crisis in the realisation that policies almost always fail to achieve their original objectives (Bardach, 1977). While policy implementation analysts have moved towards a more complex approach to analysis today, they also continue to assume that processes of implementation can be modelled and assessed to find the reasons why some policies succeed and others fail (Goggin, 1986; Saetren, 2014). A social psychology approach opens up a new set of questions about these supposed policy 'failures'. By questioning the very idea that policy can accomplish a predefined set of social objectives, SRT can reconfigure the focus on failures to instead examine the unintended effects of policy. Within this perspective, policy is never understood as 'failing' simply because, even if it does not meet its stated objectives, it can still contribute to change in the social world. This opens up new questions, such as: What do policies *do* in a particular context? What types of social changes occur because of policy events that disrupt or challenge social representations? How does policy create new possibilities for social change outside of the objectives set by the policy itself? These types of questions have the potential to expand existing knowledge about the impacts of policies on broader society while also recognising the limitations of assuming we know what these impacts will be without first understanding the interactions between policy and the social contexts in which they are implemented.

Note

1 Cited from: www.genderjustice.org.za/onemancan, retrieved 1 July 2012.

References

Ariely, G. (2012). Do those who identify with their nation always dislike immigrants? An examination of citizenship policy effects. *Nationalism and Ethnic Politics*, *18*(2), 242–261. doi:10.1080/13537113.2012.680862

Bacqué, M.-H., Fijalkow, Y., Launay, L., & Vermeersch, S. (2011). Social mix policies in Paris: Discourses, policies and social effects. *International Journal of Urban and Regional Research*, *35*(2), 256–273. doi:10.1111/j.1468–2427.2010.00995.x

Bardach, B. (1977). *The implementation game: What happens after a bill becomes a law* (Vol. 1). Cambridge, MA: MIT Press.

Bauer, M.W., & Gaskell, G. (1999). Towards a paradigm for research on social representations. *Journal for the Theory of Social Behaviour*, *29*(2), 163–186. doi:10.1111/1468–5914.00096

Buse, K., Mays, N., & Walt, G. (2005). *Making health policy (Understanding Public Health)* (2nd ed.). London: Open University Press.

Butler, J. (1990). *Gender trouble* (2nd ed., 2006.). New York: Routledge.

Butler, J. (1993). *Bodies that matter: On the discursive limits of 'sex'*. New York: Routledge.

Campbell, C., & Burgess, R. (2012). The role of communities in advancing the goals of the movement for global mental health. *Transcultural Psychiatry*, *49*(3–4), 379–395. doi:10.1177/1363461512454643

Campbell, C., Cornish, F., Gibbs, A., & Scott, K. (2010). Heeding the push from below. *Journal of Health Psychology*, *15*(7), 962–971.

Devine-Wright, P., & Devine-Wright, H. (2006). Social representations of intermittency and the shaping of public support for wind energy in the UK. *International Journal of Global Energy Issues*, *25*(3), 243–256.

Donnelly, J. (2013). *Universal human rights in theory and practice*. Ithaca: Cornell University Press.
Elcheroth, G., Doise, W., & Reicher, S. (2011). On the knowledge of politics and the politics of knowledge: How a social representations approach helps us rethink the subject of political psychology. *Political Psychology, 32*(5), 729–758. doi:10.1111/j.1467–9221.2011.00834.x
Frank, V. A., & Bjerge, B. (2011). Empowerment in drug treatment: Dilemmas in implementing policy in welfare institutions. *Social Science and Medicine, 73*(2), 201–208. doi:10.1016/j.socscimed.2011.04.026
Freedman, A. L. (2001). The effect of government policy and institutions on Chinese overseas acculturation: The case of Malaysia. *Modern Asian Studies, 35*(2), 441–440. doi:10.1017/S0026749X01002050
Goggin, M. (1986). The 'too few cases/too many variables' problem in implementation research. *The Western Political Quarterly, 39*(2), 328–347.
Hammond, K. R. (1996). *Human judgement and social policy: Irreducible uncertainty, inevitable error, unavoidable injustice* (Vol. xi). New York: Oxford University Press.
Howarth, C. (2002). Identity in whose eyes? The role of representations in identity construction. *Journal for the Theory of Social Behaviour, 32*(2), 145–162. doi:10.1111/1468-5914.00181
Howarth, C. (2006). A social representation is not a quiet thing: Exploring the critical potential of social representations theory. *British Journal of Social Psychology, 45*(1), 65–86. doi:10.1348/014466605X43777
Howarth, C., Campbell, C., Cornish, F., Franks, B., Garcia-Lorenzo, L., Gillespie, A., ... Tennant, C. (2013). Insights from societal psychology: A contextual politics of societal change. *Journal of Social and Political Psychology, 1*(1), 364–384.
Jovchelovitch, S. (2007). *Knowledge in context: Representations, community and culture*. London: Routledge.
Kaarbo, J., & Gruenfeld, D. (1998). The social psychology of inter- and intragroup conflict in governmental politics. *Mershon International Studies Review, 42*(2), 226–233. doi:10.2307/254414
Kawashima-Ginsberg, K., & Levine, P. (2014). Policy effects on informed political engagement. *American Behavioral Scientist, 58*(5), 665–688. doi:10.1177/0002764213515219
Kislev, E. (2015). The transnational effect of multicultural policies on migrants' identification: The case of the Israeli diaspora in the USA. *Global Networks, 15*, 118–139. doi:10.1111/glob.12043
Larson, D. W. (1994). The role of belief systems and schemas in foreign policy decision-making. *Political Psychology, 15*(1), 17–33. doi:10.2307/3791437
Lipsky, M. (1983). *Street-level bureaucracy: The dilemmas of the individual in public service*. New York: Russell Sage Foundation.
Mannell, J. (2010). Are the sectors compatible? International development work and lessons for a business–nonprofit partnership framework. *Journal of Applied Social Psychology, 40*(5), 1106–1122. doi:10.1111/j.1559–1816.2010.00612.x
Mannell, J. (2012). *Practicing gender: Gender and development policy in South African organisations*. London: London School of Economics and Political Science.
Mannell, J. (2014a). Adopting, manipulating, transforming: Tactics used by gender practitioners in South African NGOs to translate international gender policies into local practice. *Health & Place, 30*, 4–12. doi:10.1016/j.healthplace.2014.07.010
Mannell, J. (2014b). Conflicting policy narratives: Moving beyond culture in identifying barriers to gender policy in South Africa. *Critical Social Policy, 34*(4), 454–474. doi:10.1177/0261018314538794

Mérand, F. (2006). Social representations in the European security and defence policy. *Cooperation and Conflict*, *41*(2), 131–152. doi:10.1177/0010836706063659

Moscovici, S. (1961). *La Psychanalyse, son image et son public* (New edition 1976.). Paris: Presses Universitaires de France – PUF.

Moscovici, S. (1985). *The age of the crowd: A historical treatise on mass psychology*. Cambridge, Cambridgeshire, New York, and Paris: Cambridge University Press.

Moscovici, S. (1988). Notes towards a description of social representations. *European Journal of Social Psychology*, *18*(3), 211–250. doi:10.1002/ejsp.2420180303

Moscovici, S., & Duveen, G. (2000). *Social representations: Explorations in social psychology*. New York: New York University Press.

Niska, M., & Vesala, K. M. (2013). SME policy implementation as a relational challenge. *Entrepreneurship and Regional Development*, *25*(5–6), 521–540. doi:10.1080/08985626.2013.798354

Republic of South Africa, Ministry of Health. (2010). *South Africa: Country progress report on the declaration of commitment on HIV/AIDS*. South Africa: Ministry of Health. Retrieved from www.unaids.org/en/KnowledgeCentre/HIVData/CountryProgress/2010CountryProgressAllCountries.asp

Saetren, H. (2014). Implementing the third generation research paradigm in policy implementation research: An empirical assessment. *Public Policy and Administration*, *29*(2), 84–105.

Speer, P. W., & Christens, B. D. (2012). Local community organizing and change: altering policy in the housing and community development system in Kansas City. *Journal of Community & Applied Social Psychology*, *22*(5), 414–427. doi:10.1002/casp.1132

Swedish International Development Agency. (2010). *On equal footing: Policy for gender equality and the rights and role of women in Sweden's International Development Cooperation 2010–2015*. Vasteras: Department for Development. Retrieved from www.government.se/contentassets/f8954ef446a54d83bbcecfbf5fb61fd6/on-equal-footing-policy-for-gender-equality-and-the-rights-and-role-of-women-in-swedens-international-development-cooperation-2010-2015

Tileagă, C. (2013). Social representations of political affairs and beliefs. In C. Tileagă (Ed.), *Political Psychology: Critical Perspectives* (pp. 62–82). Cambridge, UK: Cambridge University Press.

COMMENTARY ON PART III
Political discourse and practice

Michelle Fine

In the 1930s, social psychologists Marie Jahoda, Paul Lazarsfeld and Hans Zeisel undertook a deep ethnographic analysis of everyday life in Marienthal, a community outside of Vienna, Austria, where villagers suffered individually and collectively from what was then called the Worldwide Economic Crisis (2003). Offering a biography of what they called a "weary community," beleaguered by recession that lasted for years, these researchers captured the impact of global recession on the lives in the village which had been a stronghold for the Social Democratic Labor Movement, where one would find the Workers Library, newspapers, rich civic participation – all of which came to a halt when the factory closed. Using ethnography and time charts and conversations with and observations of everyday people, Jahoda and colleagues sought to understand the everyday discourses, embodiments and behaviors that derive from economic oppression. Refusing academic language that would distance them from their informants, Jahoda and colleagues wrote through the words and metaphors of the people to demonstrate the devastating material, psychological and existential consequences of severe and collective unemployment in Central Europe. A window on their theoretical and methodological innovation comes in their analysis of the embodiment and subjectivities of *time*, noticing that while employed people would walk briskly across the street, those carrying the burden of unemployment carried the weight of time, stretching passively over a day. One man, without job or hope of employment narrated, in the passive voice, the seeming lethargy: "In the meantime, midday comes around."

In the concluding chapter, "How long can this life continue?" the authors pierced the membrane that touches both researchers and readers when they wrote:

> We entered Marienthal as scientists; we leave it with only one desire: that the tragic opportunity for an inquiry may not recur in our time.
>
> *(2003, p. 98)*

Almost 85 years later, in these essays on political discourse and practice, we encounter "another tragic opportunity for an inquiry" into the social psychology of global economic crisis. Now again, critical psychologists return to the original and neglected wound – economic inequality and devastation. Almost a century after the Marienthal project, the subject of inquiry remains the same, today exacerbated by economic policies that privilege elites and advocate austerity, developed from the perch of corporate wealth and deaf to the cries of those who most intimately endure the scar tissue of poverty, precarity and dispossession.

I read these essays with great interest for how they can help us understand contemporary waves of right-wing ideology and nationalism, the psychic weight of loss and the slow death of hope, the perverse consequences of public policies fabricated from above and the haunting objects of despair named by those whose dignity and survival hang perilously in a contingent economy. These essays render visible the social psychological thread in the fabric of everyday lives, forged amidst voracious global capitalism, a consolidation of White supremacist identities and widening inequality gaps.

In this political and scholarly context, I was honored to be asked to comment on the set of essays gathered under the section heading "political discourse and practice," and so appreciate that these conversations are percolating within psychology. The essays teach as much as they raise critical questions about the significance of listening to the whispers below. They hint at how (deeply) politics seep under the skin, and they suggest, tentatively, how new solidarities might be forged where seemingly divergent interests converge. From across these five chapters, we learn much that is hopeful: that dominant political discourses are complex and fragile. They are multisourced, vulnerable to historic and contextual variation and often empty of content. These insights suggest that the slide to the right may be precarious, tenuous and reroutable; that we should pause, and not jump to conclusions, when national surveys are gathered and reported, when polarization seems so fierce and when people are asked to comment upon issues they know little about but defend their positions vehemently.

That said, I am simply stunned by the striking political contradictions and contrasts of our times. You see, I live in a country where Donald Trump is considered a serious and popular candidate for the presidency, and of course I don't know anyone who takes him seriously. I live in a country where just this summer, scores of Black men and women and children were killed by White police officers; most White people were "shocked" and remain in disbelief, while most Black people knew the stories before the killings took place. I live in a country, like yours perhaps, where more than a few young Muslim teens are drawn to the power of ISIS and – very differently – where #BlackLivesMatter has taken off like wild fire across the nation, a mobilizing space for wildly diverse political solidarities. And adults – particularly wealthy White adults – are surprised.

Across class/race/ethnicity/religion/region/sexuality and so on, we live in very different discursive communities, trust very different kinds of information, baste in distinct political communities and craft politicized subjectivities in hinged, but bounded, pots of soil.

I live in a country – and so do you – where the alienation of young people of color and poverty is palpable; where their identities are denied, desires are betrayed and futures are bleak. They are rightfully hungry for recognition, as their parents are rightfully hungry for employment, security, papers, status and housing. And everyone is looking for someone to blame: immigrants, Blacks, Jews, Muslims, gays, "terrorists."

Political subjectivities and desires are anchored in political and racialized economies and vulnerable to the discursive volley of blame; the social psychology of political attitudes can not be extracted from the grotesque inequities in distribution of resources and opportunities, in recognition of culture and value, and in active civic participation.

And so I appreciate the opportunity to muse in conversation with these essays that attend exquisitely to politics on the ground, in the everyday, under the skin and on the tongue. I am reminded of a stunning little book by James Scott, *Two Cheers for Anarchism*, that argues for the fundamental importance of listening in on the political underground. Scott advocates what he calls the "anarchist squint" whereby critical scholars attend to the pulse of politics on the ground:

> Infrapolitics [include] practices outside the visible spectrum of what passes for political activism . . . foot dragging, protesting, pilfering, dissimulation, sabotage, desertion, absenteeism, squatting and flight. . . . Most social scientists fail to engage . . . the political analyses of nonelites. . . . What is inadmissible, both morally and scientifically is the hubris that pretends to understand the behavior of human agents without for a moment listening systematically to how they understand what they are doing and how they explain themselves.
> *(Scott, 2014, p. xx)*

Perhaps his most devastating charge is that social science listens so carefully to the words of elites but not at all to nonelites: "Their politics is read off their statistical profile: from such 'facts' as their income, occupation, years of schooling, property holding, residence, race, ethnicity and religion." (Scott, 2014, p. xxiii) With no romance about infrapolitics, he is offended that scholars assume elites know why they do what they do, but nonelites don't. He continues:

> Their [lay] explanations are no more transparent that the self-explanations of elites . . . but the job of social science . . . is to provide, provisionally, the best explanation of behavior on the basis of all the evidence available, including especially the explanations of the purposive, deliberating agents whose behavior is being scrutinized. The notion that the agent's view of the situation is irrelevant to this explanation is preposterous.
> *(Scott, 2014, p. xxiv)*

Like the chapters in this section, Scott advances a call to interrogate how everyday people engage, enact, embody and narrate politics. There are many lessons to be extracted from these chapters. I sketch next three buckets of insights/incites these chapters provoke.

Embodiments of precarity: Objects of despair and desire

While many of the subsequent chapters focus on what people say, the first by Darrin Hodgetts, Shiloh Groot, Emily Garden and Kerry Chamberlain excavates what people yearn for, fear – the objects of despair that haunt within precarity. Hodgetts et al. elaborate a rich material analysis of mundane objects as embodiments of despair and, I would add, desire. In a hinged conceptual argument, Fine, Greene and Sanchez (2015) theorize the psychosocial doubleness of contemporary precarity: the shared experience of *existential precarity* and the deeply *stratified experience of material precarity*. We all live in a time of shared contingency but with sharply differential consequences, not knowing what is next but expecting it to be troubling. For those most impacted, there is a wound indeed but also a wisdom in precarity, what Fine et al. call "prec(ar)ious knowledge." And there is a longing and a rooting in objects, place and relationship which Hodgetts, Groot, Garden and Chamberlain so beautifully explore.

Hodgetts et al. return, with grace and intelligence, questions of class, embodiment and precarity to critical psychology. These writers encourage researchers to enter realms we have long abandoned: affect, embodiment and what indigenous scholar Gerald Vizenor calls "survivance" – a dialectic braiding of survival and resistance. Drawing on Flyvberg's use of *phronesis*, which is practically oriented knowledge, and Heidegger's interest in *mundane objects*, the writers remind us about the profound significance of cans of food, hammers, the anxiety of red lights on power meters, mold and slippers. With dignity and theory they offer us a window into embodied precarity, understanding everyday politics in the body and relations through objects of despair and desire.

On dominant narratives: More vulnerable than they seem?

The next three essays unravel what people say and interrogate how politics coat the tongues of everyday people narrating global slides to the right.

Susan Condor's stunning essay opens the trilogy on political discourse and rhetorical strategies of justification as she theorizes and excavates the rhetorical underpinnings of *empty attitudes*: "sincere opinions on matters of public debate which can be satisfactorily justified without recourse to detailed factual information." Like Figgou, in the next article, Condor expands the landscape for understanding and disrupting the wide but thin spread of neoliberal, pro-austerity, nationalistic and procapital logic that laminates the culture as she reveals the fragility, and emptyness, of such expressed positions. Condor examines with political and theoretical tools the rhetorical scaffolding that "holds up" the fragile, compulsively repeated tropes of public opinion rooted in nationalism. Drawing on classic texts by Asch and Converse, Condor suggests that empty attitudes may be virulent and extreme, but they are "subject to random variation over time and across contexts," that is, they are malleable.

Lisa Figgou draws from Moscovici's work on *thinking society* as she reflects on how everyday people make sense of the rise of Golden Dawn. By so doing, she begins to disarticulate the seemingly coherent slide to the right, unpacking the multiple motives at play – bias against immigrants for sure, but also a strong populist sense of betrayal by the state. By splicing open and separating the distinct discursive strands of a nationalist social movement, Figgou opens space for rethinking the fluid and contradictory, loosely coupled assemblage of political ideology. She implores social scientists to explore the "kaleidoscope of common sense," relying upon Billig, "instead of studying the ideological profile and attitudes of extreme voters alone." Figgou nudges our scholarly attention toward the multiorigin dynamics of ideological production and narration rather than typologies of people, again rendering nationalistic discourses more complex and perhaps more vulnerable to counternarratives than they may appear at first (frightening) glance.

Isabelle Goncalves-Portelinha, Christian Staerklé and Guy Elcheroth review the literature on social influence and political behavior, drawing on *meta-representations*, a strategic construct developed by Moscovici representing those beliefs about what other ingroup members believe, value or do regarding a given political topic. They develop a framework that explicates diffusion, propagation and propaganda as strategic enactments of majority influence and call on the malleability of meta-representations as flexible ramps for reshaping popular opinion. With mixed methods, the authors present a cross-site study of college students' political views of the right. They find that meta-representations matter, but context matters more:

> Examining the role of meta-representations in social change further requires a look at the timing and location of qualitative shifts in public opinion . . . [revealing] sociopsychological processes that enable and constrain political agency, understood as the capacity to intervene in the political sphere and bring about social stability or social change through collective action.

The work on meta-representations is so significant, but I admit that the analyses can sound too homogenizing, devoid of attention to the hairline fractures within a nation and society that split us open the more they are denied. At this moment of widening inequality gaps and highly contentious debates about who "belongs" to the state and who is state-less, it seems imperative to dive into the cracks in the dominant representations, to excavate the fractures and to deepen our understandings of the variations within.

These essays are curiously silent on how social media affects the dissemination, circulation and traction of these opinions, and given my current consternation about structural and cultural fault lines, the essays are underattentive to fractures and variations within nations and communities. Nevertheless, these papers signal an ironic optimism about the vulnerability of right-wing ideologies. Perhaps the most offensive public sentiments have more volume than evidence, depth or sustainability. Condor explains:

> When respondents were unable to mobilize domain-specific information to support their views, they were nevertheless able to draw upon a stock of ideological values and knowledge concerning political rights, responsibilities and social justice to enable them to formulate their opinions as justifiable and acceptable interventions in a current public controversy. Individuals who were more actively engaged in political life could explicitly mention the political principles on which their views were based. However, less politically sophisticated respondents could still employ rhetorical heuristics that drew implicitly upon general ideological principles.

Given the apparent porosity and vulnerability of dominant narratives, it may be strategic for critical psychologists to join with activists, journalists, filmmakers, artists and organizers to cultivate and circulate counternarratives that can decouple nationalist ideologies from national ethics, partially fill the information voids, tell another story and perhaps even cultivate new solidarities borne in surprising interest convergence.

The perverse and dangerous consequence of top-down policies

If the first four essays display how everyday people speak and yearn in times of economic contingency, Jenevieve Mannell lays out the dangerous consequences of policies that ignore these subjectivities and fail to account for the crusted dispossession of bottom-up realities. Mannell writes in ways that resonate with James Scott: she articulates a highly cogent critique of masculinities policy crafted from on high. Through a systematic case study of gender policy in South Africa, Mannell cautions that policy derivative of elite perspectives can bear dangerous fruit. She examines how the meta-representation of dangerous men – in masculinity policies designed presumably to "help" women – may actually reproduce the image of women as (weak) victims in need of (male) protection, rendering women more vulnerable to male violence.

> In emphasizing the concern that men hold for the women in their lives, masculinities policies and associated programmes may be contributing to representations of women as weak or unable to cope without a male partner. . . . These negative social representations of women have the potential to influence how women perceive themselves and how they think they are being perceived by their male partners, potentially playing a role in confirming negative social identities for women.

She advocates, instead:

> The societal approach to the social psychology of policy ... frees us from an analysis of whether policy meets its objectives to explore the interactions that take place between policy and social knowledge.... [providing] a lens for understanding how social knowledge is produced and reproduced ... [drawing] into question the ability of policy makers to identify the 'reality' of a social issue and dream up effective policy solutions.

★★★

Although Jahoda and colleagues (2003) hoped we would not have to return to a social psychology of economic devastation, the essays in this section push our discipline on pressure points where social psychology has been most vulnerable and where critical psychology may be most needed. The essays penned on political discourse and practice advance a series of important interventions into our disciplinary practice. First, they interrogate politics not from the top but in the flows of the everyday. Second, they draw upon social representation theory to understand cognitive sway to the right, tithed to ideology, affect, history and context. Third, they draw from a crossnational set of studies to appreciate the "stubborn particulars" of context but also ask how people – across place – use information, narrate opinions, take up political subjectivities and how they imagine, contribute to and disrupt the political landscape in which they are situated. Fourth, they delineate the perverse consequences of ignoring everyday political life, particularly with respect to top-down policymaking.

In an epidemic of widening inequality gaps, a sea of right-wing political waves, neoliberal pressures on higher education and narrow policy mandates for austerity, critical psychology surfaces as the right place to begin a conversation about the everyday politics, patterns, surprises and ambiguities. But as these essays suggest, we need more complex theoretical frameworks and methodological tools to get beneath what Susan Condor brilliantly calls "empty attitudes." These chapters are a compelling reminder that social psychology must braid "everyday discourses and practices" with systematic explorations of history, economics, popular culture, social media and affect. This cannot be a moment when psychologists shave political attitudes off the sidewalk where politics, circuits of dispossession and privilege have fractured the walkways of community life.

These essays pick up where Jahoda left off and advance our work alongside and hopefully in solidarity with movements for justice. The writers lay a foundation for critical work interrogating how politics penetrate subjectivities, discourse, desire and policy. We need not wait another 100 years to develop a dedicated cohort of critical scholars, working across national lines, who will interrogate the *fractures within discursive communities*; scholars who will tithe our projects in *solidarity designs* with artists, activists, journalists, educators and resistance movements, and activist scholars interested in *ruptures and their transformative sustainability* who will interrogate not only the rise of right-wing nationalism but also the ruptures of political possibilities such as those envisioned by Occupy, Arab Spring, Podemos, Indignados, #BlackLivesMatter and other mobilizations erupting across the globe like staccato fireworks, too quickly burning out but shining light on the pain and desires that circle the globe. These essays are a call for sustained critical inquiry into the political penetration of our subjectivities, privileging voices of the "everyday," forged in solidarity with movements on the ground.

References

Fine, M., Greene, A. C., & Sanchez, S. (2015). Prec(ar)ious knowledge and neoliberal blues. *Harvard Educational Review*.

Jahoda, M., Lazarsfeld, P., & Zeisel, H. (2003, reprinted). *Marienthal: The sociography of an unemployed community*. New York: Transaction Publishers.

Scott, J. (2014). *Two cheers for anarchism*. Princeton: Princeton University Press.

Vizenor, G. (1999). *Manifest manners: Narratives on Postindian survivance*. Lincoln: Nebraska.

CONCLUSION

The social psychology of everyday politics:
Beyond binaries and banality

Paul Nesbitt-Larking

Introduction

According to standard definitions, to describe social forces or social relations as "everyday" is to regard them as ordinary, routine or commonplace. The everyday connotes the mundane and the banal and references circumstances and events that are unexceptional, boring, uneventful and repetitious. The everyday is the world of the taken for granted and the unexamined. Everyday worlds are those scenarios held at a distance under the scrutiny of anthropologists investigating the unselfconscious ways of a distant people or those daily routines and folkways under the more local and contemporary scrutiny of the ethnomethodologists.

To scrutinise the everyday is to set boundaries between the ordinary and the original, the routine and the unexpected, and the commonplace and the exceptional. Such boundaries are understood as binaries, opposing and mutually exclusive conditions under which critical reflexivity is the property of the observer, while those under observation simply know "how to go on" (Giddens, 1984) with their daily routines. Nowhere have these binaries been more starkly drawn than in the tradition of Western political science. The founder of modern political science, Machiavelli, strategises the relationship between the ruler and his subjects in *The Prince* (1532/1973): "Men are so simple, and so much creatures of circumstance, that the deceiver will always find someone ready to be deceived" (p. 100). Contemporary political sociology was born in the late 19th century elite theories of Pareto, Mosca and Michels (Nye, 1977). Classical elite theory established clear-cut boundaries between those few men at the top who among themselves strategised for political ascendency and the bovine and benighted masses who were readily persuaded to follow along. Contemporary empirical political science emerged with behaviouralism (not to be confused with psychological behaviourism) in the 1960s and 1970s. While less rigid than elite theory, behaviouralism dichotomised state and society in the systems theory of David Easton (1965) and the adaptations of structural-functionalism undertaken by Gabriel Almond and his colleagues (Almond & Coleman, 1961; Almond & Powell, 1966). Unlike the legal-constitutional institutionalist approaches to governments that it supplemented, the behaviouralist approach recognised and examined the workings of political societies. This represented an advance on the somewhat lifeless descriptions of the formal rules and procedures of central political institutions which had been the focus of political studies for the first half of the 20th century. However, in the hands of behaviouralism, neither state institutions nor the social relations and forces of civil society were adequately theorised and examined. In the hands of the behaviouralists, political societies were conceived as static, homogeneous and lifelessly abstracted from the messiness and turbulence of a dynamic world.

The various contributions to *The Social Psychology of Everyday Politics* move our analyses of political life definitively away from the essentialist binaries of leaders and led, state and society, and thereby establish a rich and nuanced investigation into political life beyond the state. Each chapter in its own way explores the workings of political life at multiple levels, from the informal and local to the formal and institutional, without reifying either state or society. Across the entire collection, the banal is not always obvious, the mundane may not be routine, and, in the words of Dorothy Smith, the authors conceive "the everyday world as problematic" (Smith, 1987). While the studies undertaken in this volume bring to bear sophisticated and academic social psychological understandings of everyday worlds, they are also grounded in the possibility that everyday actors are equally sophisticated in the reflexive understandings of their circumstances and that their daily theorisations and lived political creativity are instructive.

Social science – including both political science and social psychology – inhabits a world that has undergone paradigmatic changes since the era of behaviouralism in the 1960s and 1970s. The late modern or postmodern condition has called into question the ideological and sociological solidities of the 20th century. As Lyotard (1984) argues, we have witnessed the end of grand narratives, and people no longer so readily adhere to the familiar "-isms". Those institutional and associational certainties that organised political life throughout the 20th century – social classes, mass political parties, industrial unions, gender roles, established religious denominations, the mass media and community organisations – have in various ways been eroded and in many cases have faded to insignificance. From a political perspective, if institutionalism privileged the state and behaviouralism privileged society as the locus for political agency, our current circumstances prompt us to look for the political at multiple levels and in multiple sites. Eurocentric perspectives on the world have been radically decentred through the postcolonial developments. The historical experience of contact between imperial powers and the colonised world has conditioned political identities that are contingent, situated, partial and hybrid. Such liminal identities may be suffered as the consequence of dislocation and marginalisation. However, they can also generate strategic and tactical advantages to those who learn how to live in a complex and uncertain world, who see opportunity rather than danger. Many of the chapters in this volume address such conditions. Contemporary society has, therefore, been undergoing processes of desocialisation and individuation in certain respects. Social identities have never been more open. However, this does imply an end to sociality, but rather more complex and uncertain social forces and social relations. Using the techniques of critical social psychology, the studies undertaken in the present volume examine in detail how people negotiate their political identities in circumstances that are increasingly complex and in which social belonging and social cues are increasingly ambivalent. These are the settings in which politics takes place and in which patterns of conformity, belief and resistance are formulated.

Taken together, each of the chapters in *The Social Psychology of Everyday Politics* contributes to an opening up of the nature of social being and social representations, as well as exploring the nuance and complexity of social identities. While not dismissing the state as a critical site of political life, the authors enrich our understanding of politics in the dialogical spaces of civil society as well as the lived complexities of the private sphere. While social groups are taken to exert a powerful influence in political relations, their influence is not construed as uniform, absolute or predictable irrespective of time or place. Three core ideas emerge throughout the book: first, that attitudes, opinions and representations are the consequence of complex individual choices made under certain situated circumstances; second, that we can examine how people develop their perspectives on central political issues through exploring talk and text in context; and, finally, that in their political worlds, people develop certain identity strategies to handle the pressures of social forces and the ambivalences of social relations. This conclusion explores these core ideas in the three subsequent sections.

Complexity and choice: The openness of attitudes, opinions and representations

The study of human society in its contemporary postmodern/postcolonial setting can no longer take the solidity, continuity or predictability of groups and communities or individual attitudes and identities for granted. Such views underpin the logic of traditional psychological experimental design. In Chapter 7, Reicher and Jogdand refer to this as "the atomised world of the psychological laboratory – a world in which it is impossible to capture the complex, slippery and noisy process through which humans, sometimes consensually and sometimes combatively, collectively make meaning". Their insights enable a critical revisiting of findings central to social psychology which have hitherto been taken as canonical, notably the conformity to authority findings of the Milgram obedience studies and the Zimbardo prison experiments. In both cases, Reicher and Jogdand underscore the choices made by research participants, their reflexive decision to take certain paths and the consequent decision to avoid other options, at least for the time being. In the cases of both Milgram and Zimbardo, "this work does not show that people are somehow inherently inclined to assume roles or obey orders (and thereby harm others)" (Reicher and Jogdand). Importantly, they stress the role of leaders as agents of persuasion in political settings, referring to leaders as "entrepreneurs of identity" and "entrepreneurs of emotion". Using the example of Dalit ("untouchable") humiliation and political mobilisation in India, Reicher and Jogdand present a detailed analysis of how leaders and followers engage with each other and how bids to invoke certain identities or identity claims may or may not work. People choose to get involved with a cause, role or authority figure, and leaders work hard to influence those people through the establishment of a good enough inclusive "we" relationship between the leader and the group. Everything depends upon the extent to which these people and groups come together under the conditions of a particular time and place. The implications of this research for political analysis are profound. First, people are not destined to fill particular social identities, categories or individual choices. Second, much depends upon the success of entrepreneurs of identity and emotion and who can most adequately identify and mobilise a collective sense of us and them among a certain group or community. Third, the choices that people make are always conscious and reflexive choices and they can change.

Just as Reicher and Jogdand identify "the atomised world of the psychological laboratory" in Chapter 7, Condor in Chapter 12 criticises standard public opinion polling methodologies as being too narrowly conceived and abstracted from their social settings. In the case of both chapters, the common critique is the tendency for existing research to search for individual ideas in contexts that are divorced from everyday lived experiences. On the basis of over 1,900 recordings with English citizens on Scottish devolution and the Scottish Parliament, Condor concludes that despite the absence of knowledge or information regarding the topic, there is a consistency over time in both attitudes and the underlying reasons or rationales. Condor refers to such phenomena as "empty attitudes":

> Empty attitudes comprised sincere (if not especially salient, central or strongly held) evaluative stances. When respondents were unable to mobilize domain-specific information to support their views, they were nevertheless able to draw upon a stock of ideological values and knowledge concerning political rights, responsibilities and social justice to enable them to formulate their opinions as a justifiable and acceptable interventions in a current public controversy.... Empty attitudes could be highly internally coherent and consistent over time and tended to be justified in highly abstract terms.
>
> *(Condor)*

What Condor is able to demonstrate through her extensive and detailed interviews with English citizens is that many people, even without access to factual information and political knowledge, are able to generate consistent attitudes rooted in abstract frames of reference. In many instances, these citizens employ rhetorical heuristics to identify and access relevant ideological principles. Moreover, these positions are grounded in a sense of obligation toward fellow citizens rather than framed in terms of group self-interest. It is probable that many of Condor's research participants would score inconsistently if confronted with a battery of factual questions on Scottish devolution and Scottish constitutions. This might then be taken to indicate the absence of coherent and rational thinking. Condor's qualitative research demonstrates how people manage their own attitudes through established heuristics, even in the absence of detailed knowledge. Far from being self-interested ignoramuses, the English citizens in Condor's study are frequently revealed as principled and altruistic.

In Chapter 14, Goncalves-Portelinha, Staerklé and Elcheroth criticise the traditional study of political behaviour on the grounds that it "apprehends individuals as isolated figures and in abstraction from the social contexts in which their behaviours are embedded" (Goncalves-Portelinha, Staerklé and Elcheroth). As with Reicher and Jogdand and Condor, Goncalves-Portelinha, Staerklé and Elcheroth argue that both social settings and political relations are changeable and that individuals are agentive in processes of change. In the context of the social representations approach, Goncalves-Portelinha, Staerklé and Elcheroth work with the concept of "meta-representations". These are the powerful overarching bids to define ingroup norms and realities that are frequently invoked by entrepreneurs of identity and emotion. However, they are not merely imposed: "Instead, individuals are actively involved in the construction, contestation and dissemination of meta-representations, and thus also in shaping political behaviours of others" (Goncalves-Portelinha, Staerklé and Elcheroth). Based on their experimental studies among European students in Lausanne and Nanterre, the authors conclude that normative beliefs are adaptable and subject to strategic attempts to change them. While majority meta-representations are usually powerful, under certain circumstances, minority meta-representations can influence and change majority perspectives and thereby reorganise social relations. Goncalves-Portelinha, Staerklé and Elcheroth point out that while meta-representations can influence the expression of political opinions, the degree of influence is far from certain and is never pre-given. Much depends on the strength of pre-existing representations and the robustness of group categorisations as well as the degree of openness and ambivalence with respect to pertinent group norms.

Mannell's emphasis in Chapter 15 is on the field of social relations and how policy outcomes are realised in these contexts. Going beyond the conventional policy analyses and assessments, monitoring and policy evaluation, Mannell removes our attention from the ostensible purposes of the policy, normally defined top-down, and alerts us to the complex ways in which policies enter into everyday social relations, often in unanticipated ways. For Mannell, policy is "a socially embedded practice", and the ways in which policies come to affect us are mediated through our social representations, which themselves are both active and contested. In her ethnographic analysis of how international donor policies regarding gender-related issues have been adopted and adapted by South African gender practitioners, Mannell explains how representations embedded in the original policy may be adapted and changed by representations in the local setting. Rather than seeking to learn whether — in terms of the original policy objectives — policies succeed or fail, Mannell asks us to consider what policies accomplish or do in the contexts of their reception and circulation. In so doing, she adopts a broader experiential and interactive view of social policy in our lives, rather than the linear "policy effects" and "policy outcomes" approaches adopted conventionally. The policy effects she unearths in South Africa include a range of unintended outcomes. As with the other authors in this section, Mannell pays attention to the creativity and autonomy of individuals in their everyday political practices, while not removing them from those broader frameworks of discursive and ideological forces that condition their lives and set the agenda.

Talk, text, and context: Changing minds

This section features chapters that illustrate, through studies of race, gender, ethnic nationalism, multiculturalism and the environment, how people form their social representations and political identities in practice and how they change minds — both their own and those around them — and, in so doing, disrupt those metarepresentations, dominant discourses and prevailing ideologies that appear to be established.

In Chapter 1, Howarth demonstrates that conventional understandings of multiculturalism — as ideology and policy — are undercut by the practices of those actually living multicultural existences in their daily lives. In these respects, multiculturalism is not failing, it is vibrant. Moreover, given the citizenship demands of the plurality of cultural groups in society, multiculturalism has not eroded nationalism, but is rather redefining it through a range of articulated identity claims. Rejecting the "failure of multiculturalism" narrative, Howarth explains how it has in fact worked, in the sense that hitherto marginal groups now have a voice and a place. Of course, for those who rhetorically wish to sustain an ethnoracial rigid categorisation of "us and them," multiculturalism is indeed a "failure" to the extent that it in fact enlarges the encompassing definitions of "us". Multiculturalism makes the nation and nationalism more complex "as different groups with different claims to the nation assert and defend different versions of the nation" (Howarth). In Howarth's terms, nations themselves "are also reimagined as sites of struggle over meanings, ideologies and identity positions". An engaged multiculturalism is one of openness, deliberation and critique. Adding her voice to those who live and practice the broadly inclusive and caring multicultural relations of the everyday, Howarth states: "We need to reclaim nationalism and reclaim the right to collectively define what our nation is (or should be)".

Given the openness of everyday politics and the identity projects of those who reject multiculturalism and ethnoracial diversity, the presence and popularity of far-right political movements throughout Europe is as understandable as the daily lived experiences of mutual accommodation and integration. The focus of Figgou's Chapter 13 is lay explanations of the electoral performance of Greece's neo-Nazi party, Golden Dawn. Figgou conducted 12 interviews and 4 focus groups in Athens and Thessaloniki in 2012 and 2013, incorporating about 22 men and 20 women of a range of ages and political affiliations other than Golden Dawn. Using a social representations approach to the rhetorical analyses of the talk of these Greek lay actors, Figgou uncovers "cognitive polyphasia", which indicates the possibility of incompatible representations in common sense discourse. Yet, further exploration of the attributed rationales reveals a common dual explanation model. Golden Dawn received votes because of their tough views on immigration, but also, because they are an anti-political force, an unconventional party, voting for them acted to punish mainstream politicians. In their attempts to distance themselves from the socially undesirable Golden Dawn, Figgou's participants also distance others who might have voted for them, in order to save their legitimacy. Figgou's analysis is an important explanation of how common sense often deals with perceived extremism. It is deliberately distanced, both personally and vicariously, through those who have cast their votes for extremist parties, but in establishing the distance underwrites and legitimises support for some of the substantive contentions. In the case of Greece and Golden Dawn, Figgou's participants note both that immigration is indeed a problem and that politicians are out of touch.

Both race and racism are socially constructed and dialogically managed. Gibson's Chapter 3 offers a detailed conversational analysis taken from a focus group with 15-year-old Yorkshire children and examines how they navigate around race talk. Gibson's research reveals how racist discourse may be permissible when uttered in the context of stated proscriptions – saying what cannot normally be said – but is not sanctioned for the establishment of one's own perspective. What is particularly interesting in Gibson's research is how the role of the interviewer may be deeply involved in the interpretation of talk. Many of the participants are implicated in what Goffman (1982) refers to as "face-work", notably in face-saving efforts and bids to restore stable social relations following a threatened breach through a personal avowal of racism. Gibson's work illustrates important insights regarding how contemporary British children manage race, and in so doing identifies critical aspects of the micropolitics of diversity: laughter is certainly the release of repression and enjoyment at the pushing of boundaries, but it is a socially embedded practice in which boundaries are negotiated; it is possible to distinguish between acceptable prejudices and unacceptable racism; and rather than statements having a fixed attribute as an acceptable or unacceptable utterance, it is important to attend to the specific context of delivery.

Looking at race and gender representations from the perspective of elites, Augoustinos, Callaghan, Sorrentino and Worth investigate the speeches of President Barack Obama and Prime Minister Julia Gillard. How do leaders negotiate their minority and majority identities in the context of their leadership roles? Among their insights in Chapter 2, the authors question the solidity of existing social categories and illustrate the complexity of new categorisations grounded in mixed, fragmented and hybrid identities and the increasingly reflexive disengagement of signifiers from their once-familiar signifieds. They illustrate this with reference to Obama's claim that he has been criticised both for being "too black" and "not black enough" and Gillard's complex negotiation between identity as a woman and a more sex-blind affirmation of her national leadership. Neither political leader chooses to reference race (Obama) or gender (Gillard) in a direct and unmediated way. Instead, both leaders reference their personal characteristics obliquely through reference to broader cultural values. Obama integrates the broad themes and tropes of the American Dream into a narrative of broad and encompassing diversity. Race is usually implicit in his rhetoric. Gillard too largely disavows gender, as Obama disavows race. In both instances, there is a simultaneous pride in the category, but an always broader and more inclusive appeal to wider categories, such as nation, class and party. However, Gillard appeals to a specific identity while Obama claims a diverse background. Both leaders have been obliged to affirm their identities while simultaneously occluding them.

Chapter 3 investigates lay actors, while Chapter 2 is a study of the political elite. Chapter 10, by Castro, Uzelgun and Bertoldo, is an analysis of perceptions of lay actors, elites, and political activists. In their experimental analysis of the perceptions of 117 university students in Lisbon, the authors explore the extent to which radical and moderate environmental activists are perceived as either competent or warm. As they hypothesise, individuals perceived as moderate in activism are also perceived as highest in warmth. Radicals are devalued in the warmth dimension, and the authors state "we interpret this as a social penalization for failing to uphold a certain social order and challenging established norms and representations". As anticipated, radicals are favoured when they employ a concessive "yes-but" argument rather than the more categorical "yes/no" format. The authors make the important point that while it is apparent that warmth and concessions to alternative perspectives are socially desirable, when it comes to the substance of political debate, such a position might not produce the best results: "avoidance of conflict may seem to favour – in the organization of their everyday politics – an episodic, short term debate ... over a more difficult and more prolonged one. As the authors of the present text, we would consequently argue that a more difficult debate, which does not avoid conflict and does use arguments carrying counterhegemonic meaning, is much needed regarding climate change".

Identity strategies

Having revisited those chapters that disrupt the over-psychologisation of the individual or the over-socialisation of the group, as well as those contributions that examine how people form social representations and political identities in practice, I turn in this final section to those chapters that focus on the complex and varied methods through which people mobilise and utilise their identities in various ways.

Among the most important mobilised political identities is that of citizenship. Andreouli, Kadianaki and Xenitidou undertake a critical analysis of constructions of Greek citizenship in Chapter 6. At the heart of their enquiry are the boundaries that are constructed to identify who comes to be categorised as "us" and "them". The authors look at citizenship as constructed in part by state policies and practices, thereby conditioning citizen understandings and enactments. Importantly, citizens' agency is conditioned, but it is not determined by the state. The dialectic between state policy and citizen agency becomes acute when normal routines are disrupted or interrupted. Under such circumstances, established patterns and routines are no longer necessarily viable, and people become more reflexive. In the matter of Greek nationality law, changes undertaken in 2010 added a *jus soli* element to the already existing *jus sanguinis* definition of citizenship, thereby opening up the possibility for non-ethnic Greeks to be granted citizenship. Responses to this change revealed that both ethnic Greeks and immigrants oriented around a strong ethnic conception of Greekness, notwithstanding appeals to forms of civic nationality on the part of some. Some immigrants exhibited affective forms of Greekness that they felt entitled them to be included as assimilated citizens, almost as a kind of adjunct category to the "true" Greek. Ethnic and feelings-based understandings of citizenship were stronger than civic conceptions. The authors identify the complexity of constructions of citizenship between the formal policy and lay perspectives:

> negotiating the meanings and boundaries of citizenship in different ways: by restricting the scope of citizenship to ethnic Greeks, by differentiating between ethnic and civic membership, by putting forward an argument for 'true' Greekness on the basis of feelings and cultural assimilation, and by putting forward a more inclusive conception of Greek citizenship on the basis of a give-and-take social contract, although often with caveats that privileged ethnic Greeks.

In Chapter 4, Wagner, Raudsepp, Holtz and Sen examine identity formation across a range of settings: ethnic, religious, gendered and sexual orientation. The authors set out clear examples of how characteristics of biology, language and character are selected to essentialize various groups and how agentive being regulates and controls identities in formation. The micropolitics of such identities in formation are complex, illustrated by the example of a Muslim woman who is assured by magnanimous Hindu friends that they do not consider her to be "one of them [a Muslim]". In fact, the Muslim woman wishes to identify as "one of them," opening up the potential for engagement over the very issue of what constitutes "us" and "them". The woman has selected an ethnoreligious identity over the proffered social identity. Research conducted by Wagner and his colleagues argues that essentialization is not merely imposed by majority groups on minorities. Essentializations can serve both positive and negative functions, depending on the situation, and essentialized representations: "[they] are a social fact . . . a 'concert of interaction' where mutual identity work and stereotype construction endow the 'representations in interaction' with evidence". The interplay of discrimination and community defensiveness fulfils the prophesy of group cohesion and characteristics. Wagner and his colleagues open up an important distinction between positive essentialism and strategic essentialism. Minority communities that are stereotyped and discriminated against from the outside will tend to define themselves in the terms of their encounters with the majority other. This can result both in patterns of de-essentialization or re-essentialization, depending on the specific circumstances. The basis for ascribing or claiming essential characteristics can be natural (immutable) or entitative (chosen). A positive essentialism – whether of the natural or entitative variety – is one that genuinely affirms and values certain ingroup characteristics and invokes those defensively; strategic essentialism claims a certain group identity or set of characteristics in a cynical and utilitarian manner to get something. It rests on a covert disavowal of such characteristics.

Ethnocultural and national being are relatively well-established focuses of enquiry in contemporary social psychology. Social class and social status have been relatively absent from social psychological research over the past three decades. Given the context of increasing socioeconomic inequality, globalised poverty and associated perceptions of disparity, the work of Hodgetts, Groot, Garden and Chamberlain in Chapter 11 is instructive. In the context of the late modern/postmodern and postcolonial order, social psychological perspectives on class can no longer be grafted onto deterministic models of the class structure in which everything is determined by the mechanisms of the economic base and any agency that deviates from this is a matter of "false consciousness" (Archibald, 1978; Sherovkin,1985). Contradictions generated by capitalism cannot be said to give rise to a set of automatically corresponding social conflicts. Using a concept that has emerged in the context of global neoliberal capitalism, Hodgetts and his colleagues adopt the term "precariat," a neologism that has been in existence for approximately five years that combines the concepts of "precarious" and "proletariat". Importantly, for contemporary class analysis, the authors articulate their work around the concept of phronesis, that is, hands-on and practical understandings of how to go on in daily life. This is at once agentive and contingent, stressing the openness and indeterminacy of class being in an era beyond the grand narratives. Along with Scott (1990) and de Certeau (1984), Hodgetts, Groot, Garden and Chamberlain locate the meaningful, the relevant and the specific focuses of politics in everyday existences according to the ways in which the precariat navigate through oppression, privation and arbitrariness in their daily existences. The emphasis is on making do, improvising, repurposing, flying under the radar and finding minimal cost tactics of protest and survival. This is an important recovery of class analysis in critical psychology which incorporates how members of the precariat adapt to adversity and austerity with tactical skill and adaptability. Despite being the subjects of a postmodern order, the participants are far from Inglehart's (1977) postmaterialists. To the contrary, materialism is the very medium of their identity, as exemplified in the authors' analyses of food resources and the lack of them. Food – its production, distribution, preparation and consumption – exists as a locus of conflict between the classes, notably between middle-class teachers and other service professionals and the precariat. Material objects exist not just in reality and negotiated status claims, they also exist in the class consciousness of the precariat as indexical of despair, protest and escape. Material objects represent liminal markers at the edges of states of precarious being. The kind of class analysis offered by Hodgetts and his colleagues cannot be read off from a structured and abstracted understanding of the working of capitalism or even the specific conjuncture. The conditions of postmodernity make the very achievement of class consciousness and solidarity a distant matter of chance and opportunity and render the contingent and complex micropolitics of the powerless of critical importance. Who they will become is dependent on the manner of how they will become.

The ways in which ordinary people who have experienced conflict move toward reconciliation is the focus of Obradović and Howarth's Chapter 9. The strategies available are conditioned by states and legal systems, but are never dependent upon them. Obradović and Howarth explain how ordinary people engage in bottom-up approaches toward reconciliation. At the heart of the work involved in such efforts are processes of strategic identity transformation. Highlighting ingroup diversities or outgroup heterogeneities assists people in moving beyond "us and them" reasoning. Additionally, the development of superordinate categories facilitates dual identities and thereby furnishes a platform for commonality. The authors say "the rationale behind both arguments is that creating an awareness of the differences among outgroup members as well as creating mutualities across groups will allow for a 'humanisation' of the other as well as an increased perspective-taking". Among the techniques of everyday reconciliation under consideration in Chapter 9 are processes of intergenerational dialogue, intergroup cooperation, critical education and openness to sincere questioning. Under these conditions it is possible for all parties, elites and ordinary citizens, to engage in processes of reconciliation grounded in expansive and inclusive conceptions of commonality.

The theme of expansive and inclusive conceptions of community is also developed in Kessi and Boonzaier's Chapter 8 on resistance and transformation in postcolonial contexts. As with other chapters throughout the volume, Kessi and Boonzaier stress the independent impact of everyday interactions among people on their political lives and argue that such a perspective is necessary to complement the important impacts of states, governments and large-scale political organisations: "social psychological research into everyday politics in postcolonial contexts should therefore explore the encounters between its various social actors" (Kessi and Boonzaier). From the perspective of research in South Africa, the chapter calls for social psychology to expand its reach into postcolonial settings in which the politics of oppression and modes of intersectionality are complex and conditioned by forces that are not readily apparent in the social psychology of the metropole. Such an approach is necessary to adequately understand male violence against women and other men in postcolonial settings, as well as the development of negative self-perceptions among black youth:

> These examples demonstrate how racialized oppression is internalized and reenacted and how people's immediate need for power, status, and control over their lives is misdirected into acts of violence most often perpetrated towards members of their networks or communities who are weaker or closest to them.
>
> *(Kessi and Boonzaier)*

Despite this, the authors identify acts of resistance that include political practices built upon experiences of intersectionality, which enable people to identify and connect on the basis of multiple and complex elements of social being. Kessi and Boonzaier advocate both participatory action research as a critical practice and narrative methodology as potentially liberating research practices and as "empowering tools that promote critical consciousness".

The broadest conception of human identity is that of the cosmopolitical agent who regards the global arena as an encompassing home. However, as Gleibs and Reddy point out in Chapter 5, "speaking of one 'global identity' in the singular . . . is a practical impossibility". What is more viable is the development of politicised collective identities that are transnational and transregional in scope. Developing collective identities entails intergroup contact and encountering alternative knowledge systems and modes of understanding. The processes of interchange depend upon conceptions of attachment and openness toward the other with no fixed characteristics: "globalisation and attached identities are not 'given' or 'objective' but are socially constructed and socially embedded concepts that are constructed and co-constructed in our daily, global encounters" (Gleibs and Reddy). Where people experience local and global cultures to be in conflict, there are tensions in identity. Conversely, where local and global cultures are compatible, there is little challenge in a hybrid or mixed identity. The authors urge us to contemplate global identities as plural, hybridised, intersectional and contextualised in culture.

Conclusion

Each of the chapters in *The Social Psychology of Everyday Politics* opens us up to the lived experiences of political life across settings that transcend divisions of state/society and public/private and invite us into the local settings in which strategies play out, tactics are employed, coercion and persuasion are undertaken and political outcomes are far from certain.

In specific ways, many of the chapters move us beyond binary oppositions and essentialist categorisations, working instead within the framework of social structures and agencies that are most adequately captured in the specific context of the time and place of political encounter. In Chapter 7, Reicher and Jogdand underline the critical importance of understanding political influence as the always open and contingent interplay of leaders and led in which outcomes are never predetermined. Goncalves-Portelinha, Staerklé and Elcheroth demonstrate in Chapter 14 that majorities are not always able to impose their meta-representations on minorities. In Chapter 15, Mannell illustrates how policies are not always the abstract and completed outputs of states and governments and are more than top-down impositions on societies. Instead, they are worked out and lived in everyday political interactions. In Chapter 6, Andreouli, Kadianaki and Xenitidou explain how state policies, laws, cultural beliefs and values each play a part in constructions of citizenship and that a range of claims to citizenship are conceivable as policies encounter the cultural understandings of lay actors. As Gibson points out in Chapter 3, the boundaries of taste and acceptability in race discourse are not fixed, but are dependent upon the dynamics of utterance and reception in specific settings. Rather than referring to racist and nonracist discourse, Gibson turns our attention to the subtle dynamics of laughter, banter and labelling in real-world settings. The flexibility and context-dependence of race and gender signifiers are further illustrated in Augostinos, Callaghan, Sorrentino and Worth's Chapter 2, in which race and gender are identities that political leaders affirm obliquely through reference to broader and more common categories of identity and value. Social class is problematised and situated as a contingent practice rather than a pregiven social category in the work of Hodgetts, Groot, Garden and Chamberlain in Chapter 11. Three chapters (Howarth, Chapter 1; Gleibs and Reddy, Chapter 5; and Obradović and Howarth, Chapter 9) demonstrate how in everyday politics, citizens develop and move beyond the categorical confines of "us and them" thinking and develop ways of expanding or limiting boundaries of inclusion and exclusion in the development of multicultural and global identity formations.

In addition to questioning binaries, many of the chapters demonstrate how political analysis should never dismiss the everyday as simply banal and therefore uninteresting. To the contrary, the banal can be a setting of deep subtlety and nuance in which critical political choices are made and outcomes are far from obvious. Figgou, in Chapter 13, identifies how ordinary people in their common-sense explanations can both distance themselves from and yet manifest understanding of partial legitimation of extreme right-wing views and political movements. Howarth, in Chapter 1, vividly illustrates the creativity of ordinary citizens in making citizenship demands in the routine and everyday climate of multiculture. The centrality of everyday choice and decision in social identities and political perspectives are illuminated by Reicher and Jogdand as they explore the agentive in human conduct in Chapter 7. The absence of specific information does not necessarily impede the development of consistent and logical evaluations, according to Condor in Chapter 12. In Chapter 15, Mannell describes the unintended impact of living with, adapting to and creatively responding to policy initiatives in daily life. In Chapter 10, Castro, Uzelgun and Bertoldo illustrate how those with radical political agendas are most persuasive when they make rhetorical efforts to engage and affirm their opponents rather than when they present ideas as simple yes/no dichotomies. Wagner, Raudsepp, Holtz and Sen, in Chapter 4, bring out the critical importance of agentive autonomy in defining identities. They make the subtle point that while self-essentialization can be strategic on the part of minority groups, it might also be genuine. A positive essentialization affirms and values certain ingroup characteristics and invokes these defensively. In a postcolonial setting, Kessi and Boonzaier, in Chapter 8, stress the importance of daily life in attempting to understand exactly how various forms of oppression are experienced and responded to.

The Social Psychology of Everyday Politics opens up our understanding of the dynamics of power and influence in a world in which the familiar moorings of nation, class, religion, ethnicity, race, gender and other ostensibly fixed identities are increasingly in question. This is a globalising world in which political agents live uncertain lives and experience their identities as fragmented, partial and hybrid. The authors of this book understand and work from the premise that neither social categories nor individual psychological characteristics can be taken for granted and that there is nothing routine about the everyday.

References

Almond, G. A., & Coleman, J. S. (1961). *The politics of the developing areas.* Princeton, NJ: Princeton University Press.
Almond, G. A., & Powell, G. B. Jr. (1966). *Comparative politics: A developmental approach.* Boston: Little Brown.
Archibald, W. P. (1978). *Social psychology as political economy.* Toronto: McGraw-Hill Ryerson.
de Certeau, M. (1984). *The practice of everyday life.* Berkeley: University of California Press.
Easton, D. (1965). *A framework for political analysis.* Englewood Cliffs, NJ: Prentice-Hall.
Giddens, A. (1984). *The constitution of society.* Berkeley: University of California Press.
Goffman, E. (1982). *Interaction ritual: Essays on face-to-face behavior.* New York: Pantheon.
Inglehart, R. (1977). *The silent revolution: Changing values and political styles among western publics.* Princeton, NJ: Princeton University Press.
Lyotard, J-F. (1984). *The postmodern condition: A report on knowledge.* Minneapolis: University of Minnesota Press.
Machiavelli, N. (1532/1973). *The prince.* Harmondsworth, Middlesex, UK: Penguin.
Nye, R. A. (1977). *The anti-democratic sources of elite theory: Pareto, Mosca, Michels.* London: Sage.
Scott, J. C. (1990). *Domination and the arts of resistance: Hidden transcripts.* New Haven, CT: Yale University Press.
Sherovkin, Y. A. (1985). *Social psychology and propaganda.* Moscow: Progress Publishers.
Smith, D. A. (1987). *The everyday world as problematic: A feminist sociology.* Boston: Northeastern University Press.

INDEX

Page numbers for figures and tables are in italics.

Abbot, T. 26
ABC (Australian television channel) 29–30
abstract reasoning 193
abusive relationships 121–2
academic theory 192
acceptance 69, 72
accommodation 4, 148, 266
accountability 167, 209–12, 217
acculturation 75, 239
accumulation 185
acknowledgement 50, 139–40
ACM (Auckland City Mission) 177–8
action-oriented approach 89
active representations 242, 247–9
active voicing 200, 214
  activists/activism 73–4, 104, 213; climate change (CC) 146–62, 268; feminist 148, 243; stereotyping of 148–52, 159
actor network theory 175–6
adaptation 70, 75, 147
Adi movements 109
ad populum arguments 190
advantaged groups 71
adversity 21, 173–5, 270
affect 165, 256
affirmative action policies 120
African-Americans 18–19, 22, 254
Africans 52
agency 85–170, 175, 178, 209, 212, 228, 262, 269–70

aggression 109, 138
Albanians 93–7
alienation 185, 255
all-or-nothing arguments 159
Allport, G. 102–3
Almond, G. 262
altered realities 209
altruism 150
Amazon territory 57–8
Ambedkar, B. 109–13
ambivalence 202
American Dream 20–5, 268
American Jews 53
"American Promise" speech (Obama) 24–5
anchoring 81, 185–6, 241
Anderson, B. 11
Andreouli, E. 11, 90, 166–7, 268–9; *The Social Psychology of Everyday Politics* 262–3, 272–4
anger 175
animators 209, 212
anticapitalism 82
anticolonialism 123–4
anti-fascism 210
anti-immigration 8–9, 211–13, 217–8
anti-political voting 213–6, 267
antiracism 213
anxiety 183, 223
apartheid 117–20
apologies 139

Arab Spring 260
argumentative elision 197
arguments/argumentation 89, 146–62, 169, 190, 197, 208–11, 227
Ariely, G. 239
aristocracy 60–2
Arnett, J. 67
Asch, S. 164, 193–4, 256–7
Asians 178
aspirations 21, 24–5
assimilation 14, 49–50, 53, 59–60, 66, 75, 97, 269; cultural 68–9, 90, 96–9
asymmetric representations 191
asymmetry 53, 88, 191
Athens 210–14, 266–7
atrocities 138–41
attachment 10, 13, 82, 272
attitudes 46, 102, 132, 150–2, 163–9, 193–202, 224, 263–6; empty 189, 195–203, 256–9, 264–5; individual 4; patriarchal 122–3; research on 163–4; of voters 207, 223
attraction 174
attributions 55–7, 208, 239
Auburn, T. 89
Auckland 173
Auckland City Mission (ACM) 177–8
Augoustinos, M. 82, 267–8, 273
austerity 173, 176–87, 253, 256, 259, 270
Australasian region 119
Australia 4, 13, 18, 26, 70
Austria 52–7, 253
authoritarianism 71, 210, 215
authorities 105–8, 135, 178–81
autonomy 104, 186, 212

Bakhtin, M. 165
banality 222, 261–74
banal nationalism 5–8, 11, 198, 230
Banyard, P. 105
Barnes, R. 89
baseline conditions 106
Bashir, N. 148–52
Basque independence 68
bedding 175–6, 184–5
begging 110
behaviouralism 261–2
behaviours 71, 163, 253; of activists 149–50, 268; gender-related 243; individual 67, 149, 157–8, 167; political 222–36, 257–8, 265; social 224–6
Beijing 68
being, scholarship on 175
Belgium 140

belief studies 164
belonging 9–14, 89–99, 117, 257
belonging-proper 95, 98–9
Berlin 73
Bertoldo, R. 167–9, 268, 273
best-fit practices 142
betrayal 141, 257
'Better Together' campaign 113
Bhavnani, K. 122
bias 216, 257
bicultural identities 69
bigotry 45
Billig, M. 7–8, 36, 45, 102, 168–9, 208–9, 216, 222, 257
binaries 9, 13, 261–74
biological essentialism 52–3, 60–1, 269–70
blackface minstrelsy 46n1
black feminist psychology 118–27
#BlackLivesMatter 254, 260
blackness 19, 25, 31, 119, 267–8
Black people 52, 117–20, 242, 247, 255, 271
black (term) 37–40
Black & White Minstrel Show 46n1
blame 119–21, 186, 255
blankets 178, 186
blood 52, 60–1
blue blood 60–1
Blumer, H. 192
Blunkett, D. 12
Boonzaier, F. 121, 165–7, 271–3
Bosnia 141
bottom-up nationalism 4, 12–14
bottom-up reconciliation 132, 135–8, 141–2, 271
boundaries 11, 73–5, 261, 267; of citizenship 91–3, 98–9; national 239–40; territorial 66
boundary-pushing 40, 45
Bourdieu, P. 176, 194
Braga, L. 141
Brazil 140
Brewer, M. 30, 68–9
Britain 9, 14, 90–1, 113, 139, 190–1, 267
British majority 61
Britishness 11–12, 15
British Social Attitudes survey (2003) 203n7
British values 5
Brixton 61, 242, 247
Brothers for Life 246
Bruner, J. 164–5
brutality 106, 109
Bruter, M. 206

Bryce, J. 191–2
Buddhism 110
Buhlan, H. 119
Bulgaria 13
bureaucracy 95

Calhoun, C. 7, 12–15
Callaghan, P. 267–8, 273
Cannella, G. 123
Cape Town 122–3, 243
capitalism 81, 117, 123, 173–5, 253, 256, 270–1
carbon offsetting 153–9
care 12–14
caste *sabhas* (associations) 109
caste system 109–12
Castro, P. 167–9, 268, 273
Catalan independence 68
categorisation 7, 169
category prototypes 190
causal statements 40
CC (climate change) activism 146–62, 268
Čehajić-Clancy, S. 139
censure 34–48
census 192
Central Europe 253
Chamberlain, K. 256, 270, 273
change 66–7, 83, 167–9, 265; individual *vs.* systemic 154; social 30–1, 59, 67, 85–170, 224, 227–9, 233, 238, 248, 268; voting and 216
character 269
Charlie Hebdo attacks 3
Chesterton, C.: "The Secret People" 191
child adoption 60
child care 122
children 119, 140, 180–3
Childs, H.: *Public Opinion* 189
China 65
Chinese communities 208, 239
Chinese identities 69
choice 96, 106–8, 263–6
chosen group membership 51, 58
citizenship 3–5, 9, 12, 36–46, 65, 87–101, 132–3, 268–9
civic identities 18, 137
civic participation 90, 93, 97–8, 253–5
civic society 135
civic understandings 97–8
civil rights 87–8
civil society 262
claims-making 87–90, 93–4
class 14, 82, 121, 167, 173–5, 186, 247, 254–6, 262, 268–71; consciousness 271; habitus 179–80; oppression 122; psychological research and 118–19
classical analyses 224, 232–3
classical elite theory 261–2
classism 186
climate change (CC) activism 146–62, 268
Clinton, H. 31
closeness 150
clothing 176, 184–5
cognition 165, 190, 207
cognitive accounts 233
cognitive approaches 224
cognitive bias 71
cognitive conflict 159–60
cognitive polyphasia 208, 267
cognitive psychology 203
cognitive resources 124
Cohrs, J. 71
cold nationalism 7–8; *see also* banal nationalism
collaboration 125–6, 214–5
collective identities 6, 68–9, 272
collective memories 136–7
collective mobilisation 88, 103–4, 154, 157–8
collectivist culture 134
Collins, P. 121
colonialism 14, 116–17, 120, 139
colonisation 90, 117–19, 127, 140, 262
commonalities 7, 11, 71–3, 122, 166, 271
common good 150
common identities 70–1
commonplace beliefs 198, 214
common sense 117, 202, 207–8, 218, 257, 267
communication 65, 79, 140, 147–8, 154, 165, 190, 206–7, 225–30, 240
community: activities 142, 154–60; boards 135; dialogue 140–1, 243; organisations 262; psychology 174, 237
compensation 139
competencies 79, 148–52
competition 116, 150
complexity 263–6
compliance 106
complicity 118, 121, 125–6
computers 165
comradeship 11
concessive mode 169, 268
conciliatory arguments 147–8, 157–8
Condor, S. 34–5, 217, 256–9, 264–5, 273
conflict 74, 116, 131–8, 158–60, 166–7, 223, 271

conformity 13, 226, 232
confrontation 7–8, 147–8, 153–60
connectivity 67, 73
consciousness 50, 125–6, 139–40, 270–1
consensus 39–40, 79–80, 83, 124, 147, 194
consistency 199–202
constructionism 59
constructive patriotism 12–13
consumption 147, 153
content analysis 195
contested representations 242, 247–9
context 75, 167–9, 232, 266–8
continuity 70
contradictions 124, 208, 270
contranormative statements 196
contra populum arguments 190–1
conversation 79, 148–9, 194, 267
Converse, P. 192–3, 198–9, 202, 257
Converse's black and white model 202
conversion (Dharmantar) movement 110
cooperation 131, 150
coping 50, 185
Cornish people 68
corporate wealth 253
cosmopolitanism 6
costs and benefits 103–4
counter-culture 152–3
counterhegemony 154, 158–60
counternarratives 5, 11–12, 125–6, 167–9, 257
Crenshaw, K. 122–3
cricket 109
crime 133–5
criminal tribunals 134
critical discursive psychology 211
critical education 271
critical identities 5, 9–11
critical nationalism 3–17
critical perspectives, emergent 168–9
critical psychology 253, 256, 259–60
critical race theory 121–2
critical social psychology 207, 263
critical thinking 140
Croats 137
cruelty 106
cultural assimilation 68–9, 90, 96–9
cultural barriers 65
cultural essence 57–8
cultural essentialism 5–6, 9, 14
cultural globalisation 66–7
cultural identities 65, 69, 72, 168
cultural locations 122
cultural symbols 50, 136

culture: context and 167–8; local 65; narrative and 163–70; national 90; recognition of 255; ritualised 96
Curtice, J. 194
cyclical communication strategies 206
Cyprus 60

dalits 109–13, 167, 264
Damascus 73
Danziger, K. 46
debate 7, 89, 92, 147, 190, 208
decentralization 194
de Certeau, M. 270
decisions 132–3, 197, 202, 237
decolonizing psychology 118–27
de-essentializing 51–4, 59, 270
default arguments 197
deficit models 193, 203
dehumanization 116, 125, 184
de-ideologization 118
deixical referents 39–40
Dekker, H. 4
deliberative democracy 13, 192
demagogues/demagoguery 103
democracy 13, 61, 113, 189–93, 202
Democratic Party (United States) 31
denaturalisation 58–9
deontic issues 203
depoliticization 119
Depression 21–3
descent 61, 92
description 165
desire 255–6, 259–60
desocialisation 263
despair 215–17, 253, 270; objects of 173–88, 256
deterministic models 104, 270
development 116, 247, 248
devolution 195–202, 264–5
Dhaka 68
Dharmantar (conversion) movement 110
dialogical shadows 209
dialogue 34–5, 131–5, 140–1, 165–6, 169, 242, 271
difference 10–11, 14–15, 50, 58–9, 82–3, 131, 137, 207
diffusion 226, 233, 257
dignity 110, 125, 253
dilemmatic orientations 189
disabilities 174, 178
disadvantaged groups 71–2, 88
discourses: analysis 89, 167–8, 257; citizenship 93; communities and

254–5, 259–60; electoral campaigns and 206; far right 206; of feminism 59; institutionalised 91; international development 117; lay 92–9; markers 154, 158; political 4, 7, 18, 23, 57–8, 120, 171–274; racist 34–48, 267; sexuality 44–5; state 90–1, 96
discrimination 25–6, 50, 53, 59–62, 70, 116, 174
discursive psychological approaches 18, 34–5, 59, 63, 89–91, 209–13
discussions 178, 193, 243
disjuncture 228
disobedience 106–7
disparities 173, 270
dispossession 253, 259
disruptions 89–91, 99, 124–6, 181–2, 269
dissent 227
distinctiveness 70
distributive justice 82
diversities 5, 9–11, 14, 19, 23–5, 68, 266–8; cultural 3–4, 18, 30, 82; social 24–5, 29–30; within-group 137
Dixon, J. 133
dogma 216
Doise, W. 240
domain-specific information 199, 202
domestic responsibilities 122
dominance 60–1, 71, 83
dominant groups 71, 82, 118, 125
dominant narratives 256–8
dominant representations 227, 242, 247
double accountability 217
double bind 31
doubleness 256
drawing exercises 178
Drury, J. 190–1
dual identities 137
duplicity 206, 216
Durban 243
Durrheim, K. 133
dynamic approaches 169
dynasties 60–1

earned citizenship framework 90–1
Earth Day 150
Easton, D. 262
East Timor 135
Ebola 116
economic approaches 65
economic calculation 104
economic contexts 75
economic exploitation 127

economic inequality 36
economic liberalization 173
economic oppression 253
economic recession 74
economic relationships 177
economic systems 117
economic transformations 149
education 96, 99–100n1, 178, 259; access to 117; conflict and 131–2; critical 271; policies 12; reconciliation and 139–40
Eemeren F. van 154
egging on 45–6
either/or approaches 122
Elcheroth, G. 240–2, 257–8, 265, 272
elections 91, 229–32, 266–7
electoral campaigns, discourse during 206
electoral performance, far right and 206–21
electricity, access to 181–6
elites 61, 198, 253–5, 258, 261–2, 267–8
elitism 60–1
emancipatory narratives 125
emancipatory psychological essentialism 58–9
emergence, principle of 177
emotionality 118–19, 175
emotional understandings 125
emotions 4, 102–15, 264
empirical political science 261–2
employment 117, 175
empowerment 69, 122, 125–6, 167, 272
empty attitudes 189, 195–203, 256–9, 264–5
engaged followers 108
engagement 12, 114, 126
Engender Health 246
England 60, 191, 194–202, 208, 264–5
English language 69
English nationalism 191
English speaking identities 69
entitativity 51, 62, 270
entitlement 92, 269
entrepreneurial identity 19, 30, 90, 108–13, 232–3, 264–5
environmentalism 146–62, 159, 266–8
environmental NGOs (ENGOs) 148, 152–60
environmental psychology 159
episteme versus doxa 203n1
epistemic authority 194
equality 18, 58–61, 104, 133–4, 242–3
erroneous beliefs 230
escape attempts 185
essence politics 49–64

essentialism 5–6, 9, 14, 50–63, 83, 90, 95, 98, 269–70
essentialist binaries 262
Estonia 54–7
Estonian Latin 54–5
Estonian Russophones 54–7
Estonians 52, 54–7
ethical identities 69
ethnic groups 61; essence and 51–8; essentialising of 90; identities 49–50, 58, 69–72, 269–70
ethnicity 82, 92–8, 167, 174, 178–9, 254–5
ethnic minorities 60, 269
ethnic nationalism 266–8
ethnic representations 94
ethnic revival 68
ethnocentrism 13, 71
ethnocultural identities 82, 270
ethnocultural languages 69
ethnocultural representations 97
ethnographic studies 243–50, 253, 265–6
ethnographies 192
ethnophaulisms 36–45
ethnoracial diversity 266
ethnoreligious identity 269
Eurocentrism 117–18, 123, 262
Europe 3, 8, 60–1, 206–7, 228–33, 265
European enlightenment 189
European identities 82
European Muslims 59–60
European Union 68, 190
everyday, defined 261
exclusion 7–8, 14, 34, 44, 62, 75, 88, 109, 122, 126, 141, 166, 173, 213
excuses 179
existential precarity 256
experiential wisdom 177
experimental manipulation 229–31
explanations, social 208–9
exploitation 109, 119, 182
extraction models 163–4
extreme case formulation 39
extreme right *see* far right
extremism 5, 7, 15, 267

face-saving 267
fairness 40, 132–3
Falasca-Zamponi, S. 230
false consciousness 270
false starts 39, 214
family 29–30, 70–2, 166
Family 100 project 177–8
family group conferences 135
Fanon, F. 119

far right 3–9, 14–15, 52–3, 93, 173, 186, 206–23, 228–33, 256–9, 267
fascists 214–7
Favell, A. 90
Federal Ministry of Economic Cooperation and Development of Germany *244*
feelings-based citizenship 96–9, 269
femininity 31
feminism 27, 58–61, 118–27, 148, 243–5
feminist audiences 30
feminization 117
Festinger, L. 164
feudal self-definitions 61
Figgou, L. 256–7, 266, 273
Filipino psychology 119
financial contributions 149
financial dependence 122
financial issues 178
Fine, M. 256
Flyvbjerg, B. 256
focus groups 210–17, 231, 267
followers 108, 264
food insecurities 173–81, 185–6, 270
football 7
footing 39–43, 209–14
footwear 184–5
forced group membership 51
foreign policies 123
forgiveness 137–9
formal equality 58–9
formal recognition 96
Former Yugoslavia (FY) 134, 137, 210
Foucauld, M. 4
fractured globalisation 69
fragmentation 66–9, 72, 75
framing 242, 245
France 61, 88, 141, 229–32
Freedman, A. 239
free markets 147
Freudian concept of repression 45
functionality 95
fundamentalist Muslims 62
furniture 178–81, 186
Fuss, D. 59
future, projections of 191
future-proofing 190
fuzzy logic 190
FY (Former Yugoslavia) 134, 137, 210
Fyssas, P. 210

gacaca courts 135
Gallop, G.: *The Pulse of Democracy* 192
Gandhi, M. 109
gang houses 183

Garden E. 256, 270, 273
gay people 255
gender 150–2, 167, 174, 178–9, 266–8, 267–8, 269–70; differences 58–9; equality 242–3; exploitation 127; family and 29–30; Gillard and 18, 25–9; inequality 36, 243–5; policies, in South Africa 238–9, 242–9, 258–9, 265–6; politics of 18–33; poststructural view of 245; psychological research and 118–19; relations 239; roles 262
Gender at Work 244
gender-based violence 116, 120–1, 243
generalisations 38–9
genos 92
genuine escapes 185
geographic mobility 21
German language 56
German Muslims 60
Germany 52, 61, 71, 136, 209–10
Gervais, M. 208
Gibson, S. 82, 90, 267, 272–3
Giddens, A. 159
Gigerenzer, G. 197, 203
Gillard, J. 18, 25–31, 267–8
Gillespie, A. 209
Gillis, J. 136
Gilroy, P. 3
Glazer, N. 193
Gleibs, I. 6, 82, 272
global capitalism 123, 253, 270
global governance 146, 153
global identities 65–78, 81–2, 272
global inequalities 65, 71
globalisation 80, 272; cultural 66–7; daily life and 6; definitions of 66–8; as exchange process 67; fractured 69; nationalism and 7; as a process 66–7; social and political psychology and 65–78
globalised poverty 270
global north and south 116
global politics 174
global recession 253
global South 118–19
global/transnational institutions 68
global village 68
GLO-BUGs (electricity meters) 181–3
glossing 38–9, 44–5
Glow, H. 12–13
Goffman, E. 267
Golden Dawn (Greek political party) 206–21, 257, 266–7
Goldschmied, N. 21

Goncalves-Portelinha, I. 257–8, 265, 272
good *versus* bad immigrant dichotomy 90
governance 9; critical nationalism and 12–14; global structures of 68; multiculturalism and 5; politics and 50; rational 189; strategies 4–6
government actors 239
government agencies 243
grand narratives 262
grassroots movements 142
Gray, D. 90–1
Grayson, A. 105
Greece 141; Golden Dawn party in 206–21, 257, 266–7; military junta in 216
Greek bail out 99–100n1
Greek citizenship 87–101, 268–9
Greek constitution 92
Greek nationalists 210
Greekness 93, 94–5, 98–9, 166–7, 269
Greene, A. 256
green movements 153
Greens (Australian political party) 26
grievances 74, 88
Griffin, C. 90–1
Grootendorst, R. 154
Groot, S. 256, 270, 273
groups: cohesion of 54; differentiation 68–9; diversities within 137; dominant 118, 125; essence of *55*; framing of 242; homogeneous 62; identity and 227; images of 53–7; influence of 225–7; interest 226; language and 51–2; low-status 71; membership in 51, 82, 103–4, 108; minoritised 3–5, 8–9, 133; minority 82, 91; nationality and 52; perpetrator 138–42; political behaviour and 224; proximal 54; public interest 239; race and 51; religious 51, 62; self-interest of 203; stereotyping of 61–3; user 237; victim 138; *see also* ethnic groups; ingroups; majority groups; minority groups; outgroups
group-value model 132–3
growth based models 154–5
guilt 134, 139–40, 175

habitus 174, 179–80
Hage, G. 13
Hague, The 134
Halkier, B. 176–7
Hamilton, L. 90
Hammack, P. 138
hardship 175, 183
harmony 69, 71, 74

Harpies and Quines 73
Harrison, S. 206
Haslam, A. 19
hate 74
hate words 36
Hayes, N. 208
healing 133–5, 140
healthcare 117, 173
health issues 118, 178, 182–5, 208, 247–8
hegemonic masculinity 120
hegemony 81–2, 153, 159–60, 227
Heidegger, M. 176, 182, 256
Hellenic League for Human Rights 92
Heritage, J. 196
hetero-essentialisation 54
heterosexism 117–18
heterosexuals 60
hierarchies 82, 117–18, 173, 182, 186, 225
higher education 259
hijab 49
Hindu reform movement 109–12
Hindus 49, 59–60, 109–12, 167, 269
historical narratives 136
history education 139–40
history, silencing of 140
HIV/AIDS 116, 243
Hodgetts, D. 175, 256, 270–3
Holocaust survivors, children of 140
holomorphism 62
Holtz, P. 269–70, 273
homeless people 175
Home Office 12
homogeneity 8–9, 62, 68–9
homosexuals 53, 60
Hoogendoorn, S. 4
hospitality 179
hot nationalism 7–8
household behaviours 149
houses 178
housing authorities 180–1
housing insecurities 173–5, 178–81, 185–6
Hovland, C. 223
Howard, J. 29, 266
Howarth, C. 81, 90, 166–7, 209, 242, 247, 271–3; *The Social Psychology of Everyday Politics* 262–3, 272–4
humanisation 271
humanity, identification with 70–2
human rights 71, 88, 245
humiliations 109–12, 182, 264
humour 45
hybridisation 9–11, 60, 73
hyphen identities 59

'I' and 'they' 80–1
'I' and 'we' 80–1
ICTR (International Criminal Tribunal for Rwanda) 134
ICTY (International Criminal Tribunal for the former Yugoslavia) 134
identification 108, 114
identification with all humanity (IWAH) 70–2
identities: citizenship and 90–1; construction of 81; contemporary 6–7; de-essentializing 59; denaturalising 58–9; dialectic nature of different 73; discourses on 93; dislocation of 70; dynamics of 163–70; emotion, mobilisation, and 102–15; essentialism and 49–64; formation of 56, 269–70; insecurity, nostalgia, and 8–9; as intersectional 10, 121; language and 69; management of 43–5; of minorities 68; nested 74; punishment and 134; as threatened 70–2; understanding of 67; *see also* social identities
identity politics 51, 131–2
identity processes 226
identity strategies 268–72
identity work 49–64
ideological agendas 118, 207
ideological constraint 199
ideological dilemmas 7
ideological reasoning 198–9
ideologies 153, 208, 257; changes in 58, 266–8; clashing of 69; as dogma 216
ideology-driver voting 217
ignorance 74, 119–20, 196, 216, 224, 233n1
illegal immigration 211–13
"I'll ride with you" Twitter campaign 4
images 53–7
immigrants/immigration 13, 59, 90–8, 99–100n1, 102, 132–3, 190, 211–13, 217–8, 239, 257, 267
implementation 249–50
inclusion 12, 18, 75, 81–2, 88, 166
inclusive identities 74, 137–8
inclusiveness 30, 68, 71
inclusive policies 239
income insecurities 173, 178
inconsistency 202
India 49, 109–13, 264
Indian identities 69
Indian tribes 57–8
indigenization 118
indigenous cultural essence 57–8

indigenous Greek citizens 93
indigenous psychologies 119
Indignados 260
indignation 215–17
individual behaviours 67, 149, 157–8, 167
individual changes 154
individual differences 72–3, 207
individual identities 70
individualised approaches 122, 125, 134
individualistic accounts 233
individualistic approaches 224
individualistic attribution schemata 208
individual rights 97
individuals 46, 223, 225
individuation 263
industrial unions 262
inequalities 12, 62, 104, 109, 120, 132–3, 173–4, 177, 182–3, 186–7, 247, 255–9; economic 36; gender 36, 243–5, 245; global 65, 71; social 36–46, 116; socioeconomic 270; structural 82–3
inequality gaps 253
inertia 216
information 189–205, 226, 254–5
information processing 79–80, 166
infrapolitics 255
Inglehart, R. 270
ingroups 42, 74, 265; essence and 51–3; essentialisation and 53–7, 62–3; identities 136–7, 141–2; loyalty, pride, and 8–9; membership in 20, 24–5, 39, 132–4, 257; projection 71; reconciliation 138–42
injustice 133
innovation 190
insecurities 8–9, 13, 175, 178, 182
insiders 90
institutionalisation 136
institutionalised discourses 91
institutionalism 262
institutions 65, 68, 133–5, 183–6, 224
instruction, forms of 164
instrumentality 103–4
integration 4, 53, 72, 90, 96, 136, 240, 266
intelligence, studies of 118
intentions 124
interaction 61, 207, 217, 240
interchange 272
interconnectedness 66–7, 91
intercultural encounters 3, 71–2
intercultural identities 6, 10
intercultural relations 1–84
interdependence 73, 113, 137

interdisciplinary cooperation 190
interest, construction of 104, 114
interest groups 226
interest-guided politics 58
intergenerational dialogue 131–2, 140–1, 271
intergroup contact 71, 75
intergroup encounters 82–3
intergroup harmony 74
intergroup perceptions 149–50
intergroup politics 50, 90
intergroup reconciliation 139
intergroup relations 6–7, 39, 67, 88, 135, 182, 271; communication and 225; conflict and 74, 131, 134, 138; dialogue and 135; identity work and stereotyping in 49–64; memory and 136–7; racism and 102; reconciliation and 133
international agreements 231
international conflicts 131, 223
International Criminal Tribunal for Rwanda (ICTR) 134
International Criminal Tribunal for the former Yugoslavia (ICTY) 134
international development discourses 117
international donor policies 242–9, 265–6
international protocols and treaties 146–7
Internet 52–3
interobjectivity 175, 182–3
interpersonal evaluation dimensions 152
interpersonal identities 72
interpersonal perceptions 149–50
interpersonal politics 50
interpersonal relations 135
interpersonal representations 148
interpretation 193
intersectionality 10, 73, 121–3, 126–7, 167, 178–9, 186, 247, 271–2
interviewers, role of 42–6, 267
interviews 93–8, 150–60, 195–202, 210–17, 243
intimate partner violence (IPV) 121–3
intractable conflicts 137
intragroup encounters 82–3
intragroup phenomena 111–12
intragroup reconciliation 131, 138–41
intranational cooperation 131
intrapersonal identities 72
intrapersonal processes 68–9
intrapersonal tension 70
intrastate governance 50
investors 182
IPV (intimate partner violence) 121–3

Ireland 60, 191
irregular migrants 88
irresponsibility 119–20
ISCTE-IUL (Lisbon University Institute) 150, 268
Isin, E. 88–9
ISIS 254
Islamic extremism 102
Islamic State 74
Islamification 14
Islamists 58
Islamophobia 4, 8, 14
-isms 262
isolation 164
Israeli government 239–40
Israeli migrants 240
Israelis 133, 136
Israel-Palestine conflict 136
issue voting 207
ithagenia 92
ithis 92
IWAH (identification with all humanity) 70–2
IWF 68

Jackson, L. 26–7
Jadhav, N. 110–12
Jahoda, M. 253, 259–60
Jensen, I. 176–7
Jewish folklore 58
Jews 52–3, 136, 255
jihad terrorism 58
jobs 74, 253
Jogdand, Y. 110, 164, 167–9, 263–5, 272–3
Johannesburg 243
Johanson, K. 12–13
Joppke, C. 87–8
Jovchelovitch, S. 208, 241, 245
junk food 180
jus sanguinis criteria 92, 269
jus soli criteria 92, 269
justice 82, 132–5, 166–7, 259–60

Kadianaki, I. 166–7, 268–9, 272
kai 179
Kessi, S. 120, 165–7, 271–3
Kiev 73
Kinnvall, C. 4
kinship identities 70
Kislev, E. 239–40
kitchen furniture 178–81, 186
Klein, O. 140
knowing 123

knowledge 240–1, 264–5; construction 83, 88–9; mutual 62; production 80, 124, 238; psychological 118; social 83; systems of 117
Kymlicka, W. 12, 88

laboratory experimentation 163–4
Labor Party (Australia) 26–8
language 51–2, 69–70, 207–9, 242, 253, 269
latent public opinion 191–4
Latin America 119
Latour, B. 176
laughter 40–6, 267
Lausanne 231–2, 265
law, violations of 134, 166
lay citizens 81, 87–99, 206–21, 240, 267–9
Lazarsfeld, P. 223, 253
laziness 119–20
Leach, C. 139–40
leadership 79, 206, 264; minority 18, 30–1; mobilisation and 104–14; political 18–33
Lea, S. 89
left-wing internationalism 198–9
left-wing students 229–30
legal citizenship 132–3
legal-constitutional institutionalist approaches 262
legality 96
legal status 88
legal systems 90
legislative frameworks 146
legitimacy 132–3, 153, 227
Le Pen, M. 229–30
letter writing 149
Levine, M. 133
Lewin, K. 223
liberal democracies 18, 34, 189
liberalization policies 116
liberation psychology 119
Licata, L. 140
lifestyles 68, 155–6
Lind, E. 132
linguistic context 164–5
linguistic dialogue 166
linguistic hygiene 36–8, 43–6
linguists 190
Lippmann, W. 193
Lisbon University Institute (ISCTE-IUL) 150, 268
Litton, I. 209
local cultures 65
local identities 69–72
local involvement 133–5

Index **285**

localisation 69
localism 68
local politics 174
local products 68
local representations 248
local restorative justice 135
logic 124, 165
London 68
lonely paradigms 208
low-status groups 71
loyalties 3, 6
"LSSDMIC – Lay and Social Science Discourses on Identity, Migration and Citizenship" 100n2
lunchboxes 178–80, 186
Lyotard, J. 262

Macedonia 210
Machiavelli, N.: *The Prince* 261
macro levels, globalisation at 66–8
Mahad Satyagraha protest 109–11
Mahars 110
mainstreaming 243
majoritarinism 49, 93
majority groups 5, 51, 82, 91, 138, 226–7, 233, 269–70; degrees of essentialism of 55; dialogue and 133; multiculturalism and 8–11
majority-minority relationships 54–7, 90
majority opinions 224
making do 178
Malay identities 69
Malaysia 239
male violence 120
malleability 228, 231
Malová, D. 4
manaaki 179
managerial approach 149
Mannell, J. 258–9, 265–6, 272–3
manners 60–1
Manuelito, K. 123
manuhiri 179
Māori 178–9
Maoz, I. 133
marginalisation 18, 60, 117–18, 122, 125–7, 223, 231
marginalised communities 5–7, 122
Marienthal 253–4
market forces 147
market rationality 173
Marko-Stöckl, E. 139
marriage 60
Marshall, T. 87–8
masculinities 31, 120, 245–7, 258

mass media 147–8, 228, 262
mass mobilisation 233
material imbalances 132
materialism 270
materiality 175–6
material objects 173–88, 256, 270–1
material resources 124
maternal language 52
maximum diversity sampling 195
McFarland, S. 70–1
McGrew, A. 66–7
meaning 43, 79–81, 93, 103, 125, 160, 211, 222
meaning-making 165–8
media 4, 52, 117, 147–8, 165, 210, 225, 228, 239, 262
mediation programs 135
memory 136–8
men 243–7, 258–9; environmental attitudes of 152; feminism and 58–9; psychological research and 118; in South Africa 243; violence against women and 120, 271
mentalities, changes in 58
merit 82
meta-knowledge 62, 241–2
metaphors 165–6, 253
meta-representations 223, 226–33, 257–8, 265
metasystems 81
method 103, 163–4
methodological approaches 123–7
methodology 169
metonyms 173, 181, 185
Michaloliakos, N. 209
Michels, R. 261
micro-credit 243
micro-interactions 3, 209
micro levels, globalisation at 66
micropolitics 267, 271
middle classes 179–80, 270–1
migrant organisations 92
migrants 6–8, 36–7, 87–93
migration 65, 93
Milgram, S. 106–8, 164, 223, 263–4
Milgram's Yale Obedience studies 105–8, 263–4
minaret ban 59–62
Ministère des affaires étrangères et européennes (France) *244*
minorities 59–62, 229, 233, 239–40, 269–70
minoritised groups 3–5, 8–9, 133
minority cultures 90
minority groups 51–5, 82, 91, 133

minority influence 148, 227
minority leadership 18, 30–1
minority opinions 224, 230
minority rights 88, 93
minority status 68
minstrels, defined 46n1
mirror effect 54–6
misogyny 26
misogyny speech (Gillard) 26, 30–1
mixed couples 52–3
mixed MANOVA 55–6
mobilisation 89, 233, 260, 264, 268–9; collective 88, 103–4, 154, 157–8; identities, emotion, and 102–15
mobilisers 104
mobility 21, 65–6, 82
moderate activist behaviours 149–50, 268
moderate argumentation strategies 146–62
moderate social change 146–62
modernisation 57–8
Modood, T. 10–11, 14
Moghaddam, F. 68–9
monetary subjugation 173
monoculture 80–1, 90
Monroe, K. 136
moral disdain 186
"More Perfect Union, A" speech (Obama) 19, 22–5, 30
Mosca, G. 261
Moscovici, S. 79–80, 103, 163, 208, 238–41, 257
motivated cognition 207
motivations 124, 186
multiculturalism 239–40, 266; caring 13; citizenship and 5, 87–90; counternarratives of 11–12; critical nationalism and 3–17; definitions of 3–4; essentialism and 83; ethnicity and 60; identities and 6–7, 80–1; majority groups and 8–9; national culture and 90; policies related to 4–6; self-essentialisation and 53
multifaceted approaches 169
multilayered reconciliation 138–42
multiplicity 66–7, 75
multiracial identities 18–19, 23
multivocal worlds 102, 107
mundane environmentalism 149
mundane objects 256
murders 210
Murphy, K. 132
Muslims 4–5, 8–9, 49–50, 59–62, 82, 254–5, 269
mutual essentialization 56–8
mutualism 131
mutual knowledge 62

naming 42
Nanterre University 229–32, 265
narrative research 124–7
narratives 138; cultural 163–70; dominant 256–8; historical 136; neoliberal 186; of the underclass 186; underdog 21; victim-blaming 186
nation 9–12, 268
national being 270
national belonging 93–7
national citizenship 88, 91
national consciousness 139–40
national culture 90
national essentialism 14
National Front (NF; French political party) 229–30, 233n2
national identities 3, 6–10, 18, 92, 198–200
nationalism 141, 200, 210, 253, 256–7, 260; as anti-immigration 8–9; banal 5–8, 11, 198, 230; bottom-up and top-down 3–4, 12–14; critical 3–17; definitions of 3–4; English 191; in Europe 228–33; globalisation and 7; hot and cold 7–8; multiculturalism and 3–17; progressive 12–13
nationalist social movements 257
nationality 52, 94, 239
national policies 240
National Socialism 209–10
national solidarities 14–15
nation-building projects 90
nation-states 66–8, 91
NATO 68
naturalisation 57–63, 92
naturalness 37, 50–2, 58–62, 270
Nazi Germany 136
Nazi ideology 206–21
Nazi party (NSDAP) 210
negative interdependence 137
negative male gender roles 246
negative social representations 247
negotiation 148
neoliberalism 81, 116–17, 173–4, 185–7, 256, 259, 270
neo-Nazis 206–21, 266–7
neo-Nazi websites 57
nested identities 74
Netherlands 61, 139
network of involvements 182
new racism 37, 45
New Zealand 173, 187n1
NF (National Front; French political party) 229–30, 233n2
NGOs 92, 135, 142; environmental (ENGOs) 148, 152–60

19th century republican politics 61
nobility 60–1
Noble, G. 185
nonactivist behaviours 150, 153
non-attitudes 193, 199, 202
nonbelievers 58, 74
noncampaign periods, discourse during 206
nonelites 255
non-ideology-driven votes 215–7
nonindigenous migrants 93
non-WEIRD populations 232
norms, social 224–7, 233
Northern Ireland 141
North-South relations 117, 123
North Yorkshire 36
nostalgia 8–9
novel social occurrences 227–8
November 13 Paris attacks 83
NSDAP (Nazi party) 210

Obama, B. 18–25, 29–30, 267–8; "American Promise" speech 24–5; "A More Perfect Union" speech 19, 22–5, 30; "Reclaiming the American Dream" speech 20–3
Obedience (film) 107
obedience studies 105–8
objectification 81, 180, 186
objectifying 241
objectifying social identity 53
objectivity 124
objects, material 173–88, 256
Obradović, S. 166–7, 271
Occupy movement 74, 260
ochlocracy 191
old racism 45
One Man Can campaign 246
one-man-one-vote participation 192
one-reason decisions 197
Onslow, Earl of 194
openness 272
operationalist position 192
opinion polling 192–5, 231, 264–5
opinions 263–6; consistency of 199–202; formation of 233; genuine 202; meta-representations and 227; negative 198–200; neutral 195; political 222–4, 230; positive 196–202; public 189–205, 233, 256–7; rhetorical construction of 194; uninformed 199
opportunities, distribution of 255
oppressed/oppression 118–27, 174, 253, 270–2
optimal distinctiveness theory 68–9
orders, following of 105–8
organisational social psychologists 237
organizational culture 190
origins 209
orthodox beliefs 198
'other' 141
other-attributed essentialism 51
'othered' 5–9
'otherising' 11–12
otherness 4, 61–2
'others' 7–10
outgroups 42–4, 61–3, 136; degrees of essentialism of 55; discrimination 60; essence and 51; essentialization and 53–9; heterogeneity of 137; hostility 141; identity construction of 54; membership in 134; nobility 60–1; stereotyping by 49–53
outsiders 90, 96

Pacific Islanders 178
Packer, D. 107
Palestinians 133, 136
Paluck, E. 224–5
paramilitary organization 210
parents/parenting 14, 180–1, 186
Pareto, V. 261
Paris 3, 83
Parkanyi, O. 28
parliamentary debates 92
pars pro toto reasoning 71
participation 96, 103, 126, 239; civic 93, 97–8, 253–5; multiculturalism and 5; one-man-one-vote 192; postcolonial society and 117; procedural justice and 133
participatory action research (PAR) 124–7
particularisation 7, 39, 80
partner abuse 122
party organization 206
party voting 207
PASOK (Greek political party) 214–5
past, constructing 136–7
paternalism 49, 90, 178
patriarchal attitudes 122–3
patriotism 3, 7, 11–14
pauses 214
peace-building 131, 135–6, 139–42
peace process 138, 142
Penic, S. 13
people of color 255
perceptions 103–4, 113, 132–3, 224
performance 120, 164–5
perpetrator groups 138–42
personality dynamics 207

personality typology 163–4
personal self-interest 203
perspective-taking 271
persuasion 168–9
petition signing 149
Philippines 119
phronesis 177, 183, 256, 270
physical isolation 164
physical stereotyping 36
place, self and 178
Platow, M. 19
Pliny the Elder 163
pluralistic ignorance 224, 233n1
Podemos 260
polemical representations 81–2, 209
police 122–3, 133
policy 237–52
policy-based citizenship allocations 92
Polish migrants 36–7
political action 75, 79, 88
political alliances 206
political ascendency 261
political beliefs 222–36
political debates 92, 190
political identity 49–50, 262–3
political parties 262, 268
political positioning 59–61
political practice 171–274
political psychology 46, 65–78, 207–8, 224, 232–3, 237–8
political rhetoric 13–14, 190–1, 198
political right *see* far right
political science 192, 232–3, 261–3
political sociology 261–2
political surveillance 189
political underground 255
politicians 190–1
politicised collective identities 73–4
politicization 124, 126
politicized approaches 123
politicized psychology 118
politics 89; definitions of 50, 79–80; interest-guided 58; postcolonial society and 117; social psychology of 261–74
polity membership 90
polling 192–5, 231, 264–5
populism 206, 218, 230–2, 257
Portugal 153
positivism 163
positivity 140–1
possessions 175
postcolonial contexts 116–30, 271–2
postcolonial developments 262
postcolonial narratives 167
postcolonial psychology 118–27

postconflict textbooks 139–40
postfeudal nobility 61
postmaterialists 270
postmodernity 271
postnational citizenship 87–8
postnationalism 5–7
postracism 30–1
poststructural view of gender 245
Potter, J. 34, 209
poverty 116, 119–22, 173–82, 185–7, 253–5, 270
power 53, 62, 120–3, 125–6, 174, 206, 247; asymmetries in 88; dialectics of 124; dynamics 116, 124–5, 167; global forms of 118; procedural justice and 133; relationships 40, 51, 82–3, 99, 123, 167, 179, 224–5, 245; struggles 73–4, 237; unequal 226
power companies 182
powerless 271
power meters and cords 178, 181–3, 186
practitioners 243–9, 265–6
praxis 124
precariat 173–88, 270
precarity 253, 256
precision 189–90
preconditions 95
predictability 228
pre-electoral campaigns 207
prefacing, of disagreements 158
prejudice 5, 12–14, 34–5, 53, 58–9, 71, 102–3, 186, 213, 267
prices 182–3
Prince, The (Machiavelli) 261
principle of emergence 177
prison studies 105–8, 263–4
private ballots 192
private efforts 154–60
private interests 173
private sector 239
private sphere behaviours 149–50, 153
privatization 116, 182, 187n1
privilege 5–8, 93, 108, 120–1, 125, 174, 245, 253, 259
problem-solving tasks 166
procedural justice 82, 132–3
Proch, J. 71
procreation 52
production 147, 153
proenvironmental behaviours 150–2
profane sciences 79
progress 71
progressive nationalism 12–13

progressive psychological essentialism 58
proimmigration politics 13
projection 71
proletariat 270
promiscuity 245
propaganda 148, 153–4, 159, 210, 227, 257
propagation 147–8, 154, 159, 226–7, 257
propagation-like arguments 157
protest 88, 92, 109–12, 270
protest voting 207, 211–8
protocols, international 146–7
proximal groups 54
Prozi, F. 107
psychological approaches 4, 18, 66
psychological essentialism 50–3, 58, 63
psychological research 118, 186–7
psychologists 123–4, 190
psychologisation 215
psychology: decolonizing 118–27; postcolonial society and 117–18; silence and 102–4; social and political 5–6
psychometric testing 118
psychosocial doubleness 256
psychosocial justifications 152
public caricatures 186
public emotions 4
public housing 183–5
public interest groups 239
public opinion 189–205, 233, 256–7, 264–5
Public Opinion (Childs) 189
public policies 153
public-political efforts 154–60
public reason 195
public rhetoric 206
public sphere 149
Pulse of Democracy, The (Gallop and Rae) 192
punishment 132–5, 166, 267
pure communities 8–9
purpose 79–81
puzzle-solvers 164–6

Q&A (television program) 29–30
qualitative methods 163
quantitative methods 163
quasi-random variation 202
questioning 192, 271
questionnaire-based attitude research 163–4
questionnaires 229–30
Quiet Rage (film) 106

race 18–33, 51, 108, 167, 174, 247, 254–5, 266–8
Race Speech *see* "More Perfect Union, A" speech (Obama)
racial categories 51
racial difference 118
racial identities 121
racialised binaries 9
racialization 8, 117–22
racism 14, 94, 116–19, 127, 213, 217, 267–8; accusations of 34–6, 42; in Brixton 61; essentialism and 57; intergroup relations and 102; nationalism and 11; young people and 36–46
racist assaults 210
racist talk 34–48, 267
radical messages 148
radical Muslims 60
radical psychology 118
radical social change 146–62
Rae, S.: *The Pulse of Democracy* 192
rage 110
Rancière, J. 79
rape 243
Ratele, K. 120
rationality 118–19, 190–1, 203, 217
rationing 181–2
Raudsepp, M. 269–70, 273
realities: construction of 209; geopolitical 159; postcolonial 117; shared 81; social 79, 82, 227, 249
reasoning 34, 189, 194, 203
recession 253
"Reclaiming the American Dream" speech (Obama) 20–3
reconciliation 13, 131–45, 166, 271
Reddy, G. 6, 82, 272
Reese, G. 71
re-essentialization 270
referential whole 182
refugees 135
regulations 66, 81, 147, 155–6, 189
regulative citizenship allocations 92
Reicher, S. 19, 133, 164, 167–9, 240, 263–5, 272–3
reified universe 79–80
relationships 107–8, 117–18, 166; power 40, 51, 82–3, 99, 123, 167, 179, 224–5, 245; social 178
relative knowledge 117
religion 110, 168, 254–5
religious denominations 262
religious groups 51, 62
religious identities 82, 269–70

religious minorities 60
religious superiority 58
reparation movements 13
reported speech 39–40
representational exclusion 122
representational processes 226
representational systems, changes in 58
representations 133, 209, 263–6; *see also* social representations approach (SRA); theory of social representations (TSR)
representative democracies 202
repression 45, 58–61, 191–2, 267
reproductive issues 118
Republican Party (United States) 31
Republic of Macedonia 210
Research Center for Group Dynamics 223
research methods 123–7
residence permits 92
resignification 147
resistance 65, 167, 238, 256, 271–2, 272; limitations of 175; to policy representations of gender 248; silence as 133; and transformation in postcolonial contexts 116–30
resources: access to 116, 122; competition for 120; cultural 125; distribution of 255; flow of 65–6; social 124
responsibility 139, 209
restorative justice 132–5, 166–7
restraining, of claims 158
retaliation 109
retribution 166, 232
retributive justice 133–5, 167
revenge 110, 134
revulsion 174
rhetoric: approaches to 89–90; constraints on 199–202; elision of 198; formulations of 208–11; heuristics of 194–202; political 13–14, 190–1, 198; public 206; tropes of 200
rhetorical psychology 211
rhetoric strategies of justification 256–8
Richards, B. 4
Richards, D. 21
Riesman, D. 193
rights 87–8, 97
right-wing: authoritarianism 71; extremist voters 207, 218; factions 52; ideology 253; nationalism 260; politicians 7; in Switzerland 230–2; *see also* far right
ritualised culture 96
role models 27
Rudd, K. 26
Russian Cyrillic 55

Russians 52–7
Russophones 54–7
Rwanda 134–5, 140–1

sabhas (associations) 109
sacred sciences 79
safety 72
St George's flag 14
salient argumentative forms 154
Salmond, A. 104
sameness 174
same-sex partners 60
sampling 192, 195
Sanchez, D. 19
Sanchez, S. 256
Sanskritisation 49
sans-papiers movement 88
satisficing strategies 195
scarcity 179, 182, 185
Scheiber, N. 19
schooling 96, 99–100n1, 139–40
school projects 142
science 79–80
scientific gaze 118
scientific reasoning 124
SCM (stereotype content model) 148–50
Scotland Bill 191, 194
Scottish independence 68
Scottish Parliament 191, 194–201, 264
Scottish referendum 102–4, 113
Scott, J. 258, 270; *Two Cheers for Anarchism* 255–6
Scuzzarello, S. 13
second chances 135
second-generation immigrants 93–8, 99–100n1
second-order claims 155, 159
"Secret People, The" (Chesterton) 191
secular Muslims 62
segregation 74
selective memory 138
self 169; cognitive structure of 70; construction of 104; place and 178; presentation of 125; understanding of 67
self-acceptance 69
self-aggrandising essentialism 58
self-ascriptions 53, 60
self-attributed essentialism 51, 56–9
self-categorisation 70, 227–8
self-correction 36–8
self-criticism 139–41
self-definitions 51, 58, 61, 114
self-determination 28
self-essentialization 53–7, 60

self-esteem 69–70, 120
self-images 56, 120–1, 159
self-interest 154–5, 189, 203, 265
self-mobilisation 109–13
self-presentation 34
self-representation 60–1
self-respect 110
semantics 43
Sen, R. 269–70, 273
sense-making 7
separation 60–1, 136
September 11, 2001 22
Serbia 135, 141
Serbs 137
service networks 178
sexism 18, 26
sexual behaviour, unsafe 245
sexual differences 58–9
sexuality 122, 174, 254–5, 269–70
sexuality talk 44–5
sexual minorities 60
sexual relationships 118
sexual violence 243
Seyd, B. 194
shame 110, 139–41, 178–9
shared identities 72–3, 131
shared knowledge 117
shared morality 6
shared understanding 228
Sharma, M. 69–70
Sharma, S. 69–70
Shih, M. 19
Shotter, J. 89
SIDA (Swedish International Development Agency) 246
Sierra Leone 134
signifiers 50
silence 102–4, 133, 140
similarities 70–1
Simmel, G. 177
simple affirmation 197
simplified reality 209
Singapore 69
skills 124
skinheads 214–5
slippers 178, 184–6
small enterprise activities 243
Smith, D. 262
social action 126, 238
social capital 175
social categories 70–1, 82, 169, 232
social change 30–1, 59, 67, 85–170, 224, 227–9, 233, 238, 248
social class 82, 173–5, 186, 262, 270

social cognition paradigm 223
social cohesion 9, 65
social constructionist approach 177, 233
social contact 164
social contexts 75, 117, 125, 164, 231–2
social contract 97
Social Democratic Labor Movement (Vienna) 253
social diversity 24–5, 29–30, 82
social dominance orientation 71
social hierarchies 173, 182, 186, 225
social identities 49–50, 69, 112–13, 119–20, 137–8, 238, 263, 269; of men 246; Obama and 18–20, 29–30; objectifying 53; policy and 245–7; theory of 19, 169; as threatened 70–2
social inequality 36–46, 116
social influence 226, 232, 257–8
socialization 176
social justice 116, 122, 126–7
social locations 23, 122, 174
social media 26, 149, 257–8
social mobility 21, 82, 175
social movements 66
social norms and behaviours 224–7, 233
social order 150–2
social policy 237–52
social positioning 61–3
social practices 175–7, 209, 242
social psychology 5–6, 45–6, 81–3, 159, 192–3, 259–60, 262–3; citizenship and 87–101; globalisation, global identities, and 65–78; identity, emotion, mobilisation, and 102–15; policy process and 237–52; of politics 261–74; research methods for 124–7
Social Psychology of Everyday Politics (Howarth and Andreouli) 262–3, 272–4
social regulations 81
social relationships 34–5, 66–7, 125, 135, 174, 178, 265–6
social representations approach (SRA) 10, 79–82, 136–7, 141, 152, 169, 223–7, 240, 265–7
social representations theory (SRT) 238–44, 249–50, 259
social resources 124
social sciences 93, 123–4, 189–90, 262–3
social space 174
social standing 50, 54
social status 270
social values 62, 135
social workers 178
social worthiness 50

societal approach 249
societal approaches 238
societal change 57–9
societal political psychology 224
societal politics 174
societal unrest 173
sociocultural practices, flow of 65–6
sociocultural relationships 177
socioeconomic inequality 270
socioeconomic status 150, 179
sociologists 190
sociopolitical changes 149, 158, 206
sociopsychological processes 222, 229
sociostructural oppressions 121
solidarities 14–15, 131, 254, 259–60, 271
solutions 164–5
Sonke Gender Justice 246
Sorrentino, J. 267–8, 273
South Africa 117, 120–3, 238–9, 242–9, 258–9, 265–6, 271–2
Southern Albania 94
Soviet Bronze Soldier monument 52
Soysal, Y. 88
speakers 209
speculative capital 173
speech, reported 39–40
SPE (Stanford Prison Experiment) 105–8, 263–4
spiral of silence theory 224–8
SPP (Swiss People's Party) 231–2
spurious responses 195, 202
SRA (social representations approach) 10, 79–82, 136–7, 141, 152, 169, 223–7, 240, 265–7
SRT (social representations theory) 238–44, 249–50, 259
stability 69, 83, 181
Staerklé, C. 257–8, 265, 272
stagnation 216
stakeholders 237–9, 249
standards 120
standing 60–2
Stanford Prison Experiment (SPE) 105–8, 263–4
state, betrayal by 257
state, citizenship and 87–91
State Council (Greece) 92–3, 96
state discourses 90–1, 96
state elites 61
state identities 137
state institutions 262
state interests 173
statelessness 257
state policies 87, 117, 268–9, 269

status 53, 60, 79, 82–3, 121, 150, 226, 270
stereotype content model (SCM) 148–50
stereotyped reality 209
stereotypical masculinities 246
stereotyping 36, 120, 269; of activism 148–52, 159; essence and 51; of groups 61–3; intergroup relations and 49–64; oppressive aspect of 57–8; social positioning, identities, and 61–3
Stern, P. 149
stigma 62, 180, 213, 217
stories 124–5
story-tellers 165–6
strategic ambiguity 190
strategic vagueness 39–40
stratification 256
straw polls 192
strong environmentalism 146–62, 167
structural change 67
structural-functionalism 262
structural inequalities 82–3
structural oppressions 122–3
structure, agency and 89
subgroups 71
subjective identity 169
subjectivities 9–11, 96, 185, 255, 258–60
subjects 164
subjugation 118, 173
subordination 109, 125, 174
super-diversity 3
superordinate categories 71, 81–2
superordinate identification 137
supranational categories 82
supranational forums 146
surveillance 175, 189, 256
survey researchers 202
survival 253, 256
sustainability 147, 153, 167, 260
Swedish International Development Agency (SIDA) 246
Swiss People's Party (SPP) 231–2
Switzerland 59–62, 230–2
symbolic exclusion 122
symbolic imbalances 132
symbols, cultural 136
symbols, transcription 33, 48, 203n11
systemic changes 154
systems theory 262

taboo-breaking 40
taboos 168, 217
Tajfel, H. 223
talk 266–8
tastes 168

teaching 243
technology 147
tensions 91
territorial boundaries 66
terrorists/terrorism 4, 7, 58, 74, 83, 255
text 266–8
textbooks 139–40
theatres 135
thematic analysis 167
theory 103
theory of social representations (TSR) 147–8, 190–1, 208–9
Thessaloniki 93, 210–12, 267
thick political communities 189
thinking 80, 165, 198
thinking society 83, 207–8, 240–1, 257
third wave of feminism 245
Thornberry, E. 14
Tileagă, C. 240–1
time 253
tolerance 72
tool-users 165–6
top-down justice 166
top-down nationalism 3–4, 12–13
top-down policies 258–60, 265–6
top-down reconciliation 132–5, 141–2
touchables 111–12
Touraine, A. 82
trade 65
trade unions 65
traditional elites 61
traditional psychological experimental design 263
transcription notations 33, 48, 203n11
transformation 116–30, 248, 271–2
transnational encounters 7
transnational institutions 68
transnational networks 66
transnational policies 240
transparency 228
trauma 140
treaties, international 146–7
triangulation 74
tribunals 139
Trojan Horse Affair 5
truancy 180
Trump, D. 31, 254
trustee model 190–1
Truth and Reconciliation Commission (TRC; Sierra Leone) 134
truths 124, 137, 240
TSR (theory of social representations) 147–8, 190–1, 208–9
Turkey 153

Turkish immigrant community 52–7
Turkish language 56
Turkish migrants 70
Two Cheers for Anarchism (Scott) 255–6
2010 Greek citizenship law 92–9; 2015 revision of 96, 99–100n1
Tyler, T. 132–3

UK Justice Committee Report 190–1
uncertainty 175
unconscious feelings 125
underclass, narratives of 186
underdevelopment 175
underdog narratives 21
underperformance 120–1
undocumented immigrants 88, 132–3
unemployment 175, 253
unification 68–71
unintended effects 238–43, 250
Union Jack 14
uniqueness 53, 68–9
unitary citizenry 191
United Kingdom 5, 35, 68, 141, 173, 194–202; constitution of 195; House of Commons 190–1; House of Lords 194; legislature 4
United States 18–23, 58, 65, 71, 122, 192; electorate in 193; foreign policy of 22; Israeli migrants to 240; postracism in 30–1; voting behaviour in 223
universal cognition 207
universalist beliefs 71
universal sisterhood 121
University of Lausanne, faculty of Social and Political Sciences 231–2, 265
unlawfulness 213
UNO 68
unrest 173
unsafe sexual behaviour 245
untouchables 109–13, 167, 264
unworthy migrants 90
upper 1% 74
urban poverty 175
'us' and 'them' 9, 13–14, 68–9, 93, 137–8, 268–9
US Census (2013) 18–19
use-mention distinction 42–3
user groups 237
utilities 181–2, 183–4
Uzelgun, M. 167–9, 268, 273

vague constructs 190
vagueness, strategic 39–40
value-assessing tasks 166, 255

values 82, 104, 165–8, 198–9
Vandello, J. 21
vengefulness 109
Verkuyten, M. 15
vernacular political reasoning 189
victim-blaming 119, 186
victim-offender mediation programs 135
victims 138–40
video-elicitation interviews 153–60
Vienna 253
views, exchange of 79
violence 109, 126–7, 166, 210, 232, 271; gender-based 116, 120–1, 243; intimate partner (IPV) 121–3; nationalism and 7–8; racialized 119–21; structural 186; against women 245–7
Vizenor, G. 256
voice-feedback conditions 106
voices 102–4, 107, 113, 133–5, 191
voting 91, 96–8, 192, 222, 267; attitudes about 207, 223; ideology- and non-ideology-driven 215–7; issue 207; protest 207, 213–8; rights 92–3
Vygotsky, L. 165

wages 175
Wagner, W. 208, 269–70, 273
Wales 60, 191
Walker, R. 125
Wallace, D. 140–1
war 7, 74, 83
warmth 148–52, *152*, 159, 181, 268
war opponents 223
'we' 79, 83, 108, 264
weak environmentalism 146–62, 167
wealth 60–1, 65–6, 253
WEIRD populations 232
welfare 173, 179–81, 184–6
well-being 70, 75, 181
Western India 110
western involvement 116
westernisation 49
Westernised ideology 133–4
Western political science 261
Western science 118–19
Wetherell, M. 34–5
whakama 179
White, J. 21
white male privilege 120
whiteness 5–8, 14, 118
Whites 52, 254
White supremacist identities 253
white working class communities 7
Wilmer, F. 136–7
within-group diversities 137
women 243–7, 258–9; beliefs about 117–21, 247; environmental attitudes of 150–2; feminism and 58–9; in leadership roles 25–6, 31; in South Africa 122–3, 243; violence against 120–1, 245–7, 271
work 175
Workers Library 253
World Bank 68
World War II 21–3, 192
Worldwide Economic Crisis 253
Worth, A. 267–8, 273
worthy migrants 90

Xenitidou, M. 166–7, 268–9, 272
xenophobia 116, 206, 239

Yale Communication Program 223
Yale Obedience studies 105–8
yellow press 61
'yes-but' concession 148, 154–8, 268
'Yes' campaign 113
'yes/no' contrasting format 148, 153–8, 268
Yorkshire 267
young people 6, 36–46, 120–1, 139–41, 216, 242, 247, 255, 271
Yugoslavia 134

Zeineddine, F. 139
Zeisel, H. 253
zero-sum identities 137
Zimbardo, P. 105–6, 164, 263–4
Zimbardo's Stanford Prison Experiment (SPE) 105–8, 263–4